CONTEMPORARY SECURITY AND STRATEGY

Contemporary Security and Strategy

Second Edition

Edited by Craig A. Snyder

palgrave
macmillan

First Edition 1999

Published 2008 by
PALGRAVE MACMILLAN
Houndmills, Basingstoke, Hampshire RG21 6XS and
175 Fifth Avenue, New York, N.Y. 10010
Companies and representatives throughout the world

PALGRAVE MACMILLAN is the global academic imprint of the Palgrave Macmillan division of St. Martin's Press, LLC and of Palgrave Macmillan Ltd. Macmillan® is a registered trademark in the United States, United Kingdom and other countries. Palgrave is a registered trademark in the European Union and other countries.

ISBN-13: 978-0-230-52095-0   hardback
ISBN-10: 0-230-52095-2   hardback
ISBN-13: 978-0-230-52096-7   paperback
ISBN-10: 0-230-52096-0   paperback

This book is printed on paper suitable for recycling and made from fully managed and sustained forest sources. Logging, pulping and manufacturing processes are expected to conform to the environmental regulations of the country of origin.

A catalogue record for this book is available from the British Library.

A catalog record for this book is available from the Library of Congress.

10 9   8   7   6   5   4   3   2   1
17 16 15 14 13 12 11 10 09 08

Printed and bound in China

For Marion

Contents

Notes on Contributors

Michael J. Arnold is currently working full time on his PhD on Australian defence policy at Deakin University. He was recently employed as a Course Coordinator for Deakin's provision of the Defence and Strategic Studies Course at the Centre for Defence and Strategic Studies, Australian Defence College. He holds the rank of Colonel in the Australian Army Reserve and has successfully completed the Staff College, Reserves (PSC-R) course. He is currently employed as the Director, Army Personnel Agency, Melbourne. He is responsible for the career management of Victoria's 3000 Army Reserve members. He is a graduate of the Royal Military College, Duntroon, and served in the Australian Regular Army until December 1988. He transferred to the Army Reserve in January 1989. Prior to Deakin University, Michael had a long and successful career in the audio-visual and graphic design industries as a producer/project manager.

J. Marshall Beier is Associate Professor of Political Science at McMaster University. He is the author of *International Relations in Uncommon Places: Indigeneity, Cosmology, and the Limits of International Theory* (Palgrave, 2005). His articles have appeared in *Contemporary Security Policy*, *Global Governance*, *International Politics*, *International Studies Review*, *Security Dialogue* and *Third World Quarterly*.

Nick Bisley is Senior Lecturer and Director of the Graduate Programme in Diplomacy and Trade in the Graduate School of Business at Monash University. His research interests lie in the international relations of the Asia-Pacific, great power diplomacy and globalization. He is the author of *Rethinking Globalization* (2007) and *The End of the Cold War and the Causes of Soviet Collapse* (2004), both published by Palgrave, and has published articles and chapters on a wide range of topics in international relations. He is a member of the Council for Security and Cooperation in the Asia Pacific and has been involved with the training of defence and diplomatic personnel in Britain and Australia.

J.D. Kenneth Boutin is Lecturer in International Relations at Deakin University. He was formerly a senior arms control and disarmament researcher at the Verification Research, Training and Information Centre in

London. His research focuses on the political economy of security, including the traditional and non-traditional security aspects of technology policy, technological development, arms transfers, defence industrialization and arms control. He has a particular interest in these issues in the context of transnational economic processes and in the regional context of the Asia-Pacific.

Michael Boyle is Lecturer in International Relations, and Research Fellow at the Centre for the Study of Terrorism and Political Violence, at the University of St. Andrews. His research interests range from political violence and terrorism to humanitarian intervention, peacekeeping and reconstruction of failed states. He also writes on US foreign policy. He has interned for the US Department of State and the Center for Strategic and International Studies and worked as a consultant for the Centre for Defence Studies at King's College, London. He has previously held fellowships at the Center for International Security and Cooperation (CISAC) at Stanford University and the Belfer Center for Science and International Affairs (BCSIA) at the John F. Kennedy School of Government, Harvard University. Dr Boyle was also a Fulbright fellow at the Department of International Relations at the Australian National University.

J. Peter Burgess is Research Professor at PRIO, the International Peace Research Institute, Oslo, Leader of PRIO's Security Programme and Editor of *Security Dialogue*. In addition he is a visiting professor in International Relations at the Fondation nationale de Sciences Politiques, Paris. He was trained in mechanical engineering, comparative literature and philosophy in the United States, Germany, France and Norway. He has broad experience in publishing scholarly work that is situated in the intersection between multiple disciplines. Burgess has published 11 books and over 45 articles in the fields of philosophy, political science, gender, history and cultural studies. He initiated and has led PRIO's strategic institute programmes on European political identity *Europe Looking Outwards* (2002–2004), on the ethics of humanitarian interventions *Arms against a Sea of Troubles* (2005–2007) and on the new security threats to Europe, *Europe under Threat: The New Culture of Insecurity* (2007–2009). He initiated and leads two inter-disciplinary and international research projects funded by the Research Council of Norway *The Social Determination of Risk: Critical Infrastructure and Mass Transportation in the Norwegian Aviation Sector* and *The Liberal Peace and the Ethics of Peace Building*. He is also Head of Research for the project *Threats Beyond Borders. Assessing Norwegian Societal Security in a Global Environment* funded by the Norwegian Ministry of Defence. He earlier led the interdisciplinary project *The European in the New Norwegian*, financed by the Research Council of Norway's Programme for Cultural Studies (1998–2002).

Andy Butfoy is a senior lecturer in international relations at Monash University, Melbourne, Australia. He teaches courses on US foreign policy, arms control and strategic studies. Before going to Monash he was a senior lecturer at the UK Royal Military Academy Sandhurst and a research associate at the International Institute for Strategic Studies in London. He has a BA in international relations from Sussex University, an MA in war studies from Kings College London, and a PhD from the Strategic and Defence Studies Centre of the Australian National University. Butfoy has written many journal and newspaper articles on international security affairs; his most recent book is *Disarming Proposals: Controlling Nuclear, Biological and Chemical Weapons* (Sydney: University of New South Wales Press, 2005).

Sean M. Lynn-Jones is a research associate in the International Security Programme at the Belfer Center for Science and International Affairs (BCSIA), John F. Kennedy School of Government, Harvard University, where he is Series Editor of the BCSIA Studies in International Security book series and co-editor of *International Security*. He is the co-editor of many books, including *Offense, Defense, and War* (MIT Press, 2004), *New Global Dangers: Changing Dimensions of International Security* (MIT Press, 2004), *Theories of War and Peace* (MIT Press, 1998), *Debating the Democratic Peace* (MIT Press, 1996), *The Perils of Anarchy: Contemporary Realism and International Security* (MIT Press, 1995), and *The Cold War and After: Prospects for Peace* (MIT Press, 1993). His articles have appeared in *International Security, Security Studies, and Foreign Policy*, as well as in many edited volumes.

David Mutimer is Deputy Director of York University Centre for International and Security Studies (YCISS) and Associate Professor of Political Science at York University. He has recently returned to York following a two-year leave of absence at the Small Arms Survey in Geneva and the University of Bradford in the UK. His research considers issues of contemporary international security through lenses provided by critical social theory, as well as inquiring into the reproduction of security in and through popular culture. Much of that work has focused on weapons proliferation as a reconfigured security concern in the post-cold war era, and has tried to open possibilities for alternative means of thinking about the security problems related to arms more generally. More recently he has turned his attention to the politics of the global war on terror, and of the regional wars around the world presently being fought by Canada and its allies.

Andrew Latham is currently Associate Professor of Political Science and Associate Dean of the Institute for Global Citizenship at Macalester College, Saint Paul, Minnesota. He has a PhD from York University in Toronto, Canada. He is currently working on a book dealing with the implications of the modern-to-postmodern transition on the nature of organized political violence.

Craig A. Snyder is Senior Lecturer in International Relations at Deakin University. His research interests include regional security structures in Europe and the Asia Pacific. He has been a visiting fellow at the Center for Asian Studies at Arizona State University. He was part of the Deakin team that successfully tendered to deliver the Defence and Strategic Studies Course at the Centre for Defence and Strategic Studies at the Australian Defence College. He has published articles in *Pacific Review*, *International Journal*, *Asian Perspective*, *International Politics*, *Journal of Strategic Studies*, *The Journal of Conflict Studies* and *Contemporary Southeast Asia*.

Geoffrey Till is Professor of Maritime Studies in the Defence Studies Department and was formerly the Dean of Academic Studies at the Joint Services Command and Staff College. Before that he was Professor of History at The Royal Naval College Greenwich. He has taught at the Britannia Royal Naval College Dartmouth, in the Department of Systems Science at the City University, in the Department of War Studies, King's College London, where he completed his MA and PhD, and for the Open University. With the help of a NATO Defence Fellowship he was a visiting scholar at the US Naval Postgraduate School, Monterey; later he held the Foundation Chair in Military Affairs at the US Marine Corps University, Quantico, Virginia. He was recently Visiting Professor at the Armed Forces University, Taiwan, and Senior Visiting Research Fellow at the Institute of Defence and Strategic Studies, Singapore.

Acknowledgements

I would like to thank Steven Kennedy at Palgrave Macmillan for his support and encouragement through the development of both this and the first edition of the book. I would also like to thank the anonymous reviewers of the proposal and manuscript for their insights. The individual contributors also wish to offer their thanks to those who have offered comments or research assistance with their chapters. Sean Lynn-Jones thanks Bradley A. Thayer for his helpful comments on an earlier draft of his chapter. Marshall Beier thanks Richard Stubbs for the reference to the book by Samuel Hawley, *The Imjin War* (2005). Michael Boyle thanks Duncan Bell and Alex Schmid for their helpful comments on an earlier version of his chapter. Peter Burgess thanks Naima Mouhleb for research assistance in preparation of his chapter.

Acronyms

ABMT	Anti-Ballistic Missile Treaty
ASEAN	Association of Southeast Asian Nations
AU	African Union
BCSIA	Belfer Center for Science and International Affairs
CCP	Chinese Communist Party
CISAC	Center for International Security and Cooperation
GTRI	Global Threat Reduction Initiative
HEU	highly enriched uranium
HIC	high-intensity conflict
IAEA	International Atomic Energy Agency
ICC	International Criminal Court
ICISS	International Commission on Intervention and State Sovereignty
IED	improvized explosive device
INF	Intermediate Nuclear Forces (Treaty)
IR	International Relations (the discipline, as opposed to inter-state diplomacy)
ISTC	International Science and Technology Center
MAD	mutual assured destruction
MTCR	Missile Technology Control Regime
NAFTA	North American Free Trade Agreement
NATO	North Atlantic Treaty Organization
NORAD	North American Aerospace Defense Command
NPR	Nuclear Posture Review (1994)
NPT	Nuclear Non-Proliferation Treaty
NSG	Nuclear Suppliers Group
OAS	Organization of American States
OMFTS	operational manoeuvre from the sea
OPEC	Organization of the Petroleum Exporting Countries
OSCE	Organization for Security and Cooperation in Europe
PIF	Pacific Islands Forum
POE	point of entry
PSI	Proliferation Security Initiative
PSO	peace support operation
R&D	research and development
RDD	radiological dispersal device

RMA	revolution in military affairs
SALT	Strategic Arms Limitation Talks
STOM	ship to objective manoeuvre
UNMOVIC	United Nations Monitoring, Verification and Inspection Commission
UNPROFOR	UN Protection Force
UNSC	UN Security Council
UNSCOM	UN Special Commission
WMD	weapons of mass destruction

Chapter 1

Contemporary Security and Strategy

Craig A. Snyder

Introduction

The study of security has been transformed by two major events – the end of the cold war and the terrorist attacks on the United States in 2001. These events have forced a major rethink about the basic assumptions underlying security studies. At stake are some of the key concepts in security studies, in particular, and international relations, in general – security, power, conflict and the nation state. During the cold war academic theorizing about international conflict had been dominated by bipolarity and the dangers of great power conflict. Academics and policy makers alike sought to explain, and predict, all forms of conflict within the international 'system' through the lens of the bipolar superpower conflict between the United States and the Soviet Union.

With the demise of the cold war, new concepts of security that addressed not only the military realities of the contemporary world but also the political, economic and social realities were developed. On the military side questions raised by traditional interstate rivalry – nuclear strategy, deterrence, proliferation of weapons of mass destruction and the future nature of war – continued to prevail. Added to these, however, were debates concerning the theoretical foundations of strategy, understandings of the concept of security, as well as economic, social and political sources of conflict.

The study of security

Most writing in the area of strategic or security studies either focuses on traditional approaches to traditional issues, such as Mearsheimer's (2001) examination of great power politics, or takes new approaches to new issues, such as Cynthia Enloe's (1989) work on feminist investigations of global power relationships. Others, such as Marc Levy (1995) in his work on environmental security, Brad Roberts (1990) on human rights, and Myron Weiner (1992–3) on migration, look at new issues using traditional approaches. That is, these works seek to broaden the realist conception of security to include non-military threats to security such as the environment, human rights issues and the movement of people across international borders. Yet another approach, and the one taken in this volume, is to recast the debate on traditional issues such as deterrence, proliferation and the causes and transformation of war using new approaches. This book therefore seeks to move beyond the realist analysis that has come to dominate the field of security studies and to deepen the agenda of security studies by examining different levels of security, down to the societal or individual level and up to the regional or global level. The broad approach argues that the realist focus on military threats to the state emanating from outside of its borders is no longer sufficient as a means of determining what or who is being secured, what these threats look like and from where they originate (Krause and Williams, 1996: 230). As Steve Smith (2005: 57) argues, the debate over the broadening and deepening of the concept of security has been supported by the events of and in response to 11 September 2001. While these did bring military force back to the forefront of security discourse and the US-led war on terror has primarily been a state-on-state conflict (with little or no role for international institutions), the attacks cannot be explained using traditional understandings of international security or the traditional approaches to the study of security. The attacks were made by a non-state actor who used non-traditional means and were motivated not by traditional political ideology but by a combination of antipathy towards Western forms of modernity and liberalism and also of US policies in the Middle East.

Before we can understand the nature of the debate over the approach to the study of security, we must understand where security studies fits in the wider conceptual framework of international relations (IR). It may seem logical to distinguish security studies as being a sub-field of international relations, much like international law. However, the problem with this is that one cannot separate many important elements of security studies from the political, economic or social elements of the international system. One cannot simply study the military implications of war without understanding the roots of the rivalry between actors, such as considerations of power, status, ideology and wealth (Buzan, 1987: 4). Michael Sheehan (2005: 1) argues that 'security' is at the very core of IR: it is the centrality of security issues that led to the creation of the discipline of IR in the first place and is the reason that IR can be distinguished from other related disciplines such as political science, history, economics, etcetera. However, politics remains at the very root of war, something well understood by the early strategists, especially Clausewitz, who saw war as the violent form of politics. For Richard Betts (1997: 7) this is a fundamental issue, that of 'how to make force a rational instrument of policy rather than mindless murder [that is,] how to integrate politics and war'.

While the distinctions between the various sub-fields are in many instances artificial and difficult to identify precisely for specific issues, they are important in terms of providing a framework for analysis of security issues. The broad scope of security studies provides academic legitimacy, while strategic studies provide intellectual coherence to the military core.

Strategic and security studies: what's in a name?

The term 'strategic studies' has been closely associated with a US approach to the study of the military aspects of the cold war. This has also been described as 'national security studies' because it was generally Americans studying American security (see Garnett, 1987: 7). One of the distinctive elements of strategic studies has been its focus on military strategy. To this end, the focus of traditional strategic studies has been the military means that actors in the international system employ to gain their political objectives or ends. While states are the principal actors in the international system, due primarily to their command over the overwhelming bulk of military power, non-state actors such as terrorists, separatists or national liberation movements are also included. However, the pre-eminence of states is underscored by the fact that these non-state actors are usually involved in an attempt either to gain control of an existing state or to create a new one (Buzan, 1987: 3).

But just what is strategy? Barry Buzan (1987: 3–4) offers several definitions. According to Basil Liddell Hart, strategy is 'the art of distributing and applying military means to fulfil ends of policy'. For Hedley Bull it is 'exploiting military force so as to attain given objects of policy'. Colin Grey argues that strategy is 'the relationship between military power and political purpose'. André Beaufré contends that it is 'the art of the dialectic of two opposing wills using force to resolve their dispute'. Finally, Louis Halle defines strategic studies as 'the branch of political studies concerned with the political implications of the war-making capacity available to nations'. Thus, we can say that strategy involves the use or the threat of the use of force in international relations. Therefore, strategic studies is about how the instruments of force influence the relations between states.

Alongside the US-dominated strategic studies a 'British' or 'English' school evolved which looked at a wider range of issues under the name security studies. Security studies came to the fore in the 1980s and early 1990s as a response to the militaristic focus of strategic studies. Security studies and strategic studies differ not in their basic assumptions about how the world works but in what we consider security threats.

As has been mentioned above, strategic studies is based upon the realist interpretation of international relations. Realists argue that due to the anarchic nature of the international system states should be sceptical of possibilities of permanent peace, ideas of world government, disarmament and concepts such as collective or cooperative security (Garnett, 1987: 9–10). As a result, strategic studies focuses much more on military threats to states while security studies broadens the definition to include non-military threats not only to states but also to non-state actors and sub-state groups.

Security studies also incorporates a further variant, that of critical security. This takes a critical theory approach and raises questions about the nature of the international system itself and the power relationships that form the system. Critical security questions the basic realist assumption that the international system is a predetermined entity, or given, that cannot be changed. Critical theorists argue that the international 'system' is socially constructed: that is, it exists because we have agreed that it should exist. This does not mean any conscious decisions were made but that human interaction has created the structures of the international system and they are not natural nor absolute in their nature. That is, unlike the realists, who see the international system as anarchic, the critical theorists see the international anarchy as a socially constructed structure. For critical security, therefore, the focus is on changing the way we think about security and the role, and indeed the very makeup, of the actors in the system. David Mutimer in Chapter 3 takes up this approach in more detail.

While security studies adopts a broad definition of security, and as a result is much closer to IR than strategic studies, it does have one important difference. It deals with not only the causes and consequences of war, which is the primary area of interest for many IR scholars, but also the conduct of war. This is an important area of scholarship as the decision to go to war, and the result of the war, tend to rest on the military dimension rather than the political. Betts (1997: 9) makes this point when he argues that the different patterns of the First and Second World Wars (that is, Germany's ability to control Western Europe in the early 1940s, as opposed to its inability to do so between 1914 and 1918) cannot be explained only by reference to indices of power (that is, the size of the population, armed forces and the economy; amount of natural resources available; and so on). Rather the success of the German military in developing the *blitzkrieg* strategy and incorporating new military technology and the doctrine of armoured warfare provided the key ingredient to initial German success in the Second World War. Likewise, the ultimate defeat of Germany in this war was a result of a combination of the development of attrition warfare and the strategic and political miscalculations of the German leadership.

Development of strategic studies during the cold war

Before we can fully understand the implications of the end of the cold war for strategic studies, it is important to understand how the field developed before and during the cold war. The first book to examine the broader questions of security and war prevention was Quincy Wright's *A Study of War*, published in 1942. It deviated from the work of the classical strategists (as we will see in Chapter 6), which considered war as a tool of statecraft. Rather than looking at problems of national security or alternatives for national strategy, Wright looked to diplomacy, international understanding, arbitration, national self-determination, disarmament and collective security as guarantors of international peace and stability (Baldwin, 1995: 119–20).

In the immediate aftermath of the Second World War the study of war continued along this line. In the aftermath of the defeat of Nazi Germany the anti-fascist allies (in particular the United States, Britain, France, the Soviet Union and China) sought to create a new world order that would ensure global peace and stability. International institutions such as the United Nations, the World Bank and the International Monetary Fund emerged at this time to assist in decolonization, in economic, social and political development, and in the management of international crises. In the heady days of the early post-war period, security analysts built on the work of Quincy Wright and examined four key themes. The first was that security was not the primary concern of all states at all times but merely one concern that varied in importance from one historical context to the next. Theorists in this area looked at calculations as to the trade-off between military security and other values such as economic welfare and individual freedom. Second, both military and non-military tools of state-craft would be important to national security. Third, the recognition of the security dilemma (that is, the actions that one state takes to increase its security in turn decrease the security felt by others) led to cautious use of military power. Fourth, linkages were made between national security and domestic affairs, such as the economy, civil liberties and democratic processes (Baldwin, 1995: 122).

However, this period of optimism was quickly overtaken as a result of the growing tension and mistrust between the two leading Second World War allies. The United States and the Soviet Union, divided over their polit-ical and economic ideologies of democracy and capitalism versus commu-nism, clashed over the nature of the post-war system that was emerging. While the United States sought to establish an international political economic structure that favoured capitalism (especially US capitalist inter-ests), the Soviets were more concerned with exporting the worker's revolu-tion and overthrowing capitalism at a global level (and, at a more practi-cal level, exercising its control over Central and Eastern Europe, an area of strategic importance to the security of the Soviet Union). Because of this growing mistrust, tensions between the wartime allies increased to the point where the notion of a 'cold war' developed between the US-led 'West' and the Soviet-led 'East'. The most physical representation of this East–West divide was the division of Europe between the Soviet-controlled eastern half of the continent and the US-led western half. This division included the division of not only Germany but also the former German capital of Berlin. This division was a result of the original system for the post-war occupation of Germany where each of the allies was given a zone of control. While the French, British and Americans transferred their zones to a new Federal Republic of Germany (commonly referred to in English as West Germany), the Soviets transferred their zone to the German Democratic Republic (or East Germany).

Strategic analysts, at this time, began to focus on the possibility of a major conflict between the United States and the Soviet Union. Added to the mix of conventional strategic analysis was the issue of the role of nuclear weapons. As is discussed in Chapter 8, while the United States maintained a monopoly on nuclear weapons, these were seen as just another weapon in the US arsenal, albeit a strategic rather than a tactical one. That is, nuclear weapons were considered as a war-ending or war-prevention weapon. However, the potential for a global nuclear war emerged in 1949 following the first Soviet nuclear test. This was followed in 1957 with the introduction of intercontinental ballistic missiles, with the Soviet launch of the *Sputnik 1* satellite onboard the 'R–7' ballistic missile. This development provided the Soviets with the ability to strike directly at the continental United States and removed the US monopoly on both nuclear weapons and the ability to use them as a strategic weapon vis-à-vis its cold war rival.

Although the type of security study that Quincy Wright had advocated continued throughout the cold war, it was marginalized because of the narrowing of the focus of strategic studies onto nuclear weapons and the increased chance of global nuclear war. Strategic studies flourished in this period because nuclear deterrence was, by its very nature, theoretical rather than practical. The major questions raised at this time were concerned with arms control and limited war. As a result, the cold war security agenda was conceptualized through the concept of deterrence. The complexity of the rivalry between the two ideologically based blocs was simplified to questions of alliance management and nuclear stability. It was commonly assumed that state behaviour was based on a policy of power or security maximization with the strategy of influencing rivals to act in certain ways through threat manipulation and force projection (Kolodziej, 1993: 16).

This was a major shift in thinking. While previous scholars had focused on defining security and how important it was as compared to other goals, and how it should be attained, the new focus was on how weapons of mass destruction could be used as a policy instrument without risking a nuclear exchange. This type of thought, however, placed too much attention on military tools, which led to an overemphasis on the military aspects of national security over other elements such as historical, cultural or political contexts (Baldwin, 1995: 123; Betts, 1997: 12–13).

Because of this focus on the abstract theories of nuclear deterrence and limited nuclear war, many in strategic studies in the late 1960s through to the early 1980s found themselves unable to respond to contemporary strategic issues such as the Vietnam War and other post-colonial wars of national liberation. The academic strategic analysts were so specialized in global strategic issues such as the Soviet-US rivalry that they were unable to offer insights into these regional conflicts. Indeed, they tended to explain them in terms of the cold war divide and deemed them 'proxy wars' (Baldwin, 1995: 124). Moreover, those strategists (such as Pike, 1966; Race, 1972; Blaufarb, 1977; Cable, 1986; Shafer, 1988; Lomperis, 1996) that did look to Third World conflicts tended to be practitioners rather than academic theorists. They focused on examining case studies of counter-insurgency operations, concluding that the US experience in Vietnam demonstrated that theories failed when applied to the real world (see Betts, 1997: 13).

Other scholars such as Betts (1982), Bouchard (1991), Cohen (1985), Keegan (1976), Luttwak (1987), Mearsheimer (1983), Posen (1984), Rosen (1991) and van Crevald (1977, 1985) did look to non-nuclear military issues, but continued to focus upon the cold war divide. These scholars questioned the assumptions of the (non-)effectiveness of the North Atlantic Treaty Organization's (NATO) conventional forces to fight a war in Europe. The questions asked by this group focused on the political, economic, social, technological, organizational and doctrinal aspect of the NATO forces. However, strategic studies also found itself, due to its limited focus on these types of military issues, challenged by other fields such as peace studies and international political economy, which could better explain issues such as détente, economic interdependence, Third World poverty and environmentalism. Most significantly the OPEC oil embargo brought home the idea that threats to the Western living standards came from non-military sources as well as military ones (Baldwin, 1995: 124; Betts, 1997: 20). With the revival of the cold war in the 1980s under the Reagan presidency, strategic studies was revised. The focus of strategic studies from this point until the end of the cold war remained on the study of the threat, use and control of military force – in other words the use of military means to meet military challenges (Baldwin, 1995: 124–5).

In summary, the cold war affected the focus of the research conducted in strategic studies. It focused attention away from the broader questions of how security policy fits into the larger foreign policy goals and toward technical and theoretical aspects of nuclear weapons and strategies, East–West relations, and the security problems of the United States and Western Europe. Nuclear weapons added a particular twist to the focus of strategic studies: that is, strategic analysts were studying how to use the threat of using force while they also worked to prevent such usage.

Post-cold war developments and the shift in thinking

There is common agreement among security analysts as to the implications of the end of the cold war for the field of security studies. First, the role of military power was scrutinized. While the old school of strategic studies accepted that questions of force had to be seen in the wider context of the political and economic aspects of the international system, the revival of liberal notions of multilateral cooperation that accompanied the end of the cold war de-legitimized force as a tool of statecraft. For some this meant that military threats declined in relevance, while for others military tools became less useful. Second, there was a need to re-examine the way we thought about security. For some this was a result of fundamental changes to the post-cold war environment, and for others the failure of strategic studies to predict the end of the cold war. Third, there was a need to expand what we meant by security. Again, for some this meant expanding the definition to include the effect of domestic issues on the national security agenda of states, and for others it meant treating non-military threats to the national well-being as security threats (Baldwin, 1995: 118; Freedman, 1998: 52–3; Smith, 2005).

Re-defining security

In order for security studies to continue to be relevant in the contemporary era it needs to shift its thinking about security. It needs to question three broad issues: security as a goal, the means of pursuing security, and the relation of security and domestic affairs.

First, questions as to the relevance of security as the primary goal of states need to be addressed. While strategic analysts in the past have insisted on the primacy of security, is it still plausible to insist on this today? Security is important but how much security is needed, and are there other national interests that are of at least equal importance at a very basic level? How good is security if there is no food, arable land or drinkable water in a country? How effective have our security policies been if they have resulted in 'blowback' through the rise of other threats, such as environmental issues or new rivals? In the contemporary era many in the West, in particular, question the marginal costs of security. Most would accept that the Western states have an over abundance of security, and therefore the return on a dollar spent on security will be smaller than the return that dollar would provide if spent on other goals that are less abundant. In other words if in an era where the military budget provides for more security than is considered necessary, it would be cost-effective to reduce the military budget and spend that money on other projects such as cleaning up the environment or feeding the people (Baldwin, 1995: 126–8). Even in the post-9/11 environment, questions arise about how much the West's Middle East policies have not so much caused but perhaps facilitated the rise of militant Islamic extremism. Questions are also raised about the extent and nature of the West's response to the threat. These relate not only to the cost of the military actions conducted in the name of the so called 'war on terror' but also to the extent that civil liberties have been sacrificed in the name of 'national security'.

Second, security studies has also tended to favour examinations of the means to security and not the goals of security. That is, security analysts study the use of military force without devoting equal attention to the purposes for which it is used. Barry Baldwin (1995: 128–30) calls this very un-Clausewitzian. During the cold war, most saw military force as the primary source of threats to states; therefore, it was understandable that they also considered the use of force as the primary response. However, in the contemporary era, with the recognition that threats to security can come from other issues – such as environmental degrada-tion, resource depletion, disease, forced migration and organized transnational crime – security can only come from a balance of all instru-ments of foreign policy. Likewise, the response to the attacks on the United States in 2001 have tended to focus on the military dimension rather than exploring the political, social or economic dimensions of the antipathy that groups like al-Qaeda have towards the West.

As we will see in Chapter 2, strategic studies has been closely linked to the international relations theory of realism, which regards states as the principal actors in the international system. It is therefore difficult for strategic studies to address domestic sources of insecurity (Baldwin, 1995: 130–1). In the contemporary era the object of security is shifting away from the state to the individual or sub-state group. This implies a focus on how individuals can threaten the state (or ruling regime) or how the state can threaten the security of individuals, mainly in the name of regime preservation or national security.

Structure of this book

In order to explore fully the implications of the shift from strategic to security studies, it is important to understand the theoretical basis of both approaches. As such, this book begins with an examination of the leading theoretical positions within strategic and security studies, beginning with realism and following this with consideration of alternative approaches to how we think about security. This then leads into an examination some of the current debates within the field: the causes of war, the evolution of strategic thought, the transformation of war, nuclear strategy, proliferation, terrorism, intervention and regional security.

Chapters 2 to 4 deal with more contemporary theories of security. Chapter 2 introduces realism, the dominant paradigm in international relations and strategic studies. It begins by defining realism, tracing the development of realist thought and responding to the key criticisms of realism. The chapter then addresses key debates in current realist theory, such as the offence/defence variants of structural realism and whether the distribution of power or the level and source of threats are the key determinants of state action. The chapter goes on to explore the future of realism after the end of the cold war. In this section, Sean Lynn-Jones examines realism's failure to predict the end of the cold war, its continued relevance in the contemporary world and its ability to predict future international politics.

Chapters 3 and 4 critique the realist approach to security studies, offering a different approach to the subject. In Chapter 3 David Mutimer introduces critical theories of security. The object of this chapter is to explore the thinking that has developed from a recognition of the limitations of the understanding of 'security' promoted by realism. Mutimer begins by arguing that traditional definitions of security – the protection of the state from armed attack – are insufficient. He states that the question needs to be broken down into its constituent parts. *Whose* security? *How* can this security be provided? And how should security be *studied*?

Chapter 4 focuses on non-military challenges to security. It begins by looking at the class of non-military security threats against which military force has little or no utility. These may be either local or global in character, but their impacts will register on the security of states sooner rather than later, if they are not doing so already. These include environmental issues (such as, humanly generated climate change in general, and global warming in particular), resource depletion (such as deforestation or over-fishing), health issues (such as the consequences of the HIV-AIDS epidemic), forced migration and organized transnational crime. Of course many of these matters overlap and reinforce each other. These should be regarded as security concerns for states in so far as they directly threaten the peace and prosperity of a country and its citizens, and indirectly in so far as they give rise to violence and undesirable political and strategic change.

Chapters 5 to 7 take on more traditional topics of security and conflict by looking at the causes of war, the evolution of strategic thought and the impact of the information revolution on armed forces and conflict. Chapter 5 begins this section with an inquiry into the causes of war from a number of contending theoretical perspectives. Here Marshall Beier explores successive explanations of war, its causes, and the conditions for peace, as well as critiques highlighting the weaknesses of each. In each instance, connections are made between these debates and those concerning competing conceptions of security discussed earlier in the book. The approach taken uncovers insights into the causes of war through a range of inquiries into the conditions for peace as well as through engagement with more direct cause and effect types of explanations. This gives a greater sense of both the various accounts of the causes of war and the broader political contexts in which those accounts are embedded.

In Chapter 6 Geoffrey Till explores the evolution of strategic thinking from the classical era to the contemporary world. He begins with a brief survey of the development of classical strategic thinking that rehearses the essential points made by the most influential thinkers but focuses on changing concepts of what strategy means and entails. This section concludes with a review of the widening of the concept of security and its impact on strategic thinking. In the next section Till looks at the 'novelty' of contemporary security threats and offers an analysis of the problems these set for contemporary strategic thinkers. The focus here is the shift to network-centric warfare, joint operations and the role of doctrine. The final section focuses on maritime expeditionary operations. In this Till explores the nature of contemporary maritime threats, the impact of sea-based globalization, competing paradigms of naval development and naval thinking, and state-centred and system-centred approaches.

In Chapter 7 Andrew Latham explores the rather rapid development of literatures dealing with the transformation of war. He argues that at the level of the *warfighting paradigm*, there is now an extensive body of research both describing and prescribing changes in the way the world's dominant militaries conduct combat operations on the battlefield. On a somewhat deeper level, what he calls the *social mode of warfare*, the literature traces significant changes in the way state-society complexes organize for, prosecute and experience warfare. Finally, on the temporal level of the *longue durée*, scholars have begun to analyse transformations in what Latham calls the *historical structure of war* – that is, the constellation of deep structures, practices and discourses that define the very nature of 'war' and distinguish it from other forms of politics and violence.

Chapters 8 to 13 explore contemporary security issues such as the implications of nuclear and other weapons of mass destruction, terrorism and insurgency, the implications of intervention strategies, the role of the great powers and finally, approaches to regional security.

In Chapter 8 the main question is: how do the established nuclear weapon states (China, France, India, Israel, Pakistan, Russia, the UK and the United States) view their weapons in terms of national security? In answering this question, Andy Butfoy explores key themes such as deterrence and war fighting strategies. There is a case study on the United States as the largest nuclear-armed state. After a brief overview of cold war doctrine, the nexus between nuclear weapons and developments in US strategic thinking since the end of the cold war is examined. These developments include the deployment of missile defences, US reflection on the usability of nuclear weapons, the impact of terrorism, the identification of an 'axis of evil', and the commitment to maintain US military superiority as a foundation stone for world order.

In Chapter 9 Ken Boutin examines an issue that has returned to the forefront of the security agenda, propelled by prominent examples of successful proliferation and evident interest on the part of a number of other states in following a similar path. This chapter examines the key trends and developments that are threatening the global non-proliferation regime. It begins with an assessment of the state of the non-proliferation regime at the end of the cold war. The chapter then proceeds to consider the forces driving horizontal proliferation, and structural developments that are contributing to proliferation concerns. It then examines how the non-proliferation regime is adapting to these challenges. The chapter concludes by considering the impact on non-proliferation norms of the non-proliferation and counter-proliferation policies of developed states such as the United States.

In Chapter 10 Michael Boyle examines the threat of terrorism and insurgency as they have evolved through the twentieth century and assesses the nature of contemporary global terrorism. In the chapter he evaluates the strategies and tactics of terrorists and insurgents, and their relative effectiveness in achieving their political objectives. The chapter concludes with an assessment of the effectiveness of counter-terrorism strategies of the West.

In Chapter 11 Michael Arnold looks at the effectiveness of intervention and international peacekeeping. In this he does not look at the legality or morality of these interventions, but rather at the requirements for an intervention force to succeed. It explores the nature of new wars and contemporary conflicts in which interventions will likely be undertaken. The chapter examines important changes in the forms of armed conflict that occur in the less developed world that challenge many of the assumptions of conventional thinking about security.

In Chapter 12 Nicholas Bisley assesses the role of great powers in international security. In the past their power, capacity and structural advantages have brought with them special rights and responsibilities, but in the contemporary world there is good reason to question whether the term makes sense. Given the predominance of the United States, the role of nuclear weapons and globalization, the idea of great powers seems somewhat anachronistic. This chapter considers the role of great powers in contemporary security and strategy and explores the way in which the structure of the international system provides differing incentives for state behaviour. On the one hand, the predominant power in the international system has a marked taste for unilateral approaches to security and strategy. Yet even the United States recognizes that there are times when it cannot 'go it alone'. The chapter concludes with a consideration of the tensions that exist between unilateral and multilateral means for great powers to achieve their strategic and security aims.

The final chapter in the book explores regional approaches to security. It is at the regional level that most conflict since the end of the Second World War has occurred. The chapter begins with an examination of the new regionalism theory of Bjorn Hettne (2000) and then provides an assessment of the increasing or decreasing level of regionalism found in various regions of the world.

Further reading

Baldwin, D.A. (1995) 'Security Studies and the End of the Cold War', *World Politics*, 48: 117–41.
Betts, R.K. (1997) 'Should Strategic Studies Survive?' *World Politics*, 50: 7–33.
Buzan, B. (1987) *An Introduction to Strategic Studies: Military Technology and International Relations*, London: Macmillan.

Freedman, L. (1998) 'International Security: Changing Targets', *Foreign Policy*, 109: 48–63.

Garnett, J. (1987) 'Strategic Studies and its Assumptions', in Baylis, J., Booth, K., Garnett, J. and Williams, P. (eds), *Contemporary Strategy: Vol 1 Theories and Concepts*, London: Holmes and Meier.

Kolodziej, E.A. (1993) 'Whither Security Studies After the Cold War?' in Bajpai, K.P. and Cohen, S.P. (eds), *South Asia After the Cold War: International Perspectives*, Boulder: Westview.

Krause, K. and Williams, M.C. (1996) 'Broadening the Agenda of Security Studies: Politics and Methods', *Mershon International Studies Review*, 40: 229–54.

Smith, S. (2005) 'The Contested Concept of Security', in Booth, K. (ed.), *Critical Security Studies and World Politics*, Boulder: Lynne Rienner.

Wright, Q. [1942] (1964) *A Study of War*, Wright, L.L. (abridged version), Chicago: University of Chicago Press.

Chapter 2

Realism and Security Studies

Sean M. Lynn-Jones

Introduction

Realism occupies a paradoxical place in the study of international politics. It is commonly regarded as the dominant paradigm in the field – particularly in the sub-field of international security studies. At the same time, realism is criticized frequently. Almost every issue of the leading journals of international politics contains several articles that claim to have refuted realist theory. Many articles and books pronounce that realism is dead, inadequate or irrelevant. A spate of such criticisms emerged after the end of the cold war, including Charles Kegley (1993: 131–46), Ethan Kapstein (1995: 751–74) and Richard Lebow (1994: 249–77). Others, such as Jack Snyder (1991) and Richard Rosecrance and Arthur Stein (1993), argue that realism does a poor job of explaining a particular event or type of event and that other theories – particularly those that include domestic politics – offer better explanations.

Events of recent decades have given new impetus to the perennial debate over realism. Its critics have claimed that realist theories failed to predict the end of the cold war, the collapse of the Soviet empire, and the sudden transformation of the US–Soviet rivalry from enmity into amity. Such critics have also argued that realist theories are not useful for understanding key issues of contemporary international politics, including ethnic conflict, terrorism, and global responses to new problems such as climate change and emerging infectious diseases. These and other criticisms have prompted a vigorous response from realists.

This chapter examines the following questions: What is realism? How has it evolved as a family of theories of international politics? What are the most important criticisms of realist theories? What are the current theoretical issues in the debate over realism? Is realism still relevant?

What is realism?

Critics and proponents often refer to realism as if it were a monolithic body of thought. This view overlooks the tremendous diversity in realist thinking. Realists do share some basic ideas, including the belief that people (and states) generally pursue their own interests and that power determines who gets what in politics, but they vigorously debate one another and disagree on many theoretical and practical issues. Although the realist approach to international politics can be summarized as a theory that holds that states struggle for power and security in an anarchic environment, it is important to understand the differences among realists (see Walt, 2002: 197–230).

Realism can be seen in two basic ways. First, it is a general philosophical tradition. In this sense, realism connotes a general pessimism about the human condition, scepticism about the prospects for human progress, a belief that humans are likely to come into violent conflict, and the conviction that human conflicts generally will be resolved by the application of superior power, not by appeals to notions of justice. The realist worldview sees much evil in human nature and finds recurrent patterns of tragedy in human existence. These philosophical elements of realism are strongly present in the writings of Thucydides, Hobbes and Machiavelli. In the twentieth century, Reinhold Niebuhr (1944) is a prominent example of this type of realism, although the philosophical underpinnings of realism are evident in the writings of Herbert Butterfield (1950), Martin Wight ([1946] 1978), and Hans Morgenthau (1946).

Second, realism can be regarded as an academic approach to understanding international politics. Scholars who see themselves as realists may share the basic pessimism of the first type of realist, but they go beyond it in their attempts to elucidate theoretical concepts about how independent states interact with one another. Most realist scholars attempt to build social-scientific theories that explain and predict international behaviour.

This chapter will focus on realism as an academic approach to understanding international politics. Although scholarship in security studies has often been influenced by philosophical realism, most of the contemporary debates over the theory and practice of international politics have revolved around issues raised by academic realist theories.

Realism is a general academic approach to international politics, not a single, unified theory. Critics and proponents of realism often fail to recognize that realism is a family of many related theories. Although realist theories of international politics differ, most realists share the following core beliefs about the nature of international politics (for other discussions of the elements and assumptions of realism see Keohane (1986a: 7–16), Gilpin (1986: 304–5), Mearsheimer (1994–5: 10–12) and Walt (2002: 199–200). First, realists believe that states are the most important actors in international politics. They therefore focus on explaining the behaviour of states and tend to pay less attention to individuals and transnational actors like corporations and multinational organizations. Second, realists regard anarchy – the absence of any common sovereign – as the distinguishing feature of international life. Without a central authority to enforce agreements or to guarantee security, states must rely on their own means to protect their interests. The corollary of the assumed existence of an anarchic system is thus the necessity for states to use self-help measures, including force, to protect their interests. Third, realists assume that states seek to maximize their power or their security. Some realists focus on power as an end in itself, whereas others regard it as a means to security. Hans Morgenthau is the leading example of a realist who holds that states seek power. Kenneth Waltz (1988: 40–41) exemplifies the view that power is only a means to the end of security. Fourth, realists usually assume that states generally adopt more-or-less rational policies in their pursuit of power and/or security. Fifth, realists normally agree that states will tend to rely on the threat or use of military force to secure their objectives in international politics. This does not mean that realists only study war and military force, but that realists recognize that the possible use of force always lurks in the background of international politics because states must depend on self-help measures. Sixth, most realists believe that aspects of the international system – especially the distribution of power among states – are the most important causes of the basic patterns of international politics and foreign policy. Although realists may recognize that state-level factors such as regime type, domestic politics and the personality of leaders matter, they emphasize the causal importance of international factors.

In addition to understanding what realism is, it is important to understand what realism is not. Misconceptions about it abound. First, many observers associate realism with a 'hard-line' confrontational approach to foreign policy. Realists are assumed to be hawks who are eager to intervene with military force or to take an uncompromising line in negotiations. In practice, however, realists have advocated and sometimes implemented dovish policies. In the United States, for example, the realist ex-diplomat George Kennan was a frequent critic of confrontational US policies toward the Soviet Union and Russia. Hans Morgenthau, the most influential realist scholar of the 1940s and 1950s, was an early critic of US intervention in the Vietnam War. Henry Kissinger was the architect of detente with the Soviet Union and the opening of a dialogue between the United States and China. More recently, academic realists such as Christopher Layne (2006: 7–41) and Mearsheimer and Walt (2002) have opposed US efforts to seek a position of primacy in international politics and the US decision to invade Iraq in 2003.

Some realists have been hawks. Realists differ in their personal views about foreign policy and military strategy, so it is not surprising that some realists have favoured confrontational policies and the use of force. The variety of realist theories ensures that at least some forms of realism can be interpreted as calling for hawkish policies. In general, however, the realist perspective is likely to counsel prudence and caution, because realism emphasizes a sense of limits and the importance of being aware of one's adversary's power as well as one's own. In contrast to realism, liberalism and Marxism, with their universalizing ideologies, are more likely to be invoked to support crusading imperialism (see, Doyle, 1983: 205–35 and 323–53). The neoconservative beliefs that have guided the administration of US President George W. Bush also diverge from realism, although some observers erroneously conflate realists and neoconservatives.

Second, realism is often seen as a theory that only applies to issues involving the use of military force. Realists, to be sure, usually claim that the possibility of the use of force is always in the background of international politics. Realist theories, however, have often been used to shed light on international economic interactions. Several prominent scholars in the sub-field of international political economy are realists. Stephen Krasner (1991: 336–66), for example, has employed realist theory to argue that the relative power of the countries involved is often the key to understanding international economic negotiations. He suggests that countries do not cooperate because of reciprocity but because one has superior power and can use it to persuade the other to accept an agreement. Joseph Grieco (1993) has argued that states are concerned about relative gains (that is, those that increase a state's power compared with other states) in the economic realm because gaps in gains can be translated into advantages in power. Thus states engaged in negotiations on international trade may not seek to maximize their absolute gains (that is, those that increase a state's capabilities or welfare) regardless of the gains of other states, as economists would assume, but instead seek outcomes in which they maximize their relative gains compared with other states. And Robert Gilpin (1987), author of an influential textbook on international political economy, is a prominent realist. He has argued forcefully that the globalization of the world economy and the increased role of multinational corporations have not eroded the primacy of the state in international politics (Gilpin, 1996).

Third, realists are often portrayed as denying that cooperation of any kind is possible in international politics. The image of a Hobbesian war of 'all against all' is associated with many realist theories. In general, realists are more pessimistic about international cooperation than are, for example, liberal institutionalists, who believe that norms and institutions lead to cooperation. Nevertheless, many realist theories predict cooperation under different types of circumstances. Stephen Van Evera (1999), Charles Glaser (1994–5) and other so-called 'defensive realists', for example, suggest that the international system is not the harsh environment depicted by some realist theories. Rational states may be able to devise policies to maximize mutual security (for an even more optimistic realist analysis, see Kydd, 1997: 114–54). Other realists argue that international economic cooperation is likely when one very powerful state – a hegemon – takes the lead in enforcing an international system of free trade (Krasner, 1976). Many realists argue that cooperation becomes likely when two states perceive a common threat and form an alliance to counter it. Clearly realist theories do not exclude the possibility of international cooperation.

The development of realist thought

Realist thought has a long and distinguished lineage. Thucydides (1954: 49) is regarded as an early realist because his *History of the Peloponnesian War* portrayed the struggles of Greek city-states in the fifth century BC as a conflict over power. His argument that war became inevitable because of 'the growth of Athenian power and the fear which this caused in Sparta' is a classic example of a realist explanation. Classical realists, however, remained sceptical about whether realist theories could 'solve' the problem of war through the application of social science (see, in particular, Morgenthau, 1946). Structural realists, on the other hand, generally attempted to build social-scientific theories and at least some were optimistic that these theories could be used to prevent war. Machiavelli wrote about domestic as well as international politics, but his unsentimental emphasis on the realities of power in politics marks him as a realist. Hobbes also was primarily concerned with domestic politics, but his argument that men would remain in conflict unless coerced into peace by a superior power – a governmental Leviathan – remains a central element of realist thought. During the nineteenth century, realism was exemplified by the *realpolitik* diplomacy of Metternich, Palmerston and Bismarck.

In the twentieth century, the evolution of realism was dominated by the rise of what is usually called classical realism in the 1930s and 1940s, and the articulation of structural realism (sometimes called neorealism) in the 1970s and 1980s. Both groups of writers attempted to turn realist ideas into a rigorous and systematic understanding of international politics. Inis Claude (1962), for example, criticizes the ambiguities of Morgenthau's conception of the balance of power.

Between and after the two world wars, the classical realists reacted to idealistic visions of international politics by insisting on the importance of power in relations between states. E.H. Carr (1942) and Hans Morgenthau (1948) are the most prominent representatives of this approach, but their outlook was shared in varying degrees by Reinhold Niebuhr (1944), Nicholas Spykman ([1942] 1970), George Kennan (1954), Henry Kissinger (1957), Robert Osgood (1957), Raymond Aron ([1962] 1966), Arnold Wolfers (1962) and John Herz (1962). The classical realists generally saw an inherent degree of evil in human nature. Many of them explicitly argued that human nature included an innate lust for power that drove individuals and states to attempt to dominate others. In international politics, power – not justice or ideas of morality – was the key to most important events. Classical realists thus rejected claims that better international institutions and procedures for arbitrating disputes would prevent war. They argued that states should attempt to maximize their power in international politics and that this pursuit of power would serve the national interest. A particular state's national interest would depend on its power and geographical circumstances. The classical realists emphasized the concept of the balance of power and argued that states tended to ally against more powerful and more threatening states, although their writings remained ambiguous on whether roughly equal balances tended to form in international politics and whether balanced power made war or peace more likely. For example, Inis Claude (1962) criticized the ambiguities of Morgenthau's conception of the balance of power. During the early cold war, classical realism became the dominant US school of thought in the study of international politics. Morgenthau's *Politics Among Nations* (1948) became a popular textbook and remains a classic in the field.

Structural realism is largely identified with the writings of Kenneth Waltz (1979, 1988). For Waltz, the essential feature of international politics is its anarchic structure – the absence of a common sovereign. The condition of anarchy – not human nature – shapes the basic patterns of international politics. Structural realism is distinguished from classical realism by an explicit rejection of any assumptions about an innate lust for power due to the evil inherent in human nature. States in an anarchic system do not seek to maximize their power, but instead make survival their highest priority. Power is a means to the end of survival, not an end in itself. International politics is shaped by states' search for security in an anarchic system, not by a lust for power embedded in human nature. States will attempt to survive by using self-help strategies; under anarchy, they cannot expect others to protect their security. The basic patterns of international politics recur as long as the system lacks a common sovereign, regardless of the culture, ideology or domestic politics of the states in the system. Waltz argues that weaker states will tend to form balancing alliances against stronger states. (Writing at about the same time as Waltz, Robert Gilpin (1981) argues that the history of international politics is the rise and fall of successive hegemonic powers, not the repeated defeat of potential hegemons by balancing coalitions.) Waltz also suggests that the simplicity of a bipolar world – one in which there are only two great powers – reduces the possibility of uncertainty and miscalculation, thereby making war less likely. Waltz's conception of realism produces a systematic and parsimonious theory that focuses on the distribution of power in the international system while according little weight to domestic politics or ideologies. His recasting of realism has provoked much further theoretical innovation and criticism.

In *The Tragedy of Great Power Politics*, the most important recent addition to the realist canon, John Mearsheimer (2001) builds on Waltz's structural realism while incorporating some of Morgenthau's emphasis on the quest for power. Like Morgenthau, Mearsheimer argues that states seek to maximize their relative power, but he follows Waltz in arguing that the anarchic structure of the international system is the key to understanding state behaviour. According to Mearsheimer, anarchy drives states to seek power because power is the key to survival. He therefore parts company with Waltz and argues that states will strive to become regional hegemons instead of acting with restraint. Mearsheimer adopts the label of 'offensive realist' and offers a more pessimistic vision of world politics than Waltz and other defensive realists (for an excellent summary and critique see Snyder, 2002).

Criticisms of realism

Opponents of realist theory have frequently criticized realism. Most of these criticisms have been directed against structural realism, but several also apply to classical realism. Five perennial criticisms have been prominent:

1. Realism cannot explain change in the international system.
2. Realism ignores the importance of different conceptions of identity and culture in states.
3. Realism has unacceptable moral implications.
4. Realism exaggerates the importance of states and the distribution of power among them, and neglects other key actors in international politics.
5. Realism does not explain very much about specific foreign-policy decisions.

First, critics have argued that realism – and particularly structural realism – cannot explain important changes in the nature of the international system. By focusing on the condition of anarchy and the distribution of power among states, structural realism ignores many important aspects of international politics. For example, structural realism does not account for how international politics and the idea of sovereignty changed from the medieval to the modern system (see Ruggie, 1986; Cox, 1986; Ashley, 1986; Keohane, 1986a).

Realists concede much of the criticism that structural realism does not explain change very well. After all, structural realist theory claims to explain the recurring patterns of international politics in an anarchic system. Although realists admit that conceptions of sovereignty, processes of inter-action between states, and many norms and beliefs about international life have changed, they emphasize that the essential features of international politics – the struggle for security, the importance of power, the role of the threat of force, and the balance of power – remain the same. During the feudal period, for example, when modern states did not exist, international politics still followed the realist patterns of territorial aggrandizement, alliance formation and war (Fischer, 1992).

Second, realism's critics claim that realist theories overlook the importance of culture and identity in international politics. This argument challenges the realist assumption that all states can be regarded as essentially similar rational security-seeking units. States instead act on the basis of the identities and norms that they intellectually construct for themselves.

Cultural differences lead states to act in ways that realist theories would not predict (see Katzenstein, 1996).

Realist responses generally claim that concepts like norms, culture and identity are infinitely malleable and do not make for a good scientific theory. Realists also point out that differences in culture and identity have not prevented states from behaving in similar ways. Powerful states, for example, tend to expand, regardless of their conceptions of their own identity. Some realists might concede, however, that culture and identity may help to explain variations in foreign policy that cannot be explained by the application of realist theories (see Desch, 1998; Copeland, 2000a).

Third, several opponents of realism have argued that realist theories have unacceptable moral implications. Robert Keohane (1986c: 198), for example, contends that:

> realism sometimes seems to imply, pessimistically, that order can be created *only* by hegemony. If the latter conclusion were correct ... at some time in the foreseeable future, global nuclear war would ensue. ... No serious thinker could, therefore, be satisfied with *realism.*

Other critics of realism seem to be driven by the belief that the human race is capable of a more hopeful future than the endless pattern of conflict depicted by realism.

Realists offer two types of replies to claims that realism is morally unacceptable. On the one hand, they point out that realist theories do not exclude the possibility of international cooperation. The tradition of *realpolitik* as practiced by Bismarck and Metternich includes many attempts to use diplomacy to manage crises, forge alliances and prevent war. Moreover, realists suggest that the essential realist vision captures many truths about the human condition. Recognizing the limits of any attempts to change international politics may be better than foolhardy attempts to transcend the existing system, however inadequate it may be.

Fourth, realism's critics fault realist theories for assuming that states are the most important actors in international politics. They argue that the sovereign state is becoming less important. International politics increasingly takes place between multinational corporations like IBM and Exxon, transnational actors like the Red Cross and the Catholic Church, and international institutions like the European Union and the United Nations. At the same time, groups within states tend to identify more with their ethnic or religious groups than with central state institutions. If the state is losing its sovereignty and being supplanted by other actors, the critics argue, realism will become inapplicable.

Realists reply that reports of the demise of the state are greatly exaggerated. Multinational corporations and other transnational actors are probably less important now than they were in previous centuries. The British East India Company was more powerful than today's multinational corporations (see Gilpin, 1996: 25). The Catholic Church was formerly a more influential participant in international politics. States continue to play the most important role in international politics. States create the legal and regulatory environment for multinational corporations, and even the weakest states have nationalized the assets of foreign corporations. Moreover, realists argue, realism does not insist that states are the *only* actors in international politics, but instead claims that they are the *primary* actors.

Finally, critics of realism argue that realist theories do not explain very much about international politics. In particular, critics claim that realism does not explain how and why states make specific foreign-policy decisions. They argue that realism's focus on factors like the distribution of power among states ignores important variables such as individual psychology, domestic politics and international institutions.

Realists differ among themselves on how to respond to this criticism. Some agree that realist theories only explain the broad patterns of international politics; realism does not explain why particular states adopt specific policies at a given time. Thus realist theory might explain why there were few great-power wars during the cold war, but not why the Soviet Union invaded Czechoslovakia in 1968. Kenneth Waltz, for example, has conceded that 'structure is no good on detail' but he defends his realist theory on the grounds that it can explain a few very important features of international politics. For example, Waltz's realist theory predicts that war is less likely in bipolar than in multipolar international systems and that states will tend to form balances against powerful states. Waltz and other realists with similar views admit that additional theories must be used to explain many aspects of international politics and the specific foreign-policy decisions of individual states.

Other realists such as Barry Posen (1984), Thomas Christensen and Jack Snyder (1990) and Christensen (1997) argue that realist theories can explain more than just the broad patterns of international politics. Such realists believe that realism can explain the foreign policies of individual states. They have used realist theories to explain states' choices of military doctrines and alliance partners, among other things. Realists sometimes debate one another on whether realism can explain foreign policies as well as broader trends in international politics (see Elman, 1996a, and the exchange between Elman, 1996b, and Waltz, 1996, in the same issue).

Despite their differences, both groups of realists would agree that no single theory – including realist theories – can explain all the details of international politics. In many cases, it will be necessary to rely on theories other than realism to explain foreign policies. Nevertheless, realists argue that realist theories can explain many of the most important aspects of international politics. The fact that realist theories do not explain everything does not mean that realism is fatally flawed. Critics of realism, on the other hand, continue to insist that nonrealist theories offer superior explanations of many of the most interesting aspects of international politics.

Realism and the democratic peace

The most important conceptual challenge to realism is the democratic peace hypothesis. This argument rests on the empirical observation that democracies have never gone to war with one another. Statistical evidence yields an impressive correlation between shared democracy and peace. Numerous studies have found that there have been no wars between democracies and that this finding is statistically significant. Jack Levy (1989a: 88) observed that the absence of wars between democracies is 'the closest thing we have to an empirical law in the study of international relations'. Proponents of the democratic peace proposition agree that democracies have not fought each other, but they have not reached a consensus on why this is so. Some argue that domestic institutional constraints prevent leaders in democracies from launching wars against other democracies. For example, leaders that share power with legislatures are constrained from hasty aggressive action. Others argue that democratic and/or liberal norms and values prevent wars between democracies. These scholars suggest that democracies have domestic norms of peaceful conflict resolution that they apply in their relations with other democracies, or that shared liberal values – especially respect for individual rights and the rule of law – make it impossible for democracies to fight one another (see Elman, 1997; Chan, 1997; Russett, 1993; Ray, 1995; Owen, 1997; Lipson, 2003).

The democratic peace hypothesis is an important conceptual and theoretical challenge to realist theory for two reasons. First, the absence of war among democracies undermines the philosophical pessimism associated with realism. Proponents of the democratic peace hypothesis argue that war is becoming impossible among the great powers because each is a democracy or is likely to become one. They suggest that a world of democracies would be a world without war; this argument is very much at odds with the classical realism's pessimistic views of human nature. It also contradicts offensive realism's arguments about how the international system offers incentives for aggression. Second, proponents of the democratic peace proposition challenge the realist argument that the imperatives of anarchy in the international system cause all states to compete for power and/or security, regardless of their regime type. They claim that realist theory's emphasis on the structure of the international system is undermined by the apparent importance of democratic domestic political systems as a cause of peace.

Realists have vigorously challenged the democratic peace hypothesis, provoking a wide-ranging and sometimes heated debate (for a collection of key early works from both sides of this debate, see Brown et al, 1996. For a prominent realist rebuttal of the democratic peace proposition, see Rosato,

2003). Realists have offered two major responses to the democratic peace argument. First, many realists argue that the democratic peace is a myth. Some democracies have gone to war. Britain and the United States clashed in the War of 1812. Spain was a democracy at the time of the Spanish-American War in 1898. Germany in 1914 was as democratic as Britain and France, but went to war against them nonetheless. Democratic Finland allied with Nazi Germany during the Second World War and found itself at war with the Western democracies, even if its military efforts were primarily directed against the Soviet Union.

Second, realists have argued that the theories that attempt to explain the democratic peace are flawed (see, in particular, Rosato, 2003). Institutional constraints in democracies should make democracies less likely to go to war in general, but democracies often wage war against non-democracies. If liberal or democratic norms explain the democratic peace, realists argue, democracies would not be expected to threaten one another with the use of force, but democracies do make such threats. The disputes and crises between Greece and Turkey in the Aegean are a prominent example. Realists therefore argue that cases of democratic peace can be explained in realist terms. If democracies have not gone to war with one another, it is not because they are democracies. The United States and Britain, for example, have not fought one another because they have often allied against common threats, as suggested by the realist prediction that states will balance against threats or power. France and Germany remained at peace after 1945 because each feared the Soviet Union more than it feared the other. Proponents of the democratic peace proposition have offered numerous responses to the realist critiques. Maoz (1997) and Ray (1995), for example, argue that none of the alleged cases of wars between democracies was actually a 'war' between states that qualified as 'democracies' and that the existence of multiple – and reinforcing – explanations of the democratic peace does not mean that there is no causal link between democracy and peace.

A few scholars who employ realist theories do accept that democracies may be highly unlikely to fight one another (see, for example, Kydd, 1997: 129–39; Van Evera, 1990–1: 26–8). They sometimes argue, however, that democracies remain a minority of states and that the democratic sphere may shrink. At the very least, realist principles will continue to apply between pairs of non-democracies and between democracies and non-democracies. Some proponents of the democratic peace agree that realist logic still applies to much of international politics (see Maoz, 1997: 192–3). Thus there may be some signs of convergence between realists and proponents of the democratic peace proposition, but there is no widespread consensus yet and the debate continues to rage.

The debate over the democratic peace and other debates between realists and anti-realists are unlikely to be resolved in the near future. Both sides tenaciously cling to their positions and continue to offer new arguments. These debates between realists and their critics have, however, been joined by a new set of debates among realists themselves.

Debates in contemporary realist theory

The absence of a monolithic realist theory has been made abundantly clear by the vibrant debates among contemporary realists. The division between classical and structural realism no longer fully captures the complexity of the debate among realists. Some of the most important debates are between different variants of structural realism. In addition, a new generation of classical realists has challenged important elements of structural realism. Finally, some scholars have argued for realist theories of hegemonic rivalry, which cannot easily be classified as classical or structural.

There are two important debates among structural realists. First, many scholars now distinguish between the 'offensive' and 'defensive' variants of structural realism. (Some writers have called 'offensive' realism 'aggressive' realism. See Snyder, 1991: 11–12). The offensive version of the theory holds that the international system fosters conflict and aggression. Security is scarce, driving states to seek power and making international competition intense and wars likely. Rational states are often compelled to adopt offensive strategies in their search for security. Offensive realism has much in common with the philosophical pessimism that traditionally has been a foundation of realist thought. (Mearsheimer, 2001 offers the best and most complete statement of offensive realism. For excellent discussions of offensive realism and tests of its hypothesis, see Labs, 1997, and Elman, 2004. See also Zakaria, 1996. For a critique, see Lynn-Jones, 1998).

Defensive realists, on the other hand, argue that the international system does not necessarily generate intense conflict and war. States that understand the international system will realize that security is often plentiful and that defensive strategies are the best route to security. The defensive realist perspective is exemplified by the work of scholars like Stephen Van Evera (1999: 68–9), Jack Snyder (1991), Barry Posen (1993), Stephen Walt (1989) and Charles Glaser (1994–5). Defensive realism retains the customary realist emphasis on the primacy of states, the search for security and the importance of the international system in shaping the patterns of international politics, but it abandons the emphasis on pessimism and evil prominent in other realist theories. (For an attempt to reconcile offensive and defensive realism, see Walt, 2002: 209–10, and Taliaferro, 2000–1.)

A second division is that structural realists are divided on whether the most important determinant of international outcomes and foreign policies is the distribution of power or the level and sources of threats. Realists like Waltz (2000), Mearsheimer (2001) and Layne (2006) represent the first position. They emphasize the importance of the polarity of a system – the number of great powers – as well as the role of changes in the relative power of states. Stephen Walt (1987), Stephen Van Evera (1998) and Charles Glaser (1994–5), on the other hand, argue that the overall distribution of power is less important than the level and direction of threats. Walt's 'balance-of-threat' theory claims that states react to threats. The level of threat posed by a given state depends not only on its overall power, but also on its geographical proximity, offensive power and offensive intentions. Van Evera (1998) argues that the offence–defence balance – essentially a measure of whether conquest is easy or difficult – may be more important than the distribution of power in explaining the origins of wars. (For his analysis of the indeterminate implications of polarity, see Van Evera, 1990–1. His offence–defence theory builds on and modifies ideas developed in Jervis, 1978. For further recent discussions of offence–defence theory, see Lynn-Jones, 1995; Brown et al, 2004b; Glaser and Kaufmann, 1998). Glaser (1994–5) adopts a similar approach, arguing that the severity of the security dilemma determines whether power can easily be translated into threat. When offence has the advantage, increases in power translate easily into threats, and cooperation becomes more difficult.

Structural realism has also been challenged by a new generation of classical realists who call themselves neoclassical realists. These new classical realists share Waltz's belief that the distribution of power is an important determinant of international politics and foreign policy, but they disagree with most structural realists on the goals of states and the role of domestic factors in shaping those goals. In particular, they question whether it is theoretically useful to assume that security is the prime goal of states, arguing that security is a malleable concept that states can pursue in many different ways. Unlike earlier classical realists, however, they do not posit that state behaviour can be explained by individuals' lust for power. Instead, they argue that states seek to maximize their influence or that state goals vary and include prestige and status. (For overviews of neoclassical realism, see Rose, 1998; Schweller, 2003. For examples and applications, see Zakaria, 1992; Schweller, 1994, 1996, 2004; Wohlforth, 1994–5). Some new classical realists also reject the claim that the internal politics of a state and its goals and values are relatively unimportant. (Although most structural realists do not deny that internal factors sometimes are important – especially in determining a given state's foreign policy – they construct theories that rely on systemic factors to explain outcomes in international politics. See, in particular, Waltz, 1979, Chapters 2–4.) Like some earlier classical realists, they place more weight on state-level differences, especially the distinction between revisionist and status-quo powers.

Finally, Kenneth Waltz's version of structural realism has been challenged by realist theories of hegemonic rivalry and war. Unlike Waltz's theory, which tends to see international politics as a series of attempts to balance against potential hegemons, theories of hegemonic rivalry argue that international politics has been shaped by the rise and fall of successive hegemonic states that have dominated their respective international orders. War is particularly likely during periods of hegemonic transition. (Important works that present realist theories of hegemonic rivalry and power transitions include Gilpin, 1981; Organski, 1968. A variant of these theories has been employed in the realm of international political economy to argue that international economic cooperation and stability are most likely when a hegemonic power exists to make and enforce rules: see Kindleberger, 1973; Krasner, 1976. Such theories cannot easily be classified as classical or structural, because they share the former's assumption that states are not content with security but seek to maximize their power or influence, while often attempting to build a deductive theory that is as social-scientific as structural realism.

The continuing debate between the various strands of contemporary realist theory is an indicator of the vitality of realism. It is also an important reminder that realism is not a single approach, but a body of related theories.

The future of realism

Does realism have a future? Is realist theory still relevant? Can realism explain significant aspects of contemporary international politics? These are central questions in the continuing debate over the realist approach to international politics.

Critics have argued that realist theories are undermined by their failure to explain the end of the cold war and by their inability to shed light on important contemporary issues such as the potential obsolescence of major war, internal war and ethnic conflict, terrorism, the international response to George W. Bush's foreign policy, and new issues like climate change, globalization and emerging infectious diseases. (Some of these arguments appear in Kegley, 1993). In each case, realists have offered a vigorous response. (For an important general defence of the relevance of structural realism, see Waltz, 2000.)

Realism and predicting the end of the cold war

The end of the US–Soviet cold war in the late 1980s and early 1990s stimulated many critics to argue that the inadequacy of realist theory was laid bare by its failure to predict the sudden and dramatic transformation of superpower relations and the largely peaceful dissolution of the Warsaw Treaty Organization and the Soviet Union itself. According to these critics, realist theory has been undermined because it failed to predict the single most important transformation of the international system since the 1945. In theoretical terms, the end of the cold war may be just a 'single case', but it is such an important case that it should have been predicted by realist theories. After all, the US–Soviet rivalry was the central focus in the study of international politics for over a generation (Gaddis, 1992–3: 53).

Some critics of realism go further and argue that not only did realism not predict the end of the cold war, it cannot even explain these events retrospectively. The Soviet decision to relinquish its power peacefully, withdraw from

Eastern and Central Europe, and accept the disintegration of the Soviet Union itself are all held to violate realist principles of self-help and power-maximizing (see the essays in Lebow and Risse-Kappen, 1995).

Realists have persuasive answers to these criticisms. First, they have argued that any theory – including realist theories – should be modest about forecasting the future. Few social-science theories will be able to make precise predictions about international events. Realists such as Kenneth Waltz made such points long before the end of the cold war. Waltz, for example, made his expectations about his theory's predictive ability explicit: 'Like any theory, a structural theory of international politics can fix ranges of outcomes and identify general tendencies. ... We cannot hope to predict specific outcomes' (Waltz, 1986: 344).

Second, realists have pointed out that *no* theory of international politics successfully predicted the events of the late 1980s and early 1990s. Realism should not be singled out for predictive failure when none of its theoretical rivals fared any better. Liberal institutionalists, constructivists, Marxists and proponents of the democratic peace hypothesis all failed to predict that the cold war would end when it did.

Third, at least a few realist writings *did* predict the disintegration of the Soviet Union. Randall Collins, a sociologist, argued that the erosion of Soviet economic and military resources would produce 'precipitous losses of territorial power within the next 30 years' and fragmentation 'into successively smaller states' (quoted in Hopf, 1993: 205; see Collins and Waller, 1992; Collins, 1986: 187, 196, 197–201, and Collins, 1978). The existence of one prediction cast in realist terms does not vindicate the many realists who made no such predictions. It does, however, reveal that the basic tenets of realist theory could be used to predict the erosion of the Soviet empire and the end of the cold war. The fact that few realists offered this prediction does not invalidate realist theory.

Finally, some realists have argued that realism can provide a convincing retrospective explanation of the end of the cold war. William Wohlforth (1994–5), for example, argues that the Soviet Union adopted a policy of accommodation and retrenchment because Mikhail Gorbachev and other Soviet leaders perceived a decline in the relative power of their country. This shift in power initially may have been more perceptual than actual, but beliefs about power should be regarded as a central factor in realist theories. Wohlforth recognizes that many factors shaped the precise manner in which the cold war ended, but Moscow's perceptions of Soviet relative decline were a necessary condition for the changes in Soviet foreign policy that ended US–Soviet enmity. (For the argument that the relative decline of Soviet power was a key factor in ending the cold war, see Brooks and Wohlforth, 2000–1.) Wohlforth's argument is clearly not a prediction of the end of the cold war, but it does suggest that realist theories can successfully 'retrodict' the end of the cold war and thus can explain this type of international event.

Realism and the purported obsolescence of war

If the world became much more peaceful, the influence of realist theories would almost certainly diminish. Realism has tended to become more prominent and more persuasive in times of increasing international tension. This pattern has been striking in the United States since the Second World War. The onset of the cold war and its phase of acute hostility through the 1950s and early 1960s was accompanied by the emergence of many realist scholars in the United States; Hans Morgenthau, George Kennan, Arnold Wolfers, Henry Kissinger, Robert Tucker and Robert Osgood were among the most prolific. Many of these writers adopted a particularly dogmatic and strident tone as they urged Americans to abandon their idealistic ways in the face of the Soviet threat. The demise of detente and the 'second cold war' of the late 1970s and early 1980s stimulated a second flourishing of realist thought in the United States. Kenneth Waltz, Stephen Walt, John Mearsheimer and Barry Posen wrote prominent books and articles from a realist perspective during these years.

Conversely, realist theory has lost much of its appeal when international tensions have waned. In the 1920s and 1930s, the study of international politics was dominated by idealist perspectives. As the cold war thawed during the 1960s and early 1970s, many political scientists, such as Keohane and Nye (1977), shifted their attention from the balance of military power to the role of international institutions and implications of interdependence. A similar trend emerged in the 1990s.

Has the world changed fundamentally? Is the practice of international politics now so different that realist theories are obsolete? Realists reject claims that a new era of global peace and justice has dawned. They regard the post-cold war challenge to realist theory as the most recent incarnation of several perennial – and flawed – critiques of realism.

Realists deny that international politics has changed fundamentally. They point out that the initial post-cold war euphoria over a potential new age of peace and harmony was shattered by Iraq's invasion of Kuwait in 1990 and the ensuing Gulf War, the violent disintegration of Yugoslavia and the many wars on the periphery of the former Soviet Union. This pattern of violent conflict continued with massacres in Rwanda, a border war between India and Pakistan, US wars in Afghanistan and Iraq, and many other threats to use military force. Some of these wars have been within states instead of between them, but realists find this pattern unsurprising at a time when some states are fragmenting while others are coalescing within new borders. Moreover, realists argue that the absence of war does not mean that peace has broken out. Statecraft continues to follow Frederick the Great's comment that 'diplomacy without force is like music without instruments.' The possibility of war lurks in the background during many diplomatic interactions. The events of the first decade of the twenty-first century provide ample evidence that war can easily come to the fore. For a general argument that long-term trends in the international system will ensure that wars will still occur, see Orme (1997–8).

Realism and internal conflict and ethnic war

Since the end of the cold war, internal conflicts and ethnic wars have become more prominent in international politics. Some of these conflicts (for example, Yugoslavia) were suppressed during the cold war, whereas others (for example, Rwanda) existed but were overshadowed by the US–Soviet competition.

Ethnic conflicts and other internal wars would initially appear to be problematic cases for realist theory. These conflicts are within states and thus would not seem to be explained easily by a body of theory that was developed to explain the interaction of states – particularly great powers. Nevertheless, realist theory has been used to explain the outbreak of war in multi-ethnic societies. In a seminal article, Barry Posen (1993) argued that ethnic conflicts often follow the same logic of anarchy that plays a central role in realist theories of international politics. When central governments weaken or collapse, groups face a security dilemma that drives them to use force.

Other scholars have adopted similar arguments and applied Posen's analysis to other cases of ethnic conflict.

Realism and terrorism

After the terrorist attacks of 11 September 2001, terrorism became a much more prominent issue in international relations. For most observers, the emergence of terrorist groups as powerful transnational actors who could threaten states probably seemed to be a major anomaly for realist theory. Mearsheimer (quoted in Kreisler, 2002) acknowledged that 'realism does not have much to say about the causes of terrorism.' Realist theories can, however, shed light on several aspects of contemporary international terrorism, as revealed by Robert Pape in his 2005 book *Dying to Win*. First, the most important contemporary terrorist groups – including al-Qaeda – use violence strategically. Their attacks are not random or irrational, but are calculated efforts to achieve a goal. Thus realist theories that focus on strategic action and the use of violence for political purposes may be relevant. Second, the targets of most contemporary terrorist attacks are states. Terrorist groups are attempting to influence the policies of states, and the responses to terrorism will often be taken by states acting individually or collectively. Given that realist theories analyse the policies that states pursue to achieve security, realism may contribute to the understanding of how states respond to terrorist attacks and threats.

Realism and the international response to US power

The emergence of the United States as the sole superpower in a unipolar world presented an important challenge to realist theory. Most realists argue that states tend to balance against the most powerful state in the international system. Several prominent realists, including Kenneth Waltz (1994, 2000) and Christopher Layne (1993), argued that other states would balance against the United States and that the era of US primacy would not last. William Wohlforth (1999), on the other hand, suggested that unipolarity would be stable and durable because other countries lacked the means to challenge the United States. Shortly after the terrorist attacks of 11 September 2001, Stephen Walt (2000–1: 61), consistent with his view that states balance against threats, not power, predicted: 'If US leaders assume that the current surge in international support will enable them to ignore the interests of other states in the future, they will squander the diplomatic capital that the United States now enjoys and increase the risk of a backlash when the immediate challenge recedes.'

The events six years after the 2001 terrorist attacks provide some confirmation of the realist perspectives on whether countries will balance against the United States. Although other countries – individually or collectively – are not capable of forming traditional military alliances to balance US power, they have reacted to the US pursuit of unilateral advantages by distancing themselves from the United States and engaging in 'soft balancing' (see Pape, 2005b; Paul, 2005; Walt, 2005). Realists continue to debate the extent to which other states are balancing against the United States, but there is no question that realist theory has been central in understanding the pattern of international politics after the terrorist attacks of 11 September 2001.

Realism and globalization

A major conceptual argument about the changed nature of international politics asserts that changes in the world economy have changed traditional patterns of international politics. This argument is more sophisticated than the simple assertion that economic interdependence causes peace. It claims that the populations of most advanced societies now desire economic growth more than territorial expansion, that the globalization of the international economy has constrained the independence and sovereignty of states, and that international institutions are playing a growing role in managing international economic relations. Taken together, these changes create a world very different from realism's grim vision of international conflict.

Realists reply that the globalization of the world economy is less significant than most observers realize (see Waltz, 2000: 14–18). High levels of economic interdependence in the early twentieth century did not prevent the outbreak of the First World War. States may be more interested in prosperity than power, but they continue to compete for economic benefits. Many states that have become more prosperous in recent decades – particularly in East Asia – continue to acquire more powerful military forces. And states remain reluctant to cede too much sovereignty to supranational institutions or to other transnational actors.

Realism and the new agenda of global politics

As discussed in Chapter 4, another challenge to the realist vision of world politics argues that global problems like environmental pollution, climate change, emerging infectious diseases, refugee flows, poverty and hunger have become more important threats to humankind than the traditional problems of military security. This argument faults realism for its narrow definition of security and its obsession with military threats. (The relationship between old and new security threats is discussed in Brown et al, 2004a). It holds that international politics must and will change to confront the threat of environmental and humanitarian catastrophe.

Realists do not deny that environmental and humanitarian threats exist, but they continue to view these threats through a realist prism. These new threats may not emanate from states or military forces, but they will influence state behaviour, and the international responses – if any – will include state action. Environmental degradation, for example, may not prompt greater international cooperation to prevent pollution or to limit global climate change. Instead, these problems may stimulate sharper international competition over scarce resources. Similarly, international action may be necessary to prevent and resolve humanitarian emergencies, but states are unlikely to act if they do not believe their interests are at stake. And in many famines or civil wars, parties to the conflict will try to manipulate humanitarian assistance to advance their own interests. Even if it seems obvious that problems can be addressed only by international institutions, the power and interests of states will shape the membership and role of those institutions (see Gruber, 2000). In many cases, realist logic will be able to explain how states react to new threats that appear to be changing the international system.

Conclusion

Realism will continue to be an important source of theories of international politics. Despite a continuing barrage of criticisms directed against it, realism remains a vibrant source of theoretical innovations and insights into world politics.

There are two reasons why realism continues to survive. First, no other single paradigm offers a richer set of theories and hypotheses about international politics. Realism offers a worldview that can be used to generate deductive theories that can claim to explain the recurrent patterns of international politics from ancient times to the present. No contending paradigm has been able to match realism's ability to generate logically integrated theories that apply across space and time. Marxism had the potential to match the conceptual elegance and breadth of realism, but that ideology has fallen into disrepute and tended to focus on explaining economic, political and social phenomena within states, not between them. Because there is no alternative paradigm, realism retains a central place among theories of international politics by default.

Second, realism will endure because its pessimistic emphasis on self-interest, conflict and power seems to capture important elements of the human condition. We may not like realism's emphasis on tragedy and evil, but we have yet to find a way to escape it.

Further reading

Brooks, S. (1997) 'Dueling Realisms', *International Organization*, 51, 3: 445–77. This offers an interesting discussion of the differences among realists that differs from the one presented in this chapter.

Carr, E.H. (1942) *The Twenty Years' Crisis, 1919–1939: An Introduction to the Study of International Relations*, London: Macmillan.

Chan, S. (1997) 'In Search of Democratic Peace: Problems and Promise', *Mershon International Studies Review*, vol. 41, supplement 1: 59–91. This provides an excellent overview of the literature on the democratic peace.

Grieco, J.M. (1993) 'Anarchy and the Limits of Cooperation: A Realist Critique of the Newest Liberal Institutionalism', in Baldwin, D.A. (ed.), *Neorealism and Neoliberalism: The Contemporary Debate*, New York: Columbia University Press.

Kapstein, E.B. (1995) 'Is Realism Dead?' *International Organization*, 49: 751–74.

Lynn-Jones, S.M. (1998) 'Realism and America's Rise: A Review Essay', *International Security*, 23, 2: 157–82.

Mearsheimer, J.J. (1994–5) 'The False Promise of International Institutions', *International Security*, 19, 3: 5–49.

Mearsheimer, J.J. (2001) *The Tragedy of Great Power Politics*, New York: W.W. Norton.

Snyder, G.H. (2002) 'Mearsheimer's World-Offensive Realism and the Struggle for Security', *International Security*, 27, 1: 149–73.

Vasquez, J. (1997) 'The Realist Paradigm and Degenerative Versus Progressive Research Programmes: An Appraisal of Neotraditional Research on Waltz's Balancing Proposition', *American Political Science Review*, 91, 4: 899–912. This offers a vigorous critique of Realism.

Walt, S.M. (2002) 'The Enduring Relevance of the Realist Tradition', in Katznelson, I. and Milner, H.V. (eds) *Political Science: The State of the Discipline*, New York: W.W. Norton. This offers an excellent summary of the various strands of contemporary realist theory.

Zakaria, F. (1992–3) 'Is Realism Finished?' *The National Interest*, 30: 21–32. This offers assessment of the critics of realism and a balanced defence.

Chapter 3

Beyond Strategy: Critical Thinking on the New Security Studies

David Mutimer

Introduction

In July 2006 Israel waged a short but remarkably violent war in Lebanon. While violence is all too common in the Middle East, there are still notable features of this particular war in the context of thinking about security in the contemporary world. Israel waged war *in* Lebanon, but it did not wage war *against* Lebanon. Our common expectation of war has always been that it is waged by states against other states, but in this instance Israel waged war against a non-state group, Hamas, but in the territory ostensibly belonging to another state. What is more, the primary area of fighting, in Southern Lebanon, was a region that had been occupied by Israel for more than 20 years until the spring of 2000 – an area they called the 'security zone'. The zone was supposed to provide security for Israel, security against the very Hamas it spent July 2006 fighting. Israel had withdrawn from the zone in 2000 because the occupation had not provided for Israeli security, and, what is more, when Israeli forces occupied the 'security zone' it certainly did not make those living in Southern Lebanon feel secure.

Box 1.1: *The Lebanese security zone*

A number of years ago, I had a chance to meet a group of students from Lebanon. One of the women in the group lived in 'the security zone', and so I asked her what she meant when she called the place in which she lived the *security* zone. Patiently, she explained that it provided security for Israel by maintaining a space between the Israeli border and areas Israel did not control and which thus could be used as staging areas for Hamas attacks on Israel – although, she also pointed out that Hamas continued to operate in the security zone, and there was nothing Israel could do about it. I then asked about her security. Did she feel secure in the 'security zone'. She smiled and shook her head.

The recent history of Southern Lebanon captures a large swath of the contemporary debate over the changing nature of security and the study of security. Stephen Walt (1991: 212) has written that:

> security studies may be defined as *the study of the threat, use, and control of military force*. It explores the conditions that make the use of force more likely, the ways that the use of force affects individuals, states, and societies, and the specific policies that states adopt in order to prepare for, prevent, or engage in war.

This definition is based in the traditional understandings of security. Traditionally, 'security' was the security of the state; it was threatened by the military power of other states, and defended by the military power of the state itself. While it is true that Walt makes reference to the effects of the use of force on 'individuals, states and societies', strategic studies is concerned only with the security of the state, as the institution which claims the monopoly on the legitimate use of force. The effect of the use of force on individuals and societies is well captured in the term from techno-strategic language that gained notoriety during the 1990–1 Gulf Conflict: 'collateral damage'. (See Cohn, 1987, for a discussion of techno-strategic language.) The damage caused by war to individuals and to the societies in which they live is 'collateral' to the main study of strategy – states' policy in preparing for and executing war.

It is security in this traditional sense, that of 'strategic studies', that the 'security zone' north of Israel was to provide. The 'security' in question is that of a state – in this case Israel – threatened by armed attacks from the outside, and guaranteed by the state's military forces. Despite the strength of these taken-for-granted assumptions, strategic studies' understanding of security could not account for Israel's recent history in Lebanon, despite the centrality of military force and even the role of war. Israel's occupation did not, and seemingly could not, prevent the zone being used as a staging area for Hamas attacks – it failed, in other words, to provide security even on its own terms. The provision of 'security' within the 'security zone' did not extend to the people living there – indeed, the occupation greatly reduced the feelings of security of Lebanese in their own homes. Finally, the 'threat' that is posed to Israel from Southern Lebanon has never been the possibility of an armed attack from another state, but rather is of violent attacks from non-state groups. However, to maintain the orthodox comfort, Hamas is generally considered to be 'state sponsored'. When Israel returned to Lebanon in 2006, it went to 'war' against these non-state fighters.

The object of this chapter is to explore the thinking that has developed from a recognition of the limitations of the understanding of 'security' promoted by 'strategic studies'. Walt's definition of security studies, grounded in this understanding, is in fact part of his defence of the strategic studies tradition against the literature that this thinking has produced.

The literature begins from a very simple question: what is security? However, once the strategic studies answer – that security is the protection of the state from armed attack – is recognized to be insufficient, the answer to this simple question becomes much more complex. Therefore, the question is best broken down into constituent parts: *Whose* security is at issue? *How* can this security be provided? And finally, how should security be *studied*? I will examine the various forms of answer that are being provided in contemporary writing in security studies below, but first will explore the origins of the questions themselves: how it was that they came to be asked when they did, and why they are being answered as they are.

Beyond strategy: security, critical theory and the end of the cold war

The cold war practice of security, both the strategic policies of states and the academic servicing provided by strategic studies, assumed the continuity of the East–West conflict. I will refer to 'practice' throughout this discussion. While 'practice' is quite a complex theoretical concept, it can be generally understood in this context as the actions that states (and others) habitually take in order to achieve security. Ken Booth (1991: 315–16), a former practitioner and now critic, characterized security in strategic studies in rather less flattering terms than those employed by Walt above:

> The dominating security questions were: Is the Soviet threat growing? What is the strategic balance? And would the deployment of a particular weapon help stability? In that period of looking at world politics through a missile-tube and gun-sight, weapons provided most of the questions, and they provided most of the answers – whatever the weapon, whatever the context, and whatever the cost.

With the end of the cold war and the demise of the Soviet Union, these animating questions were rendered moot: there was no Soviet Union, how could there be a Soviet threat? Without a Soviet threat in a cold war, there was no strategic balance, and so nothing for weapons deployments to stabilize.

Despite rendering these key questions moot, the end of the cold war did not remove the possibilities for looking at world politics through a missile-tube or a gun-sight, but it did make that way of seeing a little less easy to assume. This provided an opening for alternatives to strategic studies to talk about security, and for these alternatives to be taken seriously. Some of these alternative voices had been speaking, throughout the cold war, about the problems with see(k)ing security through missile-tubes. Certain of these voices and their arguments formed the basis for the new attack on strategic studies, and the development of a 'security studies' which posed the question of what security means. Probably the most important of these voices was Barry Buzan's.

Buzan (1991b) put forward criticisms of two elements of the traditional understanding of security. The first, for which his *People, States and Fear* is perhaps best known, was to argue that:

> The security of human collectivities is affected by factors in five major sectors: military, political, economic, societal and environmental. Generally speaking, military security concerns the two-level interplay of the armed offensive and defensive capabilities of states, and states' perceptions of each other's intentions. Political security concerns the organizational stability of states, systems of government and the ideologies that give them legitimacy. Economic security concerns access to the resources, finance and markets necessary to sustain acceptable levels of welfare and state power. Societal security concerns the sustainability, within acceptable conditions for evolution, of traditional patterns of language, culture and religious and national identity and custom. Environmental security concerns the maintenance of the local and the planetary biosphere as the essential support system on which all other human enterprises depend. These five sectors do not operate in isolation from each other. Each defines a focal point within the security problematique, and a way of ordering priorities, but all are woven together in a strong web of linkages. (Buzan, 1991b: 19–20)

Buzan's sectoral approach to security takes direct issue with the militaristic assumptions of strategic studies. The security concern of strategic studies – the security of the state from external, military threat – was now just one of five forms of threat the state could face. This suggestion that security could be considered in sectoral terms, and that military security would no longer be considered the exclusive form of security in the contemporary world, has spurred much of the rethinking of security. Buzan's arguments are particularly important to those concerned with 'broadening' our understanding of security, which has usually meant some form of 'sectoral' widening of the universe of security concerns.

Buzan has continued to contribute to this perspective, together with a number of colleagues, mostly based in Denmark, to produce what is now being termed the 'Copenhagen School' of security studies (see, for instance, B. McSweeney's 1996 review of the products of this collaborative effort). The Copenhagen School produced a book-length restatement of its basic positions in 1998. *Security: A New Framework for Analysis* (Buzan et al, 1998) has reworked the central ideas of *People, States and Fear* in light of a series of subsequent security debates.

In addition to widening the agenda of security studies, the second element of the traditional consensus on security with which Buzan took issue was its universal focus on the state as the 'referent object' for security. The 'referent object' is the thing that is to be secured. While strategic studies focused on the question of military threats and their responses, it further assumed that such military security meant the security of states, and so the referent object of security in strategic studies is the state. If pressed, this assumption seemed to rest on a political theory of the state as a 'container' of security. While strategic analysts might accept that the security of *people* was what ultimately mattered, the state was the only institution capable of providing that security in the face of an anarchical international environment of armed states. Therefore, states' security was all that needed to be discussed (see Krause and Williams, 1997a). (Buzan, 1991b: 364) rejected this argument, suggesting that the relationship between states and individuals was rather more problematic:

> The security of individuals is locked into an unbreakable paradox in which it is partly dependent on, and partly threatened by, the state. Individuals can be threatened by their own state in a variety of ways, and they can also be threatened through their state as a result of its interactions with other states in the international system.

In particular, Buzan (1991b: 96–107) rejected the common assumption, of both strategic studies and the wider field of International Relations (here I distinguish between the academic discipline of International Relations and the activity of relations among states, or international relations), that states could be treated as similar units. He argued that, in terms of the threats they faced and the capacities they had to respond to those threats, states could be divided between *weak* and *strong* states. Weak states are those in which the institutions and political coherence are themselves weak, whereas strong states have strong institutions and firm political coherence. For weak states, a good part of their 'security problem' concerns maintaining the state itself against *internal* threat.

Despite questioning two of the central elements of strategic studies – its exclusive focus on the military and on states as the referent objects of security – Buzan's work did not move very far from the conventional understanding of security. Buzan (1991b: 22) continued to accept that anarchy, as generally understood in realist approaches to international relations, placed formidable constraints on security, the first of which was that: '[s]tates are the principal referent object of security because they are both the framework of order and the highest source of governing authority. This explains the dominating policy concern with "national" security.' Thus, while Buzan argued that states were not necessarily similar to one another in terms of their search for security, these now varied states are still the primary referent object for security. Furthermore, Buzan accepts that states live in an anarchical environment in which the use of force is still possible. Therefore, while he introduces the possibility of a sectoral analysis of security, military security is still privileged: '[b]ecause the use of force can wreak major undesired changes very swiftly, military threats are traditionally accorded the highest priority in national security concerns. Military action can wreck the work of centuries *in all other sectors*' (Buzan 1991b: 117).

In the more recent *Security: A New Framework for Analysis*, Buzan et al (1998: 8) move the Copenhagen approach more decisively away from the traditions of strategic studies. Here they argue they have moved:

> away from [*People, States and Fear's*] implicit (and sometimes explicit) placement of the state as the central referent object in all sectors. If a multisectoral approach to security was to be fully meaningful, referent objects other than the state had to be allowed into the picture. The present book extends this argument much further.

The authors are therefore at pains to set out the different constellations of referent objects in the five sectors they continue to deploy. They have also weakened the dominance of the military sector in their analysis, although they have not eliminated it. While not repeating Buzan's earlier claim that the military trumps the other sectors, the authors continue to recognize that there are 'several good reasons' for the traditional dominance of the military sector, and particularly that '[military threats] are the existential threat par excellence' (Buzan et al, 1998: 57–8).

The close connection of Buzan's earlier work on security in *People, States and Fear* to the traditional understanding of strategic studies had two effects. The first was that it allowed the work to be received by those working within the strategic studies literature – it was seen, in other words, as largely a critique from within. The second was that it spurred others to go further, to question whether or not the state could still be seen as the principal referent object of security, and whether military security should continue to be privileged in the way Buzan argued. With the end of the cold war, scholars began to push the critique of strategic studies in these directions. To do so, they were also able to draw on a range of new perspectives on world politics that had been advanced in the previous ten years.

The 1980s had seen a flourishing of new forms of theorizing in International Relations. Some of these attempted to bring Marxist political economy perspectives to bear on world politics, others the critical theory of the Frankfurt School (see, *inter alia*, McLean, 1988; Linklater, 1990;

Cox, 1986); some turned to current theories of sociology (see Wendt, 1987, 1992), and still others to the various strands of French philosophy that are commonly labelled post-structural (see Walker, 1993; Der Derian and Shapiro, 1989). For all of their differences, these perspectives share a common view on the nature of theory, which contradicts the view of theory that has dominated International Relations in general, and strategic studies in particular. Robert Cox (1986: 207) has perhaps best expressed this view in a widely quoted passage: 'Theory is always *for* someone and *for* some purpose.' Theory, in other words, is not politically neutral, but rather privileges some political projects over others. One very important implication of this view of theory is that theory is not simply a reflection of social and political life, but rather is part of what makes political life the way it is. Realism, strategic studies and their view of security, therefore, are not simply descriptions of international relations, but rather are part of the ideological framework that makes international relations work in the way that they do. These new ways of thinking about international relations provided rich resources for scholars who wished to respond to the challenges posed by the end of the cold war, but who rejected the limitations imposed by strategic studies.

From strategic studies to the study of security

The rethinking of security is taking place on many levels and in many different ways. There is no single orthodoxy that is being forged to replace realist-inspired strategic studies – indeed, the strategic studies approach is still articulated strongly, and the critics consciously reject the possibilities of a single orthodoxy (see Krause and Williams, 1996, 1997a). Nevertheless, three closely related questions serve to draw together the disparate themes of the critics of strategic studies. The first is what is or should be the *referent object* of security. Should continue to see the state and only the state as this object, or should we be identifying other referents for security study and practice? Closely related to this question is a second: how is this referent *to be secured*? The nature of security – the threats and responses to those threats – will change as the referent object changes. What poses a threat to the state may not pose a threat to an individual, for example, if the individual is considered as the referent object of security. Therefore, as the referent object of security is brought into question, so too the nature of security must be brought into question. The answers to these first two questions – what is the referent object of security and how it is to be secured – must often be answered in ways that violate the traditions of realism and strategic studies. It is not just in the substance of the answers that realism must reject, but also the way in which those answers are provided. This gives rise to the final question tackled by the critics: what is the *nature of security study*?

Whose security?

Strategic studies was concerned with the security of the state. As I argued above, this assumption was founded on the belief that the state could be seen as a *container* of security, ensuring the security of the people within its borders. Security for individuals, in other words, was guaranteed by their citizenship in a particular state – as long as the state is secure its citizens are secure. Given this view of the state, it made sense for international security to be concerned with threats to the security of that container, and so security meant state security. Put another way, the *referent object* for the study and practice of security, was the state.

While ultimately retaining the state as the principal referent object for security, Barry Buzan (1991b: 44) had noted one of the most problematic aspects of the assumption that citizenship conferred security: '[t]he individual citizen faces many threats which emanate *either directly or indirectly from the state*. These can occupy an important place in the person's life' (emphasis added). First of all, not all residents in a state are citizens, and those who are not are much less secure than the citizens – they can, for example, be expelled. More importantly, the state can be a threat to the security of its citizens, rather than their protector. State-sponsored death squads generally associated with Central and South America, or European genocidal concentration camps in Nazi Germany and the various fragments of the former Yugoslavia are potent, if extreme, examples. The conditions of Aboriginal peoples in Australia and North America, or of the homeless on the streets of most major cities in the Western world provide further instances of individual security under threat from the state which is supposed to provide protection. If we treat security as the security of the state, then we are ignoring the insecurity of these people who are under threat from the state.

Ken Booth (1991: 319) picked up this theme and argued for a very different understanding of security, with people rather than states as its referent object:

> 'Security' means the absence of threats. Emancipation is the freeing of people (as individuals and groups) from those physical human constraints which stop them carrying out what they would freely choose to do. War and the threat of war is one of those constraints, together with poverty, poor education, political oppression and so on. Security and emancipation are two sides of the same coin. Emancipation, not power or order, produces true security. Emancipation, theoretically, is security.

We must begin our thinking about security, Booth (1991: 319) argues, from people, not from states: 'individual humans are the ultimate referent.'

This argument can be derived from the strategic studies assumption of individual citizenship providing security, once it is recognized that the state both fails to provide security for all of its citizens, and indeed actively threatens some of them. However, the argument also makes a connection to a radically different view of politics from that of political realism. The concern with an emancipatory politics, freeing humans from the constraints that are put upon them, is the concern of all forms of radical political theory, from Karl Marx to Michel Foucault.

By arguing that, theoretically, security *is* emancipation, Booth rejects the state as the principal referent object of security. However, he does not necessarily provide a single alternative. 'The individual human being' is clearly one possible alternative, and is the one Booth favours. However, humans are often constrained as groups, rather than as individuals, and so must be emancipated, or secured, as groups. Marx, for instance, argued that humans were oppressed as classes, that is through the place they held in the structure of a political economy. In the examples I provided above, the oppression of states fell on people as members of groups: Jews, gypsies, homosexuals and others for the Nazis; Aboriginals in Australia, Canada and the United States; the unemployed, by and large, in the case of the homeless. What is more, as Booth notes, the constraints imposed by war and the threat of war are threats to human security, and war is waged by states. Therefore, even considering security as emancipation, the state can be retained as *a* referent object, if not the only one.

There are any number of possible ways of grouping people together. However, only a few of these seem relevant to security, understood as Booth proposes. For a particular way of grouping humans to be relevant, it must be a categorization by which they are constrained or threatened. It thus makes sense to think about the security of indigenous peoples, while at the same time it makes little sense to talk about the security of Ford drivers – except, perhaps, as opposed to Volvo drivers. Of the various ways of reconceiving the referent object of security, several, in addition to 'the individual', have been particularly important: humanity as a whole, nations, societies and genders. There has been some considerable argument that restricting our focus to human beings is too limiting, and that we should be concerned with the security of whole planet. Each of these ways of identifying the referent object of security raises a unique series of security concerns, and therefore different methods for achieving security – issues I will take up in the next section. In order to illustrate the potential and problems of the attempts to rethink the referent object of security, I will examine one of these alternative referents in some more detail: society as the referent object for security.

Societal security and the Copenhagen School

Following the first edition of *People, States and Fear* (Buzan, 1983), but before *Security: A New Framework for Analysis*, the Copenhagen School produced two books on European Security after the cold war (Buzan et al, 1990; Wæver et al, 1993) which attempted to develop its alternative conceptions of security within the European context. In the first, the authors concluded that 'the traditional military and ideological security preoccupations of Europe would become much less important in the future.' The second book picked up 'a major implication of that thread, arguing that the idea of societal security is now the most effective tool for understanding the new security agenda in Europe (Wæver et al, 1993: ix). They argued that:

> societal security concerns the ability of a society to persist in its essential character under changing conditions and possible or actual threats. More specifically, it is about the sustainability, within acceptable conditions for evolution, of traditional patterns of language, culture, association, and religious and national identity and custom. This definition makes it difficult to give any objective definition of when there is a threat to societal security. ... Societal security is about situations when societies perceive a threat in identity terms. (Wæver et al, 1993: 23)

In place of the state as the referent object for security, Wæver et al (1993: 21) propose 'society'. Society is a rather amorphous concept, and they labour hard to differentiate it from states on one side and from other forms of social groupings on the other. This differentiation is achieved through an appeal to collective identity and a subtle widening of the understanding of institutions:

> We thus end up with a definition of society partly following Giddens: 'a clustering of institutions combined with a feeling of common identity'; or more poetically, 'a rich and complex moral reality'. Institutions should not be taken too literally (which would make society more or less equal to the nation state), but societies differ from other social groups in having a high degree of social inertia, a continuity often across generations and a strong infra- structure of norms, values and 'institutions' in the wider sense. (Wæver et al, 1993: 21)

We tend to think of institutions as formal, often bureaucratic or govern- mental bodies: hospitals, schools, parliament or the Department of National Defence. It is this 'literal' meaning that Wæver is warning against. Rather, he means institutions as clearly bounded areas of regularized behaviour governed by rules of some kind. Marriage, for example, is an institution in this sense, as are widely followed social rituals, such as 'trick -or-treating' at Halloween.

Given this understanding of the society as a large-scale community which is not the state, the authors end up arguing that 'nations' are special cases of societies, and indeed are the most pertinent to the study of societal security:

> The main units of analysis for societal security are thus politically significant ethno-national and religious identities. National or nation-like identities range from rather small groups such as the Welsh and the Romany people, through major nations such as the French, Germans and Poles, to the larger but vaguer civilisational idea of Europeans. (Wæver et al, 1993: 23)

Treating 'societies' as the referent object for security, Wæver and his colleagues are able to analyse a number of different current issues in Europe as questions of 'security'. These range from those which would fit comfortably into a strategic studies text – such as the wars in the former Yugoslavia or the re-creation of political and security organizations in Europe – to questions of migration and the threat this poses to social identity. In all these cases, however, the questions they ask are not just those of how to 'secure' state borders and how best to deploy military forces to achieve that goal. In examining the problems facing the former Soviet Union, for example, they argue that 'for the post-communist states the questions concerning what kind of social system would supersede the defunct communist system and what kind of identities would emerge [were] put on the agenda. The battle over the social system was accompanied by a battle over national identity' (Lemaitre et al, 1993: 11). From this argument they can then conclude:

> Overall, the combined effects of a breakdown of Westernization in Russia is likely to be a considerable threat to societal security in Western Europe. It is probably that West European self-identification will be strengthened if the Russians and some of the Central Europeans again assume their old role as a negative reference point. (Lemaitre et al, 1993: 130)

In other words, West European security may be *enhanced* by an antagonistic Russia, by providing coherence to the West European societies' sense of self. This runs directly counter to the common cold war assumption that such antagonism was the primary source of Europe's *in*security. It is, however, an argument that has been made quite forcefully even in the context of the cold war by Klein (1990, 1994). Klein argues that the practices of nuclear security in NATO were part of a larger strategy to forge a 'Western way of life' that was identifiable in contrast to the Eastern 'other'.

The notion of societal security is also potentially problematic. Migration, the movement of peoples to new homes, may appear from this perspective to pose a threat to the societal security of the recipients.

> Immigration can present threats to security in the receiving countries, albeit generally not directly of a military kind. The capacity of social, economic, political and administrative institutions to integrate large numbers of immigrants, and the resistance of some immigrant communities to assimilation, affects the stability of society and therefore the ability of receiving states' governments to govern. (Heisler and Layton-Henry, 1993: 162)

Such an argument can be used to support policies that direct resources to smoothing this transition, in order to enable immigration while minimizing the disruptive consequences. Treating migration as a security concern can serve to focus attention on the problems and help to mobilize resources in response. However, it can also serve to bolster explicitly or implicitly racist political agendas. Xenophobes can couch their arguments in terms of the 'security of their societies', rather than in the inflammatory language of racism (see Buzan et al, 1998: 119–40).

There are two important conclusions to draw from this observation for understanding attempts to rethink security. The first is that it draws attention to the political nature of arguments about security. Strategic studies has long claimed political neutrality. Consider, for instance, John Garnett's (1987: 13) argument:

> Most strategic writers readily admit that the moral aspects of military power is a vitally important subject, and they are delighted when theologians, philosophers, and political scientists devote their attention to it. But it is a quite separate subject from strategic studies in that it requires a quite different expertise.

In other words, it is possible to study strategy without adopting a moral point of view, and without advocating a particular moral position. By contrast, the conclusion of my preceding discussion is that attempts to define the referent object of security, and to argue that they should be secured, are not politically neutral, and this applies to the traditional assumptions about state and military security as much as to newer alternatives.

Closely related to this conclusion is a second concerning the conservative nature of most arguments for security. Because security aims to 'protect' a referent from threat, it will tend to privilege the present condition of that referent. To make the state or a society the referent object for security is to privilege its continued existence in its present form. One of the striking features of Booth's reformulation of security in terms of emancipation is that it turns this conservatism on its head.

How to achieve security

Changing the referent object of security study and practice alters the source and nature of threats to that security, and therefore alters the manner by which security can be achieved. If the referent object of security is considered to be the state, military threats to states are privileged as the principal source of insecurity, and military preparation becomes the primary means of achieving security. This may then be supplemented through negotiated and even institutionalized forms of cooperation in order to reduce the risks of war, but at the heart of security, understood in this fashion, is the belief that military preparedness is the *sine qua non* of security.

In order to see how altering the referent object of security can change, indeed can radically transform, the way in which security is guaranteed, consider the case of the Greenham Common Peace Camp. In 1981 a number of women and a few men established a protest camp on Greenham Common in Berkshire, where the United States was preparing to deploy cruise missiles in a military base on the common. The camp quickly became a site of protest against the cruise missiles, and more generally against nuclear weapons, until the cruise missiles were removed as part of the arms control process of the late 1980s. The Greenham Common experience could be seen as a 'security' problem because it involved nuclear weapons, the quintessential objects of strategic studies. However, many of those involved at Greenham had a very different view of the 'security' for which they were striving. Seen through the lens of 'strategic studies', the cruise missiles *provided* security for those in Britain by bolstering the deterrent capabilities of the Western Alliance. For the women of Greenham Common, by contrast – almost all of whom were citizens of the British state – the cruise missiles and the possibility of nuclear war they represented were a direct threat to their security and that of their families (see Sylvester, 1994). In other words, the very instruments of state security can be seen as sources of insecurity for the people they are supposed to protect.

There is no simple and necessary relationship between referent objects other than the state and the form of security practices. This uncertainty is well illustrated in the varying practices that have been identified with reference to the problem of the relationship between security and the environment that can give rise to a series of quite distinct potential security practices.

One important body of research in this area was conducted under the direction of Thomas Homer-Dixon, who headed a three-year research project into environmental change and acute conflict. The argument of Homer-Dixon (1994: 39–40), therefore, is that environmental scarcity poses a threat to security, because it can give rise to violence (or to other outcomes which can in turn lead to violence). In other words, Homer-Dixon's work does not pose any real challenge to the conventional understanding of security; rather it is an attempt to argue that there are new sources of threat in the world to which states should respond. To be fair, it seems clear that Homer-Dixon never intended to pose such a challenge: 'In my writings, I have generally avoided using the word "security", and instead focused on the links between environmental stress and violence' (Homer-Dixon and Levy, 1995–6: 189). Security is still concerned with military violence, which in turn means that its primary referent object is the state. This line of argument fills detail into the point made by Buzan in *People, States and Fear*, that security threats come from a number of 'sectors'.

There have been far more radical arguments concerning environmental security, however, than Homer-Dixon's. These arguments take as the referent object of environmental security people threatened by environmental change, or even more radically, the biosphere itself. In the former case, the argument is that degradation of the environment poses a threat to human health and well-being. In the latter case, the division between human beings and the environment is collapsed, and the two are treated as elements of a single complex system. However, in either case it is damage to the environment itself that is the threat to security, rather than the potential disruptions that this may cause. The threat to this security is that which causes environmental degradation, and the response must therefore be to alter the practices in which we all engage which lead to environmental damage. Simon Dalby (1992) has drawn the connections between environmental damage, our present political and economic systems, and the practices of security during the cold war. His conclusion illustrates how different a security agenda based on this sort of *ecological* security is from the conventional treatment of security, and from that found in Homer-Dixon's work:

> If security can be reinterpreted in terms of this kind of ecologically sustainable common security, requiring a political and social order that works to sustain resources in the long-term interest of all, and taking into consideration intergenerational equity as well as intragenerational equity, then it may offer some useful potential. Here, of course, is the link between security and the arguments for 'sustainable development.' So long as sustainable development is understood as perpetuating current forms of economic activity, the future looks bleak for the environment. But the conventional model is unconcerned with the survival of ecological systems; indeed, the haste to expand the free market system suggests the apotheosis of ecological imperialism, with all its deleterious implications for rain forests and other ecosystems. Alternative political and economic options need to be pursued; questions of equity will have to be taken seriously in their formulation. These probably will need innovative technologies, but

> certainly will need the willingness to experiment with innovative social organizations much less constrained by conventional economic calculations. (Dalby, 1992: 116–17)

Pursuing environmental security understood in this fashion, then, leads to a rejection of much of contemporary political economy as a threat to security. The state is seen as insufficient, as environmental problems span national borders (see Tickner, 1992: 97–126). More profoundly, as Dalby argues, it might require transforming the global economic system and doing so on the basis of social equity. This is a completely different notion of security and what is required to achieve security than is found in strategic studies.

The suggestions for treating the environment in terms of security have not met with universal approval. From a largely realist perspective, Marc Levy (1995: 60) asked whether the environment was a national security issue, a question which he answered:

> The assertion that many environmental problems constitute security risks is correct, and is of very little importance.
>
> The purely rhetorical line of argumentation that urges us to consider environmental problems and security problems as by their very nature inseparable is probably destined to disappear. Whatever needs for attention-getting may have been present in the late 1980s, they are past now. If the problems these writers point to are really as serious as they say, then the more pressing need is not for more 'new thinking' but for effective solutions. (Levy, 1995: 60)

Of course, by asking the question in terms of 'national security', Levy largely ignores the implications of work like Dalby's. This question asks whether environmental degradation poses a threat to the security of nation-states, when the implications of more radical work is that states are at best irrelevant and at worst a key part of the problem for environmental security. Nevertheless, Levy's response allows us to pose a central question to the whole attempt to reconceptualize security: why bother?

Phrasing the question as 'why bother' makes it sound rather more flippant than it really is. Levy is saying that environmental problems are serious problems, and so deserve serious solutions. However, he is also saying that this need not have anything to do with security. Put another way, we should ask whether we could just leave 'security' well enough alone, as the study of the threat, use and control or military force, as Stephen Walt argues. We might still want to reformulate the realist conception of security, recognizing the problem with its exclusive focus on the state, but retain a concern with military force as the defining feature of security studies. To return to Booth's assertion that security *is* emancipation, this argument would tend to treat security studies as that part of an emancipatory project concerned with the human constraints imposed by war and the threat of war. There is considerable merit to this argument, but it is one I will ultimately reject. However, before doing so, it is worth examining a very sophisticated statement of this position, because it raises crucial issues concerning why we should bother to rethink security.

Wæver and 'securitization'

Ole Wæver (1995: 54) has recently asked a question very similar to the ones I have been raising in this section. He asks, '[w]hat really makes something a security problem?' The answer he gives is both novel and potentially very creative – so much so that it now serves as the basis of the framework for analysis proposed by the Copenhagen School (Buzan et al, 1998: 21–47). Wæver (in Buzan et al, 1998: 54) argues:

> Operationally ... this means: *In naming a certain development a security problem, the 'state' can claim a special right*, one that will, in the first instance, always be defined by the state and its elites. Trying to press the kind of unwanted fundamental political change on a ruling elite is similar to playing a game in which one's opponent can change the rules at any time s/he likes. Power holders can always try to use the instrument of *securitization* of an issue to gain control over it. By definition, something is a security problem when the elites declare it to be so.

In other words, nothing is necessarily a security problem, but it is made so by calling it a security problem – in the language Wæver adopts, the issue is 'securitized'. Furthermore, the state has a particular authority in this regard: if the *state* says something is a security problem, then it almost necessarily is so. There are two particular implications of Wæver's notion of securitization that I want to draw out of the discussion.

The first implication derives from the phrase Wæver has italicized: 'in naming a certain development a security problem, the "state" can claim a special right.' The invocation of security in relationship to an issue allows the state to take extraordinary measures to combat whatever threat is thereby identified. In many cases, these measures would be unacceptable even by the state, were it not for the securitization of the issue in question. For example, most states are permitted to withhold information from their citizens in the name of national security. This is true even in the United States, which has an extremely wide-ranging 'Freedom of Information Act'. The instances of the state's special right are much more extensive than that, however. Most democratic states reserve the right to suspend civil and political rights, in particular to detain citizens without charge, and to use military force against their own people, in the name of 'national security' – all actions that in 'normal' circumstances would be considered illegal and entirely unacceptable in democratic societies.

These rights to suspend civil liberties and even to use the military against its citizens are clearly extremely important. However, the most pervasive of the 'special rights' claimed by the state is the claim on social resources that is made in the name of national security. The creation and maintenance of military forces consumes large quantities of a state's resources. Throughout the 1980s, military expenditures accounted for almost 20 per cent of the expenditures of states worldwide. In the United States, this figure was over 25 per cent and in the Soviet Union it approached 50 per cent. Even in a relatively non-militarized state like Australia, military expenditures accounted for almost 10 per cent of state expenditures (figures are from the US Arms Control and Disarmament Agency, 1995).

One answer to the question I posed above, 'why bother?', is therefore because claiming that a problem is a security problem can provide a claim on resources. More than simply an attempt to 'grab attention', as Levy suggested, the argument that environmental degradation, or human emancipation, or any other issue or problem is a security issue is an attempt to make the political point that it deserves social resources. There is a danger in this line of argument, however. As Wæver notes, the state is privileged in the process of securitization, and the tendency is for the state to militarize issues when it securitizes them. The experience of the 'war on drugs' in the United States is salutary in this regard. In 1990, the United States government identified illicit drugs as a threat to US security, and proceeded to wage a 'war on drugs', which looked in many ways like any other war. Efforts at interdiction – preventing drugs produced outside the United States from entering the country – were conducted by para-military and military police operations. The US military even became involved in physical assaults on the cocaine producers in South America. The danger in trying to securitize issues in order to claim access to resources is that the issue will become the preserve of the military.

Wæver follows this line of argument to conclude that we should not be trying to extend the scope of security, but that rather we should be working for *desecuritization*. Such a move would involve the progressive removal of issues from the agenda of security, rather than introducing new issues and objects. Such an argument takes the suggestion I explored above, of leaving the security label to the study of the military, even further. Security is seen as concerned with military force, and the goal of security scholarship and practice is progressively to reduce the scope of security – ultimately to the demilitarization of political life. This is a provocative thesis, which I cannot consider fully in this chapter, although I will have more to say in the conclusion.

The second implication of Wæver's notion of 'securitization' that I would like to highlight concerns the nature of security *study* to which it gives rise. If 'security' is whatever the state, or some other authoritative group *says* it is, then how can we engage in its study? Strategic studies poses no such problems. Security is about the protection of states from external threat, so we look to see what the threats are, and devise solutions to meet them. However, along with the nature of security and its referent object, the nature of the study of security has also come to be questioned. Wæver represents one possible answer to this question, but there are others. In the final section of this chapter, I take a look at the nature of security *study*.

How to study security

The work that aims to redefine security has necessarily been caught up in the broader debate within International Relations about the nature of study and the role of theory. This is an extremely large and complex debate, but it is an important one, deserving of some attention in this sort of discussion. While it is necessarily a simplification, it makes sense to think about two positions within security studies on the nature of that study. The first of these is the position adopted by strategic studies, and the realism in which it is based. That position assumes that there is an objective social reality about which we can generate knowledge. Critics of this position argue that such objectivity cannot be achieved in the study of society. Because the objects of social study – the people, groups and institutions we examine as social scientists – are actors who understand the world and for whom action has meaning, it is impossible to treat them in the same way that you can treat the objects of study in the natural sciences.

Security and science

Traditional, realist-informed security study aspires to a form of scholarship modelled on the 'scientific method' of the natural sciences. John Mearsheimer (1990: 9) makes this aspiration explicit:

> The study of international relations, like the other social sciences, does not yet resemble the hard sciences. Our stock of theories is spotty and often poorly tested. The conditions required for the operation of established theories are often poorly understood. Moreover, political phenomena are highly complex; hence precise political predictions are impossible without very powerful theoretical tools, superior to those we now possess. As a result, all political forecasting is bound to include some error. ...
>
> Nevertheless, social science *should* offer predictions on the occurrence of momentous and fluid events. ... Predictions can inform policy discourse. ... Moreover, predictions of events soon to

> unfold provide the best tests of social science theories, by making clear what it was that given theories have predicted about those events. In short, the world can be used as a laboratory to decide which theories best explain international politics.

This passage captures the heart of the scientific aspirations of the realists. They recognize (or bemoan) the complexity of social life, and blame it for their incapacity to become physicists for international politics. Nevertheless, their scholarly goal is to develop testable hypotheses which can be generalized into laws and theories, and test them through predicting the outcome of 'experiments'. As they cannot run real experiments, they use the only laboratory they have: history. (For an extended discussion of the scientific method and its application to international politics in the realist view, see Waltz, 1979. For valuable critiques from two distinct critical perspectives, see George, 1994; Neufeld, 1995.)

Despite these scientific goals, there is also a political goal to this research. These scientific hypotheses should 'inform policy discourse'. Indeed, the leading US journal in the field, *International Security*, *requires* policy relevance for its publications. In a contributor's guide, the criteria for selection are given as: 'The editors and reviewers evaluate manuscripts on the basis of four primary criteria: subject, *policy relevance*, observance of scholarly standards of evidence and argumentation, and readability' (Johnson, 1991: 172, emphasis added). Realist students of security see themselves mediating between the 'real world' of their historical laboratory and the political realm of the policy maker. Their science reveals the regularities in histories, and explains them through 'objective' theory. This theory generates predictions, which they dutifully pass on to the decision makers charged with running states' foreign policies. The separation between the elements of this picture is crucial; as Kenneth Waltz (1979: 6) puts it: '[a] theory, though related to the world about which explanations are wanted, always remains distinct from that world.' Mark Neufeld (1995: 33) has spelled out the assumption underlying this statement more fully:

> What then is the assumption underlying this tenet? In short, it is the assumption of the separation of subject and object. This assumption postulates the existence of a 'real world' – the 'object' – which is separate and distinct from the theoretical construction of the (social) scientist – the subject. It is held, moreover, that the theoretical constructions of the subject can be formulated in terms of a ... valid observation language that captures reality – the facts – in direct terms.

The traditional security theorist, then, explains the 'real world' in direct terms, which can then be communicate to the policy maker to inform policy.

However, there is a problem here. The 'scientist' is making predictions about the behaviour of actors in international affairs. S/he then relates these predictions to the *very actors whose behaviours are the subject of the prediction*. Prediction, remember, should 'inform policy discourse'. This prediction becomes part of the environment in which the decision maker makes decisions, and renders the prediction suspect. The 'theoretical constructions of the social scientist' are no longer distinct from the world about which explanations are wanted, but rather form an important part of that world. In fact, this is much more generally true than simply in the case of predictions communicated to policy makers. The 'real world' of the social scientist is a world made up of people explaining and understanding the world and their place and actions in it in certain ways – its object of study is people interpreting their world and acting on those interpretations. Not only are theories *about* others' interpretations, they can serve to inform those interpretations, to inform the policy discourse in Mearsheimer's words. Anthony Giddens (1985: 284) has famously expressed this as 'the double hermeneutic':

> First, all social research has a necessarily cultural, ethnographic or 'anthropological' aspect to it. This is an expression of what I call the double hermeneutic which characterizes social science. The sociologist has as a field of study phenomena which are already constituted as meaningful. The condition of 'entry' to this field is getting to know what actors already know, and how to know, to 'go on' in the daily activities of social life. The concepts that sociological [or other social scientific] observers invent are 'second-order' concepts in so far as they presume certain conceptual capabilities on the part of the actors to whose conduct they refer. *But it is in the nature of social science that these can become 'first order' concepts by being appropriated within social life itself* [emphasis added].

The way in which social science theories can become part of the world on which they comment is easily seen in the field of security. The 'logic' of nuclear deterrence, the central element in US national security policy throughout the cold war, was a construction of the social scientist. Far from being distinct from the world of war managers on which they commented, the strategic analysts of the so-called 'Golden Age' created the strategies for the US state. More importantly, perhaps, they created the very categories by which the decision makers in the US state understood the world. It was only after the strategic analysts did their work that the decision makers could think of the world in terms of 'assured destruction capabilities', 'vulnerabilities to second strikes' or 'hard target kill capabilities'. These were *theoretical* ideas of social scientists, without which US military strategy in the cold war would not have been possible. Those same practitioners of strategic studies could then make predictions about US state action in the context of its nuclear strategy, but they are predicting behaviour that is only *possible* because of the appropriation of the strategists' own concepts, which enabled that behaviour in the first place. Because these ideas were necessary before the strategic actions of the United States were possible, we can say that the theories *constituted* US strategic policy. The term 'constitution' is used frequently in work about the social construction of social life, and is best understood in this fashion, meaning that which makes social life of a particular kind possible.

Security and social construction

The recognition of the double hermeneutic, of the way social science theory is part of what makes up the social life it studies, and the problems this presents for the traditional expectations of social science, informs much of the scholarship critical of realism's study of security. There is much that divides this work internally, but it is fair to say that it shares a concern with the socially constructed nature of security. As Keith Krause and Michael Williams (1996: 242) put it:

> Rather than treating states, groups or individuals as givens that relate objectively to an external world of threats created by the security dilemma, these approaches stress the processes through which individuals, collectivities and threats become *constructed* as 'social facts' and the influence of such constructions on security concerns.

We saw a clear instance of these concerns above in the discussion of Ole Wæver's notion of 'securitization'. He argued that things are not objectively given as security problems, and explored the way in which something is created, by the state, as a concern of national security; that is, how it is securitized. However, it is not just threats that are constructed in this manner, but *all* of the elements which realist strategic studies takes as given: states, nations, interests, as well as issues and threats, and even the weapons that strategic studies so often talks about (see Flank, 1993–4).

Carol Cohn (1987) explores the way in which nuclear weapons and nuclear strategy – the very heart of strategic studies – were constructed in the way Krause and Williams suggest. The world of nuclear strategy is, as she points out, a male-dominated world. Almost all of the people thinking and writing about nuclear strategy in strategic studies (indeed, almost all of the people writing in strategic studies) were men. Cohn examines the way that the language these men use to talk and think about nuclear war shapes what is and is not possible. She reports on her own attempts, as a peace researcher, to express her abhorrence of the prospect of nuclear war to the strategists:

> I found, however, that the better I got at engaging in this discourse [of nuclear strategy], the more impossible it became for me to express my own ideas, my own values. I could adopt the language and gain a wealth of new concepts and reasoning strategies – but at the same time as the language gave me access to things I had been unable to speak about before, it radically excluded others. *I could not use the language to express my concerns because it was physically impossible*. This language does not allow certain questions to be asked or certain values to be expressed. (Cohn, 1987: 149)

What Cohn's article illustrates is the way in which a social fact – even one as concrete as a nuclear weapon and the strategy governing its use – is constructed by the way in which we talk about and think about it.

Cohn is not only analysing nuclear strategy for the way the language shapes that strategy, she is also analysing the language from a feminist point of view. What she discovers is that not only are the strategists overwhelmingly male, but the language that they use is infused with sexual imagery. However, she does not argue that this imagery reflects the 'sexual anxieties and fantasies' of the strategists:

> For me, the interesting question is not so much the imagery's psychodynamic origins, as how it functions. How does it serve to make it possible for strategic planners and other defence intellectuals to do their macabre work? How does it function in their construction of a work world that feels tenable? (Cohn, 1987: 134–5)

She proceeds to show that the sexual language that strategists use to talk about nuclear war serves to provide them with a sense of control over, of distance from, and of domestic comfort with, nuclear weapons. The feeling of being in control of nuclear war allows the strategists to plan strategies for waging nuclear war. Similarly, the sense of distance – that is, the ability to separate themselves from their position as potential *victims* of nuclear war – together with the sense of domestic comfort – the sort of comfort that derives from long-term sexual partnership – allows the strategists to plan for nuclear war without considering the horrifying human costs.

Taken together, this sort of language is part of what makes nuclear strategizing possible. If it were not for these forms of language which allow strategists to ignore key elements of the effects of nuclear war, it would be difficult, perhaps impossible, to 'think about the unthinkable'. (One of the most important texts in the history of nuclear strategy is a book by Herman Kahn (1962) called *Thinking about the Unthinkable*.) While Cohn's focus is on nuclear war and nuclear strategy, the same is true of all aspects of security. The 'facts' of security – the threats, the referent objects, the measures taken to secure – are all made possible by the way in which we think about them.

Because of this, because of the socially constructed nature of the facts of security, we must study security in ways that are different from strategic studies' attempt to study security as it if was part of the natural world, ways which recognize the constructed nature of social facts.

There are a number of important implications of this approach to the study of security, but I will focus on two. The first is that if all of the 'social facts' relevant to the study of security are constructed, it means that they can be reconstructed. In other words, change is possible; just because security is understood and practised in a particular way today, this does not mean that it has always been so nor that it must always be so in the future. History, therefore, is not a laboratory in which we conduct tests of theories, but rather a creative process in which we live individual and collective lives which are informed by theories (the double hermeneutic). The implication of this observation is that part of the function of security studies is to shape the future. Richard Wyn Jones has written of the relationship between critical security studies and political practices aimed at social change:

> Ultimately ... only political practice can bring about the development of a peaceful, secure and just world order. Whilst Critical Security Studies can assist those political practices which aim at providing real security through emancipation, it cannot be a substitute for them. ... However, Critical Security Studies can become an important voice informing and legitimating those political practices that could turn the dream of 'a world of benignly interacting particularities' into reality. (Wyn Jones, 1995: 315)

Wyn Jones is writing with a clear political commitment to human emancipation, the same commitment as Ken Booth's in his attempt to reformulate security as emancipation. Clearly, political practice does not have to be aimed at human emancipation. However, if theory informs political practice in any way, as I have suggested here it must, it therefore must necessarily have some form of political commitment. This is the second implication of this approach to study I wish to draw, one I have raised above by claiming that all theory is for someone and for some purpose. Social theory of all kinds, and this includes the study of security, is political, supporting the political project of some and therefore necessarily opposing that of others. The important point to draw from this argument is that the political nature of theory applies to the traditional approach to security studies just as it does to the critical approaches. Despite their commitment to 'value neutrality', practitioners of strategic studies are necessarily supporting a political position. The question is whose?

Strategic studies assumes that states, threats and most importantly interests are objectively given. The arguments of all forms of social construction are that on the contrary these are formed in particular historical contexts. What are the implications of saying that interests are objective and natural, when in fact they are subjective and constructed? It is to insulate those interests from criticism of any kind. To criticize a state for having an interest ascribed to it by strategic studies is considered to be akin to criticizing the planet for having gravity – possible, but rather pointless. Painting the study of security as an exercise like the study of gravity or other natural sciences is therefore a political action in favour of the status quo. Strategic studies, and the realism which gives rise to it, is therefore politically conservative, if not reactionary. There is nothing necessarily wrong with conservative politics, but there is something very disturbing about a politics that claims to be apolitical.

Critical security studies

In the past decade, following from the break with strategic studies I have recounted thus far, a literature has developed roughly under the label of 'critical security studies'. Indeed, in keeping with much of International Relations scholarship and, indeed, scholarship more generally, this literature has not only grown, but has split into rival and, at times, warring factions (see Mutimer, 2006). While any classificatory scheme does some violence to what it is classifying, it is reasonable to suggest that there are four main divisions within the security studies that have grown in response to the treble challenge I have outlined in this chapter: social construction, securitization, critical security theory and post-structural security studies.

The first body of scholarship that has grown around the critical security studies label draws largely on the theoretical tradition of constructivism in international relations. This body of work follows closely the initial work of Keith Krause and Michael C. Williams in their seminal edited volume, *Critical Security Studies* (1997a, 1997b), and a number of articles they authored together and separately (Krause, 1998; Krause and Williams, 1996), setting out a research agenda on the construction of threats, referent objects and the transformation of the security environment. Indeed, one observer characterized all of critical security studies in this way: 'Critical security studies deal with the social construction of security. The rhetorical nature of "threat discourses" is examined and criticized. ... Critical security studies consider not only threats as a construction, but the objects of security as well' (Eriksson, 1999: 311–30).

There are a range of other bodies of work that respond to the set of questions I have outlined in this chapter, but do not necessarily accept either the critical security studies label or the constructivist assumptions of Krause and Williams. Following from Ole Wæver's arguments about security as a speech act, there has grown a body of work that is increasingly termed 'securitization studies'. (For a recent review of securitization studies, see Taureck, 2006.)

This research explores the ways and consequences of the securitization and desecuritization of parts of global political life. Despite responding directly to the concerns that sparked the critical study of security, securitization studies follow Buzan et al (1998: 34–5) in arguing that these studies do not fit within critical security studies. This is justified by arguing that while both bodies of work recognize the social construction of security, securitization takes that construction to be sufficiently stable in the long term for it to be treated *as if* it were objective.

Ken Booth and his colleagues at the University of Wales, Aberystwyth, have led the development of a third body of security scholarship responding to the questions animating this chapter. The so-called Welsh School (see Smith, 2005), also distinguishes itself from the constructivism of Krause and Williams and securitization studies, but claims the critical security label for its work. This literature, recently gathered in a volume edited by Ken Booth (2005b), sets out to establish a relatively narrow conception of critical security studies as that work informed by the Frankfurt School of Critical Theory. Booth is attempting to develop a singular critical security theory, which would be able then to inform research in the realm opened by the questions which undermined strategic studies as a similar theory in the cold war.

Where Booth is largely sympathetic to both the contructivists and those engaged in securitization research, the same cannot be said for the fourth body of work to emerge in the context of the rethinking of international security. Post-structuralism, Booth (2005a: 270) claims, is marred by 'obscurantism, relativism, and faux radicalism'. I would suggest, rather, that it is only in the post-structural writing that the radical promise of the transformation of security studies comes close to being realized. The post-structural writing, perhaps best exemplified in the work of David Campbell (1998a, 1998b), does not shy away from the radical implications of the production of society in general and security in particular in and through the production of social meaning. The result is that the ethics and politics of security that flow from post-structural thinking are never finished, and so the work challenges us never to cease asking the central questions of security, or other, analysis and politics.

Conclusion

I began this discussion by suggesting that the rethinking of strategy and international security can be considered in terms of three key questions: *Whose* security is at issue? *How* can security be provided? And how should security be *studied*? We can now see that in some ways, the last of these questions should come first. By exploring the way we study security, we begin to recognize the *political* content of the answers to the other two questions. Politics is about many things, but perhaps most centrally it is about power. To identify someone or something as the referent object of security, as the person or thing to be secured, is to empower them. The state derives tremendous power from its claim to be the guardian of national security – power to claim resources and to impose extraordinary measures on its citizens. Challenging the traditional understanding of security as state security, in the name of another referent object, be it the individual, or some other social grouping, or the global environment, is therefore to pose a political challenge to the power of the state and make a claim for the political power of this other referent.

A number of ways of answering these questions have been provided in the years since they first started systematically to be asked. Most of these approaches try to provide settled answers, restabilizing our understanding of security after a period of fraught uncertainty. Those commonly labelled post-structural, by contrast, challenge our thinking about security in radical ways. They force us not only to ask these questions, but to keep posing them, and the underlying questions of power, even when we have provided both academic and practical answers. While such a stance is not only radical but profoundly uncomfortable, it is ultimately the most productive path to critical thinking beyond strategy.

Further reading

Booth, K. (1991) 'Security and Emancipation', *Review of International Studies*, 17: 315–26.

Booth, K. (ed.) (2005) *Critical Security Studies and World Politics*, Boulder: Lynne Rienner.

Buzan, B., Wæver, O. and de Wilde, J. (1998) *Security: A New Framework for Analysis*, Boulder: Lynne Rienner.

Campbell, D. (1998a) *National Deconstruction: Violence, Identity and Justice in Bosnia*, Minneapolis: University of Minnesota Press.

Campbell, D. (1998b) *Writing Security: United States Foreign Policy and the Politics of Identity*, 2nd edn, Minneapolis: University of Minnesota Press.

Dalby, S. (2002) *Environmental Security*, Minneapolis: University of Minnesota Press.

Katzenstein, P. (ed.) (1996) *The Culture of National Security*, New York: Columbia University Press.

Krause K. and Williams, M.C. (eds) (1997) *Critical Security Studies: Concepts and Cases*, Minneapolis: University of Minnesota Press.

Mutimer, D. (2006) 'Critical Security Studies: A Schismatic History', in Collins, A. (ed.), *Contemporary Security Studies*, Oxford: Oxford University Press.

Smith, S. (2005) 'The Contested Concept of Security', in Booth, K. (ed.), *Critical Security Studies and World Politics*, Boulder: Lynne Rienner.

Wæver, O. (1995) 'Securitization and Desecurization', in Lipschutz, R. (ed.), *On Security*, New York: Columbia University Press.

Wyn Jones, R. (1999) *Security Strategy and Critical Theory*, London: Lynne Rienner.

Chapter 4

Non-Military Security Challenges

J. Peter Burgess

Introduction

A certain understanding of security plays a role in every aspect of life. Despite the fact that fear, anxiety, danger and doubt are fundamental social and individual experiences, the scholarly study of security has traditionally been limited to the field of international studies, associated primarily with the status of nation-states in relation to each other. According to this conventional concept, the state is both the object of security and the primary provider of security. Today a burgeoning literature is revisiting the traditional cold-war-based notion of security (Aggestam and Hyde-Price, 2000; Alkire, 2003; Baldwin, 1995, 1997; Booth, 2005b; Brown, 1997; Buzan, 1991a, 1991b; Dalby, 1997, 2000; Der Derian, 1993; Dillon, 1996; Huysmans, 1998; Kaldor, 2000; Lipschutz, 1995; Rothschild, 1995; Tickner, 1995; Ullmann, 1983; Wæver, 1997, 2000; Williams, 1994; Wyn Jones, 1999). This literature is based on a general consensus among both scholars and practitioners that a wide range of security threats, both new and traditional, confronts states, individuals and societies. New forms of nationalism, ethnic conflict and civil war, information technology, biological and chemical warfare, resource conflicts, pandemics, mass migrations, transnational terrorism and environmental dangers challenge the conventional means of understanding threats and of assuring the security of all regions of the world. The growing awareness of these new threats is challenging the way in which the principles and tasks of security scholarship are presently understood.

Across this wide range of insecurities, two distinct features characterize threats to security: they surpass the boundaries of the nation-state and they are interconnected through processes of globalization. No one state can manage the array of threats to its own security, nor can any one state manage the threats to the security of its neighbours from both inside and outside its region. In the globalized setting, the challenge of maintaining security is no longer limited to the traditional foreign policy and military tools of the nation-state; security and insecurity are no longer considered

60

as conditioned only upon geopolitics and military strength, but also on social, economic, environmental, moral and cultural issues (Tuchman, 1989; Suhrke, 1999).

The logic of security

This mutation in our understanding of security is not only an empirical one, it is a conceptual one as well. The conceptual logic of security has evolved significantly in the past decades. By conceptual logic, we mean the interacting function of three dimensions of the concept: its object, its subject and its agency. As the present volume documents, the concept has had a relatively short and significantly turbulent history. This is coupled with observable inflation in the use of the concept. Reaching far beyond the scope of traditional national security a new economy of security has formed, identifying, analysing, re-tooling and voicing a new set of security threats to which it proposes to respond with a set of newly adapted security measures. This economy is a perpetual motion machine: threats we never knew we actually faced appear to be answered by new means of differentiation. This tendency can be characterized through five general observations.

First, security is becoming increasingly commercialized. It has become merchandise that can be bought or sold on a more or less open security market. Commercial security guards replace public police forces, the number of tasks carried out by contracted security consultants has grown sharply, and mercenaries replace national security forces. Security merchandise circulates across borders, social classes, services, organizations, interests and allegiances.

Second, providers of security, be they public or private, increasingly often have recourse to technological solutions. If security were ever considered a human enterprise (a question to which we will return), then it is most certainly less so today. Human beings are less than ever part of the security equation. The security challenges of today are more than ever resolved by investing in the tools of science with the aim of developing more certain, more precise, more invisible and more dependable solutions to security threats. Humans, the traditional object of security, increasingly stand in the way of security solutions, reducing their efficiency. The epitome of security today is a tool whose technological qualities makes possible the absence of humans.

Third, the technologization of security has lead to the advanced stages of an industrialization of security, implying a kind of internal 'product' differentiation. According to the well-exercised logic of late capitalism, demand thereby does not increase as a function of needs, but rather as a function of supply: the greater the supply of commercially available technological security solutions, the more we need them. Security is itself a merchandise: it becomes more diversified, localized, tailored to its context, to its consumer and to its user.

Fourth, security has become globalized. Traditionally linked to the autonomy of the territorial nation-state, linked to the categories, concerns and tools of political and geographical borders, where physical frontiers demarcate friend from foe and war from peace. This territorial attachment, and even predication, of security is gradually being loosened. The image of threat has become more diffuse and more ubiquitous, ambiguous and invisible. Moreover, we see the rise of the notion of risk in conjunction with the changes in the concept of security. *Risk* replaces *danger* as the object of security concerns. The discourse of risk replaces *real* danger with virtual danger, unspecified but calculable danger.

Finally, the collective effect of these transformations in the notion of security is the *production* of insecurity. In other words, insecurity increases proportionally with the accelerated reflection upon security and changing approaches to security. The battle against a variety of forms of threat most often leads to instrumental and technological responses that leave little space for the human subjects. We fortify walls, erect barriers and develop systems of detection. Yet these technological systems have only the limited effect of rendering us secure. They have the side effect of rendering us less sure, less confident, more dependent. Less confidence implies less security.

The purpose of this chapter is to take stock of the most prominent challenges to non-military security and evaluate these principles based on this empirical survey. The survey begins with the anchoring point and reference of essentially all non-military security challenges, the notion of human security. The scope and influence of this 15-year-old concept can hardly be underestimated. It links in one way or another to all the other sub-fields of the survey: societal insecurity, migration, climate change, water and resources, energy insecurity, organized crime (narcotics, arms and human trafficking), health insecurity. Each of these challenges corresponds to a literature of its own, and each in a different way embodies and problematizes the theoretical principles mentioned above.

Human insecurity

Human security has become a canonical concept, with its own origin and distinct history. Most analytical and conceptual considerations of human security take the 1994 United Nations *Human Development Report* as more or less the alpha of human security thinking (UNDP, 1994). Though the report demonstrably does not represent the first use of the concept in general, the force of its impact on global discussion is undeniable. In the wake of the cold war it has became clear that, for the developing world, 'security' held an entirely different set of priorities than what were held to be the security issues of the period of nationalized superpower 'mutually assured destruction'. The UNDP report takes its point of departure in the problem of the cloak laid over the rest of the globe by the cold war focus on security on the transcontinental scale. The report is both provocative, in the sense that it argues that the long-standing tradition of the using 'security' to refer to geopolitical issues is entirely misguided, and reconciliatory in the sense that it proposes human security as a supplement to cold war security. The crisis and rapid expansion in the concept of international security not only had little relevance for improving conditions, but indeed contributed to their detriment. In the developing world, the important questions of security were not geopolitical, not even related to issues of balance of military powers. Instead, the moments of insecurity arose from disease, hunger, unemployment, social conflicts, crime, political repression, etcetera. Questions of security and insecurity are also to be found on the personal, the sub-group or the interpersonal level.

Analysing security and insecurity from the point of view of human insecurity requires a re-tooling of security studies, a shift away from the analytic tools and observation methods of both military- and nation-state-based security thinking. Thus, a clear methodological imperative informs the new nonconventional thinking on security, suggesting that the good will of social scientific analysts and politicians will most certainly motivate them to reevaluate their premises. At the same time, however, it is impossible to ignore the ideological timber of the notion of human security, which, it is important to note, originates in the UN's Development Programme. Development has been neglected, forgotten and overshadowed by a certain use of the term 'security'.

The concept of human security emerges in a moment of history between what will probably be considered as two momentous eras, between cold war geopolitics and the geopolitics of transnational terrorism. It thus not only identifies two different kinds of security and insecurity, but grows out of an era dramatically marked by two different orders of fear and by the emergence of an entirely different environment of threat, a new concept of 'war' and a radically different sense of insecurity.

The well-known UNDP *Human Development Report 1994* begins with the premise that the large-scale geopolitical conception of security is not adequate. The cold war model builds upon a fundamental assumption that the wide-ranging threat to the global political order is the most significant threat to the well-being of all individuals. The assumption is not only one of levels, collective versus individual, as is often suggested. It is a greater difference in worldview, one in which the entire world order is threatened, that is, a certain understanding of reality, of the entire constellation of relations between people, society, state and world (UNDP, 1994).

Fear and insecurity are imaginary, based on images of what could happen, what is likely, what is threatening, what is risky, etcetera. The UNDP report suggests that a different scope of imagination is relevant for the two conceptions of security. For the global level, the threat concerns the collapse of an entire way of ordering facts and ideas, peoples and societies. Insecurity in the larger sense is related to the possibility of a general collapse, the possibility of a shift in the conditions for relating to the world at all. By reason of scale, these are always on a level that cannot be grasped by any one individual. It is supra individual. A consensus on the shared experience of insecurity is difficult at best.

Doubtless the UNDP report, like its successor, the Commission on Human Security's *Human Security Now*, is a very idealistic document. It sets out the shape of an ideal world, one in which security on an individual level is generalized across all communities in all parts of the world (Commission on Human Security, 2003). Less often noted in reconstructions of the short history of human security is that the UNDP report also provides the most powerful moral voice for the needs of those subject to human insecurity. In short, the UNDP report locates security and insecurity on the personal level and small group level. The location (or re-location) of the focus of security and insecurity is the foundation of a general ethics of insecurity and for a comprehensive analysis of its nature: in other words, at the level of *ethical judgement*.

Societal insecurity

As discussed in Chapter 3, among the liveliest research and policy debates revisited in the wake of the cold war is that concerning individual and societal dimensions of security (Buzan, 1991b; Buzan et al, 1998; Krause and Williams, 1996; Sorensen, 1996). As we have suggested, the cold war grip on research in security studies and international affairs, which was prolonged for a variety of reasons, found itself opened to re-conceptualizing (Baldwin, 1997; Bilgin, 2003; Tickner, 1995). The principal evolution in theory of security is well rehearsed in this literature: cold war geopolitics privileged a realist focus on the nation-state as subject and referent object of security. Security threats originated in a more or less anarchical international arena as confrontations between states, represented by diplomatic positions and backed up by militaries. In terms of concepts, this constellation builds on the principal formula: state = nation = society.

Nearly 20 years after the end of the cold war it has almost become a commonplace to underscore that this equivalence not only does not hold, but has essentially never corresponded to the real situation in any given state–nation–society constellation. The direct implication is that the security of the state is not equivalent to the security of the society or societies it encompasses, just as it is not equivalent to the security of individuals that reside within its borders. Here too a variety of interpretations has been advanced. The most comprehensive version understands a threat to societal security as a threat to the continued longevity of society (Wæver et al, 1993: 23). This concept of societal security, advanced in the 1990s, has been extremely influential in developing new understandings of threats to societal security.

Societal insecurity involves threats to the fundamental make-up of a society. These are aspects such as values, traditions, customs, language, religion and ethnicity. These characteristics of a given group are often referred to as identity. When speaking of societal dimensions of security we thus commonly refer to threats to the identity of a group. Understanding social identity, be it in terms of threat or not, also raises a number of theoretical issues about what determines identity and it what sense it can be threatened (McSweeney, 1999: 68–78). According to Buzan et al (1998), threats to societal security can be understood to fall along two axes, horizontal and vertical. Horizontal threats to societal security refer to identities that compete with one another within a society. The social and cultural practices of one social group are threatened because of the overriding social and cultural practices of another group or groups. It is thus the social practices or the identities of other groups that threaten the group in question. These can be all to do with language priorities, religious practices, work and leisure norms, food and resources use, etcetera. Vertical threats take the form of integrating practices from above. An overarching organization, ideology, group or even state overtakes and assimilates or integrates the social group in question, with the result that the social identity in question is weakened to the point of potential disintegration or actually repressed by political forces (Buzan et al, 1998: 121).

Migration and insecurity

Migration encompasses security issues along a number of axes. It includes people who move both within and across national boundaries, internal and international migrants respectively. It refers to people moving out of choice and those who are forced to move, and people moving for political, economic, social and environmental reasons, or a combination of these factors. It also includes people at all stages of the migration cycle – from departure through living and settling abroad to return, as well as their experiences en route, for example in transit countries (Koser, 2006).

Like a number of other security challenges, migration-related insecurity increased significantly following the end of the cold war. And like so many of these challenges, the events of 9/11 have intensified awareness of and debate about migration (Faist, 2004). The migrant is more easily construed today than earlier as a potential national enemy, and the subsequent securitization of the migrant and migration in general has had enormous consequences for both individuals and states.

Migration, and in particular migration from the developing to the developed regions of the world, has become a central focus of political discourse (Ceyhan and Tsoukala, 2002). As the global economic gap widens, the motivation to migrate in order to obtain better living conditions grows in kind. Variations in vulnerability to economic, political, environmental and health-based shocks or crises create a need to seek security by moving. Migration is thus a clear consequence of insecurity. Moreover, the experience of migration is often filled with insecurities and vulnerabilities of a variety of kinds.

From the point of view of the arrival societies of migrants, be they refugees or other, there is a distinct insecurity created (Akan, 2003; Faist, 2004; Huysmans, 1995; Kicinger, 2004; Roe, 2004). Host societies experience threats to social stability through problematization of endogenous cultures, itself answered by various forms of xenophobia. Demographic changes and with them economic changes can be perceived as threatening as a function of changes in family and group make-up. Cultural, religious and ethnic identity can be the source of conflict and security. These changes in populations carry with them changes in the ways that developed state-based societies care for citizens and those who have legal right to care. These changes motivate significant dynamics through the politics of border security, homeland, security, integration, citizenship and cultural pluralism, etcetera.

The relationship between security, insecurity and migration is also linked, to greater or lesser degrees, to human and narcotics trafficking, and associated international criminality. It is safe to say that this 'security-migration nexus' has since 11 September 2001 served political interests more or less unrelated to actual migration flows. Thus, the effects of security responses to the perceived insecurity of demographic changes stemming from migration are often unintended (Faist, 2004: 4–5).

The non-military aspects of migration are however not limited to the real and perceived threats to host societies. Clearly, migration is in the majority of cases already the reflection of one kind or another of insecurity in the migrant's homeland. Populations tend to move because they are in situations of unease, unrest or direct danger. Thus while humanitarian catastrophes of the type that provoke migration are sometimes adequately analysed and understood as security issues, migration for the migrant is a security issue of another kind altogether, one that is seldom linked to the insecurities generated in 'receiver' societies. The experience of migration itself implies a variety of security threats to the migrant. Migrants on the move generally do not benefit from the security protection offered by authorities or national police (Koser, 2005, 2006). On the contrary, they are most often in a situation of illegality or directly outside the law. In many cases, they are entirely dependent upon a mediator who arranges travel according to terms that leave the migrant little or no assurance of protection against dangers of travel, from fellow migrants or even from the mediator.

Economic explanations dominate migration research. The focus is most commonly on global economic conditions as the key determinants of population movements (Böhning, 1972, 1984; Borjas, 1990; Simon, 1999). To this clearly important dimension must also be added the security threats created by international political forces. International population movements are in many cases motivated by political causes that are only marginally related to global economic issues. Moreover, despite the post-national nature of the migration phenomenon, the immigration policies of nation-states often shape or even determine how migration actually takes place (Weiner, 1992–3: 96–7).

Climate change and insecurity

Climate change has the distinction of being transformed into a security issue even before it left the scientific laboratories. A highly ideologized debate over what the facts about environmental change actually are has carried on for decades. In December 1997, 55 parties signed the Kyoto Protocol, an international agreement under the auspices of the United Nations. The Protocol committed signatories to the reduction of the CO_2 and other greenhouse gases. The protocol, which entered into force in 2005, was famously opposed by the United States, partly on the basis that it was mere climatological charlatanism, partly on the argument that it would threaten the American way of life. In 1992 the United Nation Conference on Environment and Development, the Rio 'Earth Summit', convened on a consultation basis to review environmental and developmental issues. The United States continued to impede progress, bringing an increasingly securitized rhetoric to the sphere of debate. Yet it was not the destruction of the climate that was a national threat in the eyes of the United States. It was rather the spectre of regulations on industrial production and innovation that produced the threat. It was the environmentalists that where securitized, not the environment (Dalby, 1996). Visible changes in environment conditions in recent years have further popularized debate about the threats that may be linked to environmental change.

An important academic literature has evolved linking environmental issues with military conflict, in particular with issues of interstate conflict, civil war and inter-group conflict. The relation between degradation, scarcity and armed conflict, either in the form of civil war or inter-group violence, has been documented along a number of axes (Dalby, 2006). A strong thread of research has attempted to show that environmental scarcity is directly correlated with conflict. Scarcity, it is argued, causes despair that in turn leads to conflict. The degree to which the scarcity–violence link should be conditioned and constrained has been the object of wide debate. Homer-Dixon (1991, 1994) and others have drawn significant conclusions about which environmental conditions can be correlated with interstate warfare. This research has been nuanced by other writers (Commission on Human Security, 2003) who have argued that other political, economic and social factors condition the degree to which environmental factors, in particular 'resource' scarcity, can be linked to security issues.

The particular version of the development–security nexus that concerns security transforms environmental issues to a directly non-military mode. Environmental insecurity is dependent on the resilience of individuals and societies to environment shocks. This includes on the one hand possessing the economic robustness necessary to understand economic downturns relative to agricultural production, transport of goods or production loss caused by environmental damage. Environmental insecurity on the personal level is caused by environmental destruction of homes, neighbourhoods, or local infrastructures. Disease and malnourishment are also results of economic catastrophe. In addition, the vulnerability of states and local civil governments to crises brought about by environmental change often have immediate consequences for local groups and individuals through the loss of services or life- and health-giving infrastructures. This 'political ecology' re-visits the premises of security and development economy in a way that leaves military geopolitics relatively irrelevant.

In this way the North–South dimension and a series of difficult development questions are increasingly linked to the climate–security nexus, and must in turn be associated with the question of technology (Dalby, 2002). The affluent developed world is here regarded as the primary culprit in terms of provoking environment destruction to which the developing world is particularly exposed, and therefore insecure. This version of post-national security links it directly to the rise of human insecurity. More complex is the horizon of re-nationalization which is implied by the North–South tension. The developing world's climate-generated insecurity has recently shown signs of reversing its flow. On the one hand it is closely related to the expanding migration flows from developing to developed societies. Migration issues thus fall back onto the mechanisms of border security, more or less adapted to addressing them (Allenby, 2000).

Water and resource conflicts

Scholarship on water resources has long been a standard component in scholarship on geopolitics (Sprout and Sprout, 1965). However the link between water and security has emerged only in the post-cold war scholarly debate about the scope of the security concept itself (Tuchman, 1989; Baldwin, 1997). In conformity with the classical understanding of security as geopolitics, it emerged first and foremost out of interest for *national* strategic issues, and, at least initially, those most relevant for US foreign policy (Allison and Treverton, 1992; Romm, 1993), then extended to scholarship on the scope of international security, finally joining the ongoing debate about the scope and reach of the 'new security concept' (Ullman, 1983; Gleick, 1990, 1993; Homer-Dixon, 1991; Kliot, 1994; Tickner, 1995; Wolf, 1995; Chaturvedi, 1998; Giordano et al, 2002; Selby, 2005). These valuable studies cover a wide variety of aspects of the security–water nexus. They nonetheless share one common analytic characteristic: they all regard water as a simple and finite object of political action. They presuppose water to be a good that, like other goods, can be taken up into a predetermined calculus of strategic advantage and disadvantage. Water-security analyses of this kind are entirely possible without asking what kind of role water plays outside the sphere of geopolitics, its national, regional, or local or personal specificity.

An illustration of this type of analysis is Gleick's (1993: 501) 'Water and

Security: Resources and International Security'. The analysis opens with the observation that '[as] we approach the twenty-first century, water and water-supply systems are increasingly likely to be both objectives of military action and instruments of war.' In the age of post-bipolar conflict, water as resource slides easily into a discourse of war in which all elements are considered in terms of their contribution to or detraction from the objective aim of the conflict: thus 'even water can fit into this framework if water provides a source of economic or political strength.' By the same token, in an equally important parallel logic of war, water is routinely instrumentalized as a simple means to military ends and the use of water and water-resources as 'both offensive and defensive weapons' is not unusual. Dams (Yalu River, Korean War), irrigation waterways (Syria–Israel in the 1950s), desalination plants (Persian Gulf War, 1990) and sanitation systems (Iraq War) have long been used as means to attain strategic advantage (Gleick, 1993).

Gleick's study, like many others of its kind, is true to its premises and irreproachable as such. More recent approaches to water security underscore how effectively the old geopolitical paradigm oversees the basis for water's strategic value: the function it has as a life-giving source for the individuals that make up the local, regional, national, even global populations. In the logic of geopolitical strategy, it is not a question of the conditions under which tensions over water arise or play themselves out between actual people in concrete settings. The general pattern in this literature is that the geopolitics of water brackets entirely the issue of how water comes to be scarce, how its scarcity affects populations, what it means in terms of life from the point of view of groups and individuals who have immediate contact with the resource. Indeed, as is the tendency in geopolitical analysis in general, groups and individuals are by and large bracketed from the analysis.

In recent years this geopoliticization of water has led to a stronger, and indeed more alarmist, rendering of the instrumentalization of water. The concept of 'water wars' has emerged (Westing, 1986; Starr, 1991), provoking a new debate about whether such a conflict is likely. Others have drawn evidence of impending water wars into question (Wolf, 1999; Alam, 2002; Sinha, 2006). Yet regardless of which side one takes in this debate the discourse of water remains one of the instrumental logic of war, interrogating the geopolitical mechanics and strategic viability of waging war over water. Water remains the means to one end, which is the security of the state.

Alternative approaches seek to underscore the impacts on humans of water, in both abundance and scarcity, implicitly suggesting that the traditional picture of resource conflict is incomplete. The analytical logic of war takes water as a given, an unproblematic object of contention. Either they have it or we have. The question of its 'actual' value is never posed, only the question of its exchange value in the political economy of conflict. Yet the complete picture of these reasons cannot be simply assimilated to the growing jargon of 'resource conflict'. It not only has a multitude of meanings and values for countless people, but these aspects of water do not emerge in public debate or closed political forums. Why?

Energy insecurity

Few concepts have grown in importance in the field of international affairs as fast as *energy security*. It goes nearly without saying that energy has itself always been a central dimension in the reflection and strategy on security. Its significance has however been traditionally limited to geo-strategic dimensions: the ability to wage war in modern times is closely linked to the ability to produce weapons on an industrial scale, to support energy-driven devices and to wage war itself. Thus in the classical grammar of war and security, energy, most prominently oil, enters into any and all strategic calculations.

In the late modern era, the notion of energy security has risen in importance for other reasons. This is primarily due to the transformation of the global market into an arena for security politics. The threats stemming from energy are linked to the deep and largely unregulated integration of the global economy. The world is deeply interdependent, interlinked in ways that exceed both the instrumentality of goal-oriented international relations and the democratic systems; a central part of that economy is the global energy market. Through it, the major economic powers of the globe are interlinked less by their shared need for energy, though this is largely a given, but rather by their shared need for *stability*. What happens in the energy market has profound consequences for general economic conditions to be sure, but it has arguably far more threatening consequences for the global capital system on which all depend. The classical capitalist principles of credit, investment, distribution and profit depend on stable money markets and stable conditions of production. The correlates to this market-based logic of insecurity can be mapped along three primary themes: peak oil, climate change and the Middle East.

Add to this the fact that both China and India are postured to become world economic powers, easily surpassing the energy production and consumption levels of the United States, and energy insecurity is raised considerably. The energy market will only become tighter in the coming decades and the margin of security correspondingly acute. Stability is the key. A large part of the growth in the world energy supply after 2010 will occur in countries in transition, in unstable conditions for production and investment. The 'stability' function of energy security in this points to three fundamental security issues.

First, *peak oil* has become a touchstone for a certain kind of dramatic insecurity. It refers to the notion that we are approaching the point of exhaustion of oil resources, that the global production of energy can no longer be increased. Though new oil fields will doubtless be found, the economics of exploitation will either be prohibitive or lead to critically high energy prices, multiplying instability and thus energy insecurity

Second, global *climate change*: any lingering doubts about the reality of global warming have disappeared in only the last few years. The demonstrations between climate change and carbon dioxide emission has robust credibility. The practical consequences in terms of individual and human security are clear. Those living in conditions of fragility, be it material or economic, are more exposed to the environmental consequences of global energy consumption. Changes in the global pattern will have direct consequences for them.

Third, the *Middle East*, in which 60 per cent of known oil reserves lie, remains politically unstable. The origins of this are historical and their maintenance ideological. Indeed the instability is such that it in some sense provides a predictive stability that is relevant to the logic of energy security. Oil is to varying degrees used as a tool, not as an objective

This situation is framed by what can be called the 'Energy Security System' (Yergin, 2007), which was created in response to the oil shock of 1973. It encouraged collaboration between the industrialized countries in the event of a disruption in supply and coordination on energy policies in order to avoid scrambling for supplies, and to discourage the use of 'oil weapons'. It was networked with a set of strategic stockpiles of oil, and continuously monitored and analysed energy markets and policies (Yergin, 1991). Energy insecurity is among the most pronounced effects of globalization and international connectedness. It is a concretization of the interconnected global economy, and perhaps more importantly the concretization of the interconnectedness of information, the speed and rapidity of market reactions to information, the market's low threshold for influence, its ability to create and solve crises. The most noteworthy consequence of energy insecurity is that it cannot be eliminated by direct physical means. Integrating members of the new energy security community, including China and India, into a security regime will require tailoring knowledge to individual settings, understanding what individual actors understand by security.

Transnational organized crime

Transnational organized crime operates to a large degree along the models of today's international businesses. Essentially the same structural evolution in the international community that has accompanied the rapid expansion of a global market, global supply and provision and global distribution has not only benefited international criminal organizations but has helped them to evolve in efficient and profitable ways. In short, criminal organizations are international organizations very much like others. Increased mobility, open exchange arrangements and, not least, the overburdening of customs and international control mechanisms have all contributed to an opening of the horizon of international trade (Williams, 1994). Like legal business organizations the lifeblood of illegal international organizations is the flow of money, its invisibility and convertibility. More than ever before illegal organizations are able to transfer money from one place to another and from currency to another with considerable ease (Daams, 2003; Galeotti, 2002; Krause, 1972; Ohmae, 1990; De Ruyver, 2002).

Narcotics trafficking

The most important illegal organized activity surrounds the global distribution of narcotics. The illicit drug trade is among the largest industries in the world, with the major Columbian cocaine cartels and the Asian opium cartels dominating activities. A correlation has also been made between the production and trafficking of illicit drugs. The most clear link here is in terms of narcotics as a resource that can be seized through a successfully campaign (Cornell, 2005). Thus direct support of terrorist activities through means provided by the narcotics industry has also been widely documented (Hardouin and Weichhardt, 2006).

The direct non-military security challenge of illicit narcotics trafficking is clearly its effect on the integrity of societies. For a variety of social and cultural reasons drug trafficking poses a threat to the security of individual well-being and social cohesion. This is less because of the direct effects drug use has on individuals than because of the intimate link between drugs and violence. This link has a number of levels. First and foremost, criminal organizations, unlike non-criminal ones, are willing to adopt highly violent methods to protect their profits. Second, the potential for interpersonal violence committed by narcotics users in the pursuit of funds to obtain their substances is considerably higher than for others. Lastly, individual drug takers are far more exposed to health consequences and interpersonal violence than non-drug users (Williams, 1994: 329–330).

Thus at the organization level, security issues arise in conflicts between cartels, states, law enforcement agencies and individuals that should come in the way of economic activities. In a number of cases, particularly with respect to Latin American drug cartels, the illegal organizations are primary geo-political actors, rivalling or even dominating the state. The peripheral role and weakness of the state has clear consequences for social and economic support services provided to society by the state.

Human trafficking

Human trafficking takes a number of forms. By definition, it involves moving men, women and children from one place to another and placing them in conditions of forced labour. Among current practices are domestic labour, agricultural labour, sweatshop, factory or restaurant work and forced prostitution. According to a 2000 US Congressional Research Service report, somewhere between 700,000 and 2 million people are trafficked each year across international borders. Of these 35 per cent are under the age of 18 (CRS, 2000). Trafficking of women for the purposes of prostitution is far the most comprehensive form, both in terms of numbers of individuals and financial exchange, rivalling the global narcotics and arms trades. This multi-billion dollar industry has not ceased to expand in the last decades. Yet compared with the global drug trade, trafficking in women contains lower risks and less danger for perpetrators.

Clearly, the primary objects of lost or lowered security are the individuals who are trafficked. To varying degrees, they are removed from state-based systems of social welfare and protection. Their existences are often uncharted and undocumented. Since their own activities are often illegal or semi-legal, they have limited access to police or other public protection. Loss or weakening of security takes place at several levels. Most globally, human trafficking for the purpose of sexual exploitation deprives victims of human security in terms of the violation of human rights and dignity. Furthermore, such trafficking puts its objects in the line of danger in terms of both individual and public health, deprives them of freedom of movement and removes protections from physical, emotional and sexual abuse. Trafficking in persons is also regarded as at threat to global security in the sense that it is often part of a larger phenomenon of illegal migration and organized crime, thus threatening global governance (Jackson, 2006: 303).

Trafficking of all kinds, but in particular trafficking in women is linked to networks of international crime in general, as well as to money laundering, and weapons and drug trafficking. Illicit money made from organized prostitution and other forms of trafficking tends to remain in circulation in illicit activities. Though there are exceptions, profits tend to finance more trafficking or other forms illegal commerce (Hughes, 2000: 10).

Human trafficking can also be read as a consequence of social and economic insecurity. As in the case of migration, individuals most often fall victim to trafficking when their conditions of life are insecure, in some cases desperately insecure. Poor economic conditions are a primary cause of trafficking and thus, like socio-economic insecurity in general, poverty has knock-on effects in terms of trafficking.

Arms trafficking

The flow of small arms has grown continuously in recent decades to become a worldwide security crisis. Every year millions of weapons are produced and sold on the world arms market. Accordingly, violence caused by or carried out by means of small arms, be it in civil wars, inter-group conflicts in the developing world or domestic and gang-related violence in Western cities, has not ceased to expand. Small arms have a number of particular attributes that make them well suited to worldwide proliferation. They are relatively inexpensive, they are easy to maintain and they are portable (Jackson et al, 2005: 10).

Small arms are therefore the weapon of choice in most internal conflicts. This is to a large degree for international-legal reasons. The market for small arms defies the controls and security mechanisms surrounding larger-scale weapons used by national militaries. Thus they fall into the grey zone between the domain of national police protection and military regulations. In addition, a vast variation in national laws makes the possession and even the exchange of a wide variety of weapons legal and practical. The international disparities in control also create difficulties in terms of documenting the movement of arms.

Although men are the primary victims of small arms distributed by illegal trafficking, women and children are particularly vulnerable. In armed conflicts supported by small arms there is a clear correlation between the proliferation of weapons and sexual violence against women (Hemenway et al, 2002). A similar correlation has been documented between small arms violence and forced flight. Small arms not only contribute to people leaving their homes in conflict environments, but also endanger them in flight and hinder their return. Finally, small arms violence has important knock-on effects on security in terms of health, education and welfare (Jackson et al, 2005: 33–48).

Health insecurity

At the heart of individual security is the notion that a people-centred view of security is not only necessary for ensuring the rights and dignity of the individual, but also for securing national, regional and global stability. In protecting the rights and development of the individual, security can be ensured on a much broader scale. In this respect, health security represents an integral component of individual security and is inextricably linked to the other categories that characterize it: economic, food, environmental, personal, community and political securities.

In an era of globalization threats to health represent a more prominent insecurity than ever. At its most basic, health security entails 'the protection against illness, disability and avoidable death', according to the Commission on Human Security (2003: 96). However, good health encompasses more than just a physical state of being. Health can be defined as 'not just the absence of disease', but as a 'state of complete physical, mental and social well-being'. Health is both objective physical wellness and subjective psychosocial well-being and confidence about the future. It provides one with the capacity to make choices and exercise options.

A health approach to insecurity acknowledges both objective and subjective health, subjective insecurity being just as relevant as objective threats, and thus one of the central roles of government and its institutions is to generate public confidence and reduce fear. The degree to which governments succeed in this task is a partial measure of security in society (Chen and

Narasimhan, 2002: 12). The securitization of health suggests that health can be prioritized along the same reasoning as defence and military investments are given priority in the concept of state security. Health security highlights the interrelationship between the concepts of human security and national security in that in some cases the former is not possible without the latter.

Accordingly, a security approach to health entails ensuring that health security is a public good equally accessible to all. It consists of two fundamental components: empowerment and protection. Empowerment constitutes strategies that 'would enhance the capacity of individuals and communities to assume responsibility for their own health', while protection comprises strategies that 'would promote the three institutional pillars of society: to prevent, monitor and anticipate health threats' (Chen, 2004: 12). Implicit in this approach is the involvement of various sectors of society in negotiating threats to health. Health security is connected to and informed by social, behavioural, environmental, political and economic factors. All these factors are interlinked and do not act in isolation, raising the question as to how one is to identify and assess risks to health security.

Interconnecting social, behavioural, environmental, political and economic factors combine to contribute to an inequitable balance of health security in any given region of the world, affecting the physical and psychosocial well-being of individuals disproportionately. Threats to health are generally experienced disproportionately by the poor and marginalized segments of a population. Lower socio-economic groups experience higher mortality rates – including a higher risk of mortality due to cardiovascular disease, shorter life expectancy, higher self-assessed morbidity rates, a higher prevalence of most chronic conditions, and a higher prevalence of mental health problems and disability (Mackenbach, 2005: 5). Individuals at a financial disadvantage are on average likely to experience more psychosocial stress, which can evolve into different forms of psychological and physical ailments including depression, alienation, suicide, high blood pressure, strokes and heart attacks. Health risks shaped by lifestyle factors, such as obesity and health problems associated with smoking, also tend to be higher among individuals of lower income (Ghai, 1997).

What are the major challenges to health security? At what point does a health problem become a security threat? The World Health Organization defines risk as 'a probability of an adverse outcome, or a factor that raises that probability' (WHO, 2002: 9). In addition, the Commission on Human Security (2003: 97) identifies four criteria that influence the strength of links between health and human security: (1) the scale of the disease burden in the present and in the future; (2) the urgency for action; (3) the depth and extent of the impact on society; and (4) the interdependencies or 'externalities' that can create ripple effects that extend beyond the particular diseases, persons or locations. From these criteria, the Commission on Human Security identifies three broad health challenges that are closely linked to human security: global infectious diseases, poverty-related threats, and violence and crisis. These criteria underscore threats posed by such diseases as HIV/AIDS and tuberculosis, food-borne illnesses and avian influenza to health security.

First, among the most visible challenges to individual and societal security is the couple HIV/AIDS and tuberculosis. While the incidence of HIV/AIDS is not a prerequisite for tuberculosis and vice versa, the two are closely associated as HIV is one of the largest individual risk factors for developing TB. Thus, the segments of the world population at higher risk of contracting either are the same. Second, instances of food-borne illness, despite being relatively underreported, have increased over the last 20 years, particularly in the case of illnesses caused by salmonella and campylobacter (WHO, 2002: 6). Third, while the threat of a human influenza pandemic remains largely theoretical at the moment, avian flu is a formidable risk to health security, particularly from the standpoint of anticipation. Due to the spread of avian influenza and the fact that there have been cases of bird-to-human transmission, the WHO has issued a pandemic alert (Sandell, 2006).

Conclusion

This paradigm-breaking catalogue of 'new security challenges' at first glance lacks theoretical uniformity. Aside from the already strained and tired mantra of the post-Westphalian security concept – detached from territory, dissociated from the state monopoly of legitimate violence and security, and 'lowered' to the level of human issues – the talk of a new and non-military concept of security has a distinctly methodological side. If we are to summarize this broad and ungainly field of security concepts it must be simply noting that security is a *practice*. Security is not an idea of the world but an action in the world relative to a certain set of facts about the world, be they understood as threats to the status quo social organization, impending environmental hazards, ubiquitous fear of the threats to religious identity, or invisible diseases that seem to put into question the self-evidence of everyday health loss or security not as propositional, but rather as taking the form of a question. The so-called security threats to one person in one part of the world at one given time are simply not always, perhaps never the same as security threats to another.

For the human and social sciences, this insight transforms security studies into an ethics and moves the question of method to the centre of the problem of science. Like security, science projects a certain comprehension of life onto its object: both order objects, and link them to subjects and to other objects. They validate, promote and prioritize. The anthropologists of a thousand years from now who uncover the ruins of our time and seek to understand us will learn nothing from the objects we chose to study, and everything from discovering the way we chose them. In other words, security is a kind of ethics, a set of principles and questions about how to choose what to study. It is not about objects but about attaching values to objects, giving them a place, a position and an order in the universe of objects.

Security is a practice and presupposes an agency which itself cannot be said to be pre-security. It contains an implicit link to what is profoundly human. Or to reverse the formula: the profoundly human, the foundation of humanness itself, is inseparable from a kind of insecurity, the vulnerability or fragility of life (Butler, 2004). Life that is not put into question by the question of its own security is in the strictest sense, not life at all but rather *persistence.*

Further reading

Alam, U.Z. (2002) 'Questioning the Water Wars Rationale: A Case Study of the Indus Waters Treaty', *Geographical Journal,* 168: 341–53.

Alkire, S. (2003) *A Conceptual Framework for Human Security,* CRISE Working Paper 2, Centre for Research on Inequality, Human Security and Ethnicity (CRISE), University of Oxford.

Allenby, B.R. (2000) 'Environmental Security: Concept and Implementation', *International Political Science Review,* 21: 5–21.

Bilgin, P. (2003) 'Individual and Societal Dimensions of Security', *International Studies Review,* 5: 203–22.

Booth, K. (2005) *Critical Security Studies and World Politics,* Boulder: Lynne Rienner.

Buzan, B., Wæver, O. and de Wilder, J. (1998) *Security: A New Framework for Analysis,* Boulder: Lynne Rienner.

Ceyhan, A. and Tsoukala, A. (2002) 'The Securitization of Migration in Western Societies: Ambivalent Discourses and Policies', *Alternatives: Global, Local, Political,* 27: 21–39.

Commission on Human Security (2003) *Human Security Now: Protecting and Empowering People,* New York: Commission on Human Security.

Dalby, S. (2006) *Security and Environment Linkages Revisited,* Singapore: Institute for Defence and Strategic Studies, Nanyang Technological University.

Faist, T. (2004) *The Migration–Security Nexus: International Migration and Security Before and After 9/11,* Malmö: Malmö University.

Gleick, P.H. (1993) 'Water and Conflict: Fresh Water Resources and International Security', *International Security,* 18, 1: 79–112.

Homer-Dixon, T. (1994) 'Environmental Scarcities and Violent Conflict: Evidence from Cases', *International Security,* 19, 1: 5–40.

Roe, P. (2004) 'Securitization and Minority Rights: Conditions of Desecuritization', *Security Dialogue,* 35: 279–94.

Sandell, R. (2006) *Pandemics: A Security Risk?* Madrid: Real Instituto Elcano.

Selby, J. (2005) 'Oil and Water: The Contrasting Anatomies of Resource Conflicts', *Government and Opposition,* 40, 2: 200–24.

Sinha, U.K. (2006) *Examining Water as a Security Issue,* New Delhi: Institute for Defense and Strategic Analysis: 16.

United Nations Development Programme (UNDP) (1994) *Human Development Report 1994*, Oxford: Oxford University Press for the UNDP.

Weiner, M. (1992–3) 'Security, Stability and International Migration', *International Security*, 17, 3: 91–126.

Yergin, D. (2007) *The Fundamentals of Energy Security*, Washington: Committee on Foreign Affairs, US House of Representatives.

Chapter 5

Thinking and Rethinking the Causes of War

J. Marshall Beier

Introduction

Reflecting on what we might call the 'practice of theory' in disciplinary International Relations (IR), Marysia Zalewski (1996) recalls a colleague's posted observation that sounds a fine candidate for the enduring collective lament of the field: 'All these theories yet the bodies keep piling up.' On first gloss, it seems a fair enough complaint. We do, after all, trace the origins of our field across the better part of a century, to the devastation of the European war of 1914–18 and the widespread sense that the whole terrible ordeal had been a colossal blunder whose unprecedented toll in carnage had wrought no gain for any of the warring parties. And yet, if the founding hope of International Relations was to prevent the recurrence of such a catastrophe, it might indeed seem that our theories have done precious little to answer it – a sentiment felt all the more keenly if we pause to reflect on the bloody twentieth century that unfolded in spite of that aim, while what is now widely regarded as the latest colossal blunder grinds on in Iraq. A disapproving comment on theory thus has much to recommend it. At the same time, it bespeaks a particular understanding of the purpose of doing theory, bound up with a normative commitment to reduce the sum of violences visited on human bodies. Perhaps nowhere are these more explicitly and less contentiously the fundamental and irreducible stakes than in debates about the causes of war. And nowhere is the cynical observation of Marysia Zalewski's colleague more incisively perceptive, at least for so long as we take it on its own terms. It is the purpose of this chapter, however, to disturb those terms somewhat and, with them, what have come to be known as the 'causes of war debates'.

While scholars from a number of disciplines have contributed to the sum of literature illuminating some aspect of the sources and determinants of war, many have done so either as part of a larger narrative project (see, for example, Hobsbawm, 1975) or in the particular, detailing the origins of specific cases (see, for example, Stoessinger, 2005; Rotberg and Rabb, 1989). Animated by the social scientific objective of making generalizable claims with predictive power, the causes of war debates have been rather more insular, dominated by political scientists identifying with IR, and less affected by the work of historians and others. For some scholars, the aim has been to identify those circumstances and conditions that increase the likelihood of war. The famous Correlates of War project founded in the 1960s, for example, has compiled substantial data sets on a range of factors considered by project members to be significant determinants of war, correlating them to the details of a lengthy list of historic wars dating from the early nineteenth century. Included are geographic characteristics, territorial contiguity, levels of military expenditure, trade and much more. The project's explicit social scientific purpose is to generate and disseminate quantitative data from which significant trends and tendencies might be observed, thereby enabling conclusions about constellations of factors that make the outbreak of war likely.

Correlation, of course, is not reliable causation in the strictest scientific sense, and so other scholars have turned their attentions more fully to the identification of at least nearly sufficient causes – that is, to uncovering and elaborating a much shorter list of determinants that make war not just more likely but *very* likely, perhaps even inevitable. Foremost among these are interactive dynamics associated with the classical security dilemma. Rooted in a political realist belief in the inevitability of conflict under conditions of international anarchy, the idea of the security dilemma is that while states must attend to the requisites of their own security in the interest of ensuring survival against predation, measures such as increasing military wherewithal can also appear threatening. Other states, to be similarly prudent, must therefore respond in kind. Even though both sides might seek only to provide for an adequate defence, that in itself demands that each assumes the worst of the other's intentions and prepares accordingly. The result is a ratchetting up of tensions as mutual suspicion grows with, paradoxically, an ever increasing danger of escalation to war.

Closely related are more particular inducements to war identified by mainstream scholars, such as the preventive or pre-emptive motive according to which a state will initiate hostilities against another which it believes is preparing for an eventual attack or from which it believes an attack to be imminent. Further, a host of factors and variables have been identified and debated in attempts to account for why the balance may tip (or appear to tip) in favour of recourse to war at a given moment. These include the degree of optimism or pessimism about anticipated outcomes, shifts in power that might seem to signal a present advantage or impending disadvantage for one side, real or imagined benefits to be had from a first-strike, prevailing military doctrines or force structures that create a strong incentive for or predisposition to the offensive, and much more. These and a long list of similar considerations have been proposed as causes of war that might be broadly generalizable, but scholars are not in agreement as to which among them have the greatest explanatory value and predictive power. In fact, their relative importance is often disputed even in the cases of specific wars already on the historical record.

Though differentiated by level of analysis, the notion of rationality looms large in the majority of approaches. For many, it is the rationality of the individual state leader, weighing options in the familiar manner of cost–benefit analysis, that determines the choice to go to war. For others, the state itself is treated as the rational actor, purposively seeking to maximize its national interest. Others still find the most fundamental source of war in cyclical workings of the international system – in the rise and fall of hegemonic powers, for example – but rely nonetheless on the rationality of actors to move them to war when impersonal logics demand it of them. Territorial disputes or arms-racing dynamics are rendered intelligible with reference to these broader standpoints, which together constitute the mainstream of the causes of war debates. Even less obviously compatible ideological or religious disputes can be assimilated to them to the extent that the state is made the vehicle by which respective demands are pressed, their satisfaction thus made one with the satisfaction of the national interest. It is this terrain of debate that is the object of critical reflection in what follows.

But before proceeding a few caveats are in order. What follows is not an attempt to survey these various approaches to the causes of war debates – that has been done elsewhere and, at any rate, would greatly exceed the limits of a chapter-length offering. Instead, the focus here is on the boundedness of those debates and what they consequently exclude or, at a minimum, greatly underemphasize. As this introduction will have suggested, the focus here is directed mainly toward theoretical interventions on the causes of war that are, for the most part, self-consciously situated in IR. Treated somewhat more peripherally, then, is work coming from the diplomatic history tradition of retrospective analysis of the idiosyncratic causes of the outbreak of war in specific cases. While studies of this sort tell us a great deal about the details of descent into war in the particular, by virtue of their approach they are able to offer very little in the way of explicit generalizations that might be more broadly instructive. They are therefore less amenable to the project of harnessing an understanding of war's causes to concrete measures designed to reduce the sum of its human consequences. With this in mind, it is to the theoretical terrain of debate that we now turn with a view to exposing some longstanding and increasingly thorny limitations of its dominant currents and core commitments.

Theory and impasse

As Zalewski quite rightly points out, the expression of disapproval at too many theories amidst too many bodies bears the problematic implication that theoretical debate is a frivolous and self-indulgent enterprise that somehow stands apart from the serious business of a world that, to do some violence to Michel Foucault's (1972) memorable phrase, 'presents us with a legible face'. In cautioning us against the assumption that we have 'merely to decipher' (Foucault 1972: 229) an unproblematically visible world, he reveals something of what might be the inescapable imperative of 'doing' theory. If the world did greet us with a legible face in the sense of being objectively knowable or at least free from ambiguities exceeding our rational faculties, theoretical debate might then be only so much navel-gazing. But the charge falls flat if it turns out that the world does not so readily collaborate with our efforts to lay bare its workings. Here, an increasingly palpable impasse in the causes of war debates seems particularly instructive. In the first instance, the very fact of ongoing debate suggests a more complicated picture than that implied in the complaint about theory, to the extent that consensus is ultimately confounded by fundamental disagreement about the contours and content of the 'visible' world. It is not simply a matter of getting on with the business of the world, therefore, as though the correct course were clear and uncontentious.

Near the end of the cold war, already some seven decades into the disciplinary project of IR, Jack S. Levy (1989b: 210) noted that 'enormous intellectual energy' across many disciplines had been expended on the question of what causes war, with no definitive result: 'There is little agreement among scholars,' he wrote, 'regarding the identity of the causes of war, the methodology by which those causes might be discovered, or the conceptual framework by which multiple causes might be integrated into a coherent theoretical explanation.' Certainly, little has changed in the years since. But with no reason to suspect that those who seek to address the scourge of war through theory should be anymore eluded by the face of the world than others, it is difficult to imagine how its many violences might be better ameliorated were we to retreat from theory. It is, in any event, a feckless cry since the competing views and understandings of the world that seem intent on frustrating any hope of consensus in the causes of war debates are the selfsame ones that animate the equally fraught world of 'concrete' political possibilities. It is most fundamentally thus that practice *is* theory and vice versa. And it is for this reason that it is wrong to suggest that doing theory somehow confounds or is a distraction from the urgent business of working to attenuate war's human consequences. The content and direction of ongoing theoretical dispute have much to tell us about how we have sought to understand the sources and determinants of those consequences as well as how this has been limiting, but they do not sustain a case for drawing back from theory.

While failure to reach agreement on the terms outlined by Levy suggests something of an impasse on the accustomed terrains of the project, a less parochial matter – and perhaps a more urgent one – is that the corpus of theory addressing the causes of war is fast being overtaken by both empirical and conceptual developments that none of its constituents have well enough anticipated and which none seem equipped to answer satisfactorily.

That is, the whole of the project is increasingly out of step with burgeoning literatures both within and without IR and, at the same time, seems irreconcilable to what are widely regarded as revolutionary changes in the nature and practice of war itself. And it is this, even more than what divides the varied approaches that make up the causes of war debates, that now most profoundly signals their inadequacy to the everyday exigencies of bodies piling up. It is also revealing of an unduly circumscribed terrain of debate, belying the general sense that little in the way of shared commitments unites contending accounts and perspectives. In fact, it is where they do not disagree that the continuing relevance of the causes of war debates is called most acutely into question.

Ongoing internal deliberation and dispute notwithstanding, there is actually an important core of consensus bounding the otherwise contentious causes of war literature: it is almost entirely a debate about what causes wars, particularly major wars, between states. This, of course, is reflective of the contexts of its emergence and maturation through the violent twentieth century, an era understandably preoccupied with great power/superpower war. For a theory to gain any kind of disciplinary traction under the long shadows of two World Wars and the bipolar cold war nuclear standoff that followed them, it had of necessity to accommodate (at a minimum) this kind of major war. Not surprisingly, then, inquiry into what causes war in general has, by and large, encoded an overriding interest in what causes *major* wars between powerful *states*. This is a disposition that may be more amenable to the objective of mastering or managing warfare in consonance with the system-maintenance requirements of status quo powers than to reducing the violences visited on human bodies. That is to say, the overwhelming emphasis on major interstate war invites suspicion that the causes of war debates might have less to do with bodies piling up than with *whose* bodies are piling up. Despite their appalling human toll and more frequent occurrence since at least the mid-twentieth century, the relative lack of concern to theorize the causes of intrastate wars in, for example, Africa or Central America is very telling in this regard. Civil wars in places like the former Yugoslavia, Chechnya and, increasingly, Iraq have garnered slightly more attention, though this urges the further suspicion that their currency owes to perceptions of their greater proximity to great power interests.

From our vantage point now, more than a decade and a half since the end of the cold war, it is worth asking whether the problematique subsumed at the very heart of the causes of war debates is an artefact of an era now past. Though it might be premature to consign major interstate wars to the dustbin of history, they seem nevertheless to be undergoing significant changes in both their nature and frequency that are thus far elided by the sum and substance of the causes of war debates. Growing literatures elsewhere, however, reflect an increasing recognition that so-called 'new wars' account for an ever greater proportion of the bodies piling up and, together with new 'ways of war', disturb the accustomed ways of thinking about wars' sources and determinants. All of this further unsettles the familiar terrains of the causes of war debates. But before turning to consider what the implications of this might be and how we may better seek to understand the significance of the changes underway, it is useful to consider how the major approaches to theorizing the causes of war, though varied and at loggerheads to the point of apparent impasse, can all be found to tread just a few well-worn paths.

Causae belli: sketching the terrain of debate

For readers who are well acquainted with the causes of war literature, it might seem a galling work of mischief to play down the significance of those things on which their many interlocutors are divided. The points of intervention into the debates are, on the relatively enclosed terrain of the extant literature, both numerous and diverse. Without attempting an exhaustive list here, even a cursory survey will find, variously, inquiries into the role of fashions in strategic culture (Van Evera, 1984; Hopf, 1991; Johnston, 1995), questions of misperception (Levy, 1983a; Jervis, 1988), irredentism (Goertz and Diehl, 1992; Vasquez, 1993; Huth, 1996; Diehl, 1999), synchronic change in the international system (Organski and Kugler, 1980; Gilpin, 1981; Levy, 1987; Thompson, 1988; Lemke, 2002) and a host of others. A diversity of opinion exists as to the most appropriate level of analysis, data sets, statistical and game theoretic models, research design and much more. But whatever their differences, what these many contributions have most fundamentally in common is their greater affinity for scientific 'explanation' than hermeneutic 'understanding'. As Martin Hollis and Steve Smith (1990) describe this important distinction, 'explaining' as an analytic strategy treats social phenomena as having identifiable causal bases that are both knowable and predictable, whilst 'understanding' takes a more interpretive course that eschews the emphasis on deterministic cause-and-effect relationships. The latter approach is favoured by the more critical contributions to IR theory by feminists, post-structuralists, post-colonialists and others; the former is more readily associated with the conceptual mainstream dominated by political realists and, to a lesser extent, liberal theorists. A terrain of debate dealing explicitly with the *causes* of war is therefore congenitally tied to a particular set of epistemological commitments that are inimical to the vast majority of critical scholarship whose influence has grown markedly through much of the rest of IR over the last two decades.

It is largely for this reason that the causes of war debates have been overwhelmingly dominated by realist thinking (see Cashman, 2000; Copeland, 2000b; Van Evera, 1999). Importantly, this is a theoretical current that takes war to be an ineluctable social fact – an ontological commitment that is quite inhospitable to hopes that bodies might cease piling up. One very notable exception, and one that has directly challenged this central feature of realist ontology is, as discussed in Chapter 2, the substantial literature in the Kantian tradition of 'democratic peace' (see Owen, 1997; Russett and Oneal, 2001). But despite the challenge it raises on the inevitability of war, this work in the liberal tradition of IR theory is otherwise not substantially at odds with the terrain of the debate. In the main, it is still committed to uncovering lines of causation, if perhaps more particularly the causes of *peace* than of war. And, like the majority of both social scientific and case-specific contributions, it is also generally accepting of the debates' prevailing notion of what it is that is signalled by the word 'war'.

To what, then, do we refer when we speak of war? The answer to this question is not so immediately and unproblematically self-evident as is sometimes imagined. Like art or pornography, war is something we are expected to know when we see it, something we identify by way of appeal to our common senses and without need of conceptual elaborations. In short, our sense of what war is resides in the realm of intersubjectivity such that it may seem enough merely to invoke the word in order to signify its content. In our bid to stop the bodies piling up we might thus agree with relative ease that war is so dire a part of the human experience that we are right to seek its sources and determinants and, what is more, to do so with a certain urgency. But whatever our sense of common purpose in this, it might also turn out that in our seeming concurrence on the scourge of war we have shared a signifier but not a signified. Precisely because of its commonsense appeal, *the word* war too often escapes elaboration, with the result that even quite widely disparate understandings of its precise meaning and content can easily go undetected. For want of a clearer definition of what will count as war and what will not, it might thus be that we have scant basis for agreement on what we actually hope to do, much less whence to proceed. Crucial, then, is some explicit discussion of what range and character of dire practices we mean to address when we set ourselves the task of theorizing war's causes.

Illustrative of the problem is the mainstream interpretation of a dictum famously issued nearly two centuries ago by the Prussian general and military theorist Carl von Clausewitz, in his posthumously published masterwork, *Vom Kriege* (*On War*) ([1832] 2002: 44): '*Der Krieg ist eine bloße Fortsetzung der Politik mit anderen Mitteln*'. Usually translated as, 'War is a mere continuation of policy by other means,' this is the most influential and widely known line of a treatise described by Martin van Creveld (1991a: 403) as 'the greatest work on war and strategy ever written within Western civilization'. Not surprisingly, then, it has both exerted considerable influence over and is reflected in our most accustomed ways of theorizing war, signalling among other things the centrality of the state and what is usually referred to as its 'national interest'. If war is to be understood most fundamentally as a 'mere continuation' of the state's pursuit of its policy agenda by 'other' (read: 'violent') means, any attempt to discover its causes must, of necessity, turn vitally on some articulation of the national interest. And it is thus that approaches aligned with political realist assumptions have dominated the causes of war debates, most particularly in IR. This does not mean that mainstream theorists have worked directly from the Clausewitzian dictum as though it were the arbiter of their collective research agenda. Rather, both the idea of war as the continuation of policy by other means and the general inclinations (and disinclinations) of mainstream approaches to the causes of war debates may more usefully be regarded as artefacts of a particular worldview wherein the privileging of the state simply conforms to underinterrogated common senses.

It is worth noting in this context the quite considerable element of indeterminacy inherent in the mainstream reading of Clausewitz. Dating to the first English language version of *On War*, as translated by J.J. Graham in 1873, this reading turns out not to be as definitive as it has often been made to seem. Graham, a British army officer, was the first to render Clausewitz's definition of war as 'a mere continuation of policy by other means' (Clausewitz [1832] 1949): 23). This translation has endured in subsequent and widely read English language versions (see, for example, Clausewitz, [1832] 1982: 119). Michael Howard and Peter Paret modify it only slightly to read, 'war is merely the continuation of policy by other means' (Clausewitz, [1832] 1993: 99). But while this retains the explicit reference to 'policy', the German '*politik*' could be translated as either 'policy' or 'politics'. The choice of one over the other has critical implications both for our definition of war and for the project of seeking to reveal its causes.

'Policy' is the preserve of states, whereas 'politics' entails a much broader field of human relations through and within not only the state but other forms of community as well. That said, it is not especially surprising that a British army officer of the late nineteenth century would be moved to opt in favour of 'policy' and, simultaneously, for the Westphalian state as the operant expression of political community. This would simply have fit with prevailing common senses at the height of colonial expansion by a European power so self-assured of its own superiority over peoples with different socio-political traditions and ways of life that it could conceive of a 'civilizing mission' and even lament it as 'The White Man's Burden'. As misguided as these ideas might have been, they were nevertheless so widely held and deeply internalized as to deny the validity of other forms of community whilst making genuine war the business of professional armies raised and deployed on the European model and according to European norms and legal regimes.

Clausewitz's intent is, of course, open to debate. Though his recurring concern with an array of often visceral motives and appetites broader than what is accommodated under the rubric of 'national interest' does seem to sustain a reading of 'politics' at least as well as 'policy', the point here is not to stake out a definitive position on his text. Rather, it is to highlight that, for the same reason that Clausewitz will sustain more than just one interpretive rendering, a wider range of possibilities exists than is typically admitted with the usual treatment of war in the causes of war debates – a treatment which accords well with Graham's reading of *Vom Kriege*, but not so well with other equally plausible readings. And this, in turn, calls our attention to the fundamental indeterminacy from which those debates proceed and the inherently political standpoint betrayed by their privileging of the Westphalian state. What does this standpoint demand, delimit and denote? And in what does it implicate us? In addressing the latter of these two questions, we will already have proposed something crucial to an answer for the former.

Out of bounds: the political beyond the debates

The political standpoint bound up in the operant definition of war reflects the interplay of at least two usually unspoken yet deeply held assumptions, both long prevalent and both certainly among the defining features of the contexts in which *Vom Kriege* has been translated: that the state is the preeminent form of political community and that it enjoys a monopoly over the legitimate use of violence in service of its aims. Violence being the 'other means' to which Clausewitz refers, recourse to war is therefore reserved to states – they alone may engage in the continuation of policy by these other means. War between sovereign political communities expressed through states may well be decried as a scourge for its dire human consequences, but it is important to bear in mind that it is nevertheless formally legitimate, as reflected in international law. Under this regime, other groups and forms of community that may employ violence for an explicit political purpose are denied legitimacy in doing so. Theirs may be defined as acts of insurgency, rebellion or criminal enterprise, but there are powerful political predispositions to disallow their classification as war. Such are the operant politics of the causes of war debates.

To label any organized marshalling of violence a war is therefore to claim moral approbation on the basis of appeal to a dominant set of international legal norms and agreements of which states themselves are both the authors and the principal beneficiaries. Were war taken to be the continuation of *politics* by other means, on the other hand, encompassing but also exceeding the policy practices of states, this would then capture a much fuller complement of the practices of organized violence that so persistently see bodies piling up. It would, for instance, be less ambiguous on the question of civil wars – phenomena that articulate so awkwardly and unsatisfactorily with mainstream approaches that they have not received anything like the degree of attention that would befit the extent of their grave imprint upon the human experience. Civil wars, insurrections and, increasingly, even organized and sustained terrorist campaigns do sit well with prevailing common senses about the range of practices that constitute war in a more vernacular sense. But they are not as well abided either by the state-centric biases of the causes of war debates or by a reading of Clausewitz that would insist upon the ascendancy of 'policy' over 'politics' as the locus of wars' sources and determinants. Like Graham's reading of Clausewitz, IR's engagement with the question of war's causes is a product of its time and place, preoccupied with the problem of major wars between states in consequence of an unreflexive commitment to the state as the political community *par excellence*.

Here we get our first and perhaps most poignant glimpse into the implications of adopting such an exclusive perspective. The mainstream implicitly denies the validity of non-state forms of political community, refusing them acknowledgement as collective political agents of local and often global import (Walker, 1997: 69). It is important to recognize that this locates the mainstream of the causes of war debates in a political perspective that is deeply implicated in contemporary struggles around questions of, among other things, sovereignty and security and the challenges posed by forms of political community not well expressed by, accommodated by, or abided by states. This Westphalian chauvinism also means that the low-intensity wars of precolonial Africa, the aboriginal Americas and other places where non-state inter-national systems have existed are all but unknown to the causes of war literature, notwithstanding the promise they hold for confirmation/falsification of existing theories. No less conspicuous for the dearth of attention they have received are undeniably major wars such as the massive 1592–8 Japanese invasions of and subsequent war for Korea (Hawley, 2005). That these and other great swathes of the history of warfare are effectively left off the mainstream agenda should be a matter for some concern in the case of debates whose strongest theoretical currents are deeply indebted to claims about human nature that might turn out not to be generalizable beyond the European experience (See Beier, 2005: 160–1).

For the causes of war debates, the limitations of a perspective urged into conformity with the state can scarcely be overstated. Besides excluding a priori any forms of community otherwise constituted, it leaves us an unduly circumscribed range of conceptual possibilities as well. While the epistemological bias in favour of explanation and the orientation toward causes erect formidable barriers to the inclusion of a range of critical theoretical approaches, still others may be excluded even without directly challenging these particular mainstream commitments. Marxist-inspired approaches, for example, need not press for interpretive understanding over the analytic strategy of explanation and the mapping of causal connections. They are, however, inclined toward greater interest in the class struggle context of civil wars. This, of course, does not accord well with the operant definition of war and its subsumed insistence upon the state as the sole form of political community able to legitimately employ violence in the furtherance of its political objectives. And it is here that the importance of the aspect of the political comes most sharply into relief.

Engaging the question of the partisan as a legitimate political actor, Carl Schmitt (2004) offers a useful rethinking of the relationship between politics and war. For Schmitt, a state in wartime faces an enemy that is in some sense an abstraction, having been defined as 'enemy' only as an effect of the state's translation of an interest into policy. That is to say, enmity arises not from the population or even from the soldiers of opposing states, but between the states themselves which then direct their armies into opposition. It is therefore the state that is the political actor, engaging in the continuation of policy by other (violent) means. The partisan, on the other hand, acts on the basis of her/his own enmity toward a 'real enemy' whose immediate presence is intolerable. The partisan thus experiences this enemy as 'real' and not as an abstraction. This means that violence need only be employed to satisfy the aim of driving the 'real enemy' away – the partisan neither seeks out the enemy in other environs nor offers pursuit. And it is precisely this sort of *politics* by other means that the mainstream definition of war cannot accommodate, since the violence employed by the partisan is realized independent of the policy of the state. The partisan, like the insurgent or the terrorist, cannot be granted a legitimate subject position in war on the terms of the theoretical mainstream.

Where we really see the de facto gatekeeping function of the operant definition of war is with Schmitt's third kind of enemy: the 'absolute enemy'. Reflecting on Lenin's understanding of enmity in class terms wherein the objective is the utter destruction of the enemy, Schmitt (2004: 36) concludes that the 'war of absolute enmity knows no containment'. Class struggle, according to Ernesto Laclau (2005: 8), can thus be conceived as 'a permanent war taking place within society', the objectives of which involve the eventual dissolution of the state itself. And this, in turn, is suggestive of why Marxist-inspired work has been so marginalized in the causes of war debates. Because it conceives so differently of war that it refigures community otherwise than as the state, it cannot accommodate war within the rigid limits of 'the continuation of policy by other means'. Rather, the Clausewitzian dictum must be re-rendered with *politik* as 'politics' instead of the more limiting 'policy'. On this reading, the apparent impasse in the causes of war debates is a parochial one indeed, confined as it is to very narrow conceptual spaces that not only reject the terms of more critical theories but also seem increasingly ill-suited to thinking about revolutionary changes in the nature of warfare that are currently underway.

New ways of war and old ways of thinking

What is perhaps the most significant challenge implicit in the Schmittian conception of a progression from the conventional to absolute enemy is the circumstance that, as Laclau (2005: 8–9) notes, '[m]ore and more elements that were at the beginning outside the field of war are now absorbed' into it. But while this underscores the consequences of an insistence on 'policy' over 'politics', it is not only the possibility of accessing Marxist notions of class antagonism that is most profoundly at stake. Rather, it is war writ large that is, ironically, exceeding the conceptual grasp of the causes of war debates. This is, of course, most noticeably so in the case of civil wars, wherein the traditional rendering of Clausewitz's dictum is an uncomfortable fit at best. But even where the state maps comfortably across the visible lines of confrontation and plausibly sustains a claim to sovereign domination of the field of political contestation translated into policy, this still misses potential sources and determinants of war whose relevance proceeds from a much more complicated understanding of the location of politics.

If the choice of a Marxian lens sees more and more elements absorbed into the field of war, this is not altogether inconsonant with developments long underway even in cases of major interstate war. At least since Napoleon's *Grande Armée* and the *levée en masse*, there has been a progressive social deepening of war, beginning with the innovation of mass conscription, perversely manifest in the increasingly conventional targeting of civilian populations through the twentieth century, and presently expressed in what is now tellingly called the 'war on terror'. War defined as the 'continuation of policy by other means' cannot contain this. The particular circulations of enmity that render an idea like 'war on terror' intelligible, for example, cannot function on the basis of a comparatively thin abstraction like the national interest. Conceptually tooled to apprehend war as the business of states, the mainstream of the causes of war debates has explanatory frameworks amenable to engaging state responses to 9/11, but is much less able to locate the attackers in any accustomed site of political agency. Elsewhere, similar limitations made it impossible for many to conceive the 'war on terror' in other than the now widely discredited terms of the conflation of al-Qaeda with Ba'athist Iraq. Likewise, the politically fraught category of 'unlawful combatant' marks, among other things, the explicit denial of a broader field of bona fide political actors in respect of war.

This poses imposing problems for the future of mainstream approaches in the causes of war debates. Inasmuch as what they are most adept at engaging is major interstate war, the debates seem confined to treating phenomena that account for fewer and fewer of the bodies piling up. If, as Hidemi Suganami (2002: 308) suggests, 'war is most easily recognizable as such when it takes place between well-functioning sovereign states,' then US President George W. Bush's famed May 2003 'Mission Accomplished' proclamation on the deck of the aircraft carrier *Abraham Lincoln* might have something to recommend it. But for those who are less persuaded that the 2003 Iraq war consisted only in the interstate confrontation with the

United States and was concluded with the collapse of the Ba'athist regime, a more inclusive definition of war is called for – one that recognizes US forces in Iraq and NATO in Afghanistan as unambiguously engaged in war even after the collapse of the erstwhile regimes in those countries. Failing this, and in combination with the popular post-cold war view that major war at least verges on obsolescence (see Mueller, 1989; Fettweiss, 2006), the causes of war debates seem in danger of losing their very *raison d'être*.

Moving beyond the obsolescence of major war thesis, a growing literature on 'new wars' engages the idea that major interstate conflict is giving way to civil wars drawn primarily along ethnic lines. Mark Duffield (2001), for example, reveals a more complicated story behind these wars and the challenges they pose to centralized state authority. Duffield shows how the politics of new wars greatly exceed the boundaries of both state and interstate policy realms. New political constellations – from international development agencies to local elites – shaped by changing practices and institutions of global governance incorporate and accommodate these wars to the normalized everyday of globalization. According to Mary Kaldor (2001), the new wars have not left the state behind but, rather, are political wars in which state power turns increasingly on identity politics and is expressed not only through traditional militaries but also by way of and together with different kinds of private forces. With the rise of warlordism and paramilitarism that is at least one step removed from the state, conflict is increasingly dependent upon and sustained by more disaggregated and dispersed practices such as organized criminal enterprises, the support of diaspora communities, and outright predation against civilian populations. Though Kaldor sees the continuing importance of the state, she also peers into sites of political agency not accessible on the terms of mainstream causes of war literature. Inasmuch as it so exceeds containment under the rubric 'national interest', this is much more than just an empirically complex account of the workings of what is in the end still a state-centric perspective with war reducible to 'the continuation of *policy* by other means'. Politics here, as in Duffield's account, are much more broadly sited and variously enacted.

Further complicating matters are changes associated with the so-called 'revolution in military affairs' that have seen the United States and a few other countries develop the capacity to wage war with precision-guided munitions from positions of relative impunity well beyond the reach of their adversaries' arms. In particular, the unparalleled capabilities of the United States in this regard have given rise to notions of a 'new American way of war' (Boot, 2003) characterized by devastatingly fast-paced operations, enabled by unmatched sensing, information-handling and precision strike capabilities. But, as James Der Derian (2001) argues, unrestrained faith in and enthusiasm about 'smart bombs' and the like underwrites too ready a resort to military responses to complex political problems. This is bound up with and enabled by a 'military–industrial–media–entertainment network' that has fed popular expectations of 'costless' military solutions in the sense of popular intolerance of casualties. With the added dimension of electoral politics (Shaw, 2005), an understanding even of interstate wars such as that launched against Iraq by the United States in 2003 demands a conception of the political vastly more expansive than the narrow confines of policy.

This new way of war has also had the effect of denying a legitimate subject position to those who are not able to participate on an equal footing. Utterly outclassed by weapons technologies they cannot hope to match, they are unable to engage according to the terms of legitimacy marked out under the operant definition of war (Beier, 2006). The only viable course, insurgency, thus puts them beyond the pale of mainstream thought on the causes of war. That this is a serious conceptual lapse could not be made clearer than by the circumstance that the idea of a *'war* on terror' seems not to disturb prevailing common-sense understandings of what does and does not count as war. What is equally clear is that the operant definition of war in the causes of war debates turns on an understanding of political community that is too exclusive a basis for theorizing contemporary war and its sources. No matter whether they are comfortably accorded legitimacy in all instances, many that are not anticipated in mainstream approaches to the causes of war are nevertheless undeniably effectual and possessed of the ability to affect the course of global politics. The US decision to construct 9/11 as a war is not properly the watershed moment, but it does definitively signal a historic rupture intimately bound up with the long trend toward the social deepening of war.

Conclusion: rethinking war and the questions we ask

Rethinking what war is or can be opens up a great many possibilities for thinking about how we might reduce the sum of violences visited on humanity. An expanded conception of the political, one that includes but also goes beyond the rigid confines of policy, leads to other possibilities heretofore unexplored. To take but one example, war as 'the continuation of *politics* by other means' allows us to see its victims as more than mere proxies of a loss that is really the state's own. That is, it allows us to see them more fully as victims in their own right in the same instant that we see them as political agents in their own right. Expanding the boundaries further still, we are better able to ask new questions about violence, Clausewitz's 'other means', in service of politics and what something like Johan Galtung's (1969) notion of 'structural violence' might then mean for our understanding of war and its causes. This might just make things unduly complicated. It might cast the problem of war and its human consequences in paralyzingly immense terms. But, as we have seen, the assumptions of the mainstream turn out not to be at all uncomplicated and certainly seem to be due little credit for reducing the sum of violences.

Besides the questions we think worth asking, we should also consider the sort of questions they are. Roxanne Lynn Doty (1993: 298) distinguishes between *why* questions that concern themselves with causal lines leading to an explanation of why a particular outcome obtained, and *how* questions which inquire instead into how that outcome and its causes were rendered possible in the first place. The former take for granted that a particular war, for instance, was objectively possible, while the latter seek to reveal how that possibility was created. *How* questions therefore speak more to *sources* of war than to *causes* per se. They are more apt to involve the interpretive strategies of understanding, than the cause-and-effect accounts of explanation. And they are consequently better suited to accessing such things as identity politics or a rhetorically constructed monopoly on legitimacy as important factors enabling war.

Far from abandoning theoretical inquiry, the impasse within the causes of war debates and their inadequacy without reveal it as more necessary now than ever. This is because we are no longer so sure even *what* we're talking about when we talk about war and its causes. And if we do not know even that, then there seems little prospect of doing well in stopping the bodies piling up. What a rethinking of the whole of the project entails is first an opening up of definitional categories and theoretical possibilities. Of course, this imperils deeply held ontological and epistemological commitments of the mainstream. That said, the project has failed on its own terms: there is, as when Levy surveyed the debates two decades ago, little consensus on anything. Nor has the epistemological bias in favour of explanation yielded any meaningful predictive power. If, as Zalewski's colleague suggests, we aim to better understand the causes of war because we hope to do something about it, we may have been asking the wrong questions.

Further reading

Beier, J.M. (2006) 'Outsmarting Technologies: Rhetoric, Revolutions in Military Affairs, and the Social Depth of Warfare', *International Politics*, 43: 266–80.

Cashman, G. (2000) *What Causes War? An Introduction to Theories of International Conflict*, Lanham: Lexington Books.

Copeland, D.C. (2000) *The Origins of Major War*, Ithaca: Cornell University Press.

Fettweiss, C.J. (2006) 'A Revolution in International Relations Theory: Or, What if Mueller Is Right?' *International Studies Review*, 8: 677–97.

Goertz, G. and Diehl, P.F. (1992) *Territorial Changes and International Conflict*, London: Routledge.

Huth, P.K. (1996) *Standing Your Ground: Territorial Disputes and International Conflict*, Ann Arbor: University of Michigan Press.

Jervis, R. (1988) 'War and Misperception', *Journal of Interdisciplinary History*, 18: 675–700.

Laclau, E. (2005) 'On "Real" and "Absolute" Enemies', *CR: The New Centennial Review*, 5: 1–12.

Lemke, D. (2002) *Regions of War and Peace*, Cambridge: Cambridge University Press.

Levy, J.S. (1989) 'The Causes of War: A Review of Theories and Evidence', in Tetlock, P.E., Husbands, J.L., Jervis, R., Stern, P.C. and Tilly, C. (eds), *Behaviour, Society, and Nuclear War*, vol. 1, New York: Oxford University Press.

Mueller, J. (1989) *Retreat from Doomsday: The Obsolescence of Major War*, New York: Basic Books.

Rotberg, R.I. and Rabb, T.K. (eds) (1989) *The Origin and Prevention of Major Wars*, Cambridge: Cambridge University Press.

Stoessinger, J.G. (2005) *Why Nations Go to War*, 9th edn, Belmont: Wadsworth.

Suganami, H. (2002) 'Explaining War: Some Critical Observations', *International Relations*, 16: 207–26.

Van Evera, S. (1999) *Causes of War: Power and the Roots of Conflict*, Ithaca: Cornell University Press.

Zalewski, M. (1996) '"All These Theories Yet the Bodies Keep Piling Up": Theories, Theorists, Theorising', in Smith, S., Booth, K. and Zalewski, M. (eds), *International Theory: Positivism and Beyond*, Cambridge: Cambridge University Press.

Chapter 6

The Evolution of Strategy and the New World Order

Geoffrey Till

Introduction: on strategy in general

Like many other military terms, 'strategy' has been taken over by the business community and has become so watered down as to mean little more than the way you try to get what you want. This is not very helpful. Instead, it is better to revert to the original use of the term as it relates specifically to the 'strategic level' of war where military force is used normally but not exclusively by nation states as a means of achieving desired grand political objectives. Robert Osgood (1962: 5) reminds us that this level of war is especially characterized by the association between military means and political ends:

> Military strategy must now be understood as nothing less than the overall plan for utilizing the capacity for armed coercion – in conjunction with the economic, diplomatic and psychological instruments of power – to support foreign policy most effectively by overt, covert and tacit means.

A number of points emerge from this quotation. First Osgood, like Mahan and most other strategists, is clearly taking an unashamedly 'realistic' view of human nature and behaviour. But his is a broad definition, which emphasizes that there is much more to strategy than simply killing people efficiently for political purposes. Strategy is not restricted to the conduct of war, but extends into peacetime as well. Osgood widens the agenda by emphasizing other forms of power and differing types of strategy. It may well include using your armed forces to win friends, or to influence their behaviour, as much as coercing or deterring possible adversaries.

His phrase 'to support foreign policy' makes the point that strategy, war and conflict should be designed to accomplish a political objective. This is what justifies strategic action, and as Carl von Clausewitz remarked, this is what determines a consequent conflict's form and character:

> War is nothing but a continuation of political endeavour with altered means. I base the whole of strategy on this tenet, and believe that he who refuses to recognize this necessity does not fully understand what matters. The principle explains the whole history of war, and without it, everything would appear quite absurd. (Heuser, 2002: 34)

Basil Liddell Hart (1967: 335) made the same point more succinctly, by defining strategy as '[t]he art of distributing and applying military means to fulfil the ends of policy'.

Strategic theory, obviously, is thinking about strategy, trying to 'put it all together' through the development of a skein of connected thought about the nature, conduct and consequences of military power. Liddell Hart's definition is also useful in that it raises the perennial issue of whether military strategy is an art or a science. There have always been two traditions here (Handel, 1986: 34–95). Some strategists focus on the material and quantifiable aspects of war (the disposition of forces, the physical performance of weapons) and treat it almost as a science. Here the essentials of strategy can be reduced to neat and tidy laws. This was certainly the manner in which strategy (had there existed such a word at the time) would have been understood in the Europe of the eighteenth century.

It is true, however, that much of this applied to what we would call the 'tactical' level of war at which battles are fought, because here circumstances mean that writers could be more prescriptive in their approach. There was a right way and a wrong way of preparing camps or manoeuvring bodies of infantry in the presence of the enemy after all.

At the end of the eighteenth century, however, there was a reaction against this, inspired by the great sweeping intellectual movements of the French Revolution and the 'Romanticism' which it inspired. This stressed the complexity, diversity and passion of human behaviour that made nonsense of the notion that in war soldiers should follow the rules and go by the book. The 'art of war' said Ardent du Picq in the late nineteenth century 'is subjected to many modifications by industrial and scientific progress. But one thing does not change, the heart of man.' It was this spirit and this approach that led to French officer cadets to sharpen their swords on the steps of the German embassy on the eve of the First World War and to set off to the front with élan. It inspired a devotion to the kind of unrestrained offensive that made the most of the supposed warrior virtues of the French military and the confident expectation of glorious victory. This did not long survive contact with industrial reality in the shape of the entrenched rifleman, the heavy machine gun and artillery barrages.

Of course, strategy covers both dimensions but the mix between the two at any one time may be a function of the social, economic, technological and political context to which Osgood referred. It is for this reason, also, that the question has arisen whether the principles are permanent (in the sense that they last all the time) and/or universal (in the sense that they apply to all warriors, irrespective of their relative strength or character). Do large armies march to the sound of the same drum as small ones and have they always done so?

Some have argued that the principles of war are indeed universal in time and space. They are seen as a short, handy summary of 'broad precepts distilled from experience which influence the conduct of armed conflict and which should inform all strategic and operational decisions' (UK Ministry of Defence, 2004: 185–8). But merely having experience is not enough. Military people need to think about it – otherwise, as Frederick the Great famously observed, quite a few of his pack mules would deserve to be Field Marshals. The result, these days, is often called 'doctrine': something designed to provide military people with a vocabulary of ideas and a common sense of purpose about how they should conduct themselves before, during and after the action. Doctrine then becomes the application of strategic theory in a particular place and time. If strategy is about the art of cookery, doctrine is concerned with today's menus. Both are essential. Without strategic theory, doctrine writers would not know where they have been or where they should start and are less likely to be able to work out where they should go; without doctrine, commanders would have either to rely on luck and blind instinct or to convene a seminar to decide what to do when the enemy appears on the horizon.

The question still arises, though: are strategic theory, military doctrine and the principles of war advisory or mandatory? Even most current formulations of military doctrine (which is usually considered more prescriptive than the other two forms of military thought) refer to the need for 'judgement in its application'. 'Nothing', Sir Julian Corbett ([1911] 1988: 3–11, 322–5) also tells us, 'is so dangerous in the study of war as to permit maxims to become a substitute for judgement.' Doctrine should not be dogma. Long-established principles are there to be questioned, familiar procedures to be adapted to suit particular circumstances. There is a significant difference between principles (which have an element of free play) and rules (which do not).

Then there is the question of whether such thinking applies equally to all three dimensions of war – land, sea and air – in the same way. Some would argue against the proposition that the three need to take a different approach and that, for example, 'in the air, things are different'. Thus Admiral Chernavin (1982), the last Commander-in-Chief of the Soviet Navy:

> Today ... there is no purely specific realm of warfare. Victory is achieved by the combined efforts of [all branches of the armed

forces] which brings about the need to integrate all knowledge of warfare within the framework of a united military science.

On the other hand, navies may be argued to operate in a physical environment that makes for a distinctive emphasis on independence of command, on the overriding and continuous need actually to locate the adversary, perhaps even on the permanent advantage at sea of the offence over the defence.

Nonetheless, maritime strategy has not evolved in a vacuum, but as a subset of general strategic thinking. In many ways, it seeks to apply general strategic principles to maritime operations. Mahan called his dog 'Jomini', not apparently intending any disrespect but in recognition of the debt he owed the great Swiss master of strategy Antoine-Henri de Jomini, especially for his use of the concept of 'lines of operation'. Likewise, the debt that Corbett owes Clausewitz, particularly for his stress on the need to relate military means to political ends, is obvious from the very first page of his main book (Corbett, [1911] 1988: 1).

Putting all this together, most strategists would agree with Alfred Thayer Mahan (1911: 2, 299–301) when he concluded that war is essentially an art and 'it is for the skill of the artist in war rightly to apply the principles and rules in each case'. In other words, strategy is about the application of force for the achievement of political purposes, but the manner in which this is done depends absolutely on the strategy maker's judgement of the effect of current circumstances on the application of rules and principles derived from previous experience.

Previous experience also plays a key role in the still controversial issue of 'strategic culture', a term coined in a study of the Soviet approach to nuclear strategy by Jack Snyder (1977: 38). He argued that the Soviet approach to nuclear weapons reflected their strategic culture. In his view, Russia's geo-strategic setting, its history and its institutions 'combined to produce a unique mix of strategic beliefs and a unique pattern of strategic behaviour based on those beliefs'. This related closely to the notion that countries like Britain or the United States could evolve a distinctive 'way of war', and indeed it is easy to find books with titles based on this view such as Liddell Hart (1932), Weigley (1973) and Hanson (1989). All this has led to a sometimes impassioned debate about what is meant by the word 'culture', and about its connections first with behaviour and second with the realist approach to international politics, which is usefully reviewed in Sondhaus (2006: 1–13) and Porter (2007).

Recent events have reinforced the importance of the debate. Renewed interest in the cultural dimension of conflict has been an important part of the reaction against the technological determinism that was seen to characterize US strategies against Iraq in both 1991 and, above all, in 2003 – and indeed subsequently. The failure of the technologically superior side finally to impose its will has led many, especially in the United States, to advocate a cultural approach to war instead. We, they say, should understand the way 'they' approach war and immerse ourselves in their culture, learn their language and their ways and react accordingly. But this presupposes that you can change your culture enough to do this – a point that seems to contradict the notion that culture *determines* military behaviour! In any case, others argue, the anthropological approach to strategy all too often seems dangerously simplistic, undermining our capacity to predict the future and to understand the present by underplaying other variables in the equation, not least the possible impact of sub-cultures.

Some critics go further still and deny the value of the concept of strategic culture even in understanding the past. Returning to the Russian theme with which this brief review of strategic culture began, the historian William C. Fuller (1992: xiii) in his review of 'backwardness in Russian strategy', attacks the concept of strategic culture in robust terms:

> While some social scientists might find the concept of strategic culture congenial, because it can serve them as an analytical meat-grinder for reducing coarse and uneven historical reality to a smooth and homogeneous paste, historians have a duty to be wary of any technique that substitutes theoretical elegance for complex truth.

Conflict, it would seem, is not just what we study; it also characterizes the ways in which we study it!

Strategic thinking: the traditional schools

Changing circumstances have led to the evolution of five overlapping waves or schools of strategists. Two of the most fundamentally important strategists are Sun Tzu and Clausewitz. Their distinctive approaches are, indeed, frequently compared (Handel, 2001: 17–30).

One of the most influential texts on war is also one of the oldest. Sun Tzu's *The Art of War* appears to have been written about 500 BC in the age of the warring states in China. It is very short, in effect a chain of aphorisms which lead readers to their own conclusions about their significance and what should be done about them. The whole is consciously 'clever', enigmatic and eminently quotable. In brief, Sun Tsu (assuming he actually existed!) argued that the art of war was not to win victories, but to achieve military objectives by the fastest and least costly means. Really good generals might not need to fight battles, securing their aims instead by undermining their adversary's will or ability to fight beforehand. 'To subdue the enemy without fighting is the acme of skill,' he famously wrote (Sun Tzu, 1971: 77). Armies could be destroyed most effectively by attacking their cohesion, their supplies or their will rather than by simply killing the soldiers they comprised. Surprise, speed, manoeuvre, flexibility and political skill should achieve what was in effect a psychological effect. The adversary's will and morale were the real targets.

Carl von Clausewitz (1780–1831), on the other hand, owed much to earlier European experience and thinking, in particular the ideas of Nicolo Machiavelli. In *The Prince*, Machiavelli ([1532] 1961: 87) argued that rulers of states should understand the nature of war since it was an inevitable part of their dealings with one another. Indeed, '[a] Prince ... should have no other object or thought, nor acquire skill in anything, except war, its organization, and its discipline.' He should craft his military strategy to suit his political objectives and aim at defeating his adversaries as quickly as possible through decisive battle. Clausewitz developed these ideas still further, especially in the light of the upheavals of the French and Revolutionary Wars. For Clausewitz war was simply the continuation of politics by other means, and it followed, therefore that statesmen should remain in ultimate control. The ends should determine the means, not the other way about.

Like his Swiss rival Antoine-Henri de Jomini, Clausewitz accepted that war was a potentially chaotic business, characterized by chance, fear and confusion. This would produce 'frictions' that would make everything difficult. But where Jomini harked back to the earlier era of searching for scientific principles and certainties that would enable the commander to cope with this, Clausewitz concluded that it was necessary to 'aim high' in the expectation that things would fall short. Borrowing from Immanuel Kant, he developed the notion of 'ideal' or 'absolute' war to which commanders should therefore aspire. Accordingly, he became known, somewhat unfairly, as the apostle of all-out, total, unrestrained and offensive warfare. But to some extent in this he was simply responding to the effect of the raw passions of nationalism and the hugely increased popular involvement in war characteristic of his time.

Jomini, on the other hand in *Summary of the Art of War* (1838) defined much of the vocabulary of contemporary strategic thought, by identifying such concepts as 'decisive points', 'interior lines' and 'lines of communication' arguing that commanders who understood these concepts and could apply them properly would triumph over those that did not.

Despite his scepticism about his rivals' rules and diagrams, Clausewitz did come up with the notion of the 'centre of gravity'. The commander wishing to win his war as quickly as possible should identify the enemy's 'centre of gravity' and aim at that, because that was the best way of destroying his army since the adversary would need to defend it. The centre of gravity might in fact be his army itself, or it might be his political capital. Either way the annihilation of his armed forces would decide the outcome.

The second wave

The second wave sought, consciously or unconsciously, to apply or adapt the concepts developed by the classical writers to the new dimensions of conflict of their time. Some emphasized the importance of the political context in which military operations would take place. Both Vladimir Ilyich Lenin and Mao Tse-Tung, for example, argued that a peoples' war would take radically different forms from those of dynastic or even national wars. They developed theories of subversion, partisan warfare and guerrilla operations. Mao, unsurprisingly a keen admirer of Sun Tzu, adopted in his *On Guerrilla Warfare* ([1961] 2000) many of his predecessor's ideas, in particular the avoidance in a guerrilla war of costly pitched battles against superior forces. Weakness, Mao argued, should first be created by forcing the enemy to disperse and then attacking when their numbers were reduced and their morale low. It was important too for the guerrillas to compensate for their own weaknesses when compared with conventionally armed adversaries by securing the support of the people (manifested by more recruits, intelligence and supplies) through a clever and sustained campaign to win their 'hearts and minds'.

Other strategists of more or less the same generation sought to apply such concepts to different dimensions of war particularly the sea and the air.

The two leading contenders of maritime strategy are Alfred Thayer Mahan (1840–1914) and Sir Julian Corbett (1854–1922). Mahan's *The Influence of Seapower on History 1660–1783,* his most famous book, was published in 1890, to enormous acclaim. Many others followed. Essentially, Mahan built on existing ideas about maritime operations, which were largely tactical in their approach, and attempted to situate naval thinking in the broader context of the strategic thinking represented by the likes of Clausewitz and Jomini. To a much greater degree than is generally recognized, Mahan addressed the theory and practice of international politics and the place of maritime power within them (Till, 2004: 40).

His main concern was to correct the widespread ignorance he found around him about the role and importance of seapower, even amongst seafaring peoples. In peacetime, national power, security and prosperity depended on the sea as a means of transportation. In wartime, seapower resulted from naval supremacy and provided the means of attacking the enemy's trade and threatening his interests ashore whilst protecting your own. These advantages were so great that, as the history of Britain in the period he studied clearly demonstrated, the sea powers would prosper in peace, prevail in war and dominate world events. He concluded:

> Control of the sea by maritime commerce and naval supremacy means predominant influence in the world ... [and] is the chief among the merely material elements in the power and prosperity of nations [although it was] ... but one factor in that general advance and decay of nations which is called their history. (Mahan, 1890: 91; quoted in Livezey, 1981: 41)

Seapower revolved around a simple connection. Trade produces wealth that leads to maritime strength. Naval strength protects trade, and in turn depends on geography (access to sea routes etc), physical conformation of the coast (ports etcetera), extent of territory, population, and the character of the people and the government.

Mahan stressed the importance of battle between concentrations of heavy warships as the ultimate decider of naval power. The outcome of battle depended not merely on the quality of the ships present, however, but on training, morale, the effectiveness of command, tactical disposition (in particular, skill in concentrating all your force against a portion of the opponent's) and above all on an offensive spirit – the desire to close and destroy. It is because of Mahan's emphasis on the destruction of the adversary's main battle force, that he is sometimes likened to Clausewitz. While Mahan derived his ideas from the days of sail, he was confident that they would hold true in later technological eras and would have completely rejected the notion that the advent of submarines or aircraft carriers had somehow made them irrelevant. New technology simply meant that those principles would be applied in different ways by different platforms but, he believed, in essence would stay the same 'as though built upon a rock'.

Recent scholarship on what Mahan actually wrote (as opposed to what people without the time or energy to read through his voluminous writings have said he wrote!) shows him to have focused a good deal more on the effects of maritime operations on the situation ashore, and the impact of maritime power on the workings of the international system than his critics have alleged (Sumida, 1997). His ideas, moreover, were echoed and developed by a score of other naval writers around the world then and since.

Sir Julian Corbett (1854–1922) on the other hand is less well known. His best book was *Some Principles of Maritime Strategy*, written in 1911. Paradoxically, he did most of his writing in that particularly interesting period just before the First World War, when Britain was temporarily moving away from the kind of strategy that he advocated.

Like Mahan, Corbett took the principles of maritime warfare to be a guide to thought rather than directives to action. As a lawyer, he had a more judicious sense than Mahan of the limitations of seapower and a more overt espousal of the point that the first function of the fleet was 'to support or obstruct diplomatic effort'. The advantage of maritime operations was that since they were more discriminating in their strategic effect and more controllable in action than messy, escalatory land operations they could be a particularly cost-effective means of securing political objectives. He took a comprehensive and what we would now call a 'joint' approach, in which naval activity had to be 'nicely coordinated with military and diplomatic pressure', for one simple reason:

> Since men live upon the land and not upon the sea, great issues between nations at war have always been decided – except in the

rarest cases – either by what your army can do against your enemy's territory and national life or else by the fear of what the fleet makes it possible for your army to do. (Corbett, [1911] 1988: 15–16)

For this reason, he discussed 'maritime' rather than naval strategy, thinking it about those principles governing a war in which the sea plays an important part.

The navy that commanded of the sea could use it as a means of transportation, both commercial (to supply the war economy) and military (to facilitate the projection of power ashore). Corbett argued that properly conducted amphibious operations could indeed be the means by which sea powers could help decide the outcome of wars. Maritime supremacy allowed them to strike at their enemies' weakest points, with the least effort and the maximum strategic impact. This was a vision of a uniquely cost-effective and controllable kind of limited war.

Corbett no more wrote in a vacuum than did Mahan. Many commentators have pointed out where he was being Clausewitzian (keeping naval strategy alongside its political purposes) and where he was not (doubts about the centrality of battle and the emphasis on limited war). Others have likened Corbett's approach to the clever manoeuvrism of Sun Tzu with his emphasis on winning most at least cost and on the notion of deceptive concentration. More immediately, there were others writing on related topics at much the same time, most obviously Major General Sir Charles Callwell (1859–1928). Amongst the most significant of his works are *The Effect of Maritime Command on Land Campaigns since Waterloo* (1897) and *Military Operations and Maritime Preponderance* (1905), in which the advantages of tactical, operational and strategic synergy between the differing dimensions of war were forcefully argued.

After the searing devastation of the First World War, there arose in writers like Basil Liddell Hart (of whom more later), a determination to avoid such major 'continental commitments' again. He coined the phrase 'the British way in war' and argued that Britain and other countries in a like situation should revert to the kind of grand maritime strategy advocated by Corbett (Till, 2006: 105).

Interwar airpower theory

Airpower theory lacked the profound intellectual insights of Mahan and Corbett, presumably because its theorists had so much less previous experience from which to draw and test their ideas. A sense that it was imperative in any future conflict to avoid a repetition of the awful conditions of the Western front and the hope of embracing the exciting new technologies of flight made airpower in the 1920s seem to encapsulate everything that was modern and future-centred. It should offer military people a short cut to victory that might in fact prove less bloody than the interminable meat-grinding campaigns of the First World War.

Unsurprisingly, airpower theorists like Giulio Douhet (1869–1930), William 'Billy' Mitchell (1879–1936) and the publicist/inventor de Seversky (1894–1974) therefore commanded what was almost literally the high ground in the debate about the future of war in the interwar period.

Their basic proposition came from an extrapolation from some aspects of the experience of the First World War, reinforcing the result with anticipations about the future of airpower technology. That war had demonstrated the huge psychological and operational impact of strategic bombing behind the lines. It had also shown the importance of command of the air above the lines and at sea since this would enable greatly improved surveillance, the air defence of friendly forces and the direct attack of hostile units. Believing that airpower would be a 'shield' as well as a 'sword' Mitchell, unlike Douhet (at least in the early days), paid attention to the notion of air–land cooperation and he was certainly more interested than his Italian colleague in the direct and independent aerial attack of surface forces on land and sea.

The second of these manifestations of future airpower was not inherently controversial in conceptual terms (although its likely effectiveness certainly was!). Armies and navies around the world devoted considerable efforts (though not always as many as their own airpower enthusiasts would have wanted) to the development of organic air capabilities to support their main missions at sea and on land.

The first claim of the airpower theorists like Mitchell and Douhet *was* hugely controversial at the time as they claimed that strategic bombing was likely to be so effective as significantly to reduce the effect of, and logically the need for, the kind of operations for which armies and navies were designed. A full-scale aerial onslaught against an adversary's capital city, for example, would prove to be so devastating that it would end the war even before navies and armies had had a chance to affect its outcome. Douhet (1983: 142) believed strongly in the idea of a 'battleplane' (the aerial equivalent of a battleship) 'each capable of destroying the nerve centre of a city'.

> [T]he nation which, once it had conquered the air, can maintain in operation not 100, but 50 or even 20 such planes, will have won decisively, because it will be in a position to break up the whole social structure of the enemy in less than a week, no matter what his army and navy may do. (Douhet, 1983: 142)

Accordingly, preparing this capability simply had to be the first priority of a responsible defence programme. The only questions such theorists disputed were how the air campaign should be conducted, against what targets and the attention that should be paid to developing means to defend against it, other than by hitting an adversary first, hardest and with the most immediate strategic effect.

Sceptics in the other services argued that such strategies were immoral and unlawful since they were likely to result in large-scale civilian casualties. Furthermore, they depended on undeveloped technologies unlikely to appear in the foreseeable future, and would result in the neglect of their own essential requirements. As far as technology was concerned, huge advances were indeed made in every aspect of the development of airpower. Nonetheless, strategic bombing at the beginning of the Second World War was nowhere near developing the capabilities that Douhet had claimed, and even by the end of it, the effectiveness of conventional strategic bombing remained a matter of dispute.

On the other hand, other aspects of airpower had also come on hugely before 1939, in particular air defence. Modern monoplane fighters, the development of radar and improved anti-aircraft gunnery combined to ensure that a significant proportion of bombers would *not* 'get through'. In rather the same way, the techniques and technologies of close air-support of ground and maritime forces had advanced a great deal, although the experience of war was to show that in many cases it had not advanced enough. This partly reflected the fact that strategic bombing still commanded the airpower agenda. There were no grand theories of naval airpower or air–land cooperation. Perhaps for this reason, these alternative dimensions of airpower did not attract the resources experience was to show they deserved.

The single exception to this intellectual *lacuna*, in Britain's case at least, was the concept of 'air control': the notion demonstrated in Iraq and Somaliland in the 1920s that aircraft could stabilize tumultuous third-world regions much more effectively and cheaply than could army garrisons. Despite the relative success of the practice of Imperial policing, though, it was seen by Trenchard more as a means of keeping the RAF in being than as an alternate vision of airpower, and little strategic theory resulted from it. The idea, however, did presage the way in which airpower would be used later in the century.

Blitzkrieg ideas

Finally, there is the third group within what might be termed the second generation of strategists: those who focused on the land dimension of war and who were particularly interested in exploring the way in which modern military technology could allow the further development of advanced techniques of land warfare that were beginning to emerge by 1918. The first clear set of ideas revolved around the tank as a means of restoring mobility to the battlefield and decisive effect to the campaign.

Here two Britons, Captain Basil Liddell Hart and Major General J.F.C. Fuller, were pre-eminent.

Liddell Hart, an army officer turned strategic commentator, had an eclectic approach. He borrowed from the ideas of Sun Tzu that aimed at the dislocation of the adversary rather than his physical destruction, and in his *Strategy: The Indirect Approach* urged the use of deception and manoeuvre on the one hand and new technology (notably tanks with close air support) to create and then exploit weaknesses in the enemy line. Once through, the aim would be to fan out in an 'expanding torrent' cutting the enemy's lines of communication (echoing Jomini!) and thereby inducing a state of strategic paralysis. As Fuller (1925: 47) wrote, '[t]he physical strength of an army lies in its organisation, controlled by its brain. Paralyse this brain and the body ceases to operate'.

Much of this reflected the methods adopted by the Germans in the 'Spring Offensive' of 1918 and the British in their remarkable 'One Hundred Days campaign' in the late summer and autumn of that year. The Germans, of course, put the theory into devastating effect in the summer of 1940, as did the Israelis in 1967 and 1973.

But there were also particularly interesting ideas developing in the Soviet Union. The failure of the Red Army before Warsaw in 1920 reinforced the sense that as revolutionaries they should not automatically adopt the military conventions of the old regime. This led to an outburst of innovative thinking in the Soviet Union about the way in which military operations should be conducted, most obviously on land. The result was considerable thinking about what constituted the 'operational art': the creation of a fighting style optimized for large spaces, the operational level of war, a manoeuvrist approach and the 'deep-battle'. As far as Naveh is concerned, the result was the 'most advanced compilation of ideas ever attained in the history of modern military thought' (Naveh, 1997: 236).

The centrepiece of this 'new' way of thinking about the conduct of military operations was the so-called operational level of warfare and the very closely associated concept of 'operational manoeuvre'. Early thinking about the conduct of military operations had tended to concentrate on the conduct of battle and the tactical level of war. This was a preoccupation of the later strategists of the nineteenth century too, of course, but they were equally concerned with grand strategy – the contribution that military forces could make to the achievement of national aims in peace and war. Not much had been written about anything between these two levels of war.

The Soviet School, however, identified a new level of war that lay between the tactical (the art of battle) and the strategic (the art of war). The 'operational' level of war was said to be about campaigns – hence the operational art was the art of campaigning. The essential point, though, was that the operational level of war *links* the other two. In the words of the Soviet theorist A.A. Svechin (1926: 15–17; quoted in Naveh, 1997: 183):

> Strategy decides questions concerning both the use of the armed force and all the resources of the state for the achievement of ultimate military aims. ... Operational art, arising from the aim of the operation, generates a series of tactical missions and establishes a series of tasks. ... Tactics makes the steps from which operational leaps are assembled. Strategy points out the path.

It followed that the operational art is 'the skilful employment of military forces to attain strategic goals through the design, organisation, integration and conduct of campaigns, major operations and battles'.

At the same time, Soviet military thinkers realized that the enemy was best thought of as a hostile system, not just an accumulation of menacing forces in an opposing line of battle. Behind their deployed forces lay a complex network of supporting resources, command and control systems, reinforcements, political will and so forth. If these could be attacked directly, rather than indirectly through the attrition of the enemy forces deployed to defend them, a much more cost-effective style of war became possible. Thinking 'deep' and going for the weaknesses behind the front line was increasingly emphasized. This led to the Russian concept of the 'deep battle'. To some extent this was a misnomer, since the whole point of the approach is that the decision would be sought not at the tactical level of battle, but above it at the operational or 'campaign' level to which, of course, battles contributed. In the Russian 'August Storm' operation of 1945, for example, the Japanese military system in Manchuria was taken apart, chunk by chunk, not in a series of decisive battles but in a decisive campaign characterized by fragmenting, simultaneous strikes and the generation of operational momentum. Given the scale of forces likely to be involved in many campaigns, decisions would seldom, the Soviet General Staff believed, be attained through single engagements.

Achieving this result required what has become known as a manoeuvrist approach, a deliberate and conscious attempt to shape the campaign and to attack the enemy's cohesion (whilst protecting one's own). This could take various forms. It could be, literally, a geographic manoeuvre – an unexpected angle, or combination of angles of attack. Here Tukhachevsky's revolutionary interest in the development of large-scale parachute forces or his following through the '*blitzkrieg*' ideas of Liddell Hart and Fuller could provide radical means of restoring manoeuvre to the battlefield. In the Oder–Vistula campaign against Germany and the 'August Storm' operation of 1945 against Japan, the Red Army showed that it could put theory into impressive, indeed decisive, practice.

Building on these concepts, in the 1970s and 1980s the Russians developed the concept of the 'operational manoeuvre group' – in effect a small, hard-hitting, mobile, self-contained mechanized army optimized to spread the maximum of dismay and disruption behind NATO lines by attacking its key points, communications, supplies and sources of fire support. Much of this kind of thinking was adapted by the US Army with its 'AirLand Battle' concepts of the 1980s (Naveh, 1997: 305–13).

But the manoeuvrist approach could be conceptual too – a matter of out-thinking the enemy. The enemy's plan rather than his forces was to be the main object of attack. This meant manoeuvring the enemy by the skilful use of your forces into a situation in which all his options appear unattractive.

While the terminology may be new, earlier commanders may well have understood much of this intuitively. The concept of 'ulterior objectives' associated with de Morogues and other French writers of the eighteenth century, or the common use of the term 'grand tactics' by military commentators in the nineteenth century all presuppose a level of activity different from, and possibly superior to, the conduct of decisive, linear battle. Moreover, the concept of 'manoeuvre' was substantially explored by Raoul Castex (1994: 101–5, 169):

> Manoeuvre is quintessentially a creative activity. 'To create a favourable situation' is the proposed definition. *Manoeuvre* attempts to alter or control the course of events, to dominate fate rather than yield to it, to conceive and bring forth action.

Such thinking harks back to the 'clever' approach advocated by Sun Tzu as well as the emphasis given to preparatory subversion by the likes of Lenin. As far as the Soviet General Staff was concerned, it was vindicated by the success of later Soviet operations on the Eastern Front and in Manchuria, and provided a framework for what they called 'military science' in the post-war period.

Military thinking in the cold war

But as did all military thinkers, the Soviet General Staff had to contend with the shock of the US atomic attacks on Hiroshima and Nagasaki and what that experience might do for the military lessons recently and so hardly learned. Nevertheless, there were many continuities and carry-overs into the new era. Despite the concerns of the 'atomic shock', for example, the salience of Corbett's amphibious approach and the advantages of maritime manoeuvre was soon to be demonstrated in the famous landings at Inchon, a few miles south of Seoul, in September 1950 during the Korean War. This surprise amphibious assault, deep in the enemy's rear, unhinged the North's whole plan, threatened their lines of supply and forced a pell-mell retreat from their siege of UN forces in the Pusan area far away to the southeast. The landing and the subsequent advance completely transformed the operational scene ashore, and helped create a fluid and dangerous situation for the North Koreans until the intervention of the Chinese in November re-stabilized the situation for them.

Mahanian ideas also seemed to have been confirmed by the experience of the great powers in the two world wars. Not surprisingly, therefore, the US and the British navies went into the cold war era with a set of very traditional attitudes and assumptions, despite the advent of nuclear weapons. Hence the stress on the 'offensive spirit' and on moving forward in Europe's northern waters in order to contain a Soviet submarine threat that might otherwise prove fatal for NATO's plans to reinforce and re-supply Western Europe across the Atlantic. In the late 1940s and much of the 1950s, these ideas resulted in the 'attack at source' posture of carrier air strikes against Soviet naval bases in northern Europe (Palmer, 1988).

Interestingly, their main adversary at the time, the Soviet Navy, developed increasingly similar views, particularly in the requirement to move its naval forces forward and engage Western forces aggressively. Indeed, in the second version of his book *The Seapower of the State*, Admiral Sergei Gorshkov, then Commander-in-Chief of the Soviet Navy, claimed his Tsarist predecessors had to all intents and purposes invented much of maritime strategy, and devoted some 4000 words to an analysis of its core – what the Russians call 'sea dominance'. 'History', he concluded, 'does not know of a more ancient and hardier concept' (Gorshkov, 1979: 230). When he was charged by an American admiral with sounding very Mahanian, Admiral Gorshkov replied 'And why not? The man was eminently sensible' (Hattendorf, 1991: 4). The US Navy's 'The Maritime Strategy', the public version of which appeared in 1986, was an even more dramatic demonstration of the fact that the Mahanian tradition was alive and well in the late twentieth century. Whether those who produced it were conscious of the details of Mahan's legacy remains problematic, but the extent to which his assumptions coloured the atmosphere in which the strategy was put together is hard to dispute (Baer, 1994: 429).

Despite the evident continuities however, there were considerable forces for radical strategic change in the post-war period. The dropping of atomic bombs on Hiroshima and Nagasaki in August 1945 made the final amphibious assault on the Japanese home islands unnecessary. Many drew from this the conclusion that nuclear technology would make large conventional operations of this sort both too dangerous and unnecessary. This was what Admiral Gorshkov called the 'atomic shock', a major military-technological change that seemed to call into question the continued validity of existing strategic thinking and military systems. It led in the 1950s and 1960s to the emergence of a third generation of strategists, a 'Golden Generation', closely allied with policy makers in the United States and coming from a wide range of backgrounds and disciplines. They included Thomas Schelling (an economist), Albert Wohlstetter (a mathematician), Herman Kahn (a physicist) and Henry Kissinger (a historian). Perhaps not surprisingly, the US Air Force, which tended to regard nuclear weapons as a decisively effective form of airpower, regarded their views with sympathy.

Their fundamental thesis was that the world was in a dangerous new stage in its development, confronting a set of technological, political and strategic challenges of unprecedented severity. Not just the fate of kings but the survival of the whole human race depended on the world leaders reacting appropriately.

The approach of this generation of strategists is best exemplified by the work of Herman Kahn (1962). He accepted that nuclear weapons could not be un-invented and so insisted on the need to 'think the unthinkable' if mankind was to keep control over its own military technology. Nuclear war would certainly be dreadful but it might happen anyway, and survival demanded that it be both considered beforehand and conducted at the time with as much cool rationality as the circumstances allowed. It was no use simply abandoning the project as too difficult, since this meant that a nuclear war could easily be terminal.

Kahn (1965) created the notion of 'ladder of escalation' which sought to identify a grisly hierarchy of international conflict going from political crisis at the bottom to full-scale 'spasm' nuclear war at the top, and explored rational strategies of controlled coercion appropriate for each level. The rungs and thresholds were arranged in order of the magnitude of the political objectives that divided the adversaries, the military means employed and the targets selected. This association of military means and political objective *seemed* very Clausewitzian.

'Rung 33' of his ladder of escalation attracted particular attention. He called it 'slow-motion city trading'. Here the contestants were in lethal dispute and demonstrated resolve by 'taking out' (again the language of the time) one enemy city after another in a deadly but deliberate exchange designed to demonstrate resolve while avoiding a full-scale nuclear exchange. The side that 'blinked first', by not responding in an equally coercive manner, would lose.

This position attracted much criticism. Some argued that such a strategy assumed a level of clear-thinking behaviour on both sides that was simply unrealistic. These scientific pretensions seemed to downplay human factors in the decision makers such as fear, panic and mental exhaustion alongside the practical difficulties of transmitting exact and complicated messages to an adversary. Kahn's critics pointed out that he in fact had produced such different ladders of escalation for both the United States and the Soviet Union that their leaders might not be able communicate accurately even if they wanted to, because they had a different strategic vocabulary. The danger of this is demonstrated by post-cold war analysis of the naval confrontation during the Cuba Missile Crisis of 1962, which suggests that the world got closer to an accidental nuclear escalation than many had realized for this very reason (see Savranskaya, 2005: 233–60). Further, Kahn's treatment of how the adversaries de-escalated and closed down the crisis was much less considered than how they got into and escalated it. This echoed those criticisms of contemporary war games that typically ended on a Friday afternoon, leaving the question of 'what happens next' completely open.

Others argued that since these strategies violated the laws of war (by targeting civilians for example) it was unethical even to think about such possibilities. Still others focused on the inherent disproportionality of nuclear weapons when set against conceivable objectives. 'My own personal opinion', said McNamara, Secretary of Defense at the time, 'is that no-one would win a nuclear war, in the normal sense of the word "win".' Kahn and his neo-Clausewitzian cohorts were, it was claimed, actually violating the great man's attempt to link the political objective with the military means. Worse still, thinking about all this might make nuclear war *seem* more controllable and so more likely to happen. It was as though they thought, responded Kahn acidly, that putting lifeboats on ships was wrong because it could make their navigators reckless.

By the late 1960s and early 1970s, however, a new fourth generation of strategists was beginning to emerge who considered that the focus on nuclear warfare was arcane, talked-out and overplayed. Unless it was the result of catastrophic mechanical breakdown (flocks of geese on the radar) or the world's leaders making serious mistakes at much lower levels of conflict, nuclear conflict seemed less and less likely to happen as its strategic consequences became more obvious. Strategists could do little about the first, for that was the realm of systems engineers and weapons designers, but they could focus on behaviour at those lower levels of conflict which in fact had already killed 20–30 million people since 1945 and which could conceivably escalate into something even worse. Hence the developing interest in crisis management, control and the conduct of limited war. Such writers did not produce anything as intellectually coherent as a strategic theory but their detailed analyses of particular incidents and generalizations about a number of them were intended to offer pointers to a more general understanding of the phenomenon (Bell, 1971; Allison, 1971).

One final grouping within this fourth generation of strategists deserve to be singled out, partly because they moved away from the classic focus on state against state conflict and so began the transition into the current post-cold war generation of strategists who concentrate instead on irregular warfare and more complex conceptions of low level conflict. These included those who, inspired by the challenges posed by the Malayan emergency, the Algerian War and Vietnam, chose to focus on insurgency and counter-insurgency. The writings of people like Vietnam's Vo Nguyen Giap (1962) can be said to largely to have developed the earlier ideas of Mao, applying them to their own countries and time. Carlos Marighella (1971) on the other hand took a strategy of insurgency derived from conflicts in a rural setting and applied it to the world's growing cities.

Of course this inspired a group of theorists who focused on the philosophy of counter-insurgency. Frank Kitson and Sir Robert Thompson based their ideas on their experience in Kenya and the Malayan Emergency respectively, and the former tested them in Northern Ireland. In his *Gangs and Counter Gangs*, Kitson (1960) argued that counter-insurgency forces should aim to beat the insurgents at their own game by adopting many of their tactics and structures, and developed his ideas further in his *Low Intensity Operations* (1971). Thompson (1972) took a similar line but focused more on winning the campaign for hearts and minds and undermining the perceived legitimacy of the objectives for which the insurgents were fighting. He took a less kinetic approach and advocated an 'oil spot' approach of securing and pacifying one area before moving on to the next. This in fact harked back to the *tache d'huile* methods used by the French in Algeria in the 1840s. A century later, Algeria saw the attempted implementation of the ideas of David Galula (1966). Concluding in his *Counterinsurgency Warfare: Theory and Tactics* that the French failure in Indochina was due to their not fighting fire with fire with sufficient resolution, he advocated very hard tactics in Algeria that in fact did not turn out well. The Vietnam War likewise was a steep learning curve for the Americans and numbers of books on counter-insurgency were written, but few proved a significant advance on the pioneering work of Sir Robert Thompson (1972).

Post-cold war challenges

Intrastate conflict has proved a major feature of the post-cold war period and has created a different set of challenges upon which military strategists of the present, or fifth, generation have needed to reflect. The disappearance of the structured and controlled partial bi-polarity characteristic of the cold war has produced, or at least coincided with, increased levels of disorder. This can also be attributed, in part, to resentments about the impact of globalization, or in some cases to hostility to the very values it espouses. These resentments have led to a range of less familiar threats to the system, especially from hostile groups rather than nation states. These hostile groups tend to hide amongst the general population, and have a millennial prejudice that leads to a cavalier attitude towards the conventional rules of war and makes strategic compromise difficult; they also have access to techniques and to technology that disproportionately increases their general effectiveness. Driven by the notion that 'If we do not go to the crisis, the crisis will come to us,' conventional military forces increasingly find themselves engaged with unfamiliar, ruthless and faceless adversaries, either at a distance or indeed at home.

Several things need to be said about this situation, and the first is that it has yet to produce much in the way of a coherent grand strategy in response. Instead, there have been a number of areas in which military thinkers have attempted to produce new doctrines (in the sense of that word defined earlier) relating only to particular aspects of the general situation at a particular time.

Chief amongst these have been an increase in attention paid particularly to the overlapping concepts of expeditionary operations, airpower operations, peace support operations and security and counter-terrorism operations. Much of this thinking, however, represents a re-packaging and development of ideas that had gone before, though it also seeks to incorporate conclusions about the impact of modern technology on the conduct of such operations.

The military strategies of the post-cold war era

After the Second World War had conclusively demonstrated the importance of airpower in all its various manifestations, it was hardly surprising that visionaries and doctrine writers, particularly in the US Air Force, should rush to argue that Douhet, Mitchell and Seversky had finally been vindicated. Even though the actual impact of strategic bombing on Germany was to remain contentious for many years, Hiroshima and Nagasaki ushered in an age when it could hardly be doubted that nuclear airpower would be decisive in any major conflict between the two superpowers and their allies. This became an article of faith in the US and British Air Forces and closely elided airpower and nuclear theorists in this period.

Airpower theorists like US Air Force Colonels John Boyd and John A. Warden III went on from this, however, to examine the role of airpower in those conflicts short of total war that began to attract attention from the late 1960s onwards. Building on the eventual success of airpower in support of land and sea operations during the Second World War, they claimed that its effects could be equally decisive here too. Boyd (cited in Meilinger, 1997: 363–9) stressed the advantages modern airpower could provide in getting inside the enemy's decision cycle (his OODA loop – observe, orientate, decide and act) though its information-gathering and surveillance capacities. This depended on its rapidity, its reach and, operationally, on sufficient command of the air. Warden developed these ideas, and in *The Air Campaign* (1988) also made effective use of the deep-battle arguments of the interwar Soviet School.

The adversary moreover should be regarded as a system of concentric rings, with his deployed forces on the outside and his central decision-making capacities in the middle (Warden, 1995). Airpower could fly over the first and knock out the communication nodes that kept the system together, perhaps even paralysing the enemy's command and control system by a campaign of 'shock and awe' aimed at the very centre of the system (Meilinger, 1997: 357–98). The same could work at the tactical level. On call airpower, at last benefiting from the huge advances in information technology and consequent networking of sensors, platforms and weapons characteristic of the last several decades, could deliver fast, rapid, precise and decisive effect on enemy forces and positions, thereby making the task of ground forces much easier, catering thereby for the perceived casualty-aversion so crucial in the Western conduct of wars of choice.

Experience in the 1990–1 and 2003 Gulf wars and Afghanistan seemed to confirm this (Lambeth, 2005).

The Kosovo campaign of 1999 was a particularly interesting example. On the one hand the noted commentator John Keegan (1999), concluded:

> Already some of the critics of the war are indulging in ungrateful revisionism, suggesting that we have not witnessed a strategic revolution and that Milosovic was humbled by the threat to deploy ground troops, or by the processes of traditional diplomacy. ... All to be said to that is that diplomacy had not worked before 24th March when the bombing started, while the deployment of a large ground force, though clearly a growing threat, would still have taken weeks to accomplish at the moment Milosovic caved in. The revisionists are wrong. This was a victory through airpower.

Professor Sir Tony Mason, a retired RAF Air Vice Marshal, agreed, arguing that airpower had been NATO's *sole* military instrument and its success in such cases was likely to make it *the* weapon of choice. Moreover airpower theorists contended that space was likely to take the argument still further, since it offered the prospect of even better means of surveillance, targeting and ultimately perhaps weapons delivery.

However that might be, present-day sceptics on the other hand argued that airpower in Kosovo had not significantly degraded the Serbian army, nor had it stopped the ethnic cleansing that was the original reason for the conflict. Moreover, the civilian casualties brought about by targeting mistakes and the Serb propensity to hide amongst the civilian population made public acceptance of the campaign worryingly insecure at times. Such concerns have been reinforced by the Israel's campaign in the Lebanon in 2006, which suggested that an intelligent adversary could circumvent much of the effect of conventional airpower, even of the most sophisticated kind, by the adoption of ruthless asymmetric tactics.

The expeditionary impulse

On the maritime side, the US Marine Corps were amongst the first to consider the requirements of the post-cold war world by developing the concept of 'operational manoeuvre from the sea' (OMFTS) Their aspiration was to create conditions for successful manoeuvre ashore by making use of the unimpeded access offered by the sea. Maritime forces, they argued, have a special contribution to make in their mobility (400 miles a day compared to the 30 odd usually achieved by land forces), firepower and flexibility. This seemed an attractive way of applying force intelligently in order to seize the operational initiative:

Naval forces maneuvre from the sea using their dominance of littoral areas to mass forces rapidly and generate high-intensity, precise offensive power at the time and location of their choosing, under any weather conditions, day or night. Power projection requires mobility, flexibility and technology to mass strength against weakness. The Navy and Marine Corps team supports the decisive sea–air–land battle by providing the sea-based support to enable the application of the complete range of US combat power. (Till, 2004: 71)

OMFTS drew heavily on traditional amphibious thinking as well as on the concepts of manoeuvre, deep battle and the operational art developed during the interwar period. It coincided with a tremendous growth of strategic interest in the littorals as the area in which much of the world's economic activity was conducted, where the bulk of population was settling and most of its problems and instabilities were to be found. This thinking was enshrined in the concept of 'chaos in the littorals'. It seemed increasingly to require the capacity to operate within a demanding urban environment.

Operations in the littorals required 'battlespace dominance' though the joint action of air, land and naval forces. Here there was a conscious harking back to the theories of Sir Julian Corbett and to the sense that expeditionary operations required, above all else, high levels of cooperation between the services in an essentially maritime strategy. But new technology had something to offer too. The increased reach of sea-based projection, weaponry and sensors even offered the opportunity for what became known as 'ship to objective manoeuvre' (STOM). This concept was designed to enable sea-based forces to attack the objective directly without the need for an 'operational pause' while forces were first landed, sorted themselves out and then advanced from their bridgehead. This was itself the product of operational-level and deep-battle thinking with its emphasis on manoeuvre rather than attrition. The whole point was to fight smart, not so much to destroy the enemy's forces as to disrupt and dismantle them. The aim would be to overwhelm by precise firepower, a high tempo succession of moves, surprise and simultaneity. The concept was also held to apply to peace support operations, humanitarian operations and so forth. Critics of this approach, however, have argued that 'theatre entry' is not the problem; instead, the real issue is the stabilization operation so often required afterwards.

Peace support operations

The end of the cold war allowed, and possibly made necessary, an explosion in the number of peace support operations from 1990 onwards. For conventional military strategists this was unfamiliar territory since they were often not conducted 'against' anyone, still less against recognized states. They were distinguished by consent in various degrees and the traditional concept of 'victory' seemed inappropriate. Around the world this requirement has produced, if not a strategic theory, then at least a set of new doctrines and approaches. These are increasingly based on the notion that the maintenance and restoration of peace will usually depend on a 'comprehensive approach' in which the military join with coalition partners, other government departments, non-governmental organizations and, importantly, the indigenous people themselves (both host governments and opposition groups) to achieve the objective. In British doctrine, four types of activity are identified – prevention, intervention, regeneration and sustainment. The military's role is to help provide the operational environment in which peace is enforced if necessary, the situation stabilized and the conditions for a transition to a (more) permanent state of peace are established (UK Ministry of Defence, 2004: 3–50).

These are ambitious and difficult aspirations. Each peace support operation (PSO) situation – and the particular challenges it offers – is unique. It is not proving easy to develop the overarching theory that covers all contingencies without sacrificing the kind of specificity that operational commanders find useful. Significantly, the United Nations itself is developing its own doctrine for contemporary peace support operations.

Security and counter-terrorism operations

Many of the difficult issues in peace support operations derive from the fact that 'security' has widened from the merely military aspects to include personal, social, economic and environmental concerns, and that increasingly effective groups of people seek either to exploit it for criminal purposes or to undermine it for its own sake. Attacks on power supplies, schools or hospitals are seen by the perpetrators as legitimate tactics and full use is made of the in-depth media coverage now to be expected of all security operations. Since the attacks on New York and Washington on 11 September 2001, the facts of globalization have meant that military security operations against terrorism and international crime of all sorts have had to cover both the overlapping home and away dimensions of the problem.

Homeland security is increasingly seen as requiring an integrated approach of all the security services. In some countries this is leading to the creation of new departments of state responsible for all aspects of internal security. In others it means developing better coordination between existing departments and with other countries, regionally and globally. Again this is more an urgent matter of developing protocols and procedures rather than a settled and long-considered, over-arching strategy. Moreover new and unexpected problems (sophisticated improvised explosive devices, suicide bombers, etcetera) continually appear. Here as elsewhere in the post-cold war world it would seem difficult for theory to keep up with practice.

Further reading

Baer, G. (1994) *One Hundred Years of Seapower: The US Navy, 1890–1990*, Stanford: Stanford University Press.

Corbett, J. [1911] (1988) *Some Principles of Maritime Strategy*, with an introduction by Eric Grove, Annapolis: Naval Institute Press.

Douhet, G. (1983) *The Command of the Air*, Washington: Office of Air History.

Fuller, J.F.C. (1925) *The Foundations of the Science of War*, London: Hutchinson.

Fuller, W.C. (1992) *Strategy and Power in Russia 1600–1914*, New York: Free Press.

Giap, V.N. (1962) *People's War: People's Army*, New York: Prager.

Goldstein, L.J. et al (eds) (2005) 'The Cold War at Sea: An International Appraisal', *Journal of Strategic Studies*, 28. This special issue of the journal offers an excellent analysis of the role of seapower during the cold war.

Gorshkov, S. (1979) *The Seapower of the State*, London: Pergamon.

Grey, C.S. (1999) *Modern Strategy*, Oxford: Oxford University Press.

Halperin, M.H. (1963) *Limited War in the Nuclear Age*, New York: John Wiley.

Handel, M.I. (2001) *Masters of War: Classical Military Thought*, London: Frank Cass.

Kitson, F. (1971) *Low Intensity Operations*, London: Faber and Faber.

Liddell Hart, B.H. (1932) *The British Way in Warfare*, London: Faber and Faber.

Liddell Hart, B.H. (1967) *Strategy: The Indirect Approach*, London: Faber and Faber.

Machiavelli, N. [1532] (1961) *The Prince*, London: Penguin.

Mahan, A.T. (1890) *The Influence of Seapower upon History, 1660–1783*, London: Sampson, Low, Marston.

Mahan, A.T. (1911) *Naval Strategy: Compared and Contrasted with the Principles and Practice of Military Operations on Land*, Boston: Little, Brown.

Paret, P. (ed.) (1986) *Makers of Modern Strategy: Military Thought From Machiavelli to the Nuclear Age*, Oxford: Oxford University Press.

Smith, H. (ed.) (2001) *The Strategists*, Canberra: Australian Defence Studies Centre, Australian National University.

Sondhaus, L. (2006) *Strategic Culture and Ways of War*, London: Routledge.

Sun Tzu (1971) *The Art of War*, trans and intro by Griffith, S.B., Oxford: Oxford University Press.

Till, G. (2004) *Seapower: A Guide for the twenty-first Century*, London: Frank Cass.

Till, G. (ed.) (2006) *The Development of British Naval Thinking*, London: Routledge.

Chapter 7

The Transformation of War

Andrew Latham

Introduction

Since the early 1990s, the *transformation of war* – that is, the epochal change in the nature of organized political violence that is said to characterize the contemporary era – has come to occupy an increasingly prominent place on an already crowded scholarly agenda. Among International Relations scholars, for example, this focus is evident in Kal Holsti's (1996) study of the evolution of 'wars of the third kind', Christopher Coker's (2001) work on the transition to 'humane warfare' and the coming era of 'posthuman war', and Colin McInnes's (2002) arguments about the advent of what he calls 'spectator-sport war'. This attention to epochal transformation in the nature of war is also echoed in the wider academy, which is now replete with studies analysing the recent, ongoing or imminent transition to 'post-heroic war' (Luttwak, 1995), 'post-trinitarian war' (van Creveld, 1991b), 'new war' (Kaldor, 1999), 'network war' (Duffield, 2001), 'postmodern war' (Grey, 1997), 'virtual war' (Der Derian, 2001), and 'third wave war' (Toffler and Toffler, 1993). Although these accounts differ significantly in terms of their respective analytical assumptions, theoretical concerns and policy prescriptions, they share at least one common – indeed, defining – element: a belief that we are currently in the midst of a profound world-historical 'transformation of war' that is profoundly altering the ideas, instruments and institutions of organized political violence. They are also similar in that they are all emblematic of the deep-rooted and recently reinvigorated scholarly interest in the role of war in world politics.

Yet, as I have argued elsewhere (Latham, 2002), the extant literature ultimately fails to provide a satisfactory account of epochal change in the nature of organized political violence. To begin with, the existing body of research lacks an integrative framework or conceptual language. At one level, of course, there is now widespread agreement that the history of war is punctuated with episodes of rapid and profound transformation – the 'military revolutions', 'new wars' and 'revolutions in military affairs' about which so much has been written over the past decade or so. Despite this consensus, however, there is little agreement regarding what is being transformed in such episodes (the unit of analysis), what drives such episodic transformations (causal mechanisms), or even when such transformational episodes have occurred (periodization). Nor is there a body of common and widely accepted definitions, organizing concepts and ideal types that might be used to conduct systematic and comparative research on the dynamics of revolutionary military transformation. As a result, the extant literature tends to be conceptually cacophonous – that is, a discordant mixture of theories, concepts, definitions, taxonomies and histories that is as confusing as it is confused. While I do not subscribe to the notion that the ideal state of affairs in any field of social inquiry is a kind of Kuhnian 'normal science', I do believe that such a state of conceptual confusion is a serious impediment to the kind of modest cumulation of knowledge that can result from sustained and systematic analysis of social phenomena such as war.

Second, while the extant literature addresses phenomena ranging from changes in battlefield techniques (e.g. *blitzkrieg* operational practices) to changes in the nature of war (the new-wars thesis), it is nevertheless characterized by a general failure to isolate conceptually – and then analyse systematically – what are arguably different types or orders of 'transformation of war'. In effect, it 'fuses' the various elements of the phenomenon of organized political violence. As I have argued elsewhere (Latham, 2002), however, studying a phenomenon as complex and multidimensional as war requires that we disaggregate organized political violence (and its transformation) into three distinct phenomena – the *warfighting paradigm* (the way armed forces conduct combat operations on the battlefield), the *social mode of warfare* (the way state-society complexes organize for, prosecute and experience warfare) and the *historical structure of war* (the constellation of deep structures, practices and discourses that define the very nature of 'war' in a given world order) – successively involving a deeper and wider framing of both the 'unit of analysis' and the forces that act to transform that unit of analysis over time. The extant literature fails to adopt such a perspective, as a result often conflating all three socio-military phenomena and reducing the history of organized violence to a one-dimensional and linear series of epochs punctuated by a number of revolutionary episodes. This simply compounds the conceptual and historiographical confusion referred to above.

Against this backdrop, the purpose of this chapter is to provide a conceptually guided review of the extant literature dealing with the transformation of war – one that is sensitive to the importance of distinguishing 'what at first sight seems fused' and to the utility of approaching the question of historical change in the nature of organized violence from several distinct temporal vantage points. The chapter begins with a discussion of the principal bodies of scholarly work dealing with revolutionary changes in the *warfighting paradigm*. It then proceeds to review the 'new-wars' literature, summarizing and critiquing the major scholarly efforts to shed light on changes in the *social mode of warfare*. The third section traces the emergence of the literature dealing with the contemporary transformation in the *historical structure of war*. The chapter concludes with some thoughts on future directions in the study of war and its transformation.

Transformation of the 'warfighting paradigm'

At the most obvious level, the transformation of war can be understood in terms of profound changes in the nature of *warfighting*, usually assuming the form of a transition from one 'warfighting paradigm' (or specific configuration of military technologies, doctrines and organizational forms) to another. As such, it does not simply involve changes in either the instruments or artefacts of warfare (e.g. tanks and long-range bombers), the enabling technologies (the internal combustion engine, armour, etcetera), or the supporting or ancillary technologies (such as command, control, communication and intelligence technologies). Nor is it limited to changes in the operational concepts or techniques that shape the way in which these technologies are employed. Nor, finally, is it concerned solely with organizational innovation. Rather, at this level transformation characteristically involves the evolution of a new warfighting vision that in turn guides the reconfiguration of most (if not all) dimensions of the prevailing warfighting paradigm. Such transformations are in part driven by technological change. Importantly though, they are also shaped and conditioned by human agents who, acting through and within military institutions, are attempting to bring about significant improvements in military effectiveness (i.e. the ability to prevail on the battlefield).

Broadly speaking, there are three closely related (but analytically distinct) literatures dealing with transformations at the level of the warfighting paradigm.

The military revolution

The first school of thought dealing with the transformation of the warfighting paradigm emerged in the decades after Michael Roberts (1956) first advanced the argument that during the century or so between the mid-sixteenth and mid-seventeenth centuries, Europe experienced what he called a 'military revolution'. According to Roberts this revolution entailed two sets of developments. At the most basic level, he maintained, this era was characterized by profound changes in the nature of European warfighting – principally in the form of greater use of gunpowder weapons, the introduction of tactical and operational innovations designed to maximize the effective use of these weapons, the advances in fortifications necessitated by these weapons, and the growing scale and expense of armies associated with these technical and organizational changes. At a somewhat deeper level, however, Roberts argued that these strictly military developments had effects that extended far beyond the battlefield. Specifically, he argued that as changes in the nature of military technology and technique in the early modern era forced European rulers to develop the administrative and financial means to raise, train, equip and sustain increasingly large and costly standing armies, the fragmented and decentralized structures of feudal governance increasingly gave way to the centralized rule of the early modern state. In turn, he argued, as states developed these administrative and financial capacities they became better able to create and apply military power. Taken together, Roberts concluded, these connected changes in the technological, operational and socio-political dimensions of warfare constituted a 'military revolution' – that is to say, a profound transformation in the way states and societies organize for and prosecute war.

In the decades following Roberts' initial articulation of the military revolution thesis, a rich literature emerged dealing with the causes, course and consequences of the transformation of war in late medieval/early modern Europe and the effects of this transformation on both European military institutions and the European state (Hall and DeVries, 1990). For most of this period, the animating debates tended to focus on questions related to the timing, causes, point of origin, and military and political consequences of the military revolution. In the aftermath of the 1990–1 Gulf War, however, the analytical focus and theoretical concerns of this literature changed dramatically as historians and others began to ask whether the key concepts that had been developed during this debate could be used to illuminate the so-called 'revolution in military affairs' (RMA) that seemed to be transforming the US military – and, indeed, the very nature of warfighting – in the late twentieth century. Over the course of the 1990s, this substantive reorientation had two important effects on the military revolution literature.

First, it led to efforts to situate the RMA within a longer sequence of radical discontinuities in the history of Western (military) history stretching all the way back to the early modern era. The result was the proliferation of historiographical frameworks seeking to identify all those episodes – such as the French Revolution and the Industrial Revolution – that had altered the capacity of states and societies to create and apply military power in the same way as the original military revolution. While judgements varied as to whether the late-twentieth-century RMA constituted a true military revolution (in the sense either of causing or resulting from the kind of profound transformations associated with the early modern military revolution), there was widespread agreement among military historians and others that Western military and political history at least since the early modern era had been punctuated by radical discontinuities in military practice and organization.

A second effect of the post-Gulf War focus on the RMA was a further elaboration of the conceptual apparatus derived from Roberts' original thesis. Most significantly, as military historians began to debate whether the RMA was a true military revolution, some felt compelled to begin drawing distinctions between 'great' or 'major' military revolutions on the one hand

and 'lesser' or 'minor' transformations on the other (Rogers, 2000). This distinction hinged largely on scale and susceptibility to human direction: true military revolutions were defined as massive and uncontrollable transformations of military institutions, states and societies; lesser revolutions (dubbed 'revolutions in military affairs') were held to be less all-embracing changes in military practice that were at least potentially susceptible to human management (Knox and Murray, 2001). While heuristically useful, the ultimate result of this conceptual elaboration was the convergence of the military revolution literature with the RMA literature. Perhaps not surprisingly, once this move had been made – and once military historians began to focus on lesser military revolutions and to use the language of the RMA to describe and explain these revolutions – the conceptual distinctiveness of the military revolution approach was effectively lost.

The revolution in military affairs

In the 1990s this conceptual evolution in the military revolution literature converged with a number of other developments – including the development in Soviet military science of the notion of a 'military-technical revolution', the successful use of high-technology weapons and supporting systems in the Gulf War and the accelerating pace of technological change – to trigger the emergence of a second distinctive literature dealing with the transformation of war: the *revolution in military affairs* (or RMA) literature. The central proposition of this body of work is that innovative applications of new technologies, coupled with dramatic changes in military technique and organizational concepts, have produced (or will soon produce) major changes in the nature of warfighting and that, in turn, these changes will radically alter the requirement for victory in war. While related to the military revolution literature, this body of work is distinguished from it in several ways. To begin with, while the military revolution literature traced the causal effects of technical/tactical change on the wider realms of state and society, the RMA literature focuses largely on the battlefield effects of technological and related operational and organizational changes. Second, while it is shot through with historical comparisons and analogies, the RMA literature tends to be focused on the present and near future. Finally, the RMA literature tends to be policy oriented – with few exceptions, it is concerned with generating policy prescriptions that will unlock the military potential inherent in the new technologies. This literature is also distinguished by the fact that it tends to have an American focus. Indeed, despite the fact that many countries have now taken up the question of how the RMA will affect them, the vast bulk of the literature is almost exclusively focused on the implications of the changing nature of military technology, operational technique and organizational structure for the United States and its armed forces.

The fundamental assumption underpinning all of the RMA literature is that, *inter alia*, technological innovation will transform the battlefield of the future. Beyond that fundamental agreement, however, there is little consensus regarding what, precisely, the impact of that technological innovation will be. At the risk of oversimplification, the various arguments in this regard can be organized into a number of distinctive groups or camps, each defined by its views regarding the extent to which the RMA is truly 'revolutionary', what the battlefield of the future will look like, and how best to adapt to the challenges and opportunities associated with the RMA.

The first group, which I will call the *radical transformationalist* school, believes that innovations in information and other technologies are likely to initiate a twofold revolution in military affairs. On the most obvious level, they argue, the information revolution and its knock-on effects are radically reshaping the battlefield – so much so that, in the not too distant future, it will be largely unrecognizable to today's soldiers. Simply stated, proponents of what is sometimes called 'cyberwar' argue that as the fundamental technical bases of warfare are transformed, 'aircraft carriers, tanks, fighters and bombers will cease to have a primary role in the postmodern theater of war' (Stix, 1995: 94), and that the battlefield of the twenty-first century will be dominated, not by massed troops and armour, but by:

> networks of intelligent mines and unpiloted drones that can perform reconnaissance and launch or plant weapons. Highly dispersed special forces may scout for targets and evaluate battle damage. Remotely fired missiles may become the main instruments for destroying enemy targets (Stix 1995: 92).

For the moment, of course, such scenarios remain the stuff of science fiction and futuristic fantasy; warfare today continues to be dominated by largely by 'baroque' versions of the military technologies that achieved pre-eminence during the Second World War (Kaldor, 1981). But the proponents of cyberwar argue that the constant, continuing press of technological innovation – coupled with the associated doctrinal and organizational innovations that have been taking place at an accelerating pace since the Gulf War – is increasingly transforming the battlefield. Projecting into the foreseeable future, the cyberwarriors detect signs that the 'traditional' force-on-force engagement decided by superior capabilities in the domains of firepower, protection and ability to concentrate force at the decisive point is becoming something of an anachronism. In its place, they see evolving a warfighting paradigm dominated by dispersed forces and 'brilliant' autonomous weapons connected via an information and sensor 'mesh' that will enable the timely application of decisive lethality throughout the length and breadth of the theatre of operations.

On a somewhat deeper level, proponents of this school maintain, radical innovations in information technologies herald changes in organized violence that extend far beyond the remaking of the battlefield. According to this perspective, the RMA involves more than simply remaking the battlefield by transforming the nature of force-on-force engagements or re-writing the principles of war. It also (potentially at least) involves the creation of a new medium of conflict – the 'infosphere' or 'cybersphere' – in which future protagonists will vie for dominance and victory as they currently do on land, sea and in the air. Arquilla and Ronfeldt (1997) call conflict in this medium 'netwar', and define it as 'information-related conflict at a grand level between nations and societies'.

The second RMA camp accepts that technological innovation is producing significant increases in military capability, but concludes that these increases are unlikely to result in a fundamental transformation of the battlefield – at least for the foreseeable future. Somewhat more specifically, *cautious transformationalists* such as Michael O'Hanlon (2000) argue that the main effect of technological innovation has been to enhance the combat capabilities of *existing* weapons platforms by connecting them to 'systems of systems' that will make the battlefield more 'transparent', provide 'dominant battlespace knowledge', allow for much quicker decision making, enhance the lethality of the weapons carried on these platforms, extend the global reach of military forces, and otherwise improve the ability of existing platforms to prevail in their respective environments. They do not see these innovations as making the platforms that have dominated the battlefield for the past 50 years or so obsolete. Nor do they see technological innovation as fundamentally transforming the nature of combat operations by rendering traditional force-on-force engagements obsolete. Rather, while accepting that new technologies will continue to have effects on both the conduct and outcome of military operations, and while advocating the adoption of new technologies and techniques in order to enhance the warfighting ability of their respective armed forces, the cautious transformationalists view these effects as improvements within well-established trajectories. Consequently, advocates of cautious transformation do not favour ambitious restructuring schemes intended to reconfigure these forces around some radically new warfighting paradigm. Instead, they advocate continuous and sustained modernization of the still-dominant technologies, operational concepts and force structures that first emerged out of the experience of the two world wars.

The third major school of RMA thought, which I label the *concerned transformationalist* school, is defined by a principled worry that the RMA may prove to be a two-edged sword. This anxiety is rooted in three sets of concerns (Krepinevich, 1996; Bunker, 1998). The first is that the preferred futures of both the radical and cautious transformationalists necessarily involve increased information 'dependence' and a new set of associated vulnerabilities. The fear here is that as Western militaries become more reliant on digital information infrastructures, potential adversaries may attempt to disrupt those infrastructures, at either the theatre, national or global levels. The second is that as RMA technologies proliferate they may prove just as devastating to Western military forces as to others. For the foreseeable future, Western (and especially US) forces are likely to have a near monopoly on the most effective RMA systems. But what happens when other actors acquire these technologies? For the concerned transformationalists, the fear is that 'these technologies could make it much harder for the United States to reach foreign ports safely, keep those ports as well as airfields and other infrastructure safe from enemy attack, and protect troops on the battlefield' (O'Hanlon, 2000: 16). Finally, the concerned transformationalists worry that Western dominance on the battlefield might encourage potential adversaries to pursue asymmetric strategies – including the use of WMDs either in theatre or against the US homeland – in order to deter, compel or otherwise influence US policy (McInnes, 2002: 139).

Transformation

Beginning in the early 2000s, the debates that had characterized the RMA discourse throughout the 1990s began to give way to a somewhat less abstract discussion of the ways in which armed forces might actually adapt to the real-world challenges and opportunities generated by the 'information revolution' and related technological changes. Reflecting the 'victory' of the cautious transformationalists – as well as practical experience with 'operations other than war' in the Balkans, Africa and elsewhere – the parameters of this new set of debates can be summarized as follows: technological, social and political changes are re-making the early twenty-first century 'battlespace'; purposeful efforts need to be made within defence establishments to understand and adapt to these changes; and, profound technological, organizational and doctrinal adaptation is absolutely essential if conventional armed forces are to retain their relevance and strategic utility as the new century progresses. While recent monographs by Max Boot (2006), Tim Benbow (2004) and David Lonsdale (2004) clearly indicate that the effort to conceptualize and historicize the RMA continues, military professionals and defence intellectuals have become less concerned with conceptualizing the RMA and more concerned with correctly specifying and implementing the practical and programmatic changes need to exploit it.

Perhaps not surprisingly, prior to the Iraq War, the transformation discourse tended to revolve around the question of how to adapt to *high-intensity conflict* (HIC). Drawing heavily (if selectively) on the experience of the 1990–1 Gulf War, inspired by the newly crystallized 'common sense' regarding the RMA, and informed by a post-Vietnam War institutional emphasis on fighting *symmetrical* adversaries, the pre-Iraq transformation discourse focused primarily on the question of how best to realize radical improvements in high-technology combat against conventional state-based armed forces. With the outbreak of the insurgency in Iraq, however, the tone and tenor of the debates about transformation began to change. Echoing arguments first raised (but largely unheeded) in the 1990s by analysts such as Martin van Creveld (1991b), critics of HIC-focused transformation began to argue that such an approach was dangerously misguided in that it ignored or downplayed the seismic changes in the strategic environment that had occurred in the latter part of the twentieth century. Frederick Kagan (2006), for example, argued that in the 1990s and early 2000s Pentagon planners lost their way as they struggled to develop a new warfighting paradigm that would enhance the United States' already large comparative advantage in conventional force-on-force combat. Rather than recognizing that changes in the global strategic environment were generating a variety of new *asymmetrical* threats to US interests and values – and that these diverse threats required a real full-spectrum force capable of advancing US political goals in an increasingly complex international environment – Pentagon planners developed exotic theories of future war that reflected their own cultural preferences and desires for more traditional forms of conflict. What is needed now, the critics suggest, is a transformation effort that is grounded in the realities confronting the United States (and the West more broadly) today – specifically, a need to fight a global insurgency that is most clearly manifest in Iraq and Afghanistan, but that has the potential to erupt in many other places as well. Today, the key debates in the policy literature are about the ways in which the transformation effort can be made more relevant to revolutionary changes in what Kaldor called the 'social mode of warfare' and what I have labelled the 'historical structure of war'.

Transformation in the 'social mode of warfare'

Approaching the study of revolutionary military transformation from the perspective of the warfighting paradigm is heuristically useful in that brings into focus both the revolutionary changes in the technological, operational and organizational bases of warfighting and the nature of the transformative forces driving these changes. But while such a perspective powerfully illuminates the transition from one warfighting paradigm to another, it cannot and does not capture all of the significant changes currently taking place in the realm of organized political violence. In particular, a focus on changes in the warfighting paradigm tends to obscure or occlude a number of important transformations that are taking place beyond the battlefield – changes that may be related to the evolution of a new warfighting paradigm, but that are both broader and deeper in nature.

Approaching the history of warfare from a slightly different vantage point, however, brings into focus a picture of revolutionary military transformation that at least partly address these shortcomings. Beyond the level of the warfighting paradigm, revolutionary change appears as deep changes in what might be called the 'social mode of warfare' – that is, the way in which a state-society complex organizes for and conducts war. Viewed in this way, the current episode of revolutionary military transformation appears less as a series of (radical) changes in the dominant weapons, tactics and organizational structures of *warfighting* and more as a profound shift in the complex of social, economic and deep technological forces that shape the way in which a society prepares for, prosecutes and experiences war. Somewhat more specifically, it can be characterized as a transition from the conjuncture of what Martin Shaw (1991) has labelled 'industrialized total warfare' to a conjuncture variously labelled 'information warfare', 'spectator-sport war' (McInnes, 2002), 'post-heroic warfare' (Luttwak, 1995), 'virtuous war' (Der Derian, 2001), and even (though, I would argue, erroneously), 'postmodern warfare' (Gray, 1997).

To present the key organizing questions and analytical concepts of this literature, I can offer two examples of the kind of work that is being done in this vein. The first is Christopher Coker's book *Humane Warfare* (2001). The basic premise of this book is that, for the West at least, warfare today has evolved from the 'exterminism' and 'inhumanity' of the twentieth century to the 'humanism' of the early twenty-first. In somewhat more specific terms, Coker begins the book by arguing that contemporary Western societies not only justify the wars they fight in humanitarian terms, but prosecute (or at least *attempt* to prosecute) those wars in a 'humane' fashion. Adopting a primarily culturalist analytical approach, Coker then goes on to trace the roots of this transformation, highlighting the causal effects of socio-cultural changes such as 'the humanization of modernity', the end of Hegel's 'virtuous state', the evolution of 'risk society', the rise of individualism and 'post-materialism', the 'feminization' of Western society, the 'end of metaphysics' as a justification or legitimation for war, and the demise of classical 'militarism' and the emergence of 'post-military society'. Coker concludes that the result of these essentially cultural trends has been evolution of 'humane warfare' – that is, warfare in which 'humanism' (the belief that the individual occupies the centre of the moral and political imagination), 'humanity' (the desire to mitigate the cruelty of war) and 'humanitarianism' (the desire to alleviate human suffering) define both the ends and modalities of organized political violence. Although Coker does not use the term, the shift from 'inhumane' to 'humane' warfare is clearly an instance of the transformation of war – one focused primarily on radical changes in the way in which Western society *prosecutes* wars.

Equally emblematic of this literature, although adopting a radically different optic, is Colin McInnes's *Spectator-Sport War* (2002). In this book, which focuses less on the cultural construction of warfare than on the way in which the West *prosecutes* and *experiences* war, two related arguments are developed. The first is that, in the West, the era of 'total war' has been superseded by the era of 'spectator-sport war'. McInnes defines total war as organized conflict characterized a dynamic tendency toward escalation in violence and by the tendency toward universal social participation in war. Western states used to fight these types of wars against one another. Over the past several decades, however, major war between Western states has become an anachronism: to the extent that the West continues to fight wars at all, they tend to be limited events fought on geographically distant battlefields by relatively few professional soldiers. This form of warfare – labelled 'spectator-sport war' by McInnes (2002: 144) – is also characterized by the targeting of the enemy regime rather than society, the requirement to minimize collateral damage, the need to minimize the risk to Western society and military forces, and the belief that the enemy's forces do not need to be engaged in bloody battles. In this form of organized violence, most Western citizens are not directly involved in conflict (they neither fight nor experience war directly); rather, they have been transformed from participants to 'spectators', supporting their side in war as they might their preferred team in a sporting event. The second major argument developed in this volume is that 'airpower is the West's current preferred weapon of war … [and] the Revolution in Military Affairs represents the future'. McInnes (2002: 150–151) argues that the information-based weapons and ancillary systems associated with the RMA in particular are ideally suited to this new form of war; for, in principle if not yet in practice, they provide the means to apply force precisely at long distances with little or no risk to friendly forces or innocent civilians. He concludes the volume with a discussion of the implications of spectator-sport war, suggesting that, to the extent that the 'outcome is never really in doubt, and the heroes and villains are readily identifiable', war for the West has become a 'spectacle' or morality play rather than a competitive 'sport'. Viewed in this way, McInnes (2002: 151) concludes, war is now experienced in the West as a theatrical production which provides a site and occasion for the performative constitution of 'the West' around liberal and humanitarian values.

Transformation in the 'historical structure of war'

Viewed from the temporal perspective of epochal time, the unit of analysis that comes into focus when studying organized political violence is the 'historical structure of war'. By 'historical structure' I mean those deeply embedded configurations of social relations, ideas and institutions that both constitute actors and condition their (inter)actions (Cox, 1981: 97–101). By 'war' I mean organized and purposive violence that is applied to achieve political ends (Bull, [1977] 1995: 178–180). Thus, the historical structure of war can be conceptualized as *the prevailing configuration of social relations, ideas and institutions that define the basic nature of 'war' in any given world order.* Viewed from a slightly different perspective, such structures can thus be understood to be those elements of 'world order' that pertain directly to the role of organized violence in social and political life. They are 'historical' because they are artefacts of complex social processes and therefore vary substantially across time and space; they are 'structures' because they constitute the deep and relatively persistent ontological frameworks that generate, shape and constrain social life.

Perhaps the most ambitious effort to conceptualize epochal change in the structure of war is Coker's *Waging War Without Warriors* (2002). In this work, Coker adopts a very long-term perspective that divides the history of the human species into 'prehuman', 'human' and 'posthuman' eras. The central argument of the book is that as Western society begins a transition from the human era to the posthuman era, its associated 'way of warfare' is also beginning to become less 'humanistic' and more 'posthuman'. In somewhat more concrete terms, Coker's (2002: 165–72) argument can be summed up as follows. During the early human era, the Greek and Roman forebears of Western civilization developed a culture that placed human beings at the centre of the moral and political imagination and that gave organized violence both an *instrumental* dimension (i.e. made it an instrument of human agency) and an *existential* dimension (i.e. made it an intersubjective context within which one could express one's humanity, 'know one's self' and/or forge a collective identity). At the deepest level, Coker argues, this essentially humanistic culture and its associated way of war persisted effectively unchanged for many centuries (although, of course, its particular cultural and material expression evolved dramatically over time as a result of changing conceptions of 'humanism', developments like the Enlightenment and the Industrial Revolution, and a variety of historically contingent factors).

According to Coker, however, in recent times Western society has entered a decidedly 'posthuman era' increasingly characterized by the technological enhancement, genetic redesign and pharmacological alteration of humans. Given that each era in Coker's historiographical framework has its own associated cultural construction of organized violence, this transition to the posthuman era is having the predictable effect of transforming war. Even in the current 'transhuman' era – i.e. the era straddling the human/posthuman divide – the *existential* dimension of war has all but disappeared. As Coker notes (2002: 59), the 'Western way of warfare has become almost purely instrumental' and, for Westerners at least, war is no longer a means of forging or expressing an aspect of our humanity; rather, it has come to be considered immoral, criminal or (at best) a necessary evil.

Coker argues, however, that this is merely a transitional phase. The West is now entering the posthuman era proper, which Coker (2002: 172) defines as one 'in which human beings will inhabit the same world as machines and in which the two will evolve together coequally and symbiotically'. Looking forward cautiously to the future, Coker speculates that as the transhuman era gives way to the posthuman era, the West will undergo the next great transformation of war: the transition to *posthuman* war. In the final chapter, Coker contemplates the ontology of this new form of war, suggesting that it will be defined by the final demise of the warrior as a human type, the ultimate 'dehumanization of war', and the decisive end of war as an expression of humanity (though not necessarily as an instrument of posthuman agents). Posthuman wars, he argues, will be fought by genetically reprogrammed soldiers, intelligent/brilliant machines and cyborgs. In this sense, according to Coker at least, we are on the cusp of definitively transcending the humanism of organized violence that has defined the Western understanding and practice of war since the time of ancient Greece.

A quite different take on epochal change in the structure of war is provided by the new-wars literature. As Kaldor (1999) articulates it, the core proposition of this school is that the last few decades have seen the outbreak of 'new wars' – that is, violent conflicts that differ in important ways from the 'old wars' characteristic of the modern era. In order to highlight the conceptual distinctions between these two forms of organized violence, Kaldor proceeds through a series of oppositions in which she articulates key differences between the two forms of war in terms of the following criteria: the *purposes*, *modalities* and *economic sinews* of war.

She begins with the purposes of war, arguing that the ends or purposes of new wars are qualitatively different from those of old wars. During the modern era, the wellspring of violent political conflict was *raison d'état* and the national interest. As a result, wars tended to be geopolitical in nature – that is, they were ultimately caused by the desire to maintain the equilibrium of the modern state-system and/or to defend or improve one's position with in it. As Kaldor (1999: 6) argues, however, new or postmodern wars are more likely to be about 'identity politics', which she defines as the pursuit of power 'on the basis of a particular identity – be it national, clan, religious or linguistic'. Such wars may take place among the 'decaying pillars of the Westphalian temple', but they do not reflect the social logic of the modern state-system. Rather, she argues, such wars typically erupt as a result of efforts on the part of particularist identity formations to physically displace those who are not part of their exclusive (imagined) community. They may also erupt as a result of efforts by religiously inspired terrorist organizations to conduct a 'holy war' against state and non-state actors that are perceived to be corrupt, immoral and even 'satanic'. To a large extent, this accounts for the egregious and seemingly gratuitous incidents of atrocity that have characterized so many violent conflicts in recent years.

Kaldor then proceeds to draw a stark contrast between the locus of organized violence during the modern and postmodern eras, arguing that while old wars were characterized by statist forms of control of organized violence, as we cross the epochal threshold from modernity to postmodernity we are witnessing a 'decentring' or dispersal of control over organized violence to multiple and heteronomous non-state sites. Asking a related question – by whom are wars fought? – she sharpens the distinction between old and new wars even more. Modern wars, she argues, were fought primarily between formally organized, hierarchically structured and functionally specialized *public* institutions of organized violence – that is, institutions acting on behalf of the state. Postmodern wars, contradistinctly, are fought by a disparate range of types of fighting forces, many of which are informal and *private* (i.e. not state-based) in nature. These forces include guerrilla armies, police units, criminal gangs, foreign mercenaries, kin- or clan-based irregular forces, 'paramilitary' groups (informally organized bands raised by local warlords), semi-organized militias and local defence units, international 'peacekeepers', national armies, and increasingly globalized and de-territorialized terrorist networks.

Finally, Kaldor argues that the political economy of war-making is also being transformed, highlighting perhaps most vividly the effect of globalization on war. At the height of the modern era, she argues, military forces were supported by state-based production and finance systems organized to the greatest extent possible on an autarkic, national basis. The decidedly postmodern institutions of violence associated with new wars, however, draw material sustenance not from such formal and centralized *national* economies and defence industries, but rather from *private* production and finance networks organized either locally or on a global scale. She argues, for example, that the sources of financial support for these institutions can include plunder, pillage, hostage taking, extortion (sometime referred to as the collection of 'war taxes'), drug trafficking, arms trafficking, money laundering, remittances and other contributions from the relevant diasporic community, foreign assistance and humanitarian aid (Kaldor, 1999: 104). In a related vein, she argues that weapons – especially light weapons, which are the principal means of violence in postmodern war – are not typically produced by the combatants themselves but are acquired through globalized, private networks of lawful and illicit arms brokers. All of this suggests to Kaldor that a new mode of war-related surplus appropriation is evolving as we cross the threshold from old wars to new wars – one in which the new institutions of organized violence organically fuse economic exploitation and military-political coercion at the molecular level of the local community, while simultaneously tapping into decidedly postmodern global financial and commodity flows.

Building on Kaldor's insights, a number of scholars have extended the new-wars thesis in ways that trace the connections between world order transformation, the changing nature of political violence beyond the West, and the evolution of a new Western way of war. Mark Duffield (2001), for example, has argued that new wars – which he calls 'network wars' – are in fact structurally induced clashes between a globalizing 'liberal strategic complex' at the core of the contemporary world order and the 'non-liberal political complexes' created by globalization that have crystallized at the margins of that order. Similarly, Martin Shaw (2000) has argued that the remaking of world order around an emerging 'global-Western state-conglomerate' has transformed the role and character of organized violence, giving rise to what he calls 'degenerate war' in the periphery and 'global policing' or 'cosmopolitan law enforcement' actions emanating from the West. Finally, Herfried Münkler (2002) traces the rise of a new form of war characterized by *de-statization, asymmetry* and *autonomization*. What connects Kaldor, Duffield, Shaw, Münkler and other scholars (for example, Adamson, 2005; Bauman, 2001) writing in this vein is their commitment to a holistic or embedded account of the new wars – that is, an account that explains changing forms of organized violence in relationship to broader and deeper changes at the level of world order. While they may differ with respect to the particulars, all of the authors writing in this tradition see 'globalization' as a process that is transforming both what Kaldor calls the 'social mode of warfare' and what I have called the 'historical structure of war'. They are also bound together by a common understanding that one of the key causal mechanisms linking globalization to the emergence of new wars is the changing architecture of world order. Indeed, it is not overstating the case to argue that one of the hallmarks of this school of thought is the shared belief that as globalization is transforming the cultural, economic and political matrix of global society, it is also remaking what Shaw (2000) calls the social 'relations of violence'.

Conclusion

To sum up: recent years have seen the rather rapid development of literatures dealing with the transformation of war. On the level of the *warfighting paradigm*, there is now an extensive body of research both describing and prescribing changes in the way the world's dominant militaries conduct combat operations on the battlefield. On a somewhat deeper level, what I have called the *social mode of warfare* literature traces significant changes in the way state-society complexes organize for, prosecute and experience warfare. Finally, there is now a still somewhat underdeveloped literature on the level of what I have called the *historical structure of war* – that is, on the level of the constellation of deep structures, practices and discourses that define the very nature of 'war' and distinguish it from other forms of politics and violence.

Ultimately, though, much conceptual work remains to be done, especially with respect to the modern-to-postmodern transition and the associated transformation in the 'historical structure of war'. While the new-wars literature constitutes an important breakthrough for the study of organized political violence, thus far its potential for generating insights into the forms of organized violence that are organic to the evolving postmodern world order has not been fully realized. Put simply, despite its promise, this literature has thus far failed to come to grips in a sustained and systematic way with the relationship between war and world order transformation.

Two limitations in particular have prevented this sort of engagement. First, the new-wars literature continues to conflate changes in the nature of organized political violence on all three temporal planes. Kaldor's otherwise path-breaking work, for example, defines new wars in terms of changes in the nature of both the social mode of warfare (when she talks about the new political economy of warfare) and the historical structure of war (when she links the emergence of new wars to globalization). Second, this literature is limited in that it fails adequately to conceptualize and historicize the fundamental structure of war at the level of world order. Ideally, the study of the historical structure of war would begin with a rigorous analysis of the evolving nature of any given world order and then proceed to specify the structures and dynamics of organized political violence organic to that world order. In other words, it would involve specifying those elements of world order that pertain directly to organized political violence. The new-wars literature hints at this possibility, but ultimately fails to provide such an analysis.

Taken together, these conceptual weaknesses render the new-wars literature incapable of adequately illuminating the transformation of political violence at the level of world order. In order to address these shortcomings, what is needed now is a historically sensitive and theoretically guided account that is able to isolate what I have called the 'historical structure of war' – that is, *the prevailing constellation of deeply embedded discourses, structures and practices that define the basic nature of 'war' within a given world order* – and then historicize it. Such an account should therefore provide us first with a 'property theory' of war as a fundamental element of world order.

'Property theories', according to Alexander Wendt (1999: 86), 'explain how things or processes are put together so as to have certain features. In other words, they are *ontological constructs* that conceptually specify the nature of a social relationship, form or practice. Such theories often assume the form of *models* or *ideal-types* that provide a simplified representation of a complex reality and thus a way of grasping the variety of actual forms and tendencies in various historical settings. Using such heuristic devices to fix social patterns and dynamics lends analytical structure to a description, providing the conceptual benchmarks around which the analyst can subsequently develop meaningful interpretations of historical patterns, engage in cross-case comparison, and identify potentially significant causal regularities. Property theories are thus more than just descriptions – they are explanatory abstractions that enable us to answer constitutive (or 'explanation-what') questions regarding how social kinds are structured. While an important element of explanation in their own right, such theories are also necessary precursors to *causal* explanations; for, as Wendt (1999: 87) aptly puts it, 'without good descriptions of how things are put together any [transition theories] we propose will probably be wrong'.

With respect to what I have been calling the 'historical structure of war', such a property theory would minimally have to specify: (a) the historical configurations of violently conflictual social forces within a given world order (i.e. the *constitutive antagonisms of world order*); (b) the constituent units of world order with a significant war-making capacity as well as the system-level social structure within which these units are embedded (i.e. the *political architecture of organized violence*); and (c) the deeply embedded socially constructed beliefs that specify the nature (moral) purpose and meaning of organized violence (i.e. the *cultural discourse of 'war'*).

Finally, any systematic analysis of organized political violence on the historical structure of war should also furnish us with a 'transition theory' capable of illuminating not only the properties of war in any given era, but the dynamics of historical transformation. Typically, 'transition theories' attempt to explain changes from one state to another by specifying 'the causal mechanisms that link an explanatory variable with an outcome variable' (Wendt, 1999: 86). Such theories thus answer 'explanation-why' questions (as opposed to 'explanation-what' questions) regarding the ways in which social kinds are transformed over time. Ideally, a transition theory of war as a historical structure would illuminate the constitutive mechanisms through which revolutionary shifts in world order produce changes in the nature of war. Somewhat more specifically, it would specify the ways in which the broader dynamics of world order transformation generate new *constitutive antagonisms* of world order (i.e. new configurations of violently antagonistic social forces), new *politico-institutional matrices* through which these antagonisms are expressed, and *new cultural discourses* that legitimate, warrant or authorize certain kinds of organized violence while anathematizing others. Unless and until such theories begin to emerge, the literature is fated to remain in its current state of underdevelopment.

Further reading

Arquilla, J. and Ronfeldt, D. (1997) *In Athena's Camp*, Santa Monica: RAND Corporation.

Benbow, T. (2004) *The Magic Bullet? Understanding the Revolution in Military Affairs*, London: Brassey's.

Boot, M. (2006) *War Made New: Technology, Warfare and the Course of History*, New York: Gotham Books.

Coker, C. (2001) *Humane Warfare*, Boulder: Lynne Rienner.

Coker, C. (2002) *Waging War Without Warriors*, Boulder: Lynne Rienner.

Hall, B.S. and Devries, K. (1990) 'Essay Review – The "Military Revolution" Revisited', *Technology and Culture*, 31, 3: 500–7.

Kaldor, M. (1981) *Baroque Arsenal*, New York: Hill and Wang.

Kaldor, M. (1999) *New and Old Wars: Organized Violence in a Global Era*, Cambridge: Polity.

Knox, M. and Murray, W. (2001) *The Dynamics of Military Revolution, 1300–2050*, Cambridge: Cambridge University Press.

Latham, A. (2002) 'Warfare Transformed: A Braudelian Perspective on the

Revolution in Military Affairs', *European Journal of International Relations*, 8, 1: 247–60.

Luttwak, E.N. (1995) 'Toward Post-Heroic War', *Foreign Affairs*, 7, 3: 109–22.

McInnes, C. (2002) *Spectator-Sport War*, Boulder: Lynne Rienner.

O'Hanlon, M. (2000) *Technological Change and the Future of Warfare*, Washington: Brookings Institution Press.

Shaw, M. (1991) *Post-Military Society*, Philadelphia: Temple University Press.

Stix, G. (1995). 'Fighting Future Wars', *Scientific American*, 273, 6: 92–8.

Toffler, A. and Toffler, H. (1993) *War and Anti-War: Survival at the Dawn of the Twenty-First Century*, New York: Diane Publishing.

van Creveld, M. (1991) *The Transformation of War*, New York: Free Press.

Chapter 8

Nuclear Strategy

Andy Butfoy

Introduction

The extreme destructiveness of nuclear explosives means many people believe them to be unusable, while others see them as the ultimate weapon. Whichever way you look at them, they place special demands on strategic thinking.

Nuclear strategy is the use of these weapons to achieve international political objectives. This use can take the form of threats and promises intended to shape the diplomatic landscape, as well as military operations. The threats and promises can be implicit or explicit, and are often based on military plans. This chapter asks how the nuclear-armed states – at the time of writing, China, France, India, Israel, North Korea, Pakistan, Russia, the United Kingdom and the United States – see their weapons in these terms. Another focus is the concepts employed by analysts to illuminate the link between the weapons and national security goals. Nuclear terrorism is not examined here as currently there is no evidence of non-state actors having these weapons; however, the subject has been explored elsewhere within strategic studies (Ferguson and Potter, 2004; Frost, 2005).

A study like this faces constraints. Shortage of space, for example, prevents detailed examination of each country. In any case, lack of reliable public information means scholars are limited in what can be said about official strategies. This is why many studies veer toward speculative scenario building and generalization. Furthermore, because nuclear weapons have not been used militarily since 1945, strategic thinking here is more hypothetical than in the realm of conventional warfare. Indeed, much of the literature produced on the subject since 1945 might turn out to be irrelevant if the world ever crossed the line into an era of nuclear warfighting. Although this sounds discomforting to strategic theorists, in an emergency decision makers might well feel compelled to make things up as they went along.

The chapter is divided into two parts. The first deals with US strategy. It outlines the key turning points in the evolution of US thinking from the cold war to the 'global war on terror' and confrontation with the 'axis of evil'. Part two compares the nuclear postures of the other states with that of the United States.

US nuclear strategy

There are four reasons for using the United States as a reference point here. First, it is seen as a trendsetter in strategic thinking, and US concepts are often used to frame analyses of strategic issues affecting other states. Second, more information is available on US nuclear policy than on that of any other state. Third, US nuclear weapons have a world order function. Their role is said to stretch beyond deterrence of nuclear attack on the United States to providing leverage for US power projection, underpinning non-proliferation and reinforcing global peace. Fourth, and this is the flip side to the previous point, US strategy is controversial. This controversy sharpens debate over the strategic concepts surrounding nuclear weapons.

The cold war

History is important to this story. Current US military capabilities are largely a legacy of the cold war. Moreover, the cold war was a formative experience for many of today's policy makers, and many of the concepts framing today's thinking on nuclear strategy are inherited from that period.

The United States had a nuclear weapons monopoly from 1945 until the Soviet Union tested its first bomb in 1949. Washington used this monopoly to destroy Hiroshima and Nagasaki, ending the Second World War, and then deployed the weapons on the diplomatic stage to meet the challenges of the cold war. Because no responsible person wanted the cold war to turn into the Third World War, nuclear weapons were seen as at their most useful when used politically, not militarily. They would help shape the peacetime international landscape. US readiness for nuclear war would deter the Soviet Union from unacceptable behaviour, such as invading Western Europe. At the same time, the nuclear guarantee to its European allies, also termed the nuclear umbrella or extended deterrence, would add substance to Washington's leadership role.

Deterrence required getting inside the minds of potential aggressors in the Kremlin. It called for US planning and capabilities that would make any Soviet scheme for offensive war deeply unattractive to Moscow. Early US warplans envisaged the Soviet Union using its numerical superiority in ground forces to launch a conventional invasion of Western Europe. It was presumed this would push the Western allies back, probably to the English Channel. As this onslaught unfolded, the United States would respond by dropping as many nuclear bombs as it could to devastate the Soviet Union. By the mid-1950s when the US nuclear arsenal had grown to thousands of weapons, and was more explicitly linked to cold war diplomacy, this approach became known as 'massive retaliation'. The strategy allowed Washington to limit defence spending by reducing troop levels, whilst nonetheless increasing the fire-power of its armed forces. It called for the integration of nuclear weapons into the United States' general preparations for war, with conventional forces seen as a trip-wire to nuclear escalation. In theory any communist expansionism would be deterred by the threat of bombing intended to eliminate the Soviet Union and China as functioning states, killing hundreds of millions of their people.

In time massive retaliation was dropped because it was too blunt an instrument. Critics said that in a crisis over, say, Berlin or insurgency in Vietnam, the 'all or nothing' approach implied by massive retaliation would leave an American president either paralyzed or driven to absurd levels of violence. Furthermore, by the 1960s the Soviet Union's capacity to retaliate to US bombing was set to expand rapidly, making massive retaliation look increasingly suicidal. Analysts argued that the more suicidal a strategy looked, the less credible it would appear to an enemy, and the less credible the strategy, the less effective it would be as a deterrent.

Faced with a Soviet challenge a president might want to shift from the apocalyptic rhetoric of massive retaliation to a measured contemplation of different diplomatic and military options. This consideration led to the adoption of 'flexible response' in the 1960s, although it took decades to fine-tune the new strategy. US conventional forces were beefed-up and its allies were asked to provide more for their own conventional defence rather than simply rely on the US nuclear umbrella. In addition, a range of nuclear attack plans were added. Washington retained an option to use nuclear weapons first in the event of a conventional war, such as a Soviet invasion of Western Europe, but said 'first use' would not necessarily be a first resort and could be kept relatively small. It could be a warning shot telling Moscow to back off, or an attack on Soviet conventional forces in, say, East Germany; it was to be distinguished from a 'first strike', which was jargon for a large-scale attack to comprehensively disarm the enemy.

Plans were also devised for large nuclear attacks on the Soviet Union which spared Soviet cities. There were three rationales for this. First, plans for less than all-out war would theoretically make US nuclear forces more usable, and thus make the threat of their use more credible in a broader range of contingencies. Second, keeping Soviet cities standing, at least at the start of a war, would give Moscow an incentive to leave American cities alone. After all, US planning for limited strikes did not remove Washington's option of eventually escalating to obliterate the Soviet Union. Soviet cities were to be held hostage, to be kept alive only if Moscow accepted the rules of nuclear conflict as laid down by Washington. Third, attacks which kept the Soviet leadership in Moscow intact held out the possibility of negotiating an end to hostilities.

There was also a need to stalemate Moscow's search for its own nuclear options as it amassed greater strategic capability in the late 1970s. This is why many Americans who were sceptical about the military value of nuclear warplans nonetheless supported the refinement of them. They reasoned that the hard men in the Kremlin who were thinking about nuclear war had to be convinced the United States could beat them at their own game. Good US strategy would close off Soviet opportunities for nuclear adventurism at all levels of potential nuclear war, whether it be massive or limited. This variant of flexible response became known as the 'countervailing' strategy.

The idea of limited nuclear war got much critical attention. One reason was because planning for limited use of the weapons nonetheless kept open the risk of escalation to all-out war with the Soviet Union. This was considered both good and bad. It was good because maintaining the chance of all-out war would keep the potential costs to Moscow out of proportion to the likely gains of their contemplated misadventure, thereby reinforcing deterrence. It was bad because everyone realized that if this chance of total war turned into reality it would constitute an utter strategic, political and moral failure.

In addition, many considered the sort of limited options envisaged in flexible response nonsensical. They thought that during a war involving, say, scores of nuclear weapons, it would be impossible to maintain the type of command arrangements and level-headedness required to ensure escalation did not get out of control.

Yet others believed that as nuclear weapons might be used, analysts had a responsibility to think through what a nuclear war could look like – and how best to win it. One concept that emerged, which was integral to the notion of initially sparing Soviet cities, was 'intra-war deterrence'. This was the idea that the United States could, even after war had broken out, deter the Soviet Union from raising the intensity of violence or the scope of the fighting through 'escalation dominance'. This was to be achieved through US strategic superiority. Moscow would be so impressed by the United States' range of nuclear warfighting capabilities that it would never make sense for Moscow to escalate, because it could never find a level of nuclear war in which it held an advantage. In theory, US superiority would enable Washington to dictate the scope and intensity of a war. It would be this superiority that would, for instance, permit the United States to respond to a Soviet conventional invasion of West Germany with a limited first use of nuclear weapons, and then deter the Soviet Union from further upping the ante.

However, US hawks worried that Washington lacked the superiority this approach required (indeed, some claimed it was Moscow that was acquiring escalation dominance, which would pull the rug from under US strategy). They called for higher military spending, a more capable nuclear force and a missile defence system. On the other hand, the peace movement believed flexible response moved us closer to a superpower nuclear war fought in Europe. They reasoned that if the United States believed it could achieve superiority and limit a nuclear war to Europe, it would be more likely to go nuclear, with devastating consequences for the continent.

The mainstream view was in between the hawks and the peace movement. It tended toward the idea that there could be no such thing as meaningful nuclear superiority in the cold war context. Most Western and Soviet leaders accepted they were stuck in a condition of mutual assured destruction, or MAD. Soviet and US forces were so diversified and so large that each had numerous secure 'second-strike' forces. This meant each could guarantee retaliation and the destruction of the other, no matter what happened on the battlefield or during a missile duel. Acceptance of MAD was reflected in the signing of the 1972 Soviet–American Anti-Ballistic Missile Treaty (ABMT), an agreement not to deploy nationwide defences against missiles. Both sides accepted such defences would be costly, likely to fuel the arms race and, in any case, would not provide an escape from MAD (after all, even if defences were 99 per cent effective, that would still mean many cities could be wiped-out). Many in Moscow and Washington recognized the futility of looking for a military solution to nuclear vulnerability.

Thus nuclear weapons could not be treated as just another weapon. No political objective seemed worth the cost of using the things. Many saw this as perversely reassuring because MAD appeared to make nuclear weapons unusable. MAD, it seemed, meant nuclear strategy had become an oxymoron. This was a reasonable opinion, given that Moscow and Washington eventually amassed more than 50,000 nuclear warheads between them, many with more than ten times the power of the bomb that destroyed Hiroshima.

After the cold war

The end of the cold war led to a rethink. This was done in a perhaps overly conservative manner. US cold war strategy had apparently been vindicated, so why fix what was not broken? Furthermore, caution seemed warranted by uncertainty about the unfolding global landscape. Still, some adjustment was inevitable. Large Russian and US force reductions were announced, and Washington reached agreement with Moscow and Beijing to de-target nuclear missiles. The 1994 Nuclear Posture Review (NPR) pointed to a policy of 'leading and hedging': 'leading' referred to advancing arms control; 'hedging' referred to maintaining smaller but powerful nuclear forces as insurance in the event of the international scene taking a serious turn for the worse.

The end of the cold war took much of the edge off US nuclear strategy in terms of public debate and military career ambitions. Still, thousands of weapons remained and someone had to think about what might be done with them in an operational sense. In the 1990s three concerns shaped US nuclear planning. First, there was the requirement to retain a hedge in the event of ideological backsliding in Moscow or the emergence of radical Russian nationalism. Second, there was a need to maintain superiority over

Beijing, to facilitate the deterrence and perhaps defeat of Chinese power (e.g. in the event of things going badly over Taiwan). Third, there was the question of how US nuclear weapons could help in dealing with 'rogue states', an elastic category of countries which included the likes of Iraq, Iran, Libya, North Korea and Syria. Qualifications for membership of this category included having an anti-democratic government, supporting terrorism, attempting to acquire 'weapons of mass destruction' (WMD, said to include biological, chemical and nuclear weapons), and hostility towards the United States and/or Israel.

Dealing with rogue states required new thinking about nuclear weapons. During the cold war US nuclear forces were a type of equalizer, off-setting Soviet numerical superiority in conventional forces. After the cold war, it was Third World nuclear forces, and sometimes biological and chemical weapons, which were seen as equalizers to US conventional superiority. A type of role-reversal had occurred.

These Third World weapons posed a threat to regional stability and a constraint on US policy that was premised on the option of military intervention. If US nuclear weapons could deter cold war Soviet adventurism, why couldn't Third World WMD do the same to post-cold war US adventurism? In response to this changed setting, US nuclear strategy sought to deter rogue states from using WMD against the United States or its allies. This deterrence could even extend into wartime. Washington, in theory, would deter rogue states from using WMD even while US troops defeated them on the conventional battlefield. This was a new variant on the old concept of intra-war deterrence. It partly arose from a particular reading of events in the 1991 Gulf War, when Saddam Hussein accepted a conventional defeat rather than escalate to the use of chemical weapons because, supposedly, he feared US nuclear retaliation. (An alternative explanation is that Saddam feared use of chemical weapons would lead Washington to switch its war aims from evicting Iraq from Kuwait, to regime change in Baghdad; there is no evidence Washington was preparing for nuclear escalation.)

So, during the 1990s the United States retained the cold war idea that it should be prepared to be the first to use nuclear weapons. The most common first-use scenario was a threatened nuclear response to a rogue state's use of chemical or biological weapons, although the option of a nuclear counter to an enemy's conventional forces was also retained. Given the small number of nuclear targets in rogue states, it was sometimes difficult to maintain the old cold war distinction between first strike and first use; in practice the two could mean much the same thing.

Into the twenty-first century: the 'global war on terror' and confronting the 'axis of evil'

When George W. Bush became President in early 2001, the unilateralist element in US foreign policy was strengthened. The Anti-Ballistic Missile Treaty was dumped, making way for a national missile defence system, and the White House withdrew its signature from the Comprehensive Test Ban Treaty. The United States would keep all its strategic options open.

The 9/11 terror attacks later that year reinforced the trend. It led to speculation about how to stretch US nuclear strategy to deal with what was identified by President Bush as the 'axis of evil', which was short-hand for the idea of Iraq, Iran and North Korea teaming-up with terrorists. In practice, however, all the feasible options for dealing with these potential targets were conventional, not nuclear. In particular, it soon became apparent that groups like al-Qaeda offered nothing in the way of sensible nuclear targets.

In 2001 the administration conducted its own Nuclear Posture Review (Wirtz and Larsen, 2005; GlobalSecurity.org, 2002). It said Washington would not allow arms control to constrain US strategy, endorsed calls for a national missile defence system, retained the first-use option, and listed states of interest to US nuclear planners (Russia, China, Iraq, Iran, North Korea, Syria and Libya). In the uncertain post-9/11 environment, emphasis was also placed on 'adaptive planning' for nuclear strikes. This called for impressive weapons accuracy, an ability to target weapons rapidly, enhanced command and control arrangements, and weapons with a range of explosive yields able to 'hold at risk' a spectrum of targets, especially deeply buried bunkers and mobile missiles. It was suggested this would not only be useful operationally but could also help deter rogue states from even building WMD. The proposition was that hostile states would recognize it was both hopeless and dangerous to compete with Washington. Not only would they realize this was a no-contest, but they would also be sobered by concern that their WMD programme could be a lightening rod for an American attack.

Critics worried that the review reflected a militarization of policy. The missile defence system, for example, looked as if it was about enhancing the United States' nuclear warfighting options. In particular, it seemed to be aimed at China's nuclear deterrent, although this was denied, with the administration emphasizing the danger from rogue states, especially North Korea. Concern was also raised that the NPR 'lowered the nuclear threshold' – that is, made nuclear weapons more usable, and thus more likely to be used, in a wider range of circumstances. This overlapped with a worry that Washington was blurring the line between nuclear and conventional forces, that it wanted to normalize or 'conventionalize' nuclear weapons. However, the Pentagon pointed out that the NPR continued efforts began decades earlier to find conventional replacements for nuclear weapons in some scenarios. This could *raise* the nuclear threshold in some contingencies. Although the United States wanted to keep its nuclear options open, it certainly did not want to be dependent on them. This made sense given the unquantifiable but certainly enormous political costs of using nuclear weapons, and the US lead in 'smart' conventional weaponry.

Nevertheless, Bush's often negative stance on arms control, his invasion of Iraq in 2003, and his implicit threat to extend so-called pre-emptive war to Iran and North Korea provided a context for the NPR's implementation which alarmed some observers. With Iraq the President blurred the line between pre-emptive and preventive war. Preventive war is attacking a state that might strike some time in the future; it is based on speculation, and is illegal in international law. Pre-emption is about getting in the first blow when faced with an imminent attack; it is supposed to be based on solid intelligence and can be legal. Although the invasion of Iraq was presented as preemption, Baghdad had not the capability, plans or intention to attack the United States.

Critics worried that Washington was harming the broader fabric of world order (Walker, 2004). This criticism partly arose because of Washington's complex relationship to the status quo. For good or bad, the biggest military challenges to the international landscape apparently came from the United States, not from rogue states. Although US nuclear strategy had only a marginal place in all this, it implicitly helped underpin an approach to world order (including a refusal to rule out first use against Iran) that some found unsettling rather than reassuring.

Five themes seem set to persist in US nuclear strategy over the next decade. First, the primary objective will remain deterrence of nuclear attack on the United States. Second, Russia's military will continue to be a yardstick for US force sizing. War with Moscow seems most improbable but the abstract idea of it is useful in keeping the bar high on the United States' nuclear capacity, although this does raise the risk of fuelling an arms race (McDonough, 2006). Third, US forces will retain their world order functions. The nuclear umbrella will continue to influence the shape of Washington's nuclear policy. Some linkage between potential conventional military operations (e.g. concerning the defence of South Korea and Taiwan) and nuclear scenarios will continue. Fourth, this linkage means questions over first use will remain (Butfoy, 2002). Fifth, US leaders will continue to be exceedingly reluctant to use nuclear weapons. There are all sorts of good reasons for this reluctance, and no good ones for being the first, since 1945, to cross the line to nuclear war.

The other nuclear powers

Although US strategy provides a reference point for looking at other countries, Washington does not provide a universally applicable benchmark nor is it a model of how the others approach nuclear weapons. The other nuclear-armed states are not trying to copy Washington (Russia comes closest, but even it has a differently oriented posture). The reason for employing the United States as a reference point is not predictive but illustrative: how do the strategies of the other states converge with, or diverge from, that of the United States?

First, it must be emphasized that nuclear strategy only makes sense in terms of political context, and this is obviously different for each state. For example, since 1991 Moscow has had to deal with its lot as a collapsing superpower, followed by efforts to resurrect itself as a major Eurasian player facing numerous challenges. Its nuclear forces are important here not only in terms of deterrence but because Russia's capacity for inflicting destruction is one of the few areas in which it can meet Washington as a near equal at the negotiating table. Beijing apparently sees its nuclear weapons as a signifier of emerging superpower status, although it seems to be keeping its nuclear forces at relatively modest levels. If London and Paris had not acquired nuclear weapons during the cold war, it is an open question whether they would choose to get them now. Today their nuclear forces are seen as boosting possibly anachronistic pretensions to great power status and as insurance in the face of an uncertain future. Indian and Pakistani nuclear weapons serve as symbols of mutually antagonistic types of national identity, with India also considering a potential threat from China. And so on.

However, some generalizations can be made. All nuclear-armed states seem to think that nuclear weapons carry political weight. To take a stark example, North Korea's nuclear weapons are one of the few reasons why the international community takes any notice of the place. It seems North Korean nuclear policy is driven as much by a desire to be taken seriously on the diplomatic stage as by any way nuclear weapons might contribute to the North's military options. Another type of example is provided by Pakistan's nuclear forces. They have made the nation's future a more significant matter of concern to the world's great powers.

The idea of political weight crosses into the difficult to define realms of national pride and international status. Status issues are often said to have been important to many past nuclear decisions. For example, in developing its deterrent force, France made much of the idea that an independent nuclear strategy demonstrated tangible sovereignty and full nationhood. However, it is difficult to measure just how much additional status nuclear weapons confer. For instance, do nuclear-armed France, Pakistan or North Korea have more international prestige or diplomatic muscle than, say, non-nuclear-armed Germany, Brazil or Japan?

The more closely one looks at the individual nuclear-armed states, the more the differences present themselves. No two states have exactly the same approach to nuclear weapons. Their capabilities vary widely, and their strategies differ in terms of political signalling (the public message the weapons are intended to send), strategic conceptualization or doctrine (the ideas used to frame planning), and operational planning (the matching of weapons to targets).

Capabilities

Only Russia can match the United States' capacity to conduct large-scale nuclear operations. Indeed, Russia currently has more nuclear warheads than the United States, although the general state of the Russian strategic infrastructure is in doubt. In addition, Russian and US forces are both supported by missile defence systems which are patchy but nonetheless might prove useful in limited contingencies.

In terms of second-strike forces, nuclear-armed submarines are often assumed to be best suited for the role because they have a relatively good chance of staying out of harm's way early in a war. US capabilities here are clearly superior to all the others. France, Britain and Russia also have well-established, but less capable, nuclear submarine forces. There are rumours Israel has a limited capability to deploy nuclear missiles at sea. China and India have explored their options in this regard, but it is unclear how far they have got. For these, and other nuclear weapon states like Pakistan, policy for survivable second-strike forces must lie with mobility, dispersal, deception, underground basing and a good deal of hope.

In strategic theory this is disturbing, as the less confidence a state has in the survivability of its nuclear forces during a crisis the more pressure there may be to fire first. Imagine if both sides to a conflict (e.g. Pakistan and India) were in this situation. This could produce a 'use-them-or-lose-them' dilemma. In the worst case these pressures could tip one or both sides over the brink even if both preferred peace.

There is also uncertainty over how different states stack up in terms of their first-strike capabilities – that is, in their capacity to destroy an enemy's nuclear forces in either a pre-emptive or 'bolt-from-the-blue' attack. For example, whether Washington could wipe out China's or Russia's nuclear forces is a matter of debate (Lieber and Press, 2006). However, the United States' qualitative edge here is marked and seems to be increasing, fuelling speculation that Washington is expanding its nuclear superiority over all comers, including Moscow (McDonough, 2006), although how meaningful this idea is in practice must remain questionable.

Assessments of the first-strike capabilities of the various nuclear-armed states are heavily dependent on circumstances. The most obvious factor to consider in weighing this capability is who the target state is. For example, Britain's nuclear-armed submarines might offer a first-strike capability against some enemies, but not others. Assessments would have to consider the warhead-to-target ratio, weapons accuracy, quality of intelligence, command and control systems, and the effectiveness of the enemy's defences. It would take strategic analysts and weapons specialists with access to classified information to provide a solid assessment of, say, India's first-strike capability against Pakistan and vice versa.

Deterrence

Most analysts naturally view deterrence from a strategic perspective and with an eye to military factors. However, there is another viewpoint that can be called *a*strategic. This is the idea that deterrence does not rely on military plans or preparations to use nuclear weapons at all. It relies on the fact that nuclear explosives symbolize a potential to destroy the world as we know it, regardless of planning. In this sense deterrence can be seen as relatively easy, almost automatic, as long as a state has some nuclear bombs. The assumption is that no matter how impressive its strategy was, no aggressor would risk even a small chance of its own destruction. No aggressor could reasonably expect the benefits of war to outweigh the costs of nuclear weapons exploding on its cities. This idea overlaps with MAD-type thinking and is what analysts mean by 'existential deterrence'. Here the deterrent effect of nuclear weapons comes from general, even visceral, perceptions of their destructive nature, not from specific strategies for how they might be used.

Most non-experts, or the public, tend to view the idea of existential deterrence as convincing, while many experts have serious doubts. Experts tend to think deterrence should rest on finely tuned capabilities, well-crafted strategies, and the recognized resolve to implement them. They see this combination as reducing the chance of inadvertent war, enhancing the credibility of deterrence threats, and making any use of nuclear weapons more, rather than less, rational; moreover, experts are more inclined to see rationality in terms of advancing the cause of victory. To the public this way of looking at nuclear weapons can sound twisted and dangerous.

All the states discussed here see nuclear weapons as primarily a deterrent to nuclear attack. However, beyond this generalization, things get more complicated. Precisely how deterrence is translated into strategic concepts, force structure and contingency plans will vary between cases. Most states have a narrower notion of deterrence than Washington does. They mostly focus on simply preventing attacks on the national homeland. A narrower perspective is unsurprising as these states carry fewer (or no) alliance obligations and less world order baggage than Washington. These other states are also often assumed to view nuclear deterrence largely in terms of targeting cities, although not to the exclusion of other options. Counter-city targeting reflects the idea that deterrence is about threatening the most horrific disaster imaginable, and is encouraged by the fact that cities make easy nuclear targets. Compared with the others, Washington puts more of an emphasis on targeting military forces and command infrastructure, although it reserves the option to obliterate cities as an ultimate threat. Washington has more military-oriented targeting partly because, given its more capable forces, it can. Washington also sees a military-oriented approach as making its threats more credible and more rational in terms of advancing its interests. A focus on military targets is also easier to justify in terms of the laws of war, but this issue rarely receives much attention in strategic analysis and policy statements.

The role of nuclear weapons is not always limited to deterring nuclear strikes. It is commonly asserted that nuclear weapons also have a role in deterring biological and chemical attacks. In addition, as noted above, during the cold war the United States viewed its weapons as also deterring conventional invasions, especially of its allies in Europe. This view was shared by France and the UK and integrated into their nuclear policies. It is also the logic used by Pakistan, pointing to the role of its nuclear forces in deterring Indian conventional invasion.

For these reasons the United States, Britain, France and Pakistan have pointedly refused to rule out first use of nuclear weapons. In an echo of US thinking, Britain and France have also suggested their nuclear capability is useful in providing a shield for conventional expeditions to the Third World. The chief of staff of the French navy could have been speaking for his US and UK counterparts when, in 2004, he said: 'Without it [the nuclear deterrent], we would no longer be able to intervene in regions with nuclear weapons' (Yost, 2005: 126). In this sense, both France and Britain have scaled-down approximations to US approaches. Even France, traditionally very sceptical of the warfighting connotations of flexible response, accepts the possible usefulness of limited nuclear strikes. However, Paris publicly rejects the idea nuclear weapons have a specifically military role. Paris insists its nuclear forces exist to signal the national resolve required for deterrence. This includes a declared willingness to escalate quickly a dire situation to the highest level of destruction possible, rather than using the weapons to reverse events on the battlefield (Yost, 2005). The aim is to keep the idea of total destruction alive as a deterrent, not to invent ways of 'conventionalizing' nuclear forces.

The British appear to be somewhere between the French and Americans here, with a common theme among the three being ambiguity about exactly when they would order a nuclear strike. The most prominent former UK nuclear bureaucrat to write on the subject has written:

> There is no basis for speculation on what contingency planning may secretly be undertaken within the Ministry of Defence or operational headquarters. It is possible, given now the very general 'to-whom-it-may-concern' character of UK nuclear deterrence, that there is currently little or no such planning in specific terms. (Quinlan, 2004: 274)

Each state will have it own factors to consider when contemplating first use. Take, for instance, Pakistan. Just what type and scale of Indian attack are Pakistani nuclear weapons supposed to deter? At the top end of the scale, the Pakistan nuclear forces are to deter an Indian nuclear strike or an overwhelming conventional invasion aimed at destroying the country, but what else? They would not be used to deter or retaliate against a minor border incursion. A deterrent threat over a relatively minor matter would likely carry little credibility, would devalue the currency of the threat, and – if carried out – would be universally condemned as insane and wicked. So where is the threshold of Indian attack beyond which Pakistan would threaten to escalate, and then really escalate, a conflict into a nuclear show-down? We do not know, nor do we know how Pakistan plans to operational-ize such escalation in terms of matching weapons to targets. Similarly, we do not know much about just how the Indian military thinks about deterring – or perhaps pre-empting – Pakistani escalation. Specific geopolitical circum-stances, rather than ideas gleaned from Western strategic studies, are likely to frame this sort of thinking.

Over the years only Russia, China and India have made unambiguous statements ruling out first use. However, Russia has since changed its posi-tion in an effort to get more leverage from its nuclear capabilities, and India has given mixed signals on the matter. At the time of writing China stands alone in clearly renouncing first use, although whether and how this declaratory stance – or any other declaratory stance – translates into constraints on planning is unknown.

Compellence, 'crazy' states and 'known unknowns'

Historically, an emphasis on deterrence has overshadowed the notion of 'compellence'. Compellence (as will be discussed in Chapter 11) is the use of threats to coerce a target government to do something, such as give up a piece of territory or compromise its sovereignty. Deterrence threats (e.g. 'don't attack us or else') are generally seen as more believable, effective and legitimate than compellence threats in support of aggressive demands (e.g. 'give us that piece of land or else'). So far compellence has been a mostly theoretical issue. All nuclear-armed states claim their weapons serve the cause of peace and stability. Although many argue that recent proliferators like North Korea challenge the status quo, these states have not yet tried to use nuclear weapons to overturn the international system. It is worth remembering that when China acquired nuclear weapons in the 1960s, it was considered far more dangerous than recent rogue states, including 'crazy' North Korea. Yet China's nuclear stance has been basically defen-sive. (At the time of writing Tehran is said by some to be in a different cate-gory because of its hateful perspective on Israel and supposed indifference to cost–benefit calculations. Iran's more extreme leaders are said by some people to be the closest the world has to a government with 'suicide-bomber' characteristics. However, at the time of writing Iran has no nuclear weapons and the case does not belong in this chapter.)

Of course, it may be we have simply been lucky. For example, if Saddam Hussein had acquired nuclear arms by 1990, could he have intimidated the Kuwaitis to agree on annexation without war? Then, having occupied Kuwait, he could have tried to deter any counter-intervention to reverse events. Could Saddam perhaps have used compellence to make his gains and deterrence to keep them, persuading the international community to look the other way?

Each nuclear-armed state is likely to have drawn up target lists, and to have worked through some sort of scenario development. These lists and scenarios are likely to involve a mix of military and political targets. Just how sophisticated the planning is would vary from state to state. It will depend on the number and types of available weapons, and the nature of the security environment. There is also the political culture of the state to consider: is it essentially defensive, opportunistic, or aggressive? It is one thing to say a nuclear-armed country has the *capability* to do something; it is another to say they *plan* to do it, and another again to say they *will* do it.

Analysis of non-Western nuclear strategy involves considerable speculation (see, for instance, Lavoy et al, 2000), and this can be highly abstract and politicized. This was symbolized in a 2002 press briefing by then US Defense Secretary Donald Rumsfeld. He raised the possibility of Iraqi WMD being passed to terrorists. The implication was that Saddam had a strategy to build a nuclear bomb and allow Islamist terrorists to use it against an American city. Presumably it was believed Saddam's strategic aim would have been a mix of compellence – forcing the United States out of the Middle East – and vengeance for putative past wrongs done to Iraq and to Arabs more generally (or, to accept some US views on the nature of terrorism, the aim could have been to destroy US democracy). A journalist suggested there was no evidence of such a strategy; Rumsfeld's response was:

> Reports that say something hasn't happened are always interesting to me, because as we know, there are known knowns; there are things we know we know. We also know there are known unknowns; that is to say we know there are some things we do not know. But there are also unknown unknowns – the ones we don't know we don't know. (United States, Department of Defense, 2002)

Saddam was portrayed as being beyond rational deterrence and as willing to pay any price, indeed suffer any consequence, to inflict mass murder on Americans. By 2003 Washington was so adamant that deterrence would not work with Iraq that it insisted military action was imperative. One must hope a similar logic never pushes a state toward nuclear pre-emption.

Conclusion

As far as can be gleaned from the public record, all nuclear-armed states see their nuclear forces as having primarily a simple deterrent function. In addition, the United States gives its nuclear weapons a wider role. They provide a nuclear umbrella for allies, thereby reducing the pressure for proliferation among them, they act as a deterrent shield for conventional

US intervention against troublesome governments, and they threaten rogue state WMD programmes.

It is unsurprising some targets of US hostility have given serious thought to how best to enhance their own capacity for deterrence. This does not mean Washington's stance has been the determining factor behind the nuclear planning of, say, China or rogue states. But it would be remarkable if US behaviour, especially its reflections on intervention, pre-emption and first use, was not a factor in shaping their plans.

It is reasonable to assume these other countries view their nuclear weapons as quasi-equalizers. Ideally, from their perspective, the weapons make Washington rethink its first-use policy, neutralize the United States' conventional military superiority, and deter US conventional military intervention. It seems nearly everyone accepts that nuclear weapons tell enemies they cannot achieve a meaningful or cost-effective military victory.

So deterrence remains the core idea – so far. Nuclear weapons are seen as useful for dissuading enemies from launching large-scale attacks, such as invasion. Whether they have much of a role in preventing lesser attacks is subject to debate and would depend on circumstances.

Although the link between nuclear weapons and deterrence is powerful, it should not be taken too far. It is naïve to assume deterrence will always work, and it is complacent to assume every nuclear-armed government will always take deterrence to be the overarching concept for managing its weapons. It may be only a matter of time before we see a government adopting a compellence strategy. Another worrying possibility involves a crisis getting out of control, leading to pre-emption. The extreme nature of nuclear weapons means any state that feels imminently threatened by them, and which has an offensive capability of its own, will at least think about getting in the first punch if this means it can lessen the chances of its own forces being wiped out and its population being slaughtered. This, along with the idea that the best way to deter war is to prepare for it, is why there will be a continuing call for expertise in the dark arts of nuclear strategy.

The best place to end this discussion is with a reference to how destructive these weapons can be. This destructiveness ought to cause scepticism about the very possibility of devising a nuclear warplan which is not recklessly ruinous of civilized values. Many would argue the chain of devastation that could be caused by these things means only a criminal or lunatic would want to use them. A related factor to consider is that it is improbable any political or military leader could have much realistic confidence in projections of the consequences of exploding a nuclear bomb. Weapons experts could tell them the likely physical impact, but not much else of value. The first step to nuclear war could be mapped out, but projections of steps two, three and four might well be more or less fiction.

It is no wonder many believe the only acceptable nuclear strategy is one designed to deter others from using such weapons. Other rationales (such as using nuclear weapons to deal with chemical or conventional threats, or options for loosely argued pre-emptive attack) often seem dangerous. The problem here, though, is that even a stress on narrow ideas of deterring nuclear war can still be an encouragement to proliferation.

The British government under Prime Minister Tony Blair provided an inadvertent example of this. Blair claimed UK nuclear forces were necessary because 'we cannot be sure that a major nuclear threat to our vital interests will not emerge over the longer term', but *no* state can be 'sure' of this; he also discussed the need for these forces in the context of countering 'the threat posed by a nuclear North Korea' (Blair, 2006: 5), but there was no evidence of a North Korean threat to the UK that needed deterring.

If Blair's arguments hold water for the UK, they could just as easily apply to many – perhaps all – other states. The UK also suggests nuclear forces are needed because 'most industrialized countries have the capability to develop chemical and biological weapons' (UK Ministry of Defence, 2006: 6). But this capability is intrinsic to modern life; if it needs to be deterred by nuclear weapons, non-proliferation is not only a lost cause but also dangerous.

This is one reason why many believe the primary focus in international security policy making should not be on nuclear strategy at all – not even if it is framed in terms of deterrence. Since nuclear strategy is about ways to exploit rather than get rid of the bomb, its value to humanity is at best provisional, a way of buying time through deterrence until we find a better way of arranging human affairs. Those sceptical or horrified by the very notion of a nuclear strategy will focus more on arms control, especially efforts to make the use, and perhaps ownership, of the weapons illegitimate. In the meantime, the 'respectable' members of the nuclear club, as recognized by international treaty (the United States, Russia, China, UK and France), will continue to insist their weapons have utility and are essential. Simultaneously, they will try to keep a straight face as they preach sermons to others on the necessity for, and virtue of, nuclear abstinence.

Further reading

Butfoy, A. (2005) *Disarming Proposals: Controlling Nuclear, Biological and Chemical Weapons*, Sydney: University of New South Wales Press.

Freedman, L. (2003) *The Evolution of Nuclear Strategy* 3rd edn, Basingstoke: Palgrave Macmillan.

Gormley, D. (2006) 'Securing Nuclear Obsolescence', *Survival*, 48, 3: 127–48.

Kaplan, F. (1991) *The Wizards of Armageddon,* Stanford: Stanford University Press.

Kristensen, H., Norris, R. and McKinzie, M. (2006) *Chinese Nuclear Forces and US Nuclear War Planning*, Report for the Federation of American Scientists and the Natural Resources Defense Council,
<www.nukestrat.com/china/chinareport.htm>.

Nolan, J. (1989) *The Guardians of the Arsenal: The Politics of Nuclear Strategy*, New York: Basic Books.

Quester, G. (2006) *Nuclear First Strike: Consequences of a Broken Taboo*, Baltimore: The Johns Hopkins University Press.

Quinlan, M. (2005) 'India–Pakistan Deterrence Revisited', *Survival*, 47, 3:103–16.

Sokolski H. (ed.) (2004) *Getting MAD: Nuclear Assured Destruction, its Origins and Practice*, Carlisle Pa.: Strategic Studies Institute of the US Army War College.
<www.strategicstudiesinstitute.army.mil/pubs/display.cfm?pubID=585>.

Stoker, J. (2007) *The United Kingdom and Nuclear Deterrence*, Adelphi Paper 386, London: Routledge for the Institute for International and Strategic Studies.

Chapter 9

Emerging Nuclear States and the Challenge of Non-Proliferation

J.D. Kenneth Boutin

Introduction

There is a heightened sense of threat in many quarters regarding the proliferation of weapons of mass destruction (WMDs), particularly nuclear weapons. Long-standing policy concerns over horizontal nuclear proliferation – the acquisition of nuclear weapons by actors that previously did not possess them – have been exacerbated by recent trends and developments. Milestones such as North Korea's detonation of a nuclear device in 2006, Iran's ongoing efforts to develop nuclear industrial capabilities consistent with a weapons programme, and apparent interest on the part of a number of non-state actors in acquiring a 'mass-casualty event' capability involving nuclear warheads or radiological dispersal devices (RDDs or so-called 'dirty bombs') provide a powerful stimulus for renewed efforts to address horizontal nuclear proliferation. The continuing proliferation of nuclear-capable delivery systems, particularly tactical and strategic ballistic and cruise missiles, is contributing to the heightened sense of concern. Current trends suggest that the issue of nuclear proliferation will remain at the forefront of the international security agenda for the foreseeable future.

The course of horizontal nuclear proliferation has significant implications for the non-proliferation regime. Changing patterns of nuclear proliferation and structural changes in the nuclear supply environment constitute major challenges for the international arms control community. The difficulties inherent in attempting to prevent nuclear proliferation by 'rogue' states and insurgent groups are compounded by the changing context of proliferation, with some emerging nuclear states now in a position to pursue the qualitative and quantitative enhancement of their nuclear weapons capabilities, having successfully crossed the nuclear threshold. Efforts to prevent horizontal proliferation are complicated by the emergence of transnational industrial processes that are difficult for states to monitor and control, and by the development of secondary nuclear suppliers. These industrial trends provide increasing scope for the circumvention of controls on the proliferation of materials, equipment and technologies crucial to the development and production of nuclear weapons.

While concerned authorities are redoubling their efforts to curb the ambitions of nuclear proliferators, maintaining the integrity of the non-proliferation regime is likely to prove increasingly difficult. The non-proliferation regime will need to adapt significantly if it is to address post-cold war nuclear proliferation and supply trends. These trends are generating diverging policy responses that are potentially counterproductive over the long term or which otherwise undermine the non-proliferation regime. The political foundations of the Nuclear Non-Proliferation Treaty (NPT) may be threatened by the requirements of addressing vertical proliferation in emerging nuclear states, for example.

This chapter examines trends in horizontal nuclear proliferation and their impact on the non-proliferation regime. It focuses on the long-term implications of the policy requirements generated by the impressive strides being made by emerging nuclear states, rather than on particular nuclear weapons programmes, the strategic consequences of proliferation, or the host of normative questions raised by efforts to prevent nuclear proliferation. The chapter begins by examining the changing nuclear proliferation environment, assessing key proliferation trends and the processes of structural change that are facilitating the nuclear programmes of emerging nuclear states. It then turns to the impact of these trends and processes on the nuclear non-proliferation regime, where policy requirements are taking arms control into uncharted territory. The chapter concludes by examining the implications of the eroding political basis of the nuclear non-proliferation regime.

The challenge to the nuclear non-proliferation regime

The transformation of the nuclear proliferation environment is more evolutionary than revolutionary. The trends involved are the product of complex economic and political processes, the extent and impact of which vary considerably between cases. Many of these processes are transnational, and involve states other than the emerging nuclear states that are the subject of proliferation concern. The international scope of these processes potentially limits the effectiveness of many national and multilateral non-proliferation instruments.

The processes that are transforming horizontal nuclear proliferation are not mutually exclusive. The evolution of nuclear agendas in emerging nuclear states and the structural transformation of the nuclear supply environment are mutually reinforcing, for example. Interest in developing and producing nuclear weapons is driving efforts to develop advanced indigenous nuclear industrial capabilities. This is contributing to changing patterns of research and development (R&D) and production in nuclear and related high-technology industries and to the emergence of secondary nuclear suppliers, and this in turn provides a basis for changing proliferation strategies and potentially renders the development of nuclear weapons a more attractive proposition.

The nuclear non-proliferation regime

The nuclear non-proliferation regime encompasses an extensive array of national and international instruments developed with the objective of limiting or preventing altogether the proliferation of nuclear weapons. It is necessary to distinguish between what are effectively two distinct arms of the non-proliferation regime. One addresses vertical nuclear proliferation – the qualitative and quantitative enhancement of existing nuclear arsenals. This branch of the regime focuses on limiting the size of and ultimately eliminating the nuclear arsenals of those states that are officially accepted as nuclear weapons states under the NPT, though progress to date toward the objective of nuclear disarmament has been disappointing. The other arm addresses horizontal nuclear proliferation in states that are not formally accepted as nuclear powers by the international community. This focuses on deterring nuclear aspirants and preventing any acquisition of nuclear weapons, but now is faced with the requirement of reversing nuclear proliferation when this occurs.

The nuclear non-proliferation regime is structured around a complex, overlapping network of multilateral arrangements. Vertical and horizontal nuclear non-proliferation efforts are largely pursued through distinctive sets of multilateral mechanisms. The Strategic Arms Limitation Talks (SALT) and the Intermediate Nuclear Forces (INF) Treaty were developed to address the specific requirements of vertical nuclear non-proliferation, for example. The NPT was developed to address both vertical and horizontal nuclear proliferation, but has had little apparent impact on the former. The NPT, which has constituted the cornerstone of horizontal nuclear non-proliferation efforts since its entry into force in 1970, is supported by a dedicated 'safeguards' system designed to encourage and verify compliance with horizontal non-proliferation obligations. This requires states parties to report on their peaceful nuclear activities and to provide for the inspection of nuclear facilities by the International Atomic Energy Agency (IAEA). It is important to note the contribution to the horizontal nuclear non-proliferation regime of initiatives targeting the proliferation of nuclear-capable delivery systems, including ballistic and cruise missiles, but instruments such as the Missile Technology Control Regime (MTCR) are beyond the scope of this study.

As well as providing a basis for collaborative efforts to prevent nuclear proliferation, multilateral instruments such as the NPT constitute the framework for many national non-proliferation measures. The integrity of multilateral mechanisms depends on the level of commitment of participating states. The development and effective implementation of national measures is crucial to states' efforts to meet their international non-proliferation obligations, such as controlling nuclear-related exports. The failure of some states to recognize and act on this helps to explain the very uneven coverage provided by the non-proliferation regime, despite the broad membership of the NPT.

Many features of the nuclear non-proliferation regime survive largely unaltered from the cold war. Established approaches to addressing horizontal nuclear proliferation reflect the perspectives of political authorities in the developed industrial states that were at the forefront of efforts to prevent the emergence of new nuclear powers in the decades following the Second World War. The nuclear non-proliferation regime remains geared to the context of a state-centric and hierarchical proliferation environment. Until recently, most of the materials, equipment and technologies necessary to develop and produce nuclear weapons were only available from a select group of suppliers, the composition of which was relatively static. Supply-side controls continue to manifest the historical ascendancy of the established nuclear suppliers. While the NPT has a general requirement that states parties refrain from assisting nuclear weapons programmes in other states, practical multilateral measures dedicated to this objective are limited to export control regimes such as the Nuclear Suppliers Group (NSG) and the Zangger Committee (also known as the NPT Exporters Committee) which are based around the established nuclear exporters.

Another legacy of the cold war is the relative inattention to particular aspects of the proliferation equation. This includes the political and economic factors driving demand for nuclear proliferation. While the NPT does offer states parties the benefits of increased access to peaceful nuclear support in exchange for agreeing to forgo acquiring nuclear weapons, it does not address the politico-military factors underlying horizontal nuclear proliferation other than by reducing the potential nuclear threat posed by other states. Initiatives focusing on non-state actors and their potential contribution to nuclear weapons proliferation and on the development of nuclear industrial capabilities in emerging nuclear states are similarly underdeveloped. Many members of the international arms control community continue to assume that the commercial sector is under effective political control, despite the evident capacity of multinational enterprises to operate with little or no regard to the dictates of political authorities in any particular state. This perspective is the product of a time when transnational high-technology R&D and production processes were much less the norm.

Established non-proliferation norms also have a crucial impact on post-cold war efforts to address the nuclear proliferation challenge. This legacy includes the norms of engagement and voluntarism. These features have characterized nuclear non-proliferation initiatives, even in cases where they have been built around a relatively restricted member base. The norms of engagement and voluntarism continue to provide the political underpinnings of the nuclear non-proliferation regime. The fact that multilateral mechanisms have been based on these principles has rendered them more politically acceptable. The widespread acceptance of these norms has been reflected in the scope of key multilateral mechanisms; only a handful of states remain outside the NPT, for example.

One further norm inherited from the cold war is that of equality. This crucial norm involves the ideal parity of states in terms of their right to possess nuclear weapons. While non-proliferation mechanisms do not necessarily treat states as equals – the NPT from the outset has accepted a select group of states as signatories without requiring them to first abandon nuclear weapons, for example – compromises such as this have been regarded as a temporary expedient. Supporters of non-proliferation still expect the nuclear weapons states to disarm. This norm has played a key role in securing widespread support for the non-proliferation regime, particularly in cases where states possess the necessary resources and yet have elected to forgo developing nuclear weapons capabilities.

The norm of equality persists despite the failure of the acknowledged nuclear powers to eliminate their nuclear arsenals. Its resilience in the face of the lack of progress toward this objective testifies to the importance attached to engaging the nuclear powers on the issue of non-proliferation, in the hope that they might yet proceed with nuclear disarmament. At the same time, this reflects biased assumptions about the rationality of particular state actors that are difficult to sustain. The possession of nuclear weapons by developing states is considered inherently destabilizing in a way that their continued possession by the accepted nuclear powers is not, despite the record of those developing states that have successfully crossed the nuclear threshold.

The formal acceptance of the possession of nuclear weapons by a select group of states effectively legitimizes their status as nuclear powers in the eyes of many, despite the fact that this is incompatible with the spirit and letter of the NPT. The privileged position of these states and their failure to extend the consideration they are accorded in the non-proliferation regime to the vast majority of states has resulted in the unbalanced application of nuclear non-proliferation measures. While the inequalities of the non-proliferation regime have been a source of considerable concern for some time, it was only recently that this has begun to threaten widespread support for mechanisms such as the NPT.

The nuclear non-proliferation regime inherited from the cold war has been useful in terms of providing the arms control community with a common framework within which to pursue general non-proliferation objectives, despite the exceptionalism of the established nuclear weapons states. Participation in the non-proliferation regime continues to offer obvious benefits for the development of civil nuclear programmes while providing a high level of reassurance about the nuclear ambitions of the majority of states that adhere to their international non-proliferation obligations. The regime is being undermined, however, by the ongoing transformation of horizontal nuclear proliferation and the structural environment within which it occurs.

Beyond horizontal proliferation: the evolution of nuclear programmes

Recent years have seen substantial progress in the development of general nuclear industrial and in some cases weapons capabilities in a number of states that are not recognized as nuclear weapon states under the NPT. While the Iraqi and Libyan nuclear weapons programmes have been terminated, North Korea has successfully reached the nuclear threshold, and Iran's nuclear agenda may include the objective of developing nuclear weapons. Among the most striking progress is that of India and Pakistan, which are following in the footsteps of the acknowledged nuclear weapon states. Despite the concerted efforts of the international arms control community, India and Pakistan have successfully crossed the horizontal/vertical nuclear proliferation divide.

The policy transformation involved in progressing to vertical nuclear proliferation is considerable. The nuclear programmes of states engaged in vertical proliferation are characterized by attention to the political and military utility of nuclear weapons, as well as to quantitative issues. This may involve a focus on aspects as varied as nuclear force posture and strategy, developing delivery systems, and promoting sustainable nuclear industrial development. In the case of India, for example, there is evident interest in enhancing the utility of the nuclear arsenal, including through providing effective delivery systems, and a determined effort to develop advanced indigenous nuclear industrial capabilities capable of sustaining its weapons programme (Tellis, 2002: 66–70).

The vertical proliferation focus of the Indian and Pakistani nuclear weapons programmes constitutes a significant departure for states that generally are still considered 'developing.' This testifies to the importance political authorities in emerging nuclear states potentially attach to acquiring nuclear weapon capabilities. In both these cases, successive governments have considered nuclear weapons sufficiently important to justify the allocation of substantial resources. The developmental level of the emerging nuclear states has contributed to the general reluctance on the part of the international arms control community to view their nuclear programmes through any lens other than that of horizontal proliferation, and to downplay their significance in terms of the nuclear non-proliferation regime (see Bracken, 2003: 401).

While political authorities in India and Pakistan strive to consolidate their nuclear arsenals, other emerging nuclear states are focusing on the objective of developing initial nuclear weapons capabilities. Differing starting points and the uneven developmental pace of nuclear programmes are producing a widening gap within the ranks of the emerging nuclear states.

The traditional horizontal proliferation paradigm remains valid for those states whose nuclear programmes have yet to result in the successful detonation of a nuclear device or in weaponization – the development of nuclear explosive devices that are compact and robust enough to be deployed operationally. These states are the subject of proliferation concern due to their actual, suspected or potential efforts to enter the ranks of the nuclear powers. This group of states includes one (North Korea) that has thus far only demonstrated a rudimentary nuclear weapons capability, and a number of 'threshold states' that may be close to acquiring initial nuclear weapons capabilities. Determining the status and objectives of the nuclear programmes of threshold states can be quite difficult, even where nuclear industries are subject to external verification, as the cases of Iraq prior to the Gulf War of 1990–1 and Iran more recently illustrate (see Blix, 2005; Fitzpatrick, 2006).

The potential scope for horizontal nuclear proliferation is growing. The demands of developing nuclear weapons are likely to prove progressively less daunting as relative costs fall and the learning curve steadily contracts. According to one estimate, for example, India required only about 2500 person-years to develop its first nuclear weapon in the 1970s, compared with the 40,000 it took the Allies during the Second World War (Clancy and Seitz, 1991–2: 3). As outlined below, the development of indigenous nuclear industrial capabilities and improved access to external industrial support will facilitate efforts by states to pursue the development of nuclear weapons. It is likely that the ranks of the emerging nuclear states will further expand, and that North Korea will not be the last to breach the nuclear barrier. There are good prospects as well that, once across the nuclear threshold, other states will join India and Pakistan in progressing to vertical proliferation.

The bifurcation of the emerging nuclear states has major implications for the non-proliferation regime. The need to address both vertical and horizontal nuclear proliferation in emerging nuclear states complicates non-proliferation efforts by generating distinctive sets of policy requirements, which are potentially incompatible. That it has not had a notable impact in this respect to date is due in large part to entrenched reluctance to entertain the possibility that emerging nuclear states could progress to the stage of vertical proliferation and the resulting dearth of appropriate policy responses, despite the impressive strides of the Indian and Pakistani nuclear weapons programmes.

Beyond dependence: nuclear industrial development

Key aspects of the non-proliferation regime are threatened by the ongoing evolution of the nuclear proliferation environment. A number of long-standing assumptions, such as the static nuclear-industrial hierarchy of states and the limited potential for the circumvention of supply-side controls, are increasingly problematic.

Until recently, there were a limited number of potential suppliers of crucial nuclear materials, equipment and technologies. It generally was only those European and North American states with well-established nuclear industries that were in a position to export items such as centrifuges for nuclear enrichment. The hierarchy of the nuclear supply environment was reinforced by the national structure of nuclear industries, with R&D and production organized on a relatively autonomous basis in individual states with little international collaboration. Supply-side controls such as those promoted by the NSG were feasible due to the potential to secure the adherence of most of the limited number of states capable of supplying sensitive nuclear materials, equipment and technologies. The potential effectiveness of this approach was demonstrated by the case of Iraq, which was forced to develop a clandestine nuclear supply network at great cost.

The ongoing structural transformation of the nuclear supply environment is providing increasing opportunities for determined proliferators to overcome the formidable obstacles posed by supply-side controls. There is growing scope for emerging nuclear states to exploit non-traditional sources of supply for the sensitive nuclear materials, equipment and technologies needed to develop and produce nuclear weapons. The structural environment for nuclear proliferation is being transformed both by easier access to the products of industry based in the developed industrial states, and by what Kampani (2002: 107) refers to as 'second tier' proliferation involving new state suppliers. The growing competence of nuclear industries in these emerging secondary suppliers is undermining the established oligopoly of exporters that has existed since early in the nuclear era. The emerging secondary suppliers are not covered by the NPT safeguards system and are not bound by the initiatives that (at least in theory, if not always in practice) restrict the traditional nuclear exporters.

Increasingly advanced nuclear industrial capabilities are a characteristic feature of the emerging nuclear states that have progressed to the stage of vertical proliferation, as well as some of those that have yet to reach this point. Recent years have seen the progressive development of a growing capacity to produce sensitive nuclear materials, equipment and technologies on the part of states such as Pakistan. In the process of developing a capacity to meet local needs, these states are acquiring a significant nuclear export capacity. Such suppliers may be capable of supporting other emerging nuclear states well in advance of the successful development of nuclear weapons, as the case of Pakistan demonstrates (see Corera, 2006: 59–60).

The export capacity of particular emerging secondary suppliers depends on a number of factors, including their level of nuclear industrial development and the extent of their integration into transnational R&D and production processes. Emerging secondary suppliers may be in a position to supply items ranging from materials such as specialty alloys and composites to production equipment and centrifuges or technologies contributing to the local capacity to produce fissile material or design effective nuclear warheads. The support provided by emerging secondary suppliers potentially extends to the re-transfer of sensitive nuclear materials, equipment and technologies obtained from third parties, as well as the provision of those manufactured or developed locally.

Emerging secondary suppliers have made a substantial contribution to horizontal nuclear proliferation. An illicit nuclear supply network based in Pakistan supported the nuclear weapons programmes of Libya, Iran and possibly North Korea, for example (see Corera, 2006; Bowen, 2006: 36–42). While this now-defunct network appears unrivalled in terms of its duration and scope, similar capabilities exist, or are being developed, in other emerging nuclear states. The progressive industrial development of emerging nuclear states will continue to undermine the established hierarchical structure of the nuclear supply environment, potentially contributing to an accelerating pace of horizontal proliferation.

The development of emerging secondary suppliers is being facilitated by general industrial trends. High-technology R&D and production are increasingly characterized by transnational processes of technological development, application and diffusion. A polycentric collaborative approach to R&D and production is supplanting the practice of concentrating R&D and final assembly in the 'home' state of a firm. This trend is the product of mounting commercial pressures, as firms strive to offset the spiralling costs of developing and applying advanced technologies through increased specialization, which they offset through horizontal industrial integration. This deepening technological globalization involves increasing inter-subsidiary and inter-firm collaboration, often on a transnational basis (Boutin, 2004: 5–12). Although political restrictions have limited the impact of these trends in the nuclear field, polycentric R&D and production is a feature of many high-technology industries involved in the development and production of nuclear-related 'dual-use' equipment (see Hibbs, 2006: 38).

The local scope for exploiting the opportunities provided by technological globalization varies considerably. Some national industries are more deeply embedded into transnational R&D and production processes than others, and consequently some states are better situated than others. Extensive integration into transnational R&D and production networks characterizes many export-oriented developing states, often with the encouragement if not support of local political authorities. Technological globalization has contributed to the successful development of nuclear industrial capabilities in a number of emerging nuclear states. Transnational industrial processes were successfully exploited by Iraq in its quest for nuclear weapons, for example (Beck and Gahlaut, 2003: 12).

The potential contribution of transnational industrial processes to nuclear proliferation is greatest in the absence of effective supply-side surveillance and control mechanisms. Polycentric industrial processes and expanding transnational technological diffusion are providing multi-national enterprises with an increasing capacity to develop and supply sensitive technologies and equipment free from effective political oversight. As Scholte notes, while states may be able to influence supraterritorial activities, they lack the capacity to control them effectively (Scholte, 2000: 136–7). This represents a major policy challenge even in the case of the United States, which despite a series of initiatives dating back to the cold war still struggles to ensure that locally based high-technology industries do not contribute to proliferation (see Gansler, 2006: 34).

The proliferation challenge resulting from the industrial trends outlined above has been exacerbated by the demise of the Soviet Union. A decade and a half after its collapse, concern remains over the security of nuclear materials from under-protected sites within the territory of the former Soviet Union. For example, it is thought that some two-thirds of Russia's estimated 600-tonne stockpile of weapons-grade plutonium and highly enriched uranium (HEU) is inadequately protected (Galeotti, 2006: 48). There are ongoing concerns as well about the estimated 50,000 nuclear engineers and technicians that were under- or unemployed following the demise of the Soviet Union (Mozley, 1998: 218). So-called 'technological mercenaries' drawn from the ranks of former employees of the Soviet nuclear industry have considerable potential to contribute to nuclear-related technological proliferation with their specialized knowledge and skills (see Moody, 1997: 21–3).

The increasing availability of crucial nuclear technologies, equipment and materials from state and industrial suppliers potentially reduces the difficulties, costs and time involved in developing and enhancing nuclear weapon capabilities, and provides greater scope for determined prolifera-tors to overcome the developmental and production obstacles imposed by concerned members of the arms control community. As will be discussed below, the existing nuclear non-proliferation regime is poorly equipped to address this structural transformation, despite growing concern over its potential impact on horizontal nuclear proliferation. This is leading concerned authorities in some states to reconsider their approach to nuclear proliferation.

Responding to the nuclear proliferation challenge

The contemporary challenge to the nuclear non-proliferation regime is multifaceted. The regime has been under increasing stress since the end of the cold war due to the continued failure of the established nuclear weapon states to meet their disarmament obligations. Long-standing disquiet over this issue is being supplemented by concern in some quarters that the non-proliferation regime is less relevant to efforts to prevent horizontal prolif-eration than was once the case. This view is the product of the evident scope for states to pursue nuclear programmes despite the regime. The

NPT, for example, has been called into question both by the failure of the acknowledged nuclear weapons states to eliminate their arsenals and by the non-compliance of signatory states that have pursued nuclear weapons programmes (Rathbun, 2006: 227). Iraq, Libya and possibly North Korea made significant progress even while covered by the provisions of the NPT, and of these North Korea withdrew from the NPT prior to its first nuclear test, while processes independent of the NPT terminated the nuclear weapons programmes of Iraq and Libya.

While political authorities in many states appear reluctant to acknowledge the extent to which the requirements of non-proliferation are changing, others recognize the significance of this transformation. The view that the established institutional pillars of the nuclear non-proliferation regime are inadequate is readily apparent on the part of political authorities in the United States, which traditionally has constituted one of the principal supporters of efforts to curb horizontal nuclear proliferation. US recognition of the changing context of proliferation in the emerging nuclear states is manifest in the recent adoption of a position implicitly accepting horizontal nuclear proliferation for the first time.

Heightened concern has served as a catalyst for concerted efforts to strengthen the nuclear non-proliferation regime. Concerned authorities have sought to address the perceived shortcomings of the regime by developing supplemental measures that target particular gaps or weaknesses in the existing coverage of mechanisms such as the NPT. This includes measures focusing on aspects such as nuclear stockpile stewardship, the nuclear fuel cycle and the nuclear supply environment. Some of these initiatives focus on enhancing the capacity of existing non-proliferation instruments such as the NPT. As a result, verification provisions strengthened to better detect undeclared nuclear activities now support the NPT. States parties to the NPT are being encouraged to sign Additional Protocols that provide a basis for greater assurance of their compliance with their non-proliferation obligations under the treaty (Cooley, 2003: 30–1).

A number of states have introduced strengthened national non-proliferation measures to support or supplement their international obligations. In some cases, these initiatives target particular actors. There are a number of initiatives designed to address the specific case of the former Soviet Union, for example. These include the International Science and Technology Center (ISTC) established in 1992 to provide employment for scientists and engineers in nuclear and related fields who might otherwise find employment as 'technological mercenaries', and the Global Threat Reduction Initiative (GTRI) launched by the United States in 2004 to address concerns about the security of nuclear material stockpiles (Rogers, 1992: 472).

There have been a number of initiatives targeting proliferation in the emerging nuclear states. This approach is most apparent on the part of the United States, which has led the way in moving to establish a capacity to identify and analyse nuclear proliferation networks (Starr, 1993: 23). The United States has developed country-specific sanctions targeting the industries and suppliers supporting particular emerging nuclear states, such as those provided for under the 2000 Iran Nonproliferation Act and the 2005 Iran and Syria Nonproliferation Act (Anderson, 2007: 21). Some of these measures even target specific firms, such as the punitive US sanctions applied to the China Precision Machinery Import and Export Corporation, in an attempt to avoid causing undue damage to important bilateral relationships ('Taming Nuclear Tigers', 1991: 1106). Some of these initiatives reflect awareness of the increasing contribution of commercial enterprises to nuclear proliferation.

Interest in supplementing the established mechanisms of the nuclear non-proliferation regime has led some states to develop initiatives that break with the model established during the cold war. One important area of difference involves the scope of multilateralism. A number of recent non-proliferation initiatives rest on a relatively narrow base of supporters. While the NSG and the Zangger Committee also involved limited numbers of states, recent initiatives have been notable for the changed context that is involved. Key actors are eschewing developing a broad-based consensus in favour of collaboration with limited 'coalitions of the willing' established independently of the usual framework provided by the United Nations or other non-proliferation mechanisms. This approach has been necessitated by interest in adopting a more overtly political response to the challenge of nuclear proliferation.

A much more confrontational approach to non-proliferation has emerged since the end of the cold war. The policy shift from engagement and multilateralism to more unilateral and confrontational policies is being led by the United States. The new US emphasis on counter-proliferation is manifest in a number of initiatives it has led, some of which are unilateral in nature, and if multilateral have largely been developed outside existing non-proliferation mechanisms and based on quite different principles. This includes the US-led Proliferation Security Initiative (PSI), which provides for the interdiction of nuclear and other WMD-related transfers by 'rogue' states (Valencia, 2005: 25–6). This important policy shift emerged soon after the end of the cold war under President Bill Clinton, who oversaw the introduction of a doctrine of counter-proliferation and who initiated air strikes against Iraqi WMD sites without first securing the approval of the United Nations Security Council (Walker, 2004: 50–1). The emphasis placed on this approach has deepened under President George W. Bush, who in 2002 indicated that the United States was prepared to use force to prevent the proliferation of WMD-related technologies (Steinbruner, 2003: 3).

The post-cold war period has seen an unprecedented politicization of nuclear non-proliferation efforts. While the non-proliferation regime has been inherently political from the outset, this is becoming much more blatant. This is the case in terms of the development of instruments focusing on particular states, the approaches employed, and the language associated with such efforts. Declining confidence in the effectiveness of the multilateral pillars of the nuclear non-proliferation regime has led political authorities in some states to develop more 'robust' non-proliferation initiatives that involve much more pre-emptive and confrontational approaches to addressing nuclear proliferation, as noted above.

The post-cold war popularity in some quarters of applying the label 'rogue' state to emerging nuclear states such as Iran and North Korea situates these states in an entirely different political context than formerly by suggesting that these states are beyond the pale of the accepted norms of the international community, and that their actions are potentially destabilizing. At the same time, this helps to legitimize confrontational non-proliferation approaches to these states. This has been combined at times with efforts to discredit existing non-proliferation instruments and actors, particularly the IAEA, in the interest of short-term political objectives. This was evident prior to the US-led invasion of Iraq in 2003, when it sought to legitimize its efforts to promote regime change by calling into question the capacity of the IAEA and the United Nations Monitoring, Verification and Inspection Commission (UNMOVIC) to ensure Iraq's compliance with its obligations to terminate its WMD programmes (Blinken, 2003–4: 41).

Finally, recognition of changing patterns of proliferation in some of the emerging nuclear states is leading political authorities in some states to explore innovative policy responses that approach this in terms of vertical nuclear proliferation. This was manifest in the groundbreaking arrangements negotiated by the United States and India in 2005, which reflected the willingness of the former to accept India as a de facto nuclear weapons state and to focus on managing India's nuclear weapons programme instead of attempt to abolish it outright.

The implications for the nuclear non-proliferation regime

The trends outlined above constitute a significant threat to the nuclear non-proliferation regime. The nature of efforts by concerned members of the international arms control community to address what they regard as a heightened post-cold war proliferation threat, exemplified by Iraq and its nearly successful efforts to develop a nuclear weapons capability, have major implications for nuclear non-proliferation efforts. Both the conceptual basis of the non-proliferation regime and the norms by which it operates are threatened by some of the policy responses now being generated by the perceived requirements of non-proliferation. The trend toward more robust non-proliferation instruments is undermining the established multilateral basis of the non-proliferation regime, while the issue of how proliferation in the emerging nuclear states is conceptualized has major implications for efforts to promote nuclear non-proliferation. Addressing the challenge of nuclear proliferation is likely to prove increasingly difficult due to the more complex nature of post-cold war patterns of proliferation and the structural transformation of the nuclear supply environment and the potential for this to encourage counterproductive policies.

The conceptual basis of non-proliferation

The established conceptual basis of proliferation involving the emerging nuclear states has proven quite resilient. It remains the norm to approach the nuclear weapons programmes of all of these states in terms of horizontal proliferation, despite the fact that it has been more than three decades since India first demonstrated a potential nuclear weapons capability by detonating a nuclear explosive device. Even the newly adopted US approach to India stops short of formally accepting it as a nuclear weapons state, though it effectively treats it as such (US White House, 2005).

While a re-conceptualization of proliferation has arguably been long overdue as a result of the transformation of the nuclear programmes of states such as India and Pakistan, this is not a straightforward proposition. Recognizing and accepting vertical nuclear proliferation on the part of states such as India threatens to undermine the basis for promoting traditional horizontal nuclear non-proliferation objectives with respect to other emerging nuclear states and complicate efforts to develop coherent policy approaches, while failing to do so ensures that such states will continue to remain outside the non-proliferation regime.

There are major obstacles that stand in the way of reconceptualizing proliferation in emerging nuclear states to accommodate the potential for vertical proliferation. The entrenched perception of the limited capacities of developing states to pursue nuclear weapons programmes of a nature traditionally associated with the developed states is likely to continue to influence official attitudes. This is due in part to the implications of recognizing vertical proliferation on the part of emerging nuclear states: doing so suggests that this is no less legitimate than vertical proliferation on the part of those states currently recognized as possessing nuclear weapons under the NPT. These political implications may work against the general adoption of such an approach. While the acceptance of states such as India and potentially Pakistan as 'legitimate' nuclear powers is facilitated by the fact that they are not considered 'rogue' states, accepting vertical nuclear proliferation on the part of states such as Iran and North Korea will prove much more difficult for political authorities in a number of states, including the United States. Such an approach has long been resisted by states that strongly support the nuclear non-proliferation regime for this reason. This position has only recently begun to change, led by the United States and its revised approach to India. For the present, however, the United States is treating India very much as an exception, which includes exempting it from existing domestic non-proliferation-related legislation, rather than amending the relevant legislation.

To the extent that that the international arms control community follows the lead of the United States in accepting the transformation of nuclear proliferation in states such as India, this will have major implications for non-proliferation. This stems from the potential incompatibility of the measures that logically result from this shift and those that stem from the requirements of addressing horizontal nuclear proliferation in other emerging nuclear states. Vertical nuclear proliferation is addressed through proliferation management, which involves measures that are quite dissimilar from those developed to prevent proliferation. While many aspects of the two approaches to addressing proliferation are not necessarily incompatible in a technical sense, in that they can be pursued relatively independently of each other as demonstrated by the distinctive arrangements developed during the cold war for those states which were recognized as nuclear states and those that were not, they are incompatible in political terms.

There is an additional difficulty in that the acceptance of vertical proliferation suggested by policies of proliferation management effectively legitimizes nuclear proliferation. This has the potential to erode the norms that have underpinned the non-proliferation regime, undermining the understanding reached with the majority of states that have agreed to forgo acquiring nuclear weapons. The acceptance of a select body of nuclear weapons states has long been the source of some resentment, and this is likely to increase if states such as India are accepted as nuclear weapons states (see Erickson, 2001: 41). This has serious implications for the process of engagement that has in the past enabled nuclear weapons states and non-nuclear weapons states to work together to prevent horizontal proliferation, despite the inequitable nature of instruments such as the NPT.

The political implications for the nuclear non-proliferation regime make it difficult to operationalize a shift to accepting and responding to vertical proliferation on the part of emerging nuclear states. This potentially generates a major policy dilemma, and it is unclear whether the non-proliferation regime has the capacity to accommodate simultaneously the perceived requirements of addressing both vertical and horizontal nuclear proliferation. It will prove much more difficult to develop broad-based non-proliferation approaches, including in terms of developing a consensus on how particular cases of proliferation should be addressed. However, persisting with an outdated conceptual map that views nuclear proliferation in states such as India and Pakistan in terms of horizontal proliferation is just as problematic if such states are to be brought into the non-proliferation regime.

Non-proliferation norms

The erosion of the norms underpinning the non-proliferation regime also is helping to undermine its political basis. The more overtly political and confrontational trends of post-cold war nuclear non-proliferation approaches are exacerbating long-standing concerns over the objectivity of the non-proliferation regime. This is threatening the legitimacy of the non-proliferation regime by casting the efforts of particular states to prevent, impede or reverse proliferation in a much more threatening light. The impartiality of the nuclear non-proliferation regime is increasingly open to question. It has not gone unnoticed, for example, that the United States' efforts to address nuclear proliferation in emerging nuclear states are closely tied to broader political objectives such as regime change (Cirincione, 2003: 4).

The integrity of the global nuclear non-proliferation has been open to question for many decades. This is because of the well-established division between those states that are formally accepted as possessing nuclear weapons and the much larger group that are not. The NPT attempted to address this lack of integrity of the regime by obliging the nuclear weapons states to reduce and ultimately abandon their arsenals. However, not only is it the case that the nuclear weapons states have retained nuclear weapons, some are adopting policies that are steadily eroding the established basis for non-proliferation. Progress toward the development of new or strengthened multilateral instruments that reflect the traditional approach to non-proliferation has slowed considerably in recent years. This has been replaced by an increased emphasis on unilateralism in key states that have supported traditionally multilateralism.

More robust, unilateralist non-proliferation approaches are also counterproductive in that they have the potentially to undermine the effectiveness of multilateral non-proliferation instruments. This would reinforce the tendency to promote robust non-proliferation instruments with the potential to alienate the non-nuclear weapons states whose support for the non-proliferation regime has been crucial to the success of efforts to prevent widespread horizontal proliferation. The concerns that have driven more confrontational non-proliferation approaches in the United States and elsewhere are likely to remain, and may well grow more acute if other states succeed in crossing the nuclear threshold.

The erosion of the non-proliferation norms of engagement, voluntarism and equality through the development of non-proliferation mechanisms which are based on a limited group of states, which do not seek to engage proliferators, or which are inequitable has the potential to discourage participation in the non-proliferation regime. This has serious implications for the regime, as this would reinforce perceptions of its inability to deal with determined proliferators and lead to greater reliance on measures that discourage participation. This would complicate efforts to develop the broad international consensus on proliferation issues that has been crucial to mechanisms such as the NPT.

Conclusion

The ongoing transformation of nuclear proliferation and the nuclear proliferation environment is opening up new policy terrain. The contemporary non-proliferation challenge is evolving in concert with changing patterns of proliferation and structural changes in the nuclear supply environment, but their impact varies considerably, depending on factors such as the relative importance attached to nuclear non-proliferation.

The salient feature of horizontal proliferation at the present time is not the determination with which it is being pursued or the structural changes in the proliferation environment that are facilitating the development of nuclear weapons capabilities in emerging nuclear states, important as these trends are. More significant is the changing political context, which complicates traditional approaches to what is still generally conceived and approached as a horizontal proliferation issue. The difficulties inherent in meeting the contemporary nuclear proliferation challenge ensure that there is no straightforward solution to the problem, and can be expected to drive concerned political authorities to more carefully consider their non-proliferation objectives and approaches. In some cases, this may force them to make difficult decisions involving incompatible policy responses that may exacerbate the nuclear proliferation challenge.

Further reading

Beck M. and Gahlaut, S. (2003) 'Creating a New Multilateral Export Control Regime', *Arms Control Today*, 33, 3: 12–18.

Blinken, A.J. (2003–4) 'From Pre-emption to Engagement', *Survival* 45, 4: 33–60.

Blix, H. (2005) *Disarming Iraq*, revised edn, London: Bloomsbury.

Boutin, J.D.K. (2004) *Technological Globalization and Regional Security in East Asia*, Working Paper no. 65, Singapore: Institute of Defence and Strategic Studies, Nanyang Technological University.

Corera, G. (2006) *Shopping for Bombs: Nuclear Proliferation, Global Insecurity, and the Rise and Fall of the A.Q. Khan Network*, Melbourne: Scribe Publications.

Mistry, D. (2003) *Containing Missile Proliferation: Strategic Technology, Security Regimes, and International Cooperation in Arms Control*, Seattle: University of Washington Press.

Mozley, R.F. (1998) *The Politics and Technology of Nuclear Proliferation*, Seattle: University of Washington Press.

Scholte, J.A. (2000) *Globalization: A Critical Introduction*, New York: St Martin's.

Steinbruner, J. (2003) 'Confusing Means and Ends: The Doctrine of Coercive Pre-emption', *Arms Control Today*, 33, 1: 3–5.

Tellis, A.J. (2002) 'Toward a 'Force in Being': The Logic, Structure, and Utility of India's Emerging Nuclear Posture', *Journal of Strategic Studies*, 25, 4: 61–108.

Valencia, M.J. (2005) *The Proliferation Security Initiative: Making Waves in Asia*, Adelphi Paper no.376, London: International Institute for Strategic Studies.

Walker, W. (2004) *Weapons of Mass Destruction and International Order*, Adelphi Paper No.370, London: International Institute for Strategic Studies.

Chapter 10

Terrorism and Insurgency

Michael Boyle

Introduction

The events of 11 September 2001 placed the issue of international terrorism at the centre of the agenda of contemporary security studies. For many in the West, this asymmetric attack by the terrorist group al-Qaeda on the world's last superpower heralded a dramatic shift in what it means to be secure. No longer could states safely assume that the chief threat to their survival were rival states; instead, in a world of increasingly porous borders and high rates of transfer of technology and ideas, small groups of terrorists could pose a mortal risk to even the most powerful states. The apparent evolution of terrorism from a highly localized threat to a transnational phenomenon, fuelled by the mix of modern technology and radical Islamist ideology, also implied that the traditional state-based responses to terrorism might no longer be sufficient. Beyond its immediate cost to human life, the 11 September attack ushered in a new age of fear and insecurity for many in the West, and suggested that the decisive political and ideological struggle of the post-cold war world would be fought without frontlines or clear victories.

In response to these attacks, the United States, supported by its allies, declared a 'war on terror' and invaded Afghanistan to close al-Qaeda training camps. Calling the war on terror a battle for the civilized world, President George W. Bush vowed to hold states that support or host terrorist groups responsible for their actions. In March 2003, the United States and its coalition partners widened the front on the war on terror by invading Iraq and overthrowing the Saddam Hussein regime, in part due to the fear that Iraq could transfer weapons of mass destruction to terrorist groups. This invasion was followed by an intense insurgency, driven by a mix of al-Qaeda operatives and local Iraqi militias opposed to the occupation. Ironically, what had been perceived as a new response to a new type of threat led the United States and its allies into a very old problem: that is, 'small wars' in which insurgent forces vie with a foreign power for control of an occupied state. Today, the wars in both Iraq and Afghanistan represent a new mixture of a traditional insurgency against an occupying force with the mass-casualty terrorism of al-Qaeda and the so-called 'new terrorist' movement.

The purpose of this chapter is to investigate the extent to which the concepts of terrorism and insurgency should be updated in light of the events since 11 September. It will ask the following questions. What is terrorism? What are the causes of terrorism? Does al-Qaeda represent a kind of 'new terrorism' dissimilar to that of the past? How can we define insurgency? Do the traditional schools of thought on insurgency and counter-insurgency apply to the crises in Afghanistan and Iraq? Finally, what is the relationship, if any, between terrorism and insurgency in the modern world?

What is terrorism?

One of the perennial problems in the study of terrorism is the lack of a clear definition. While terrorism has a very long history, efforts to offer a precise definition are relatively recent. The first formal definition was offered by the League of Nations in 1937: 'all criminal acts directed against a state ... and intended to create a state of terror in the minds of particular persons or the general public' (quoted in Laqueur, 2003: 233). Due to a lack of political support by member states, the League of Nation's proposal for a definition of terrorism was never ratified (Wardlaw, 1989; Laqueur, 2003). Subsequent attempts to offer a definition have encountered difficulties over distinctions drawn about the kinds of acts deemed to be terrorism and the types of perpetrators who may engage in terrorism. The widely used US Department of State's (2002: xvi) definition describes terrorism as 'premeditated, politically motivated violence against non-combatant targets by sub-national groups or clandestine agents, usually intended to influence an audience'; this specifies that the act must be political in motivation and directed against non-combatants. Yet this definition runs into trouble both over what constitutes political motivation, given that mixed motives are usually present for violent acts, and over who might count as a non-combatant, particularly in cases where those targeted are the civilian officials or the police of an occupying state.

This definition of terrorism also implicitly excludes the possibility that states could be the agents of terror, despite the fact that there are clear historical cases where states have used terrorist violence against their populations. The term 'terrorist' originated in the Reign of Terror (1793–4) in the French Revolution, during which the Committee on Public Safety and the Revolutionary Tribunal, headed by Maximilien Robespierre, hunted down thousands of French citizens loyal to the old regime and imprisoned or executed them. In the 1930s, the term 'terrorism' was most closely associated with totalitarian states such as Nazi Germany and Stalin's Soviet Union (Hoffman, 2006). More recent examples of state-led terror would include Cambodia under the Khmer Rouge and Iraq under Saddam Hussein. More controversial, however, is the claim that 'terrorism' applies to the use of force during wartime. An oft-cited example of state terrorism during wartime is the Allied bombing of Dresden in 1945, which produced a firestorm that devastated the city and killed at least 25,000 people. As this bombing raid was clearly designed to create fear in an audience beyond its immediate target, it at least merits comparison with more traditional forms of terrorism. Whether – as Hoffman (2006) suggests – the fact that state actors such as the Allied forces make an effort to be discriminate and submit their actions (at least in principle) to the distinction between combatant and non-combatant makes a difference in categorizing their action as terrorism remains a debatable point.

But the relationship between terrorism and the state cannot be described solely in terms of perpetrators and victims. Many modern democratic states were founded by revolutionary groups who employed a mix of insurgent tactics and terrorism. The United States, for example, was a state borne out of a revolution against an imperial power, and its principal fighting force, the Continental Army, regularly used insurgent tactics such as ambushes to harass British forces. The state of Israel was founded in part due to the activities of two terrorist organizations (the Irgun and the Lehi, alternatively called the Stern Gang), both of which used assassinations and bombings to convince the British that they should abandon their efforts to control Palestine. Terrorism was part of their regular repertoire of action; the Irgun's bombing of the King David Hotel in Jerusalem in July 1946 killed 91 people and remains one of the most lethal terrorist incidents of the twentieth century (Hoffman, 2006).

Such examples of terrorism as a tactic within an insurgency points to the difficulties involved in maintaining a nominal distinction between a 'terrorist' and an 'insurgent' or 'militant' (Laqueur, 2003). When terrorist tactics are employed in the context of a national liberation struggle or a struggle against occupation, the international media tends to shy away from the word 'terrorist' in favour of more neutral terms (Hoffman, 2006). This terminological neutrality implies that the perceived legitimacy of the cause obviates the fact that indiscriminate harm to civilians has been caused. This parsing of language is particularly evident in the Middle East, where Palestinian suicide bombers are alternatively described in the international media as 'terrorists' or 'militants', sometimes within the same story (Hoffman, 2006). Jenkins (1980) and Hoffman (2006) point out that the term 'terrorist' is a pejorative one, so making sure that that label is attached to one's enemy and not oneself is a primary concern for armed groups and insurgents. This clear element of subjectivity in application of the term 'terrorist' suggests that achieving a perfect definition of terrorism is difficult, if not impossible (Laqueur, 2003).

While there will always be difficulties in defining terrorism, there is nevertheless no reason to succumb to the total relativism of 'one man's terrorist is another man's freedom fighter'. As a social and political phenomenon, terrorism does have distinct characteristics which can be captured, however imperfectly, in a definition. In a comprehensive review of the common elements of over 109 definitions of terrorism, A.P. Schmid (1988) produced a consensus definition which successfully captures much of the complexity of the phenomenon: 'Terrorism is an anxiety-inspiring method of repeated violent action, employed by (semi-) clandestine individual, group or state actors, for idiosyncratic, criminal or political reasons, whereby – in contrast to assassinations – the direct targets of violence are not the main targets' (Schmid, 1988: 28). While no definition perfectly describes every instance of terrorism, this definition highlights the key features – extra-normal victimization, variable motives and the infliction of psychological fear or stress on an audience beyond the target – which are the distinguishing indicators of terrorist violence.

The causes of terrorism

The causes of terrorism are equally, if not more, complex. There are five general approaches to the causes of terrorism, though none have been proven to provide a comprehensive explanation for the phenomenon. The first is a simply a strategic rationale: that is, that the terrorist perceives that the benefits – either tangible or in terms of publicity – associated with inflicting indiscriminate harm on others outweigh the expected costs (Crenshaw, 1981; Wardlaw, 1989). In many cases, the strategic necessity for terrorist violence is a function of the relative power disadvantage that the terrorist faces. 'Cast perpetually on the defensive and forced to take up arms to protect themselves and their real and imagined constituency only,' Bruce Hoffman (2006) writes, 'terrorists perceive themselves to be reluctant warriors, driven by desperation – and lacking any viable alternative – to violence against a repressive state, a predatory rival or ethnic group or an unresponsive international order' (Hoffman, 2006: 22). In such a desperate situation, terrorist violence can provide a low-cost way of publicizing grievances (Wardlaw, 1989). Moreover, because terrorists operate from the shadows and attack at chosen moments, it is hard if not impossible to deter them or to fully protect a vulnerable society, especially from independent or semi-independent terrorist cells. The pervasive fear generated by terrorist violence can, under certain circumstances, allow a terrorist group to win concessions from a far more powerful opponent (Jenkins, 1974b; Wardlaw, 1989).

It is important to emphasize that terrorism is not always successful in generating a strategic payoff. The strategic payoff from symbolic terrorist acts (such as the Oklahoma City bombings) or from catastrophic or mass-casualty terrorism (such as the 9/11 attacks or the Aum Shinrikyo gas attack on a Tokyo subway) appears to be negligible; if anything, these attacks tend to strengthen the resolve of governments to crack down on terrorist groups and their supporters. Symbolic terrorist attacks are those directed at a symbol of political, religious or ethnic significance, while catastrophic terrorism tends to aim at mass casualties. These types can overlap, as they did with the 11 September attacks. Indeed, there is some question as to whether it makes sense to attribute a discrete payoff to such attacks, because they may just be 'propaganda of the deed' or an attempt to mobilize populations for a particular cause. Such acts of terrorism also have diminished strategic payoff because of the blowback effect, whereby the outrage caused by the attacks itself induces fewer concessions from the target than the perpetrator would otherwise have achieved. But terrorism does occasionally deliver power to its perpetrators, either as part of bargaining within an ongoing conflict (for example, the LTTE's use of suicide attacks in Sri Lanka) or at forcing the eventual withdrawal of an occupying power (such as FLN attacks against the French in Algeria). Although achieving political change or gaining control of the state is rare for terrorist movements, even the hope of achieving such a goal is sufficient to convince some groups to follow a deliberate strategy of terror (Hoffman, 2006). Moreover, what may matter more is not that terrorism 'works' as a strategy, but rather than terrorists perceive that it does (Jenkins, 1974b).

Such a rational cost–benefit approach to terrorism has recently been invoked to explain the ultimate in apparently irrational acts of terror: suicide terrorism (Pape, 2003; Bloom, 2005). According to Robert Pape (2003), suicide terrorism is not usually the work of random fanatics, but rather part of a distinct and organized strategy by a group to win political concessions at a relatively low cost. While the act may be irrational at the individual level, because the perpetrator does not survive to reap the benefits of the attack, suicide terror can be a successful strategy for a group if it forces states to end an occupation of contested territory. By sacrificing his or her life, the terrorist becomes a kind of altruist who serves a cause with a distinct payoff for his or her real or imagined constituency (Hoffman, 2006). Affecting the strategic payoff from this kind of violence, in particular by offering political concessions to drain support for terror from aggrieved communities, is seen as essential for ending suicide terrorism.

But the strategic logic alone cannot fully explain the phenomenon of terrorism. There are many communities with distinct political grievances, but only a select few turn to terrorism; moreover, some radical or 'lone wolf' terrorists appear to act without reference to widespread political grievances or discrete strategic payoff. This has raised the question of whether radical or extremist ideologies naturally lead groups to terror. Historically, there has been a close relationship between radicalism or extremist ideologies (whether religious, Marxist or otherwise) and terrorism (Laqueur, 1999). In the nineteenth and early twentieth century, terrorism was often the weapon of radicalized outcasts such as the

European anarchists in the late Victorian era or the violent opponents of the Tsarist regime in Russia. As Laqueur (1999) points out, the terrorist movements of the mid-twentieth century included extremist movements on the left (Red Army Faction, Red Brigades, IRA, ETA, Palestinian terrorists) and on the right (neo-Nazis in Germany, right-wing American militias). Extremism can come in odd, sometimes contradictory forms. For example, some current animal rights groups see no apparent contradiction in terrorizing humans for the sake of protecting non-humans; leftist terrorist groups such as the Red Army Faction saw no tension between holding a commitment to socialism and succumbing to the kind of extremism that produces terrorist violence. Across the political spectrum, extremist ideologies, particularly those that provide a pervading sense of desperation in a battle against a far superior opponent or a powerful sense of fighting for a noble cause, have been an important factor in turning idealistic, politically engaged people towards terrorism.

But while extremist ideologies may play a role in setting the preconditions for terrorism, they are neither necessary nor sufficient to bring about a turn towards terrorism. There are many radicalized groups that do not engage in terrorist acts, no matter how extreme their rhetoric is. Moreover, some terrorist acts come out of motives (such as revenge or crime) which are unrelated to any extremist ideology (Schmid, 2004). Radicalization is not always followed by violence; rather, there are a series of intervening variables that steer an individual either towards or away from terrorism. Sageman (2004) argues that the steps towards radicalization are a function of social networks and inter-group dynamics, rather than individual pathologies. Recent promising work in psychological approaches to this problem sees 'terrorism as a process', that is, a sequence of interdependent steps through which individuals become drawn towards terrorist groups (Horgan and Taylor, 2006). A number of factors – such as the social and political context and the individual's personal circumstances – that can explain why people shift in and out of extremist groups affect this process. Such an approach has many virtues, not the least of which is to account for cases under which individuals are drawn to extremist ideologies but not to terrorism.

Beyond extremism, however, lies the issue of religion. Since 11 September, considerable attention has been given to the role of religion, in particular Islam, in fuelling terrorism. Religious terrorism is not a new phenomenon. Terror has been employed in a wide range of religious traditions, including Judaism (the zealot revolt against the Roman Empire in 66–70 AD), Islam (the attacks by the Order of the Assassins on political leaders from 1090–1272 AD) and Hinduism (the sacrificial killings by secret society enforcers to please the Hindu god Kali) (Laqueur, 1999; Juergensmeyer, 2001). Since 11 September, the chief focus of the study of religious extremism has been on Islam, in particular the radicalized Islam of Sunni-dominated groups like al-Qaeda. To some observers, such groups represent a worrying evolution of religious fanaticism, with an emphasis on waging a worldwide *jihad* through attacks on civilian targets to roll back the influence of the West or to establish a new caliphate in the Middle East (Bergen, 2002; Burke, 2004; Gunaratna, 2003). The interrelationship between terrorism and radical Islam is explained alternatively as a function of the perceived failure of modernization in the Arab world (Lewis, 2002) or the clash between secular Western values and religious fundamentalism in the Middle East (Barber, 2003). Still others suggest that terrorism is a manifestation of an internal doctrinal war within Islam, similar to the bloody Reformation in Christianity in the sixteenth century (Aslan, 2006). Some – but not all – of these accounts imply that the West happens to be an unfortunate bystander and scapegoat in an internal war not of its own making.

Yet there are at least three reasons to be sceptical of overly simplified explanations of the link between terrorism and Islam. First, as in many religions, the central ideas and texts of Islam are polyvalent and can be used to justify many different things. *Jihad*, for example, can be interpreted merely as a non-violent struggle against hardship or as a call to arms against all those who do not subscribe to the 'true' form of Islam. Second, as Louise Richardson (2006) points out, it may not be religion which is having the persuasive effect on radicalizing Muslims. Many Muslims live in states marked by intense political conflict in which radicalization might have occurred no matter what religion was prevalent. It may be that religion is only a convenient organizing device in places where transformative politics are attractive but risky. The religious imagery of Islam, in this view, is employed in justifying terror not because of any inherent features of the religion itself but because it has an enduring resonance with the terrorist's self-ascribed constituency. Finally, grand theories linking Islam with terrorism tend to downplay the role of discrete foreign policy choices made by Western governments – for example, support for Israel or the invasion and occupation of Iraq – in motivating groups like al-Qaeda to engage in terrorism (Scheuer, 2004).

Another explanation for terrorism concerns poverty, especially in the developing world. Strong forms of this argument suggest that it was not coincidental that the 9/11 attacks were directed at the symbol of global capitalism, the World Trade Center, as the attacks reflect a reaction to the growing gap between the rich and poor (Honderich, 2002). A more conventional form of the link between terrorism and poverty holds that widespread and endemic poverty, coupled with high rates of unemployment for educated young men, creates conditions conducive to radicalization and later terrorism. There is some superficial evidence to suggest a link between poverty and terror; terrorist groups, especially of the Marxist, Maoist and revolutionary varieties, tend to adopt language that emphasizes their support for the poor and disenfranchised. However, as a general rule the historical record for the relationship between terrorism and poverty is mixed at best (Laqueur, 2003). Neither the leaders nor the rank-and-file of terrorist groups come exclusively from the poor or the dispossessed. For example, the leadership of al-Qaeda is neither poor (Osama Bin Laden had a fortune estimated in the tens if not hundreds of millions before the 11 September attacks) nor uneducated (Ayman al-Zawahiri was a prominent Egyptian eye doctor). Among the rank-and-file, the pattern is similar. Educated young people who hailed from the middle class drove the leftist terrorism in Europe in the mid-1970s; similarly, the 11 September hijackers were educated in the West and came from middle-class or affluent backgrounds. Many insurgent groups who use terrorism, particularly Maoist groups like the Shining Path in Peru, claim to work on behalf of the dispossessed, but how much this is a genuine motivation, rather than a rhetorical strategy, remains debatable (Weinstein, 2003). Certainly, the record of terrorist groups who take up the mantle of the poor does not always match their rhetoric. The Shining Path, for example, regularly brutalized the peasantry, conducting show trials and executions to intimidate the poor into supporting them (Manwaring, 1995). Finally, the poverty explanation for terrorism must also explain why many other desperately poor countries have a non-existent or negligible record of producing terrorists. It may be that widespread unemployment among young men is conducive to radicalization, but this is also correlated with organized crime and related activities. Poverty and desperation is endemic throughout much of the world, but terrorism is not.

Another contending explanation for terrorism relates to political regime type. After the 11 September attacks, President Bush endorsed the view that the lack of democracy in the Middle East produced widespread alienation from normal politics, which in turn fuelled radicalization and terror (US White House, 2002). The lack of legitimate avenues for political expression in non-democracies, according to this theory, produces a seething cauldron of discontent, which tends to lower the costs associated with mobilizing young people for terror campaigns. Autocratic regimes would thus produce conditions conducive for recruiting terrorist operatives and turning otherwise normal activists towards forms of violent political expression. Turning these states towards democracy would presumably 'drain the swamp' of terrorist support and lead to the collapse of terrorist movements (Windsor, 2006).

As was the case with poverty, however, the evidence for this explanation of terrorism is mixed. It is certainly true that autocratic regimes dominate the Middle East and terrorist groups such as al-Qaeda hold long-standing grudges against some of these regimes. However, the historical record does not show a strong correlation between autocracy and terrorism, or between democracy and the absence of terrorism (Gause, 2005). Many liberal democracies have had to contend with home-grown terrorist movements (for example, the Red Army Faction and the Red Brigades in Western Europe and the right-wing extremists in the United States).

Moreover, there is limited evidence that democracy lifts the lid off discontent and diverts radicalized people away from terrorism. Many tolerant European states are confronted with home-grown radical groups in their midst who have chosen not avail themselves of democratic expression within the state or, worse still, have exploited it for their activities. These examples suggest that democracy is not the panacea for terrorism, and indeed that even the term 'democracy' may be too broad to be able to draw hard conclusions about its relationship with terrorism (Crenshaw, 2005).

There is also the negative case problem: any explanation based on a lack of democracy would need to explain the dozens of cases of non-democratic states that do not produce terrorism in any form. Highly autocratic and repressive regimes, such as North Korea, are generally the least susceptible to terrorist violence. States with semi-autocratic regimes, or weak democracies, appear to be more likely to produce terrorists than those states that ruthlessly exercise control over their population. But if weak autocratic regimes or democracies do occasionally produce terrorist groups, it does not automatically follow that democratization would put an end to terrorism. The transition towards democracy tends to produce instability and political violence in many states, and the process towards democratization in states with a 'terrorist problem' may be bloodier and even more dangerous (Snyder, 2000; Gause, 2005) than other cases. Finally, many terrorist groups such as al-Qaeda have issued statements declaring their unyielding hostility to democracy in any form. While democratization may reduce the number of people who find their message attractive, it is unlikely to make al-Qaeda and other similar groups close up shop in the Middle East or elsewhere (Gause, 2005).

The final set of explanations for terrorism relates to the psychological dimensions of terrorism. At the most basic level, terrorism is clearly a form of psychological warfare, in that it aims to induce fear in a target audience and to generate a reputation of strength and resilience for the terrorist group (Jenkins, 1981; Schmid, 2005; Hoffman and McCormick, 2004). The intended psychological effect is the reason why terrorists use spectacular or highly lethal attacks to attract public attention, and why terrorist organizations devote resources to controlling the message in the media (Wardlaw, 1989; Hoffman, 2006). Some of the earliest analyses of terrorism emphasized that it was a form of theatre, carefully choreographed for maximum psychological effect, for as Brian M. Jenkins put it 'terrorists want a lot of people watching and a lot of people listening and not a lot of people dead' (Jenkins, 1974a: 15). Moreover, there is evidence that social psychology can explain why people brought into terrorist organizations, and cut off from ties to family and other social groups, remain invested in these organizations for a long time (McCauley, 2002)

However, there is no reason to assume that a single psychological profile of a 'terrorist' exists. Public reaction to acts of terrorism generally reinforces the notion that a terrorist must be a lunatic drawn to nothing but destruction and death. Certainly some individual terrorists demonstrate evidence of distinct pathologies which set them apart from other people. Theodore Kaczynski, the Unabomber who sent letter bombs to various locations in the United States, may be afflicted by some psychopathology (McCauley, 2002). But across the population of people involved in terrorism there is no distinct and identifiable terrorist profile (McCauley, 2002; Horgan, 2005). Most studies have concluded that terrorists are not psychopathic killers and that there are no unique psychological features which set terrorists apart from the general population. Terrorists operate like ordinary people in most of their lives, and in many cases behave in ways quite similar to their victims. The notion that that there is an inherent emotional or psychological make-up of terrorists provides a seductive but misleading impression that terrorists can be identified and, even stopped, *ex ante*. This is unlikely to be the case. Aside from the insights that social psychology provides into group dynamics, the most important contribution that psychology will make to terrorism studies is in identifying the processes of radicalization and the social and political context for terror, rather than producing a generic psychological profile of a terrorist.

None of the five causes presented here – strategic, ideological, political, economic, or psychological – have proven to be sufficient to fully explain terrorism. This is perhaps because no single causal explanation can capture a complex phenomenon like terrorism, which is the product of an interaction of causal factors operating at both the individual and social or political levels. Moreover, the search for causes of terrorism may be facilitated by disaggregating the general category into its component sub-types (for example, national liberation terrorism, radical Islamic terror, etc.) and by assuming that a different set of causal variables may be associated with each sub-type. By rejecting mono-causal explanations for terrorism, and by breaking the phenomenon down to its component parts, the next generation of research may provide greater insight into the causes of terrorism.

Al-Qaeda and the future of terrorism

One of the central debates in the literature on terrorism concerns whether groups like al-Qaeda represent a new form of terrorism, unique and distinct from the past examples of terrorist movements. Advocates of the 'new terrorism' hypothesis argue that modern terrorists are less concerned with minimizing civilian casualties than their predecessors (Laqueur, 1999; Stern, 1999; Allison, 2004). Evidence for the growing barbarity of terrorist violence is not hard to find. The historian Eric Hobsbawm (1995: 13) pointed out that revolutionaries of the nineteenth century such as Friedrich Engels were horrified at attacks which targeted non-combatants. By contrast, the agents of 'new terrorism' appear to relish the possibility of mass casualties. Nine months after the 11 September attacks, Abu Gheith, a spokesman for al-Qaeda, suggested that al-Qaeda had the right to kill 4 million Americans, including 2 million children (quoted in Allison, 2004: 12). Bin Laden has been explicit that the killing of innocents is permissible in the context of *jihad* (Bergen, 2002; Scheuer, 2004). The conventions and laws of war and the general strictures of morality, which gave pause to even the most radical terrorists of the early twentieth century, appear to pose fewer problems for modern terrorists who are committed to death and destruction on a massive scale.

Especially since the 11 September attacks, many experts have been concerned that this commitment to mass killings may be facilitated by the spread of modern technology, especially nuclear, chemical and biological weapons, around the world. Considerably more attention has been paid to the threat of nuclear terrorism than chemical or biological, though the risks associated with the latter may be greater. This is in part because the casualties associated even with a rare event of nuclear terror would be so extraordinary. A 15-kiloton device placed in a major city would devastate several square miles and produce casualties ranging from 30,000 to 100,000 (Laqueur, 1999: 72). The resulting social and economic chaos, and environmental and public health aftershocks, would be incalculable. Graham Allison (2004) concluded that terrorist organizations with significant capabilities, such as al-Qaeda or Jemaah Islamiyah, would be the most likely perpetrators of nuclear terrorism, but that any number of small splinter groups could presumably have access to loose nuclear material on the black market or to material stolen from nuclear-armed states such as Pakistan. Moreover, there is no longer a question of intent. Osama bin Laden, for example, has signalled his intent to acquire nuclear capabilities and to use them on the United States and its allies (Scheuer, 2004).

The risks of chemical and biological terrorism appear to be equally severe. Materials for both are low cost and easier to obtain than nuclear weapons, and require a less substantial infrastructure to launch a successful attack. The anthrax attacks on various locations in the United States in late 2001 indicate that even a 'lone wolf' terrorist could cause significant disruption to social and political life with sporadic attacks. If chemical attacks were conducted with reasonable levels of efficiency, the death toll could be substantially higher. Likewise, biological attacks would be at least equally lethal and hard to track. A US government estimate in the early 1990s concluded that over a million casualties could be produced over a short period with an efficient and sophisticated biological attack (Laqueur, 2003: 227). The ease of movement around the world, in particular air travel, suggests that the spread of a biological agent could be quicker and more lethal than at any other time in history.

The nexus between terrorism and weapons of mass destruction has received considerable attention since the 11 September attacks, especially as evidence emerges that al-Qaeda has repeatedly sought to acquire such capability. In both academic and policy circles, this has led to intense debate on how best to eliminate state support for terrorist groups. While the 'new terrorist' movement is transnational and highly mobile, some experts point out that groups like al-Qaeda nevertheless need to a base of operations within a state to survive (Byman, 2005b). State support can vary from direct support to a kind of benign neglect where terrorists are left to run their operations independently of their host. This argument holds that the Achilles heel of 'new terrorism' is the states that sponsor or host them, who can be held legally, politically and even militarily account-able by other states. Threatening states which support or give political space for terrorist groups would presumably deter others from supporting terrorism and force weak states to ruthlessly pursue terrorists within their borders. Other experts suggest that terrorist groups can be deterred through measures short of war, particularly if it is clear to them that valu-able goals will be sacrificed if they choose to engage in certain terrorist acts (Trager and Zagorcheva, 2005–6).

This line of argument has led to an intriguing disjuncture in the debate over the 'new terrorism'. While the threat is amorphous and transnational, the remedy proposed is usually framed in terms of state choice. Is this suffi-cient to counter terrorists of nearly global reach? If al-Qaeda has emerged as an international brigade for terrorism across the world, adopting a response which is hemmed in by state borders may be insufficient. If al-Qaeda has gradually become 'a global instrument with which to compete and challenge Western influence in the Muslim world', it poses an unprece-dented challenge to these states (Gunaratna, 2003: 1). The spread of radi-cal Islam to Europe, Asia and elsewhere appears to give al-Qaeda and related groups a kind of 'strategic depth' that they would otherwise lack (Simon and Benjamin, 2005). Radical ideologies of terror in the past, such as anarchism in the late nineteenth century, sought a wider, even global audience, but were limited by the technology of the time to pamphlets and other forms of communication with a modest reach. By contrast, the 'new terrorists' can extend their activities around the globe by taking advantage of modern innovations such as the Internet and cheap air travel (Kiras, 2007). One of the essential questions in contemporary security studies is whether state-based responses are sufficient for a threat whose shadow extends beyond national borders.

The 'new terrorism' exemplified by al-Qaeda may also have a different leadership structure than previous terrorist organizations. In contrast to the hierarchical or cell structure of older terrorist organizations, groups like-al-Qaeda tend to resemble a leaderless resistance, with no chain of command or membership roll. Such an organization comprises individuals who are inspired by a particular leader or ideology, but who take no direct orders from any particular person or organization (Hoffman, 2006). This is even more decentralized and diffuse than the cell structures that dominated terrorist organizations in the 1960s and 1970s. Such a nearly independent structure complicates efforts by law enforcement to track those involved in terrorist activities or to prevent attacks. With a looser and flatter organizational structure, new terrorism represents a 'network of networks' rather than an organization in the conventional sense.

Hoffman (2004) and others have become concerned that the 'new terrorist' groups al-Qaeda and Jemaah Islamiyah might have morphed into a kind of 'franchise terrorism', comprised of almost fully independent secret cells, rather than an organization with a distinct structure. A related fear is that al-Qaeda may have become a brand name of sorts – a McDonald's of terrorism – that will then be adopted by many disgruntled groups. There is some evidence to suggest that this has occurred. In early 2007, for example, an Algerian Islamist militant group sought and received permission from Bin Laden to rename itself 'al-Qaeda', in the hopes of improving its fortunes in its insurgency against the secular government. Such spreading of the brand name now extends to insurgencies: the splinter group al-Qaeda in Iraq appears to have some kind of relationship with the nominal heads of al-Qaeda, Osama Bin Laden and Ayman al-Zawahiri, but the extent to which it takes orders from the al-Qaeda leadership is unclear. Some independent terrorist groups appear to adopt the language and tactics of al-Qaeda for propaganda purposes, even if their goals are very different. Despite carrying out their attacks in the name of al-Qaeda, neither the Muslim immigrants who attacked a commuter train in Madrid in March 2004 nor the British Muslims who launched attacks on the London Underground in July 2005 appeared to have regular or direct operational communication with the al-Qaeda high command.

All of these factors – the indifference to civilian casualties, the clever capitalization on modern technologies and weaponry, the leaderless cell structure, and the development of a brand name of radical Islam – suggest that the current problem of international terrorism may be of a different nature from what has existed in the past. In some ways, this new terrorism may be a reflection of globalization, as it involves small, decentralized networks of terrorist groups capitalizing on an increasingly borderless world to increase the vulnerability of those who had lived in the safety of the developed world.

Yet there are at least two possible critiques of the concept of 'new terrorism' which warrant serious consideration. First, it may be that the novelty of al-Qaeda is overstated, for previous groups had nearly independent cell structures (for example, Russian revolutionaries against the Tsarist regime) and ideologies that purported to have global reach (such as Marxist terrorist groups). Al-Qaeda's chief innovation may be technological, in the use of the Internet, air travel and modern technologies like mobile phones, rather than its political orientation or global reach.

Second, there are important sceptical voices who suggest that the fear of 'new terrorism' is overblown. Accusing the terrorism industry of inflating the threats of terrorism, especially since 11 September, John Mueller (2005) attacks in particular those who focus attention on the connection between terrorism and weapons of mass destruction. Mueller points out that the spread of nuclear arms has actually been reasonably slow, and that the costs involved in building and launching a nuclear device for an act of terrorism might be higher than expected. Similarly, he points out that the risks of casualties with chemical and biological weapons are often overestimated, given the low rates of lethality from both types of weapons (so far) and the expected difficulties of using them successfully. Yet Mueller's focus on the relatively small risk of dying in terrorist attack may overlook the devastating effects of such an attack, which justify the expense spent on prevention (Byman, 2005a).

How does the emergence of a 'new terrorism' shift the way that states handle terrorism? Some critics have suggested that fighting terrorism in traditional but narrow ways, such as punishing state support for terror to drain terrorist resources, may be misguided. The historian Michael Howard (2006–7) suggests that the remedy for new terrorism will be found not by defeating al-Qaeda or punishing states like Iraq but by transforming the sullen resentment and antipathy towards the West that fuels the new terrorism. This is a political task that a strategy of holding states accountable for terrorism, to the point of preventive war, does not address. Others, such as David Kilcullen (2005), suggest that the battle against the 'new terrorists' should be reconceptualized as a global counter-insurgency where the goal is to disaggregate the various groups allied under the banner of al-Qaeda into constituent units and defeat them separately.

What is insurgency?

Just as was the case with terrorism, 'insurgency' is a term that eludes a consensus definition. Broadly understood, insurgency is the strategic use of violence by armed factions against a state or occupying force for the purpose of overthrowing the existing political order. In most cases, insurgency is a form of asymmetric warfare, because the insurgent forces are generally weaker than the government or occupying army, which has the coercive power of the police and army at its disposal. Insurgent warfare is marked by the absence of fixed battle lines, by the use of secrecy and ambush, and by the competition for the support of the population between the insurgents and their opponents (sometimes called 'incumbents') (Kalyvas, 2006). The term insurgency is nearly synonymous with a number of other phrases – including small wars, guerrilla wars, people's wars, partisan wars and wars of national liberation – all of which capture the essential idea that the insurgent hopes to overcome its weakness against a conventional foe with stealth, mobility and ruthlessness.

The conceptual attributes of insurgencies are as follows. First, insurgent warfare is operationally closer to harassment of the opposing force, than to open warfare. Its focus is primarily denial: that is, to stop the government or opposing force from establishing functional control over a contested territory. Only at the final stages of an insurgency do the battle lines begin to resemble those in a conventional war. Second, insurgents typically have inferior technology to their opponents. Third, because insurgencies are comprised of small units or cells of fighters, they have greater flexibility in launching operations, and mobility for adjusting to circumstances than conventional armies. Fourth, the insurgent force generally capitalizes on its superior knowledge of the terrain for concealment and surprise. Finally, the insurgent force typically seeks to create networks of information among the local population in order to facilitate its operations and to provide a ready base of support should it be successful against its enemy. Mao Tse-Tung ([1961] 2000: 93) famously remarked that the guerrilla must move among the people as a fish swims in the sea.

As a social and political phenomenon, insurgency is not new. While there are numerous examples of insurgent forces fighting alongside conventional armies in the past, the most significant modern example was the uprising against France's occupation of Spain (1808–14), from which the term 'guerrilla warfare' – meaning 'small war' in Spanish – arose. The strategy and tactics of the Spanish guerrillas would not be unfamiliar today; they used ambushes to hold down Napoleon's army in cities, while their irregular militias cut supply lines and harassed army units in the countryside. By 1810, over 300,000 French troops were in Spain fighting the insurgency, which in turn diminished Napoleon's ability to fight on other fronts. The asymmetry of power between the French Army and the Spanish people had been overcome by a denial strategy that raised the costs of occupation to unacceptable levels. Napoleon came to conclude that this national uprising was the cause of his undoing, for 'that unfortunate war destroyed me. All my disasters are bound up in that fatal knot' (quoted in Smith, 2006: 159).

There is an extensive canon of theories of insurgency and guerrilla warfare, largely borne out of individual experiences of success or failure. The first major theorist of guerrilla warfare was the British adventurer T.E. Lawrence, who fought with Arab irregular forces in the Arab uprising against the Ottoman Empire (1916–18). Lawrence and his forces used ambush and destruction of rail lines to harass the Ottoman forces, who were too few in number to crush the revolt. Mobility, he believed, was essential; the insurgent must 'tip and run', and use 'not pushes but strokes' to force retreat on the enemy (quoted in Laqueur, 1998: 170). On the basis of his experience, he came to believe that a science of guerrilla warfare could be constructed, based on an 'algebraic' relationship between material and spiritual factors (Laqueur, 1998). Lawrence's approach to guerrilla warfare remained a collection of observations rather than a coherent theory, but he is well remembered for his warning to counter-insurgent forces that 'to make war upon rebellion is messy and slow, like eating soup with a knife' (quoted in Nagl, 2005).

The second major theorist of guerrilla warfare was Mao Tse-Tung. Drawing from his experience leading Chinese Communist Party (CCP) guerrillas against the Chinese government of Chiang Kai-Shek, and later the occupying Japanese Army, Mao developed an elaborate three-stage theory of guerrilla warfare. During the first stage, the guerrilla avoids pitched battles and conducts operations to stretch enemy resources and to demonstrate the moral strength of the guerrilla. In the second stage, the guerrilla fights the conventional army to a stalemate and begins to force the enemy to evacuate towns and contested territory. Once the guerrilla force has a base of operations, it can shift into offensive operations and use over-whelming force to devastate the enemy and to capture control over the state (Mao [1961] 2000; Kiras, 2007). Patience, and a keen awareness of the stages of a guerrilla war campaign, were essential in Mao's theory. Without a sense of timing and political acumen, the guerrilla army could not launch a successful revolution on its own.

Subsequent theorists of guerrilla warfare, however, were less willing to wait until the objective conditions for success in a campaign had been reached. Ernesto 'Che' Guevara, who trained as a medical doctor before fighting with Fidel Castro in the Cuban Revolution, believed that small bands of organized guerrillas could jumpstart a revolution on their own, in the absence of any pre-existing 'objective' conditions. This *foco* theory of guerrilla warfare emphasized that popular forces alone can win against a conventional army provided that they have the support of the population (Guevara, [1961] 2003). This emphasis on taking the initiative to start guerrilla warfare was adopted by a Brazilian theorist, Carlos Marighella, who argued in his 'Minimanual of the Urban Guerrilla' that acts of terror can create the conditions for revolution, even in cities under the control of the government (Laqueur, 1998). The key to Marighella's theory was the population's reaction to the cycle of response and counter-response by the governments and insurgents; if the government failed to act with restraint it would alienate the population and drive them towards the insurgents, even if the insurgents had been the ones initially responsible for the terror-ist acts. This would ultimately create a no-win scenario for the government and lead to victory for the insurgents.

While many of these classic theories of insurgency and guerrilla warfare found adherents across the globe, their value as theories are debatable. Most of the chief theorists of insurgent warfare drew directly from their own experience as fighters without accounting for case-specific variations, either in terrain (desert or jungle fighting, for example) or type of oppo-nent. Moreover, many of the theories presumed that guerrilla war could be fought and won independently of the behaviour of external actors. Mao, for example, does not attribute his success in winning the support of the

Chinese people to the fact that a foreign invader, Japan, conducted a brutal occupation of his country. Yet there could be little doubt that his resistance to Japan allowed the CCP to demonstrate its nationalist credentials and build a base of support. This systematic underestimation of the unique conditions for success in an insurgency raises some serious questions about whether these theories can be fruitfully applied to other cases.

Yet there is at least one feature of the later theories of insurgency that clearly applies to more recent cases: the embrace of terrorism. The early theorists of insurgency, such as Lawrence, were deeply concerned that violence should be minimized to preserve as much public support as possible for the eventual takeover of the state. Mao was similarly concerned and issued a series of rules to ensure that the Red Army treated the Chinese people fairly. While no guerrilla campaign was ever gentle in its treatment of the non-combatant population, for pragmatic reasons both Lawrence and Mao did not embrace the tactic of terrorist violence against non-combatants as part of their strategy. By contrast, Marighella (1968: 36) endorsed the use of terrorism in his writings, for:

> the terrorist act, apart from the apparent ease with which it can be carried out, is no different from other guerrilla acts and actions whose success depends on planning and determination. It is an action which the urban guerrilla must execute with the greatest calmness and determination.

This embrace of indiscriminate violence against non-combatants for the purposes of agitation and publicity is characteristic of terrorism and increasingly of modern insurgencies.

The dilemmas of counter-insurgency

Counter-insurgency is defined broadly as 'those military, paramilitary, political, economic, psychological and civic actions taken by a government to defeat an insurgency' (US Department of the Army, 2006). Like insurgency, counter-insurgency has a long history of theoretical approaches built on best practice from the direct battle experience. There are two schools of thought for counter-insurgency theory. The first is the direct approach, which assumes that fighting an insurgency operates by the same general logic as fighting a war (Nagl, 2005; Greenhill, 2007). Direct approaches try to play to the strengths of the more powerful counter-insurgent force by drawing insurgents into open combat and destroying them. In one of the first counter-insurgency manuals, C.E. Callwell argued that the counter-insurgent wins by 'overawing the enemy by bold initiative and by resolute action, whether on the battlefield or as part of a general plan of action' (quoted in Kiras, 2007: 177). Aside from its impact on combatants, the direct approach to counter-insurgency assumes that punishing insurgents and their supporters can transfer allegiance in the population back to the government or occupying army.

The 'hearts and minds' or indirect approach to counter-insurgency places less of an emphasis on coercing the population to support the government and more on winning their support through political concessions and aid. The term 'hearts and minds' was coined by Field Marshal Gerald Templar, who served as a commander in the Malaya Emergency between 1952 and 1954. He summarized this approach as constituting three 'oughts':

> Governments ought to secure their population from insurgent coercion. They ought to provide competent, legal and responsive administration that is free from past abuse and broader in domain, scope and vigour. And they ought to meet rising expectations with higher living standards. (quoted in Schafer, 1988: 62)

Both the direct approach and the 'hearts and minds' approach favour population-relocation efforts to separate insurgents from their population and to encourage the population to defect to the incumbents (Greenhill, 2007).

Since the 'war on terror' began, there has been a renewed interest in counter-insurgency theory and practice, with many asking whether the insurgencies in Afghanistan and Iraq bear any resemblance to previous insurgencies. That recent insurgencies appeared to be waged by a coalition of the willing, as opposed to a discrete organization with a coherent ideology and leadership, was surprising to some observers. Beckett (2005) remarked that, especially in Iraq, the insurgency appeared to be driven by groups that would emerge suddenly and cooperate in a joint strike against US and British forces, then disappear back into the population and not cooperate again. The overriding emphasis on denial as an objective, and the apparent lack of efforts to build an alternative political infrastructure, appear to set the Iraqi insurgency apart from previous cases. Yet an in-depth RAND study of counter-insurgencies during the cold war period revealed that other insurgencies (such as the FMLN in El Salvador) started similarly and only coalesced into coherent organizations after external pressure was applied (Long, 2006). That state structures in Afghanistan and Iraq are so weak would imply that external pressure has not been applied and that the armed factions have not been forced to coalesce. Without historical distance, it is impossible to know whether the insurgencies in Afghanistan or Iraq will be fully or only partially consistent with previous examples.

The big picture question, however, is whether developed Western countries are still willing to bear the political and moral costs of fighting brutal counter-insurgency campaigns. In the past, this was not in doubt. European colonial powers fought and won dozens of small wars throughout the nineteenth century and early twentieth century, often employing their advantages in technology (such as the machine gun) to ruthless effect (Beckett, 2001). They were also willing to mete out collective punishments to drain support for the rebellion. But, as Andrew Mack (1975) pointed out in a famous essay, Western states steadily became less successful at winning small wars in the late twentieth century. This is in part because the insurgents' aim is increasingly to destroy the incumbent's will, rather than capacity to fight. Part of the insurgent strategy for doing this is to prolong the conflict and to increase the costs in blood and treasure to the incumbent, to build up domestic opposition and force the occupying power into retreat. In Vietnam, for example, the Viet Cong campaign tied down increasing numbers of US forces and in doing so produced such intense domestic opposition that the United States was forced to withdraw. This dynamic is reinforced by the asymmetry of interests between insurgents fighting for their lives and occupying powers fighting for uncertain political goals in a foreign land (Mack, 1975). As long the insurgents could deny victory to the counter-insurgent forces, the waiting game would favour victory for the insurgents over the long term.

Aside from simply refraining from waging small wars, it is not clear how those wishing to fight 'small wars' can overcome this dilemma. Recent counter-insurgency theory has focused attention on how the competition for the population could be won at manageable political, economic and moral costs. Humanitarian aid and economic inducements are increasingly seen as necessary because in an age of worldwide media coercion comes with higher costs than it did in the early twentieth century. If true, this would place higher organizational and resource burdens on armies fighting counter-insurgency campaigns. An influential study by John Nagl (2005) emphasized the role of organizational learning as the key determinant of success and failure in counter-insurgent campaigns. If counter-insurgent forces cannot adjust to changing circumstances, and keep the delicate balance of coercion and inducement necessary to win the population to their camp, they are unlikely to succeed. The challenges posed by counter-insurgencies in such changing circumstances have led some critics to conclude that classic counter-insurgency theory will provide limited guidance on how to fight a campaign when every move that one makes is instantly broadcast around the globe (Kilcullen, 2006–7).

Conclusion

The events of 11 September, as well as the subsequent US invasions of Afghanistan and Iraq, have redefined the debate over the nature of terrorism and insurgency in the modern world. The insurgencies in Afghanistan and Iraq point to an increasing fusion of these two concepts, where terrorist violence is increasingly employed as a force multiplier within insurgent campaigns. As noted earlier, this is not entirely novel; terrorism has always been employed as a tactic within warfare (Schmid, 2004). What is novel is that terrorism is increasingly becoming the predominant strategy of insurgents, shifting from being one part of a wider strategy of opposition (as it was for the Irgun in the revolt against British rule) to the chief way that the insurgents do business (as it is for al-Qaeda in Iraq). This can be seen as a strategy of compensation, as terrorists try to overcome the conventional superiority of Western armed forces with violence against unprotected non-combatants (Bacevich, 2006). But terrorist violence such as suicide bombings is also now used as a catalyst for conflict between ethnic or sectarian groups, to induce the kind of chaos that makes it hard, if not impossible, for the occupier to win. This elevation of terror from an occasional tactic to a dominant strategy within insurgencies suggests that mass-casualty violence against non-combatants will increasingly become the preferred way to even the score in asymmetric conflicts. If this occurs, this fusion of terrorism and insurgency promises to lead to more bloodshed and barbarism as the war on terror continues.

Further reading

Hoffman, B. (2006) *Inside Terrorism*, 2nd edn, New York: Columbia University Press.

Laqueur, W. (2003) *No End to War: Terrorism in the Twenty First Century*, New York: Continuum.

Mueller, J. (2005) 'Six Rather Unusual Propositions about Terrorism', *Terrorism and Political Violence*, 17: 487–505.

Nagl, J. (2005) *Learning to Eat Soup with a Knife: Counter-insurgency Lessons from Malaya and Vietnam*, 2nd edn, Chicago: University of Chicago Press.

Pape, R. (2003) 'The Strategic Logic of Suicide Terrorism', *American Political Science Review*, 97, 3: 343–61.

Chapter 11

Intervention

Michael J. Arnold

Introduction

The end of the cold war and the subsequent implosion of the Soviet Union left its successor state, Russia, diminished and flailing with democratic and free-market reforms. That other great cold war protagonist, China had earlier rejected Mao's communist economic agenda for capitalism and it, like Russia, became heavily reliant on the West for investment, technology and access to its lucrative markets. The United States sat atop a new unipolar power configuration, seemingly unchallengeable as the sole superpower. With the East–West divide of the cold war gone, the march of democratic governance and free market economics was inexorable.

The tumultuous forces of what was to become known as globalization began to reshape the international landscape with a vengeance. Along with the information technology and financial revolutions, powerful new ideas regarding human rights and security gained traction, colliding with the old notions of the inviolability of state sovereignty. This was coupled with an evolving body of international law, and it is now apparent that the days of state rulers committing atrocities and hiding behind the state sovereignty were numbered. Future Pol Pots and Idi Amins could reasonably expect to be held to account by the international community for their crimes against humanity in a new International Criminal Court (ICC) that came into being at the start of the new century. State sovereignty was becoming conditional: that is, state leaders were expected to confirm to universally recognized standards of good governance. With these developments has grown an expectation that the international community would now intervene when the conditions of sovereignty were violated, with military force where necessary.

After the cold war's end, the United Nations' ability to manage security increased significantly, as the deadlock which had characterized the Security Council (UNSC) during the cold war eased markedly. The five permanent members of the UNSC were more able to find common ground on matters of security, particularly given the influence of the United States. A new optimism grew and a new freedom of action for the international community to intervene in military conflicts within states emerged. The early successes of the 1990–1 Gulf War and 1992 Cambodian intervention seemed to augur a bright new era for UN-sanctioned military interventions.

Since the Gulf War we have witnessed a succession of military interventions. The initial successes were followed by a string of what can only be described as unmitigated disasters, with only occasional operations deserving of being described as truly successful. In this chapter I will define military intervention, describe the types of military interventions, overview the debate on when an intervention is appropriate, and finally outline the requirements for successful interventions.

The future of military intervention

Global security in the first decade of the twenty-first century is as complex and paradoxical as ever. The forces of globalization are recasting developed and developing states alike. The interdependence of states is increasing, and even the most powerful are more vulnerable than at any other time in history. Weak actors, such as failed or failing states, and *jihadist* warriors such as al-Qaeda compete with the traditional interactions between competing strong states for the attentions of leaders and their policy makers. Military technology, both conventional and that relating to weapons of mass destruction (WMD), continues to diffuse throughout the globe. As al-Qaeda demonstrated, non-military technology can also be put to military use. Thus, military interventions are potentially becoming more risky, both militarily and politically.

Yet, at the same time, some of the forces mentioned above are increasing the likelihood of certain types of military intervention. The diffusion of military technology, particularly that related to WMDs and ballistic missiles, has created a greater willingness by the international community to undertake interdictions and contemplate preventive and pre-emptive operations against rogue states. However, the problems experienced by the United States and Britain in Iraq are likely to curb their enthusiasm for further major types of interventions, at least those that involve significant numbers of ground troops, in the short to medium term.

Given the problem of overstretching the highly capable militaries of the West, the notion of a standing force under the UN or a regional organization such as the European Union (EU) or more desirably NATO, given its access to the armed forces of many of the European states as well as the United States, Britain and Canada, has great appeal. Due to the entrenched political views of state sovereignty, there is little likelihood of a UN-based force coming into existence in the near future. However, NATO's expanding scope of operations has made it a more viable option.

In the long term, history tells us that military interventions of all types will occur as a matter of course. It is hard to imagine a world in which leaders of states will not resort to the use of military force when strategic circumstances demand it. Those circumstances, to be sure, will change. As will the reasons for military intervention. And while the evolving body of international law should, in theory, make the leaders of states and sub-state entities more accountable for their actions and thus reduce the incidence of conflicts requiring intervention, recent events demonstrate emphatically otherwise. Perhaps international law has created additional pressure on leaders to intervene in circumstances of gross violations of human rights where once arguments of state sovereignty and non-interference would have sufficed as reason enough not to intervene. Today it is increasingly difficult to justify non-intervention when either genocide or other forms of extreme human suffering are occurring and, most importantly, where the global media have highlighted the plight of the victims. The horrors of the Rwandan genocide of 1996 and the atrocities perpetrated in the Balkan's during the 1990s, and more recently the ethnic cleansing and genocide in the Sudan are clear examples of what is intolerable to the majority of citizens of the major western powers. Popular demand for intervention in future humanitarian crises is likely to remain strong.

On the other hand, the preventive war rationale that formed the basis of the Bush Administration's 2003 Iraq intervention and, it can be argued, Israel's 2006 intervention against Hezbollah in Lebanon ordered by the government of Ehud Olmert, has been discredited. The highly damaging political fallout that has resulted will serve as a salutary lesson for political leaders and will create, for at least the short term, a reluctance to intervene.

Definition of intervention

By intervention, I am referring to action by one state or group of states against another state or group of states designed to halt or change a course of action or policy deemed undesirable by the intervening state or group of states. Such interventions feature regularly throughout the history of humankind and seem to be a permanent feature of the anarchic international system where states continually vie with each other to gain an advantage in their general security. General security equates to a combination of favourable economic circumstances and freedom from military-based threats including those posed by other states and non-state actors such as terrorist groups.

Interventions can be roughly divided into those that are essentially military in nature, which in turn can involve the direct or indirect use of force, and those that are non-military, that is, primarily political, diplomatic or economic in nature. Non-military economic interventions include: inducements, such as one state or group of states offering another state access to markets, on favourable terms, in return for a change in its behaviour; punitive trade sanctions designed to adversely affect a state's economy; and so-called smart sanctions designed to impact on the ruling elite, such as freezing of personal financial assets and barring them from international travel.

Diplomatic efforts usually precede other forms of intervention and are akin to lobbying or pressuring a target state's key constituents (that is, its ruling elite, business elite, or even the general public). These may then in turn persuade policy makers to abandon an activity or course that is deemed a threat to international security, international trade, the well-being of the biosphere, etcetera. If diplomatic efforts fail and the stakes are considered high enough, then economic and/or military measures may result.

Military interventions differ from the other types in that there is usually the prospect of the use of deadly force and therefore the lives of everyone involved in the operation are at risk. Likewise, the lives of citizens of the state subject to the intervention, be they members of groups hostile to the intervention or non-combatants, are also potentially at risk (Haass, 1999: 2). Tony Coady (2005: 15) defines a military intervention as 'one power singly, or several powers jointly, acting without the express consent or invitation of the state invaded'. This succinct but rather narrow definition excludes those many instances where the target state has invited an outside force to intervene. Using Coady's definition Australia's 2006 military assistance to East Timor and the Solomon Islands, or the 1999 Australian-led InterFET mission in East Timor would not qualify as interventions as they all received approval from the host governments. I argue that at least in the latter case the example is not so cut and dried, as the Habibie government was coerced into allowing the intervention by the United States. Its assent was begrudging in the extreme but given the parlous state of the Indonesian economy after the 1997–8 Asian financial crisis and the US threat of blocking IMF loans and other aid it had little choice. Moreover, the brutal repression that the Indonesian army-controlled militias in East Timor inflicted on the local population was a form of proxy military action.

Richard Haass's (1999: 20) definition is broader and is the one favoured here: '[a]rmed interventions entail the introduction or deployment of new or additional combat forces to an area for specific purposes that go beyond ordinary training or for scheduled expressions of support for national interests.' This definition includes the broadest array of classic military activities such as wars of aggression as well as those circumstances where the aim of the intervention is benign and the target state's consent is given. These include peacekeeping, humanitarian assistance and some stabilization missions such as those in East Timor and the Solomon Islands in 2006.

Military interventions vary in their objectives; scale of operations; duration; force composition, that is, troop types (combat versus non-combat, ground versus air versus naval forces, the number of different national contingents); and their intensity. They range from deterrence, the threat of force, to the waging of a major war (warfighting), to preventive and pre-emptive actions, to nation or state building and humanitarian assistance, and small-scale rescues of hostages and police actions. Haass (1999: 49–65) has developed a useful categorization of types of interventions which will be overviewed later in this chapter.

Types of intervention: a typology

As stated above, military interventions can be direct or indirect in nature. They can also range in scale from small incursions into a foreign state's territory by special forces, like the Israeli operation to free hostages at Uganda's Entebbe airport in 1976, to larger-scale interventions with conventional forces, such as the United States' massive intervention to assist Britain, France and Russia against the Axis powers in the Second World War. Their objectives vary from humanitarian concerns such as the provision of food and medical succour to victims of natural disasters, such as relief efforts after the 2004 Boxing Day Tsunami in the Indian Ocean, to the destruction of a dangerous capability, real or potential, of another state, such as Japan's attack on the United States' Pacific Fleet at Pearl Harbour in 1941.

Haass (1999: 50) classifies interventions according to their purpose: deterrence, prevention, compellence, punitive, peacekeeping, warfighting, peace-making, policing, nation-building, interdiction, humanitarian assistance and rescue. He also identifies indirect uses of force, such as the provision of military assistance without engaging in direct intervention. Alex Bellamy and Paul Williams (2005: 157) offer an alternative classification of 'non-UN peace operations'. They have established a useful typology of six categories of intervention based on the type of actor (single state, regional organizations, and ad hoc coalitions of the willing) that undertook the intervention, and whether it received UNSC sanction or not.

By combining the Haass approach with that of Bellamy and Williams, a useful categorization of interventions can be developed. Haass provides the basis of identification of the species within the genus of military interventions while Bellamy and Williams provide guidance as to the identification of intervention sub-genera. This more refined categorization is useful in assessing the confusing melange of conflicts that have emerged in the post-cold war world. Bellamy and Williams' (2005) two sub-genera are: peace interventions and non-peace interventions. Peace interventions, as implied by the name, are operations designed to end conflict and/or provide succour to a suffering population. They include peacekeeping, peace-making, humanitarian and post-conflict stabilization operations. Non-peace interventions are simply all the other forms of intervention and are conducted with self-interest as the primary motivation of the intervening state(s).

Of course, classifications can become blurred and one form of intervention can lead to another. For example, the provision of military advisers by the United States to South Vietnam in 1959 quickly escalated into the mass deployment of combat troops and warfighting throughout the 1960s and early 1970s, while the 2003 Iraq warfighting intervention evolved into a state-building operation probably well beyond the scope initially envisaged by the Bush administration.

Non-peace operations

Deterrence

Haass (1999: 51) defines deterrence as an indirect form of intervention premised on the persuasion of an opponent that a particular course of action will have unacceptably high costs or risks. Deterrence strategies have been successfully employed by states either individually or in coalitions. Deterrence requires the state to possess the required military capability; the threat needs to be credible, and clearly communicated to the rival state.

There has been much debate, however, since the terrorist attacks on the United States in 2001 over the utility of deterrence as a strategy. The bloated nuclear arsenals of the cold war with their viable 'second strike' or retaliatory nuclear capability ensured that the superpowers and their major allies avoided direct military confrontations. However, with their basic assumption of an adversary's rationality (Sperandei, 2006: 264–5), they are increasingly seen as unnecessary or irrelevant to contemporary deterrence needs.

Compellence

Compellence can be considered the sibling of deterrence in that the former is seldom undertaken successfully without the latter being articulated or implicit in the strategic relationship between two or more states. (Sperandei, 2006: 253). Compellence then is the use of force in a discrete and limited way, designed to sway the decision making of the government of a state. An obvious historical example is the gunboat diplomacy of the colonial era. To differentiate compellence from deterrence there is a requirement for the actual use of force. That is, a state must destroy or clearly demonstrate its ability to destroy carefully chosen targets that are of high value to the target state, with the aim of altering the calculations about the cost of undesirable actions that state intends to undertake. The 1998 US and British air strikes on Iraq in response to the Iraqi decision to suspend cooperation with UN Special Commission (UNSCOM) and International Atomic Energy Agency (IAEA) inspectors is an example.

Haass (1999: 53–5) contends that in the contemporary world, given the proliferation of military capabilities, demonstrations of force such as gunboat diplomacy are not likely to be successful. Sperandei (2006: 278–9) suggests that this may not be so if a coherently linked deterrence–compellence strategy is designed and articulated rather than each being implemented discretely and sequentially. Demonstrations of force also have a significant political cost as the target state, more specifically the ruling elite, may suffer a loss of prestige or face and may in turn be more difficult to be swayed. The outcome heavily depends on how the decision makers in the target state react to the use of force. If they do not react in the way wanted, then the action will be seen as a failure, and unless the compelling state follows through with even more punitive action, it may suffer its own loss of face and potential long-term political consequences. The attempts by the United States and Britain to compel Saddam Hussein to bring Iraq into compliance with UN Security Council resolutions, lasting more than a decade and ultimately unsuccessful, demonstrate the problems that a compellence intervention can bring. Saddam Hussein's intransigence in the face of mounting pressure from the United States and Britain raised his profile among many in the Arab world and highlighted the limitations of military measures in forcing a state to bend to one's will.

Preventive attack

A preventive attack is one that is designed to destroy or degrade a capability of a state – or of a non-state actor – before it becomes a threat, or to destroy that capability if it has already become one. Israel's successful attack on Iraq's Osirak nuclear reactor in 1981 is an example of such an action. The aim of the action was to stop Iraq's nuclear weapons programme in its nascent stage. Likewise, the strike by Japanese naval forces against the US Navy's Pacific Fleet at Pearl Harbour in 1941 was designed to deliver a 'knockout blow' to buy time while Japan achieved its war aims in East Asia. The success of such actions is totally dependant on good intelligence that is both accurate and timely. Thus, the objective is to strike a crippling blow early, well before the capability is fully developed. Pre-emption – a subspecies of preventive attacks (Knopf, 2006: 395) – is different from preventive actions due to its timing and context. Pre-emptive strikes are made when a state feels the threat of imminent military action by an enemy; that is, the enemy capability represents a 'clear and present danger'. For example, Israel's 2006 intervention in Lebanon sought to destroy the missile-launching capability of Hezbollah and to release captured Israeli servicemen. Pre-emptive actions can be either defensive or offensive in their intent.

Likewise, the United States adopted pre-emption as a key strategic principle in aftermath of 9/11. While preventive attack (Knopf, 2006: 395) more accurately describes the new approach, the 2002 National Security Strategy (US White House, 2002) indicates that the United States reserves the right to act pre-emptively against states that provide succour to terrorists and the regimes of rogue states that develop WMDs. This was the premise for the US-led invasion of Iraq in 2003: that is, the aim of the operation was to destroy

Saddam's WMD programme. A major information campaign preceded the invasion emphasizing the imminent nature of the threat. However, the United States and Britain lost credibility, as did the notion of pre-emption (in actuality 'preventive action'), when they failed to discover any WMDs in Iraq.

A problem with such preventive actions is the possibility of unintended consequences. For example, a strike on a WMD production facility could result in major civilian casualties, and of course, there is the danger of retaliation by the attacked state.

Punitive attacks

A punitive attack is the use of military force to inflict pain and exact a cost from a target state: that is, it pays a price for undesired behaviour. In order to justify such actions the punishing state(s) need clear evidence that the target state actually committed the offence. The punishing state also needs to be aware that such an action may trigger further hostilities. An example was the 1986 US air strikes on Libya as punishment for Libyan support of terrorist groups, specifically the attack on a Berlin disco frequented by US servicemen and women (Haass, 1999: 5).

Punitive attacks are intended to inflict punishment on the target state but not necessarily to change the situation. They are reactive in nature and, in contrast to compellence, the initiative remains in the hands of the attacker. The calculation of how much force is enough is arbitrary and can be either proportionate or disproportionate. The intention of the attacker is to send a message to the target state, its own public, and possibly to allies and other potential enemies. The US-led attack on Afghanistan, in the aftermath of 11 September, while it can be described as a warfighting intervention with the purpose of regime change, also had a punitive aspect. There was a large element of revenge in the motivations for initiating the campaign. In addition, the United States sent a message to those states that harboured or provided succour to terrorist organizations that they too could face its wrath; and there was an element of the United States reassuring and galvanizing its allies, as well as demonstrating to the rest of the world its resolve to act decisively against any attack on its sovereignty.

A state undertaking a punitive attack may ultimately have compellence or deterrence as goals. The message delivered to the target state could also include a desired mode of behaviour or the abandonment of an undesired course of action (Haass, 1999: 56). Public presentation of purposes behind an attack is most important and is often the only thing that differentiates between a punitive attack, deterrence or compellence.

Warfighting

Warfighting is the highest level of intervention and involves the conduct of elaborate and large-scale military operations. Warfighting has always been the ultimate measure of a state's military power (Hastedt, 2006; 365). Prior to 1945 warfighting was a fairly regular occurrence between major powers – usually for territorial gain, the maintenance of the status quo or balance of power, or in self-defence. The First and Second World Wars are the most obvious examples of the almost unlimited scope of warfighting. However, since the advent of nuclear weapons warfighting can be characterized as limited, that is, restricted either geographically or in terms of the means employed. Conflicts in the nuclear age are usually contained within clear territorial boundaries and virtually always employ only non-WMD weapon systems.

Military assistance

The indirect use of military force, namely military assistance, is another of Haass's (1999: 64–5) categories of intervention. Not to be confused with deterrence, it refers to the provision of various types of military assistance by one state to another, including weapons and other military equipment, training of security forces and intelligence. While such military assistance can be support for an ally, the intent of the intervening state may also be to shape a conflict in an adverse way for a third party. For example, during the Vietnam War, China and the Soviet Union assisted the North Vietnamese in their struggle against the United States and South Vietnamese. The United States returned the favour to the USSR by providing assistance to the forces opposed to the Soviets during their intervention in Afghanistan.

Interdiction

Interdiction operations involve the discrete and direct use of force to prevent military equipment, materiel or personnel reaching a battlefield, port or terminal. It also can be undertaken to enforce sanctions imposed on a state, as was the case with Iraq after the 1990–1 Gulf War. It can occur on land, in the air or on the sea (Haass, 1999: 61). A more recent example of an interdiction intervention is the US-led Proliferation Security Initiative (PSI), which is a response to the growing problem of WMD proliferation. Under the PSI, member countries are committed to the disruption of the illicit trade in WMDs by interdicting vessels, aircraft etcetera that are suspected of carrying suspicious cargo in their territory or territorial waters.

Rescue

Haass (1999: 63) define rescues as a very limited type of military action, in hostile circumstances, generally undertaken by special forces. The aim of such missions is to rescue actual or potential hostages. Recent examples of this type of rescue mission include the unsuccessful attempt to free US hostages in Iran in 1980 and Israel's 1976 successful rescue of hijack victims from Entebbe airport in Uganda. This category can also relate to the rescue of potentially large numbers of persons who are in physical danger but not necessarily potential hostage victims. This group could include expatriate citizens and tourists caught up in a local conflict, as in Lebanon in July–August 2006. Rescue operations can occur with or without the concurrence of the ruling elite of the target state.

Peace operations

Humanitarian assistance

A humanitarian assistance intervention is the deployment of forces to save lives without necessarily altering the political context within the target state. Such interventions include the supply of medical assistance, food, water and shelter in circumstances where the central authority is either unwilling or unable to assist its own people. It can be either consensual, in which case the intervening force is usually unarmed or lightly armed, or imposed, in which case the intervening force is heavily armed.

In consensual circumstances, the military's technical skills and capabilities to lift or sustain persons are used. For example, the international response to the 2004 Boxing Day Indian Ocean Tsunami focused on the deployment of various military assets to provide assistance to those countries affected. An example of an imposed humanitarian assistance operation – that is, one in a hostile environment – was the protection provided to the Kurds in Northern Iraq by US and British forces following the end of the 1990–1 Gulf War. The extension of the UN Protection Force (UNPROFOR) to provide humanitarian aid to civilians trapped in the civil war in Bosnia between 1992 and 1995 is another example of this.

Peacekeeping

Traditional peacekeeping evolved during the cold war and had as one of its key aims the prevention of superpower intervention in regional conflicts. Such operations can be defined as the deployment of unarmed or lightly armed troops whose mission is to restore order or to buttress a fragile political situation between two or more contending political groups within a state. The peacekeeping forces, among other things, monitor the separation of opposing forces, troop withdrawals and ceasefires. The intervention force plays an almost passive and impartial role within extremely limited guidelines. A peacekeeping operation is supposed to be impartial in its conduct: that is, all contending parties must be treated the same and there needs to a level of consensus reached by them (Talentino, 2005: 15). Most importantly, the operation needs the support of the United States or sufficient numbers of the other militarily capable powers, and the imprimatur of the permanent five members of the United Nations Security Council. While traditional peacekeeping missions during the cold war specifically excluded troops from the United States and the Soviet Union, they would often include troops from members of NATO or the Warsaw Treaty Organization. For example, the Second United Nations Emergency Force (UNEF II) deployed in Egypt in 1973 included Canadian and Polish forces that cooperated to provide the logistical support for the mission.

Since the end of the cold war, peacekeeping has evolved and has become something of a growth industry. The passive role as an inter-positional force has been largely jettisoned for a more proactive approach with much stronger mandates for the use of deadly force, both for the self-protection of the peacekeepers themselves and for that of non-combatants (ICISS, 2001: 62). This evolution is the direct result of atrocities committed in conflicts such as Rwanda and the Balkans where traditional peacekeepers, hamstrung by overly restrictive mandates, were limited to being unarmed observers, unable to intervene.

Peacekeeping operations usually fall under the mandate of a multilateral organization, usually the UN or a regional organization such as NATO, the European Union or the Economic Community of West African States, but also can be undertaken by ad hoc coalitions, as with the 2003 intervention by US, South African and Moroccan forces in the Liberian civil war.

Peace-making

Peace-making can defined as the combination of coercive and non-coercive efforts to bring belligerent groups to a negotiated peace agreement, with external players serving as mediators to participants in the violence (Talentino, 2005: 15). Unlike ordinary warfighting there is a significant degree of restraint, largely due to the lack of clarity of the situation. The aim is to restore a degree of order (and to introduce a peacekeeping force) from which peace can eventually be restored and state control can be re-established. Conflicts in which peace-making operations are mounted are usually messy and confusing situations with a large number of contesting parties, of which, one or more is hostile to a return to the status quo.

Peace-making forces are usually more heavily armed than 'peacekeepers' and may have to overcome considerable local resistance from well-equipped and highly trained forces. The interventions are considered transitional and are expensive to maintain. Thus, there is usually considerable pressure to restrict the duration of this type of intervention and hand over to peacekeepers as soon as is practical. The US-led intervention in Somalia (UNITAF) in 1993 and the Australian-led East Timor intervention in 1999 are examples of peace-making (Haass, 1999: 60).

Nation building and peace building

Nation building and peace building are terms used interchangeably in relation to post-conflict reconstruction. Peace building is the process of reforming or rebuilding a government's institutions and processes, and sometimes also encompasses social and economic institutions. Nation building, or probably more accurately state building, is the creation of political, social and economic institutions and processes where few or none previously existed (Talentino, 2005: 16). It is usually undertaken in the case of a failed or failing state and is designed to culminate in the creation, within that state, of institutions that will in turn sustain peace (and since the end of the cold war, the development of democratic governance and free-markets, particularly if the United States is involved). In such an intervention, overwhelming force is applied while indigenous security forces are trained and institutions generally associated with democratic governance are established (Haass, 1999: 61).

Nation building is an option for failed states or defeated states such as Germany and Japan at the end of the Second World War, Iraq in 2003 or Afghanistan in 2001. It is usually very expensive in both a financial sense and in terms of casualties sustained by the intervening forces, particularly if large parties opposing the intervention remain undefeated or are able to regroup after initial defeat. In Iraq, for example, there was the added complication of the intervention triggering an internecine conflict between the Sunni, Shia Muslims and the Kurds that, at the time of writing, had evolved into a civil war.

Policing

Policing is quite different from peace-making and has some similar characteristics to peacekeeping. These include the limited use of force: that is, they are carried out by lightly armed troops given very strict rules of engagement (ROE). Such interventions are designed to quell conflict between local opposition forces and re-establish a peaceful or stable environment. Such policing operations can involve the deployment of forces in a quasi-hostile environment, as was the case with the British Army in Northern Ireland. In this example, the opposing military actions are, in the main, terrorist attacks and the aim of the intervening force is damage limitation. That is, it does not attempt to solve the underlying causes of the conflict or defeat the opposition; rather the aim is to place a ceiling on the violence so that diplomatic and political solutions can be found. Commitment to this type of conflict is usually open ended, and therefore likely to be very difficult to sell to the intervening state's public (Haass, 1999: 60). The 2006 Australian interventions in the Solomon Islands and East Timor to help indigenous security forces to restore law and order are further examples of this type of intervention.

Stabilization operation

The term 'stabilization operation or mission' has recently entered the strategic lexicon. Colin Gray (2006: 4) describes stabilization operations as post-war activities aimed at enhancing the stability of the social and political spheres of a state. As its title shows, the 2006 United Nations

Stabilization Mission in Haiti (UNSMIH) is considered a stabilization mission. The term can be seen as an alternative to 'nation or state building', which has negative connotations within the US domestic political arena. James Dobbins (2004: 1) articulated this in testimony to the US Congress in 2004. He described 'post-conflict stabilization' in relation to the conflicts in Bosnia, Haiti, Somalia, Iraq and Afghanistan as exercises in 'nation-building'. Indeed, 'stabilization operations' and 'nation-building' are used interchangeably in his report. Most importantly, he articulates the need for an inter-agency approach in the conduct of these operations.

Stabilization operations range from assisting local security forces to re-establish law and order as was the case with Australia's East Timor and Solomon Islands interventions in 2006, to the state or nation-building phase after another type of intervention, most likely to be either warfighting or peace-making – as is the case with Afghanistan and Iraq. Thus, they are varied in scale and cost but in most cases require a long-term commitment by the intervening state(s).

The aim of this type of intervention is to facilitate the (re-)establishment of government control and help local security forces re-establish law and order. This is likely to include raising and training new security forces, and more often than not quelling insurgencies and other forces opposed to the government.

An 'all-of-government' or 'inter-agency' approach is required to overcome the multi-layered and highly complex challenges that these missions present. A 'military only' approach is likely to be too narrow in its approach and lacking in critical areas of expertise.

To intervene or not to intervene?

Since the conclusion of the Second World War, the use of military force has become an increasingly difficult proposition for the leaders of states to justify. That war and its terrible predecessor, the First World War, created a general resolve to avoid the massive destruction and loss of life characteristic of industrial-age warfare. The formation of the United Nations was the direct result of this resolve. With the UN the world had, in theory, an institution with a mandate to prevent war in the first instance and, in the event of war breaking out, the wherewithal to effect a quick resolution. The advent of the cold war and the veto power of the five permanent members in the UN Security Council meant that the UN was effectively stymied. In reality, it was the omnipresent fear of nuclear holocaust that curbed warlike ambitions. The superpowers maintained a firm grip on the activities of their allies and were usually very wary in undertaking military interventions. The aim and scope of any cold war military intervention had to be limited. Even major conflicts such as those in Korea and Vietnam were limited – geographical limits were identified and strictly enforced, and the use of even tactical nuclear weapons was never considered.

In addition, during this period the long-established theory of 'just war' came out of the shadow cast by total war. The tenets of this theory can be summarized as: to be just, a war must be for a worthy cause, undertaken as a last resort, waged by legitimate authority, use reasonable force and respect the rights of non-combatants. The ultimate aim of this body of thought is to make it more difficult to go to war, in a political sense, and to place strict constraints on military commanders in their conduct of operations (Walzer, 1992).

Another factor that has had the effect of both limiting the scope of leaders to go to war and moderating their own behaviour and that of their military commanders, once at war, is an evolving body of international law. Building upon just war theory, the aim of this body of law is to impose strict limitations on the state's use of force. The essential, premise is that a state's right to self-defence is the only justification for the use of military force (Haass, 1999: 10).

Since the end of the cold war, notions of state sovereignty, in particular the principle of non-interference in the domestic affairs of states, have been subject to sustained challenge. Partly this is due to the well-documented forces of globalization, and the growth in number and power of both intergovernmental organizations and non-governmental organizations, but also, I would posit, due to the increasing incidence of intra-state conflicts and the threat of non-state actors, whose ambitions often bring them into direct conflict with states.

Scholars and jurists such as Geoffrey Robertson (1999: 347–51), state leaders such as Tony Blair (1999), and UN Secretary General Kofi Annan (1999) have articulated a concept of conditional state sovereignty. In essence, their argument is that the first duty of a state's government is the protection of all its citizens. If it wages genocide or ethnic cleansing or commits other crimes against humanity against a section of its population, the world community has an obligation to intervene. Furthermore, its leaders should not be able to hide behind sovereign immunity and should be held accountable for their actions. Likewise, if a state's government is either unwilling or unable to avert mass starvation or alleviate suffering, then, once again, the world community has an obligation to intervene. Thus, it is likely that we will see the current level of military interventions sustained or even increased into the future.

Criteria for success

The allure of military interventions for political leaders is that they appear to offer a quick fix to often urgent problems. In addition, their initiation demonstrates decisive and resolute leadership. There is also a galvanizing influence on the population if it can be demonstrated that the cause is just. However, military interventions often lead to unforeseen and often more complex future problems. History is replete with examples where military action has triggered undesired outcomes that are often worse than the original problem – the Iraq War, at the time of writing, being the latest example.

The criteria for successful interventions vary, to some degree, depending on the nature of the intervention. However, on the basis of the principles established by the ICISS, the 'Blair Doctrine' and an assessment of successful past interventions, a successful intervention can be predicted if certain criteria are met.

First, the cause must be just and it must have political legitimacy, from either the UN Security Council or an appropriate regional organization (Blair, 1999; ICISS, 2001). Some interventions are relatively easy to portray as just and readily acquire political legitimacy. The relative ease with which Western political leaders mobilize public support for humanitarian assistance and peacekeeping or peace-making missions whose aims are to prevent or halt genocide or ethnic cleansing, or to restore law and order is well documented. Rescues and certain interdiction operations, such as that conducted against Iraq in the aftermath of the 1990–1 Gulf War are also usually relatively easy to justify. Higher-end interventions such as punishment and warfighting interventions may be more difficult to justify in the event that the rationale is not evident.

The second criterion for successful intervention is that all other avenues to resolve the conflict must have been exhausted; this helps to add weight to political legitimacy. However, this must be measured against the costs of delaying military intervention, particularly in the event of genocides, mass starvation and ethnic cleansing (ICISS, 2001). The differing approaches of the United States to the 1990–1 and 2003 wars with Iraq demonstrate the value of exhausting the diplomatic and political options before recourse to warfighting. In 1990, the United States acquired an immediate UN Security Council resolution demanding Saddam's withdrawal from Kuwait followed by a resolution imposing immediate economic sanctions on Iraq. A series of resolutions from the UN and the Arab League calling for Iraqi withdrawal followed as the United States began diplomatic efforts to build a broad-based coalition of forces to liberate Kuwait. This latter effort had two purposes: first, to ratchet up the political pressure on Saddam Hussein by showing the international community's resolve; and second, to assemble the force necessary to evict Iraqi occupation forces. In 2003, a unilateralist United States put in desultory effort, at best, into securing UN support for its planned invasion of Iraq. Moreover, what effort was made was at the insistence of the British. The United States had little real interest in building a broad-based coalition, preferring to assemble a 'coalition of the willing'. Effectively, it wanted a force comprising the highly capable militaries of the United States, Britain and Australia. Thus, while the coalition was ruthlessly effective in defeating the Iraqi forces, it lacked the legitimacy a more broad-based coalition might have conferred. The subsequent non-discovery of WMDs – the pretext for the intervention – destroyed any of the intervention's limited initial legitimacy.

The third criterion for successful intervention is that it must be viable and improve on the circumstances that created the need for intervention in the first place (Blair, 1999; ICISS, 2001). In general, this means interventions should be limited to small to medium and/or weak states. O'Hanlon (1997: 51–2) suggests that interventions into large, powerful states should not be considered and intervention into states with WMDs and the means to deliver them over significant distances would also almost always qualify as being unviable. Certainly, the leadership of both North Korea and Iran have come to this conclusion. In addition, O'Hanlon suggests that some specific types of conflict – such as protracted guerrilla wars and insurgencies, or conflicts that will probably evolve into protracted insurgencies or trigger civil war or are likely to draw in large, powerful states – should be avoided if at all possible.

Fourth, there needs to be political resolve that will not falter should domestic public approval wane or if higher than expected casualties occur, or the duration of the mission is extended due to unforeseen circumstances (Blair, 1999). Despite the worsening situation in Iraq in the aftermath of the initial invasion, President Bush has remained resolute in his determination 'to see the job through', despite falling opinion polls and protracted criticism from other prominent world leaders.

Fifth, there should be a clear political aim that translates into an unequivocal military mission for the force commander. It should be supported by robust rules of engagement: that is, a clear and appropriate articulation of the limits on the use of military force that can be used during the intervention (ICISS, 2001: 60). If the aim needs to change during the course of the intervention then the force structure of the intervention force should be re-assessed and modified, as appropriate. The Australian-led intervention in East Timor in 1999 is an excellent example of a mission with a clear political aim: namely, the neutralization of the pro-Indonesian militias and the cessation of their vicious campaigns against the East Timorese people. The military force had clear and robust rules of engagement: that is, they were authorized to use deadly force to protect the East Timorese and to defend themselves, if necessary (Prins, 2002: 142). Conversely, the debacle at Srebrenica in July 1995 in which a battalion of Dutch UN peacekeepers were forced to evacuate by the Bosnian Serb Army which then murdered 6000 Bosnian Muslim men and boys is testimony to the passivity and ambiguity of traditional peacekeeping and overly restrictive ROEs (Prins, 2002: 60–61).

The sixth criterion for a successful intervention is that the intervening force should have unity of command. In the event of a complex and difficult intervention, the core of the force must be comprised of highly capable combat and combat support troops. The rapid success of the ground offensive phase of the 1990–1 Gulf War and the initial invasion and occupation of Iraq in 2003 demonstrate the veracity of this principle. This contrasts with the inept performance of the UN Mission in Sierra Leone in May 2000. The force, a mix of Indian troops and troops from several

African states, was powerless to stop the rebel Revolutionary United Front advance towards the capital. In the end, a wholly British intervention force was needed to rescue the situation (Prins, 2002: 60–61).

Finally, the intervening force should have sufficient capabilities to prosecute the intervention successfully. That is, the intervention force needs adequate force balance, tactical mobility, firepower, command and control, logistics and tactical intelligence gathering assets. The US intervention in Somalia is a salutary negative lesson in the dangers of changing the aim of an operation but not re-assessing the force size and structure needed for the expanded role. The operation's original aim of humanitarian assistance was expanded to state building, but this change was not accompanied by an increase in the resources available to the force commander.

What are the mechanics of a successful intervention?

This question refers to the more complex (and dangerous) interventions such as warfighting, peace-making and post-conflict stabilization operations. The majority of these are likely to occur in regions far away from those states that are likely to be motivated to intervene and militarily capable of doing so. Military capability equates to general military competence and a highly developed ability to conduct expeditionary warfare. Only a very small group of states have such capability.

Most states have militaries that have a local or, at best, regional focus; that is, their defence forces are configured to defend their borders and territorial waters. While they may have some ability to project force into the territories of nearby neighbours, they have little capability to project power at any distance beyond this. Few states have significant capabilities to conduct expeditionary maritime operations: that is, that combination of naval, air and land forces (such as aircraft carriers, strategic lift aircraft, amphibious ships, suitably trained and equipped ground forces), as well as the logistical ability to sustain troops in the field at a significant distance from a state's home territory (O'Hanlon, 1997). Few states have the ability to conduct such distant interventions, and of these, only the United States has the global reach and the expeditionary competence as well as the sheer mass to intervene anywhere on the planet and do it alone if necessary. Compared with the United States, Britain and France have much smaller militaries, with smaller force projection capabilities. They are likely to require assistance with even medium-scale interventions. Nonetheless, by world standards, both have significant expeditionary capabilities and, certainly, both have the military competence to lead distant interventions in the event of American unwillingness. Some middle powers such as Australia and Canada also have limited intervention capabilities that can be used to supplement the forces of the aforementioned powers and, most importantly, help confer legitimacy to an operation (Kurth, 2005: 93).

On the other hand, the pool of militarily competent armed forces is somewhat broader, including virtually all Western states, many non-Western states such as China, India and Russia, and some in the developing world, such as Singapore and Malaysia. This factor is critical when an intervention, whether sponsored by the UN, a regional body or the United States, is likely to be of long duration. A large pool of military forces from a range of states is critical for the operation's long-term viability and its ongoing legitimacy.

Assuming an intervention force has sufficient military capability, what are the mechanics of a successful intervention? As previously discussed, the first requirement is a clearly articulated political objective that is militarily viable. In most cases, this will be a limited objective such as to halt genocide, force a cessation of hostilities between warring factions or create an environment for a political settlement.

Sufficient time must also be allocated for the critical first step: that is, a detailed assessment of the mission. In this, military planners need to undertake an extensive study of the target state in its entirety, including its geography, its key civil and military infrastructure, the population's demographic structure, the key political and military groups, key leaders, relations with other states and their likely reactions and so on. Planners will also identify the critical intelligence shortfalls and plan for their amelioration. This process will calculate the likely opposition to the intervention, and from this an assessment will be made of targets such as military cantonments, communication nodes, air defence batteries, or bridges that may need to be destroyed or degraded by air and naval forces as the intervention force deploys. It will also calculate the size and structure of the force required for the intervention, including its command and control arrangements (these are particularly important if the intervention force is to be comprised of contingents from a wide variety of states). The assessment will also include the intervention's logistical and administrative requirements. The product of this assessment will be a detailed operational plan, detailing each phase of the operation, complete with subsidiary contingency plans to facilitate rapid responses to enemy actions considered unlikely in the initial assessment.

The mix of forces in an intervention force – that is, the mix of air, land and naval combat forces as well as the ratio of combat to logistic and construction troops – is dependent on the nature of the mission, as each will have a different mix of standard military tasks and non-security related tasks. The intervention force will need sufficient combat troops to establish control in the target state. It may also require engineers to repair infrastructure and undertake water purification, additional medical personnel to treat injured non-combatants and hostile combatants alike, and logistic troops to orchestrate the movement of aircraft and shipping as well as the supply of food and water to elements of the civil population.

The next step in the intervention is the establishment of lodgements. Combat troops comprising airmobile elements such as paratroopers, helicopter-borne light infantry and special forces will secure points of entry (POE) – ports and airfields. Once secured, these will enable the rapid build up of the main body of the intervening force and will eventually provide for their ongoing sustainment. The POEs will be defended against all reasonable contingencies, particularly during the build-up phase. The intervening force will attempt to complete the insertion of the main body as rapidly as possible. The aim will usually be to achieve surprise and present the opposition forces with as many simultaneous and then rapidly successive tactical problems as is possible with the aim of creating paralysis in their decision making.

The next step is the establishment of strongholds that will help facilitate the rapid establishment of a 'general presence'. The need to establish a presence rapidly will influence the selection of lodgement points. Where the intervention force has to contend with warring factions it will attempt to establish presence in as wide an area as possible, but not to the extent that it is too 'thin on the ground' and vulnerable to enemy attack.

Neutralizing hostile forces and extending control throughout the country is the final and most difficult stage of the operation and may either take years or not be achieved at all. There are two main strategies for establishing control (O'Hanlon, 1997: 33). The first is the establishment of a unified indigenous security force comprising both a military and a civil police organization under the political control of the government. This will take a significant period, during which the intervention forces will be responsible for neutralizing forces hostile to the intervention. The indigenous security force will gradually assume responsibility for neutralizing the insurgency, once sufficient members have been recruited and trained. The second strategy is for the intervening force to destroy or critically weaken the hostile forces before handing over to the indigenous security force. In effect a third strategy is a combination of both of these approaches and we have seen this adopted in Iraq and Afghanistan, albeit somewhat tardily. Up until the end of 2006, the intervention forces in both states were primarily responsible for both defeating the insurgency and training an indigenous security force. Once an area is deemed low risk or largely free of insurgents, the intervention force hands over responsibility for security to the indigenous force.

The types of hostile capabilities an intervention force are likely to engage are essentially low technology in nature. That is, their weaponry will comprise, in the main, small arms, improvized explosive devices, hand grenades and perhaps some light anti-armour weapons and mortars. The insurgents are also likely to employ guerrilla tactics, including raiding, ambushing and acts of terror. In the long term, it is difficult to contain dedicated, well-organized large groups of irregulars in complex terrain, as the US-led forces in Iraq and Afghanistan continue to learn. Inevitably, the forces hostile to an intervention will adopt a long-term strategy designed to erode the intervention force's will to continue with the occupation.

Thus, as Iraq and Afghanistan demonstrate, the key objective of any intervention is to prevent an insurgency from developing in the first place (O'Hanlon, 1997: 32–8).

Further reading

Bellamy, A.J. and Williams, P.D. (2005) 'Who's Keeping the Peace? Regionalization and Contemporary Peace Operations', *International Security*, 29, 4: 157–95.

Grey, C.S. (2006) 'Stability Operations in Strategic Perspective: A Sceptical View', *Parameters*, 36: 4–14.

International Commission on Intervention and State Sovereignty (ICISS) (2001) *The Responsibility to Protect: Report of the International Commission on Intervention and State Sovereignty*, Ottawa: International Development Research Centre.

O'Hanlon, M. (1997) *Saving Lives with Force: Military Criteria for Humanitarian Intervention*, Washington: The Brookings Institution Press.

Taletino, A. (2005) *Military Intervention after the Cold War: The Evolution of Theory and Practice*, Ohio: The Ohio University Press.

Chapter 12

Great Powers and the International System: Between Unilateralism and Multilateralism

Nick Bisley

Introduction

Great powers have traditionally played a distinctive role in the international system. From Bismarck's Prussia to George Bush's United States, having substantial military and economic prowess, and the diplomatic heft that this creates, has historically provided these states with a special status in international society. Their interests have been thought to be the most vital to systemic stability and hence warrant protective action that would be unavailable to normal members of international society. This distinctive role is particularly apparent in the realm of security and strategy. Yet in many ways the idea of an international system managed by the concerted action of a small number of great powers is anachronistic. In a world linked by complex webs of interdependence, where great power can be acquired on the black market by even the most underwhelming of states, the notion of a select group of states who manage the system through the projection of their power and influence appears to ring hollow. Although there is good reason to be sceptical of the continuing relevance of the idea, however, one should not dismiss altogether the way in which concentrations of power shape the structure of the international system as well as the particular role of those who hold that power. Moreover, the constitutional document of the current order, the UN Charter, accords a central place to five ostensible great powers in the workings of international security.

The status of great powers in the current order is thus less than clearcut. To that end, this chapter examines the role of great powers in the contemporary international system, with a particular focus on their place in the system's security and strategic setting. The chapter will look first at the traditional role of great powers and then consider the primary challenges that this faces in the contemporary world. The third part of the chapter then examines the approach of the singular great power in the current system and concludes that while the traditional concept of a small group of powers managing the system is badly out of date, the realities of power in an anarchical international system means that those who hold significant concentrations of power still have a distinctive place. The current order is unusual in that only the United States has the kind of systemic interests that one associates with the great power role and is the only power willing to project force to underwrite its interests in the system as a whole. The influence of the United States and its position, caught as it is between the imperatives of unilateral and multilateral approaches, show both the continuing importance of power and the complex new realities that shape the contours of international security.

Great powers in the international system

There is a tendency to assume that great powers determine life in the Hobbesian state of nature that is international politics. As such, there is a decidedly realist bias to assessments of their nature and role (e.g. Gilbert, 1999; Miller, 1995). Such views do not assume an inherent Manichean streak to all great powers, but rather that they are driven to put national power at the centre of their actions in the international system. Yet the association of great powers only with the application of military power in the service of interests narrowly defined misunderstands the particular role that great powers have historically played. Before this is discussed, however, it is important to be clear what the term itself means.

What makes a power great? In Von Ranke's famous essay, *The Great Powers*, he argues that they are those states that can defend themselves in conflict with all other powers, even in the event that their opponents combine their efforts (in Von Laue, 1950). In this classical depiction it is relative military power that lies at the centre of the determination of a power's status in the system. The historian Paul Kennedy (1988: 697) modelled his best-selling survey of 500 years of great power conflict on Ranke's 1833 essay, noting that a great power is 'by definition a state capable of holding its own against any other nation'. While vague, the implication of this conception is clear. A great power is one that must be able to defend itself against any other. Mearsheimer's recent effort to devise a grand theory of great power politics also draws on this military-determination tradition. In his work of self-styled 'offensive realism' he argues that to deserve the great power appellation 'a state must have sufficient military assets to put up a serious fight in an all-out conventional war against the most powerful state in the world' (Mearsheimer, 2001: 5). This puts military power at the centre of consideration, but he emphasizes that a great power does not need to be able to defeat the strongest power, merely to be able to take it on and force a stalemate situation. In essence, his definition follows Kennedy's more succinct conception – being a great power means being able to hold one's own.

This influential military-capacity understanding derives from a broader assumption that force determines the pattern of international relations and those few states that have the lion's share therefore have a decisive role to play. In this view the international system is defined by the distribution of power amongst states, and as such the holders of substantial power are disproportionately influential. This is typical of what Raymond Aron ([1962] 1966) has described as an oligopolistic conception of the international system. These views are not without merit but only go some of the way to explaining the particular role that great powers play in the broader landscape of world politics for while military wherewithal matters it is also the case that the underlying attributes of a great power involve more than just military capacity.

Martin Wight's analysis of the great powers makes just such a point. For Wight ([1946] 1978: 50), the determination of great power involves not only assessing the quality and nature of power but the relationship of that power to the system as a whole. For Wight, power alone is not a sufficient criterion, even if understood in relative terms. The particular place of the great powers derives from the nature of the relationship between its concentrations and the workings of the international system. To that end he approvingly cites Toynbee (1926: 4, cited in Wight, [1946] 1978): 'a great power may be defined as a political force exerting an effect coextensive with the widest range of the society in which it operates.' The distinctive role of great powers comes not only from the fact that they have extensive military capacity but also from the political influence that derives from the spread of interests that such power creates. Yet even in this conception, great power is ultimately about military capability. It does pay attention to the political elements of that power, and is in that sense an improvement on the determinism of the previous definitions, but it does not go much further than that.

Hedley Bull's formulation provides a clearer set of reasons for the unique place of great powers in the modern international system. Bull ([1977] 1995) places the role of great powers alongside his other pillars of international society – international law, diplomacy, the balance of power and war – and sees them as operating to ensure the existence and perpetuation of international order. From the outset, it is clear that his view sees a particular functional place for great powers that goes beyond the strictly military. In his tripartite definition of what constitutes the category he makes this explicit. The first is that it is necessarily a plural concept. For Bull there is no such thing as a singular great power. The category requires at least two roughly comparable states. The second aspect relates to the character of power. Great powers must be, in his view, the most powerful military states in the system and this is defined as the capacity to be able to advance their interests without their allies' assistance. Third, great powers are recognized by others as having special rights and responsibilities. Great powers are not only those that have the greatest military strength; they are seen by others as having a special role. In part this recognition derives from the realization that the nature of power differentials in an anarchical system means that concentrations of military might deserve recognition. But it is also a reflection of the fact that states in the system see benefits, what these days might be called global public goods, that derive from a managerial function that is performed by the great powers. In this sense, they must have power beyond simply the military. In a similar vein, Levy (1983b: 16) argues that they are marked off from others by 'their military power, their interests, their behaviour in general and interactions with other Powers, other Powers' perception of them, and some formal criteria'. Thus they are not only defined by a maximalist conception of military prowess; in his view, they are states that have extensive interests in the system, the capacity to advance those interests and, due to these attributes, conduct relations amongst themselves and others on a different basis from normal states.

Both Bull and Levy see great powers as distinctive members of international society. This is not only because of their importance in matters relating to security and war, but because they help to provide stability to a system lacking a central authority. Bull ([1977] 1995: 201–20) determines that the great powers provide order to the system by preserving the balance of power, managing crises between one another, exploiting their local preponderance, respecting each other's spheres of influence and engaging in joint actions to police the broader principles and practices of order. In essence it is the inequality that great powers represent which provides order to a system that is built on formal principles of egalitarianism. It is this slightly unusual proposition that gets to the heart of the role that great powers play and the historical evolution of that role. In the modern international system, anarchy – the condition denoting the absence of a formal centre of authority – is the defining feature. In response to the challenges posed by this, states have devised the principle of sovereignty and legal equality as the basis on which their interrelations should be conducted. Yet as realists remind us, in an anarchical system, sovereign equality is a convenient fiction. They insist that the legal basis of the international system is of little significance to the matter of power politics, and the place of great powers – able to dispense with the niceties of laws and other constraints due to their ability to transform will into action – serves as a reminder of this.

In some of the more extreme moments, this depiction carries some weight, but in most circumstances things are not as dire as the realists insist. Indeed, for so long as there have been efforts to construct systems to order relations between states there has been a recognition that the inequality of power has a broader role to play. To that end, Simpson (2003) argues that the notion of legalized hegemony describes the awkward middle ground that exists between the formal equality that is the letter of international law – and the core principle of international politics – and the substantive inequality that produces decisively different roles and duties. Legalized hegemony refers not only to some de facto recognition of the realities of power but also efforts to construct some formal basis to the dominant and distinctive role of great powers. In this sense then, great powers are notable not only due to their hypertrophic military capacity but to the particular status that international society conveys to them. Great powers have responsibilities to the international system, and these responsibilities convey certain rights and, as such, great powers are not beholden to the sorts of constraints that impinge on normal members.

Since the emergence of a distinctly modern international system, one can identify four phases in the evolution of this role involving a steady increase in its formal recognition and institutionalization. Although some have argued that modern Western wars began in 1494 with France's use of gunpowder in its war in what is today Italy, a more useful starting point is more orthodox: the conclusion of the Peace of Westphalia in 1648. Of course, modern international relations did not instantaneously emerge out of the ashes of the Thirty Years War, but the core principles of sovereignty, territoriality and non-interference that have become the cornerstones of the modern system were codified for the first time there. The first phase of the modern role of great powers spans the period from the Westphalian peace to the creation of the Congress system in 1815. The treaties of Osnabrück and Münster, which form the Peace of Westphalia, name France and Sweden as its guarantors. In some senses this is the first formal recognition of a particular role for great powers. Beyond this, however, while great powers were of key importance to the broader developments in international relations between Westphalia and Vienna, their role was informal and lacked any institutionalization. The first phase involves an informal dominance of great powers that is a function of their power and interests, not of expectations of rights and responsibilities.

This changed distinctly with the creation of the Congress of Vienna in 1815 that followed the defeat of Napoleonic France. Between 1815 and 1830 the European powers codified a diplomatic system which formally accorded the great powers a specific managerial role in international security. Under the direction of the Congress of Vienna's principle architect, the Austrian Foreign Minister Klemens von Metternich, the four victorious powers, Austria, Britain, Prussia and Russia, along with the reinstated monarchy in France, created a group to manage European international security (see Kissinger, 1957). The system was based on the view that the great powers needed to manage both the power aspects of the international system and the principles which underpinned it. The system reflected the view that the great powers needed to work together to head off any future challenge not only to their position but to the ideas which determined legitimate conduct in the international system.

This involved regular meetings and action to resolve particular challenges. During this time the great powers defined themselves, and were seen by others, as acting not only in their own interests, but in the broader interests of the European international system.

While it formally limped on until 1830, the closely managed system did not last long, and effectively came to an end in 1822 with the death of the British Foreign Secretary Viscount Castlereagh. After 1830, however, the four continental powers created the 'Holy Alliance' which continued to manage challenges to international security from both military and revolutionary ideas, although it lacked the formal congress approach of the immediate post-Vienna period. While the tightly knit system of 1815 did not last beyond the creation of the Holy Alliance, the system of great power responsibility was firmly entrenched and survived, albeit in more limited form, until the First World War. This phase established the core idea that has survived to this day: that great powers have an obligation to help underwrite the smooth functioning of orderly relations, in return for which they have distinctive rights: that is, Simpson's notion of legalized hegemony.

Following the First World War, the victorious powers determined to create an institutional mechanism to prevent the recurrence of such carnage. The League of Nations was an attempt to protect international security through institutionalizing international relations, promoting the rule of law and enhancing transparency in diplomacy. Its basic mechanism was to embody the principle of collective security to prevent the recurrence of war. This third phase of the development of the role of great powers in the international system saw the League accord a special status to the great powers by providing them with permanent membership of the League Council, the primary body of authority within the League structures. The intended membership was to be Britain, France, Italy, Japan and the United States. The United States did not ratify its membership and hence never took up its place in the Council. Although this did accord a formal status to great powers that reflected their interests and represented responsibilities, the constitutional structure of the League meant that the Council was virtually unable to make decisions (due to the unanimity requirement). This meant that the substantive role of great powers followed a pre-1914 pattern, even though the formal structures had created something new.

The creation of the UN system in 1945 represents a curious development. While it finally brought about the creation of a genuinely egalitarian, universal international system, where all members of international society were accorded equal status, it also built into the Security Council (UNSC) the most clear-cut recognition of the inequality inherent in international politics which the distinctive role of the great powers reflected. The key problem of the League Council was that it did not pay sufficient attention to the realities of power. More precisely, it showed that unless one could provide great powers with some control over matters, then they would not participate and thus undermine the system's very purpose. As Chris Brown (2004: 9) points out, the 'only way in which a Great Power can be controlled is by the actions of other Great Powers'. Votes or censure are not enough. To overcome indecision, the UNSC adopted qualified majority voting, but to assuage the great powers it provided each permanent member with a veto. The notion of great power responsibility is explicitly stated in Article 24 of the UN Charter, which confers on the Council the primary responsibility for maintaining international peace and security (UN, 1945). Yet for the bulk of the duration of the cold war the ambitions of the charter's framers were thwarted as both the USSR and the United States vetoed resolutions which they felt impinged on their interests. Moreover, they conducted their security relations with one another almost entirely outside the UN framework. Although the 1945 settlement set up a system of law that provided a clear incentive for great power participation, cold war politics meant that great powers did not follow the intended path.

Great powers have, since 1815, been accorded a distinctive formal role in international security. They have a vital role to play in securing stable international relations – they police their spheres of influence, they keep the ambitions of smaller powers in check, act to resolve crises and use force to stabilize international relations – in return for which they are exempted from certain aspects of international law. Central to this conception is the assumption that they act in concert with one another. Yet during the twentieth century the idea of concerted great power management of the system has been largely elusive. Since the end of cold war hostilities, there has been some revival of great powers acting in concert, as in the response to the Iraq invasion of Kuwait in 1990–1, although this has been the exception rather than the rule. In practice, the great power role envisioned by the framers of the charter has not been realized. It was generally thought that the cold war froze the possibilities of the modified version of collective security embodied in the structure of the UNSC. Yet in the nearly 20 years since the thawing of Soviet-US hostilities it has become increasingly clear that there is no consensus for great power management of the international system, at least not of the kind envisaged by the charter. There are many reasons for this, the least of which is the rather dated feel of those accorded 'great power' status and the extent to which those afforded a veto power continue to conceive of their interests in narrow terms. But a more significant reason is that the very premise of a system managed by a club of great powers is increasingly out of step with the realities of contemporary world politics.

Great powers: a quaint anachronism?

In some respects, the emergence of the idea that great powers had a particular role to play was a reflection of the realities of power in an anarchical international system. But it was also a function of a specific design in which the great powers were thought to be able to act, from time to time, to protect the underlying system. The key to this proposition was configuring the interests of the powerful with the underlying values that the system advances. Minor powers may be frustrated by the evident hypocrisies of international society, but they put up with them not only because they must but because they recognize that the existing configuration of the international system depends upon it.

The general view that great powers play a managerial role in international society derives from a number of more basic assumptions about their power and capabilities. The first is the belief that there exists an appropriate fit between the power that they have and the means to provide order. If there was not a sense that their military or political capacities could effect the sort of management function that is assumed, then clearly they would not have their place in the system. The premise is that the concentration of military, political and economic weight was traditionally sufficient to keep ambitions in check, to order the system and ultimately ensure that the system survived. The second element is the existence of a shared mindset among the great powers about their interests and values. As both nineteenth and twentieth century experiences made plain, the success of concerted action among the great powers is dependent upon a consensus on the underlying values that their collective action promotes. The greatest challenge to the effective working of the UNSC following 1945 was not the clash of interests between the United States and the Soviet Union, but the absence of a common view as to the values and ideals that the UNSC, and the UN more broadly, should act to promote.

The failure to accord great powers special status – that is, expecting them to behave as a state like any other – greatly increases their propensity to operate outside the system. Great powers cannot be entirely tamed, goes this third assumption; any effort to construct a system with rules and norms shaping behaviour requires that great powers be given some leeway. The balance struck in the UN Charter is the most explicit statement of this assumption in action. Without special treatment then, the great powers would not participate in the system, thus robbing it of much-needed importance, legitimacy and functional efficacy. Finally, the idea that the great powers have a special managerial role derives from a more basic belief that there is a need for management. If there were confidence in the reasonable behaviour of other states or in the efficacy and spontaneity of the balance of power then the self-conscious creation of a directorial role for great powers would be markedly diminished.

In the opening decade of the twenty-first century, when globalization's impact is more evident than ever before, the idea of a unique role for great powers is largely out of step with the prevailing conditions. Central to the traditional place of great powers in international order was the sense that concentrations of military, political and economic power provided an effective ability to underwrite the system. It is no longer clear that there is a fit between the traditional capacities that are associated with great powers and the ability to manage the system. To put it plainly, it is not clear that the contemporary system of international security can be managed in the traditional way. As Brown (2004: 15–6) notes, the agential capacity of great powers has been diminished by changes in the nature of global capitalism. This gets to the broader point. It is not clear that great powers, acting alone or even collectively, can effectively advance the expected goals of system stability through underwriting international security. The reasons for the disjuncture between traditional conceptions of great power and the ability to provide an order-promoting role derive from the rise of nuclear weapons, the unipolar structure of the current international system and the changes associated with globalization.

As Ken Boutin discusses in Chapter 9, nuclear proliferation is once again a central issue in contemporary international security. In 1998, India and Pakistan joined the nuclear club, following on from North Korea's flirtations with nuclear weaponry that began in 1994 and have continued since 2002, and Iran's nuclear ambitions are clear. In part, North Korea and Iran's actions are the result of traditional security concerns, as well as the more specific fears that the United States has stoked since 2002. The message these two powers took from US foreign policy was unmistakable – the best means to deter US intervention is to get a nuclear capability and do so quickly. For India and Pakistan the motives behind nuclearization were more mixed: there was a security dilemma aspect (most notably for Pakistan) but there was also a more symbolic purpose. The acquisition of nuclear weapons was seen, in both New Delhi and Islamabad, as a sign that they had joined the top table of states. In their minds, nuclear weapons are a sign of membership of the great power club. While nuclear weapons have an association with great power status – unsurprisingly given their destructive power – their strategic and political significance is less than clear-cut. Even when they form part of the arsenal of unquestionable powers of the highest rank, their influence on strategic behaviour is cause for considerable debate. For example, it is still not a settled issue whether nuclear weapons were a cause of conflict or a source of strategic restraint in the cold war (see Lebow and Stein, 1998).

Although nuclear weapons send a clear signal to international society and to one's domestic constituents, on their own they are not sufficient to catapult a small or weak state to the top of the global tree. At a basic level, a state needs to acquire a second strike capability and a substantial arsenal to be comparable to the major powers. More directly, John Mearsheimer (2001: 128–33) points out, with the exception of the unlikely event of genuine nuclear hegemony, deterrence acts to undermine their ability to assuage insecurity. As such, great military power is a function of conventional land warfighting strength. In Mearsheimer's view, nuclear weapons alone do not take a state to the top table.

This brings us back to the paradoxical situation in which states see nuclear weapons as a sign of great power status but their strategic importance fails to support this logic. In part, this is due to the mistaken assumption that nuclear weapons always trump conventional military force. But it is also because nuclear weapons helped to undermine the traditional role that great powers were intended to play through the UNSC. At a basic level, their sheer destructiveness diminishes the political effectiveness of the projection of great power. Moreover, nuclear weapons provide a disincentive for great powers to conceive of their interests in the systemic fashion that is needed to play the traditional role. Since the end of the cold war, this tendency has been pronounced. During the cold war, however, both the USSR and the United States spread their interests about as widely as could be imagined. Does this not confirm the idea that nuclear weapons were of secondary consideration to the traditional role? The problem was that while they clearly managed their spheres of influence they did not manage their bilateral strategic relations within the UNSC. Rather, because of nuclear weapons they dealt with this crucial element themselves, entirely outside the institution intended to manage all aspects of international security (Freedman, 1995). The point is that nuclear weapons make management of the system in the traditional way much more complex. War becomes much less effective as an institution, the incentives of the great powers to conceive of their interests in a manner sufficient to play the traditional role are significantly reduced and the acquisition of nuclear weapons by lesser powers, while not making them great, acts to undermine the strategic effectiveness of the major players.

To be clear, nuclear weapons have not served to make powers less great or of lesser significance to the broader patterns of international security; rather they undermine the traditional managerial role of great powers by making the fit between the character of power and its effective application to advance international order more difficult to make.

The second significant reason for the move away from the traditional role is the overwhelming systemic dominance of the United States. By almost any measure it is the most important power on the planet and has no rivals in a range of vital sectors (Kennedy, 2002; Wohlforth and Brooks, 2002). Its military is the largest, most powerful and most technologically sophisticated in the world, and is the only one capable of projecting significant power to any part of the globe. Its political and diplomatic heft is unmatched; its economy is not only the largest, its firms dominate global business and finance and it is at the leading edge of many high technology industries. In science, higher education, entertainment and culture it is the world leader. Its position of primacy is unique in modern history. But it is precisely this unique status – that it is unrivalled and unchecked by others of roughly equal stature – which serves to undermine the traditional place of great powers and their influence on the system. From Bull's point of view, the United States' status as the lone power of significance, by definition, transforms both the system and the role of great powers. Bull ([1977] 1995: 194–5) argues that, 'if the US were indeed the single dominant power, it could no longer rightly be called a great power or superpower.' But the point is not purely definitional. The underlying premise of the classical conception of the great powers is that they constrain each other and act to limit their systemic ambitions, and this works to structure their interests so as to promote orderly conduct. Without peers, then one must assume that the tendency for great powers to act in an order-promoting way – which in turn justifies great power exceptionalism – will disappear. More importantly, this seriously undermines the pillars on which international stability is traditionally thought to rest.

The absence of a great power function means that the system is liable to be influenced by the dominant power's conceptions of its interests, and its particular view of how international relations should be conducted and the values on which these should be based. The traditional role of the great powers was to promote order by forging a consensus on legitimate action and working to ensure stable relations were maintained within that framework. Multiple powers meant that the stakes for any significant disagreement amongst themselves over the values and principles on which the system should be built would be high (although it would not prevent great power conflict over these values, as we saw with the cold war). A unipolar world lacks this, and thus the approach of the dominant power to the structure of the system can involve the desire not only to advance its interests but to project its own conception of the underlying principles and values of international relations. In the foreign and security policy of the contemporary United States one sees some elements of this going on. In the absence of a state or group of states that can act to induce the United States to see a value in order over the projection of its interests and values, what we have seen in US intervention in Iraq, its diplomatic support of Israel's 2006 invasion of Lebanon and its approach to Iran and North Korea is the result of it being able to feel that it has the ability and the right (if not the duty) to press home policy that advances its conception of both a just and stable international order.

This sentiment is in part fuelled by the third major reason for the anachronism of the great powers: globalization. Globalization refers to the way in which the increased rate and speed of the movement of goods, people, capital and knowledge around the planet is forging denser transnational networks of economic, political and cultural relationships that are in turn reconfiguring state perceptions of their interests and their security environment (see Bisley, 2007). While the kinds of changes that this process is thought to be bringing about have tended to be overstated, it is clear that the nature of economic and political interests have been changed in important ways. Economic interdependence, brought about by the growing rate and significance of international trade and production, means that states not only have a vested interest in avoiding conflict, their approaches to crises and to security policy more generally reflect these circumstances. Equally, the networks of trade, finance and production of which globalization consists are themselves sources of vulnerability and insecurity. Globalization has brought about a subtle shift in the strategic environment and it casts doubt on the logic underpinning the traditional approach to the great power role. Globalization has widened the nature and character of threats against which states and societies need to secure themselves. From terrorism to infectious diseases, globalization's network of transnational linkages has decisively changed the character of threats as well as state perceptions of these. As such, it demonstrates that traditional approaches to international security are in need of significant change. Military power projected by major powers is of little help in combating pandemic influenza, and terrorism needs to be combated not by serried ranks of tanks and artillery but by a complex array of political, economic and military policies among powers great and small. Finally, globalization has increased the range and number of actors in the international strategic environment and their access to sophisticated weapons and tactics. The balance of private and public power in international security has changed; the character of threats and the way to respond to them are such that traditional ways of thinking about statecraft and security policy is increasingly out of step with global circumstances and, more precisely, with particular state interests. Thus, globalization makes it patently clear that the old-fashioned approach of great powers managing the system through judicious use of military force belongs in another era.

Beyond these more broad-ranging issues, it is clear that there is little appetite among the wealthy states to think of themselves as military great powers. Unipolarity is not only a function of US power and success; it is a reflection of an absence of any other power willing to undertake such a role. Of course, Britain and France have the formal trappings of this status but no one is really fooled. More importantly, neither is particularly interested in spending what would be necessary to begin to match US power, even in a proportionate manner. The only possible exceptions to this come from Russia and China. Both are nuclear powers and permanent members of the UN Security Council, and both are somewhat uneasy with US primacy. Yet even here neither is at all close to being a peer of the United States and both insist (though perhaps a little too much) that they have no interest in going down such a path.

Underlying all this is the simple fact that states perceive their interests and their security environment in a decidedly different way from in the past. Although the notion of a global policeman providing public goods has some resonance, especially within the United States (see e.g. Gray, 2004), there simply is no appetite for old fashioned great power approaches to international order and security. This derives from changed interests, a different security environment and changed domestic circumstances such that constituencies are not willing to the bear the costs – understood in financial, political and human terms – of being an old-style great power. Yet this should not be confused with an argument that says that power no longer matters. Power all too clearly is of fundamental importance; what has changed is the way in which this power is deployed.

Great powers and contemporary security and strategy

It is important to emphasize that although the traditional managerial role of great powers has been undermined by recent developments, powerful states still matter for the international system as a whole. Even while they do not fulfil the role envisioned in the UN Charter, the significant powers in the system provide public goods through, for example, providing the bulk of the costs of institutions such as the UN and the IMF. They are centres of wealth and provide leadership in their regional spheres, and in the case of the United States underwrite military security in three different continents. But the question that this chapter is most interested in is the way in which great powers advance their security interests, given the breakdown of the managerial role that has traditionally been associated with their status. If the old ways are no longer appropriate, what kind of role have they come to play? The focus in this section will be on the United States, for two main reasons. Space constraints mean that we cannot consider the behaviour of other weighty powers such as Russia or China who matter at the global level but who still lack the decisive position of the United States. Second, only the United States acts in a way that resembles a great power, in the sense that it understands its interests in the widest terms and acts to advance them in the broadest way.

Since the adoption of what has come to be known as the Bush Doctrine, most clearly articulated in the 2002 National Security Strategy (US White House, 2002), the defining feature of the US approach to security is the perpetuation of its present position of primacy and the willingness to use this advantage to protect itself from threats (Daalder and Lindsay, 2003) both through traditional deterrence and through novel means, such as pre-emptive war. From this flows a number of essential aims and approaches which have driven US security and strategy in recent years. The first is the ambition (however unrealizable) of total security. The predominance of the United States and the technological sophistication of its power, along with the growing vulnerabilities of a globalized world, have driven key decision makers in Washington to embrace a totalizing approach to security (see Van Ness, 2006). The aim is to use all available means to ensure that the United States is entirely secure. This is understood to mean efforts to ensure that no power, great or small, state or non-state, is in a position to provide an existential threat to the US political community. At base this means ensuring a military preponderance such that no power would consider trying to compete with the United States, and then using this power to remove threats that do exist. Thus, security policy is not about mitigating threats but about removing them, and doing so on a global stage. In this sense, commitments to allies are not understood as a function of geopolitical calculus, but as a means to protect the US political community. In the pursuit of ballistic missile defence and the neo-Wilsonian ambition of promoting democratic transformation around the world, one sees examples of the pursuit of total security.

The second approach is a unilateralist tendency in power projection. Unilateralism is driven both by the prerogatives of primacy and by the sense that the complexities of the world require action in which the trouble of building consensus on appropriate action among members of international society is thought to undermine effective policy. Unilateralism does not mean strictly doing things on one's own. The Iraq intervention is an example of unilateralism, not because the United States was the sole power – by definition the 27-state coalition made it clearly multilateral – but rather because it was the result of an unwillingness to be put off by the protests of one's friends and allies. While this kind of unilateralism has a longer-run history in US foreign policy (see Holloway, 2000), the tendencies of the Bush presidency have been of a markedly different kind, both in tone and substance. Moreover, the central proposition is that only the United States is willing and able to make the sorts of changes necessary to secure not only US security interests but US values and ideals themselves. This ambitious and overtly assertive approach has led many to conclude that the United States is undertaking a possibly imperial foreign policy (Ikenberry, 2002; Johnston, 2004). Indeed some go so far as to say that an imperial approach to security is necessary in a globalized world (see generally, Cox, 2003). The third element of this has been a subtle transformation of the United States' cold war alliances into partners (when willing) in this global security strategy. NATO's support for the Afghanistan campaign, both in the invocation of Article V and the more recent handling of the stabilization force, is a key aspect of this. In East Asia this shift is even more palpable as both Japan and Australia tighten their alliance relationships and commit to international force projection to advance these ends (Bisley, 2006).

The problem with the current US predilection for a primacy-driven approach to security, and the unilateral approaches that it has bred, is that there are very serious doubts about the extent to which such a path will achieve the intended level of security. For example, Nye (2002) argues that the nature of US interests are such that multilateral paths to security – understood in their broadest sense – are the only alternative that will achieve real security. To neglect international institutions, to ignore global trading rules or the opinions of one's allies not only undermines the broader system but hurts US interests. Moreover, as the Iraq intervention makes clear, to achieve security policy objectives one needs to do a great deal more than apply physical force. The lack of fit between the military means and the policy objectives in Iraq, and indeed elsewhere, is increasingly clear (see generally Gray, 2005).

Underlying this are two distinct issues. The first relates to the suitability of a military approach to the kinds of security challenges that predominate in the current system. After the WMD justification for Iraq melted into the sand, the intervention was justified in terms of democracy, human rights and the war on terror. This move was not only an exercise in cynicism, but also reflected a belief that the absence of democracy and human rights presented security threats to the United States and the world. Yet the ability of military means to promote these ends, whether conceived as security matters or as ideals in and of themselves, is questionable at best. The second relates to the limits of US power. At the heart of US strategy is a belief that with sufficient technology, money and will, security can ultimately be achieved. The reality is that absolute security is a chimera and that strictly military means to advance security goals will always fall far short of the desired outcome. In very basic terms the cost of advancing a military vision of US security understood in a global sense is quite simply unaffordable, and that is before one counts the political and cultural costs of the current approach.

Thus the United States is caught between a conception of its security interests in which unilateralism is thought to be appropriate and broader global conditions which would appear to give greater succour to those who argue for a more multilateral approach. Moreover, one need not agree entirely with Nye's vision that US interests require a multilateral foreign policy to see that there is a need for cooperation of a considerably more advanced kind than the United States has embarked upon, both for functional and political reasons. In functional terms, if the United States is to continue down the path it has gone down then it requires burden sharing. Even in spite of its predominance, the United States cannot afford to pursue the security policy it is undertaking. The intervention in Iraq makes this clear. But beyond having more hands and more money to advance its conception of a secure international system, cooperation is needed to add political legitimacy to US grand strategy. It is this dimension of US policy that appears out of step with the times. The politics of US security policy has been very badly handled, with a high-handed and arrogant demeanour and an unsophisticated public diplomacy posture that is plainly undermining US aims. Key to the success of the nineteenth-century role of the great powers was the perceived legitimacy of their actions. The United States clearly needs to improve this element of its international policy (see Walt, 2005).

The United States is in a conundrum. It perceives that it must act in a particular way to secure its interests. That is, the character of security threats provides incentives for it to act unilaterally, and the structure of the international system allows it, as a great power, to act in this sphere with a certain degree of leeway. Yet, there are times when such an approach seems positively counterproductive. The political and economic environment appears to pull it in a different direction: that is, towards pursuing a more cooperative and consultative approach to security. This is the real tragedy of US power. It is caught between two conflicting approaches to security, ones which, given the tone of its present approach, are almost mutually exclusive. At the very least one must conclude that the current structure of the international system can be interpreted has having wildly different incentive structures for security policy.

In some respects we return to the basic point made earlier, that in the absence of other great powers, the dominant state is able to act in ways it otherwise could not. In US approaches to security one sees the dominant power trying, however vainly, to make the world more secure by trying to make it more like itself. The contemporary security environment is such that the application of force by great powers is not the most effective means to achieve a stable order. Moreover, the character of globalized societies and states involves an inherent risk or vulnerability that will never be resolved. States must learn to live with these risks or, conversely, pay the price to resolve them. At present, there seems little appetite for the latter and an almost palpable sense of denial about the former. The current situation is in no small matter a function of the unipolar character of the system. Until other great powers emerge (and we cannot be confident that this will occur), a return to a managerial role for the major powers (whether self-conscious as in the Congress system or a function of rivalry as in the cold war) is unlikely. Yet even in the event of the rise of several great powers who can forge some minimal consensus on appropriate action, there appears no chance of a return to the managerial life of nineteenth-century great power politics. The character of power in a globalized world and the structure of economic and political interests act to prevent this old-style conduct of international order. This should not be confused with the liberal argument that globalization neuters the great powers. If anything, the opposite is the case, the United States' place in international security demonstrates beyond doubt that power matters. States with concentrations of power will have a distinctive and determinative role to play for some time to come. The point is that the nature of greatness is less clear-cut than in the past and the practical constraints of the effective deployment of great power to stabilize the system are much greater. In short, power matters but its capacity to provide system stability through judicious application has been significantly reduced.

In the case of the current order, US perceptions of security and its policy preferences for pursuing its interests are the fundamental determinants of the character of the international security environment. These preferences appear to oscillate depending on the United States' perceptions of its interests, the changing conceptions of its responsibilities and the policy approaches to make good on these, and most importantly of all, the character of domestic influences on the security policy makers. For so long as the international system is unipolar, US constituents will have a disproportionate influence on the shape of international security. It is this, as much as in any other sphere, that shows just how much the role of the great powers has changed in the past two hundred years.

Further reading

Aron, R. [1962] (1966) *Peace and War: A Theory of International Relations*, London: Weidenfeld and Nicholson.

Bisley, N. (2007) *Rethinking Globalization*, Basingstoke: Macmillan.

Brown, C. (2004) 'Do Great Powers Have Great Responsibilities? Great Powers and Moral Agency', *Global Society*, 18: 5–19.

Bull, H. [1977] (1995) *The Anarchical Society: A Study of Order in World Politics*, 2nd edn, Basingstoke: Macmillan.

Daalder, I.H. and Lindsay, J.M. (2003) *America Unbound: The Bush Revolution in Foreign Policy*, Washington: Brookings Institution Press.

Freedman, L. (1995) 'Great Powers, Vital Interests and Nuclear Weapons', *Survival* 36, 4: 35–52.

Gilbert, A. (1999) *Must Global Politics Constrain Democracy? Great-Power Realism, Democratic Peace and Democratic Internationalism*, Princeton: Princeton University Press.

Gray, C.S. (2005) *Strategic Surprise*, Carlisle: US Army War College.

Gray, C.S. (2004) *The Sheriff: America's Defence of the New World Order*, Lexington: University Press of Kentucky.

Ikenberry, G.J. (2002) 'America's Imperial Ambition', *Foreign Affairs*, 81, 5: 44–60.

Johnston, C. (2004) *The Sorrows of Empire: Militarism, Secrecy and the End of the Republic*, New York: Holt.

Kennedy, P. (2002) 'The Greatest Superpower', *New Perspectives Quarterly*, 19, 2: 2–18.

Kennedy, P. (1988) *The Rise and Fall of the Great Powers: Economic Change and Military Conflict From 1500 to 2000*, New York: Random House.

Mearsheimer, J.J. (2001) *The Tragedy of Great Power Politics*, New York: W.W. Norton.

Miller, B. (1995) *When Opponents Cooperate: Great Power Conflict and Collaboration in World Politics*, Ann Arbor: University of Michigan Press.

Nye, J.S. (2002) *The Paradox of American Power: Why the World's Only Superpower Cannot Go it Alone*, Oxford: Oxford University Press.

Simpson, G. (2003) *Great Powers and Outlaw States: Unequal Sovereigns in the International Legal Order*, Cambridge: Cambridge University Press.

Toynbee, A.J. (1926) *The World After the Peace Conference*, Oxford: Oxford University Press.

Walt, S.M. (2005) *Taming American Power: The Global Response to US Primacy*, New York: W.W. Norton.

Wohlforth, W.C. and Brooks, S.G. (2002) 'American Primacy in Perspective', *Foreign Affairs*, 81, 4: 20–33.

Chapter 13

Regional Security and Regional Conflict

Craig A. Snyder

Introduction

Throughout the history of the twentieth century, states have looked to their immediate and near neighbours as well as key external or regional powers as potential sources of threat or of protection. By focusing on these neighbours, states have sought to devise rules and norms for how states in a particular region should act. Rather than at the global or local level, the region is where most post-1945 success in achieving security arrangements has been experienced. Louis Kriesberg (1994: 155) argues that 'all international conflicts have a regional base, but also have some links to countries or other large-scale actors from outside of the region.' Barry Buzan (1991b: 187) argues that the relational nature of security makes it impossible to understand the national security patterns of a state without a firm understanding of the pattern of regional security interdependence in which it exists. As such, the region is the most appropriate level of analysis to examine international order issues.

This chapter provides an assessment of the level of regionalism that is developing in the various regions of the world. It will use Bjorn Hettne's (2000) 'new regional theory' to assess the level and direction of regionalism that has occurred in these regions since the end of the Second World War and in the post-cold war era. It is argued that the development of regionalism is dependent on the support of the regional great power(s), the extent of reciprocity that exists in the relations of the states in the region, and the level of strategic reassurance that exists among these states. The chapter first considers what constitutes a region and regionalism. Following this, the main body of the chapter is divided into three sections. The first will explore the theoretical underpinnings of Hettne's 'new regionalism'. The second will assess the level of regionness and regionalism that has developed in a number of key regions around the globe. Finally, the chapter will explore the nature of the threats faced by regions. Traditionally these concerns involve the avoidance of war and the preservation of, or peaceful management of any change to, the material distribution of resources among the great powers in a region. The danger of inter-state conflict in any region stems from historic tensions, any unresolved territorial disputes, the modernization or expansion of military forces and capabilities, the proliferation of weapons of mass destruction and their means of delivery, and competition over resources, especially among the great powers. However, there also exist other important non-traditional security threats. These range from challenges to the norms and institutions of the region to threats to the political and economic stability of the states within the region. Finally, environmental issues and threats can challenge the security of the region (see Ayson, 2005).

What is a region?

At its most basic, a region is a group of states in proximity to each other within a geographic area. However, proximity is not the only consideration in regards to defining a region (and indeed, as we will see below, is not necessarily a requirement). In addition to living in geographic proximity to each other, people and states need to have a common set of cultural values, social bonds and historical legacy (Hettne and Soderbaum, 2002: 39). Robert Jervis (1999: 6) argues that a region (or system in his terminology) can be defined as groups of interconnected states where a change in any relationship within the group will influence the others and where the region as a whole develops characteristics and behaviours that are distinct from those of the individual states. It may seem logical to identify each of the major continents as a region based on cultural and historical patterns, but while this is a good rough guide, many regions exist only in a portion of a continent and others overlap continents. Southeast Asia is an example of the former while the Middle East includes, at least, parts of Northern Africa and Southwest Asia.

Other writers such as Peter Katzenstein (1997: 7) refute the geographic determinants of regions, as not being 'real', 'natural' or 'essential'. Rather regions are 'social and cognitive constructs that are rooted in political practice' (Katzenstein, 2000: 354) and are open to change. Therefore, for Katzenstein (2000: 354) a region is a grouping of states that share a communal identity. For example, the fact that Italy (a Mediterranean state) and Turkey (an Islamic state on the southeastern edge of Europe) are members of the *North Atlantic* Treaty Organization (NATO) is not 'natural', that is, a result of geography or even of cultural ties or historical legacies. Rather, each of their memberships in the alliance is due to acts of political imagination on the part of the North Atlantic political leaders in the early cold war era.

Another example of a region not bound by geography is the concept of the 'Anglosphere'. James Bennett (2004) argues that as the Anglosphere is

'a network civilization without a corresponding political forum' its boundaries are by their very nature vague. At the core is the relationship between
the United States and the United Kingdom while Canada, Australia, New
Zealand, Ireland and South Africa constitute a much more fluid peripheral
group. These states share a common historical narrative such as parliamen-
tary democracy and the rule of law that is taken for granted. The tightness
of the group, and indeed the core–periphery division, is much more fluid
than a geographically bounded region and is closely tied to the domestic
politics of the various states. For example, Canada under the Cretian
Liberal government had a close relationship with the United States during
the George Bush Senior and Bill Clinton administrations in the 1990s but
moved to the outer group with the election of George W. Bush as US
President in 2001. Similarly, Australia's relations with the United States
have fluctuated with changes in government in Canberra and in
Washington. Under the Hawke and Keating Labor administrations,
Australia took a more independent line, especially in regards to the Asia
Pacific. With the election of the Howard Coalition government in 1996,
the alliance with the United States was reinvigorated, even more so when
Bush replaced Clinton as president, leading to Australia joining the UK as
the only other member of the US-led coalition to deploy combat troops in
the invasion of Iraq in 2003.

Regionalism

Regardless of the nature of the regional grouping, the degree to which
regionalization occurs depends upon the amount of regionness that is felt
amongst the regional powers. During the cold war regional analysis existed
in an atheoretical framework, or at least with an uncritically realist or neorealist approach. Here the focus was on the material distribution of
resources throughout the region and on balances of power between the
great powers and their alliances. Following the end of the cold war the
prevailing realist orthodoxy came under critical analysis as assumptions
about the nature of international security and the ways states interact
strategically were re-examined. In this, reconsiderations were made of the
assumptions states had about how their security interactions enhanced or
detracted from their security. Realism initially came under criticism from
neoliberal institutionalist approaches, but was increasingly challenged in
the 1990s by critical and constructivist theories of international relations
(Acharya and Stubbs, 2006: 126). The focus of the debate between realism
and neo-liberalism for regional security was in how they relate to prospects
for security cooperation among and between the regional actors.

Following the end of the cold war a new school of regional analysis
adopted a constructivist/critical security approach and began to raise
questions about how notions of regional identity were being advanced.
This 'new regionalism' school differs from previous study of regions in

that the earlier study focused on the 'functionalist' nature of integration that emerged in Western Europe in the 1950s and 1960s. The problem here is that while functionalism can explain how regional structures operate and how they generate 'spillovers' that spur even greater integration, they are unable to explain how regional orders are created in the first place. Nor do they address the important role that the development of regional identities plays in regionalism (Breslin and Higgott, 2000: 335; Beeson, 2005: 971–2).

The debate between each of these theories reflected the importance of the transformation. The debate centred on how realists, neoliberal institutionalists and constructivists differed in their assessment of the rationales for state cooperation. Realists, as discussed in Chapter 2, argue that as states are power or security maximizers, they may not cooperate with each other even when they share common interests because the 'self-help' international system makes cooperation difficult (Grieco, 1990; Mearsheimer, 1990, 1994–5; Waltz, 1979). Institutionalists such as Robert Keohane (1984; Keohane and Martin, 1995) argue that institutions help to overcome international anarchy by helping to shape the interests and practices of states.

While realist and institutionalist approaches appear to be alternatives, policy makers are able to choose between them to address different issue-areas or even different issues within a specific issue-area. Indeed, Robert Keohane and Joseph Nye (1987) argue that realism and institutionalism are compatible with one another as they share a utilitarian view of the international system in which individual actors pursue their own interests by responding to incentives. Both doctrines posit similar conceptions of international political action: a process of political and economic exchange, characterized by bargaining among states. They both assume that rational decision making drives state behaviour. The difference between the two rests in their assumptions about the goals of the actors in the international system. For realists military force is the most important determinant of states' power due to the 'self-help' international anarchy in which they exist.

For institutionalists, however, economic and political incentives are just as important as concerns for military security (Keohane and Nye, 1987: 728–9). Hedley Bull ([1977] 1995: 67) argues that states will accept limitations on their actions when they recognize the benefits of reciprocity for strengthening cooperation. Such reciprocity rests upon two aspects: contingency and equivalence. 'Contingency' is the principle of rewarding positive actions of others while punishing negative actions. It thus rewards cooperation while deterring non-cooperation through the threat of punitive action. Reciprocity, therefore, returns ill for ill and good for good. 'Equivalence' refers to a rough equality in the level of reward exchanged between states. In cases where the actors have unequal power capabilities, equivalence will generate reciprocity of goods and services that hold mutual value to the actors but are otherwise incomparable. 'These exchanges are often, but not necessarily, mutually beneficial; they may be based on self-interest as well as on shared concepts of rights and obligations; and the value of what is exchanged may or may not be comparable' (Keohane, 1986b: 5–8). This is essential to reciprocity, as a 'lack of equivalence is likely to lead actors to misunderstand the strategy and tends to produce escalating feuds rather than cooperation' (Milner, 1992: 471). The importance of reciprocity in facilitating inter-state cooperation is demonstrated in nature of the cooperation between France and Germany following the Second World War. In this Germany provided the economic might for, and the French exercised political control over, the emerging West European regional cooperative structures. Through this, the Germans gained increased recognition as a 'normal' state while France benefited from, rather than feared, a German revival. In turn, this led to the development of a strong Franco-German amity that had been almost inconceivable during, at least, the previous 70 years.

Unlike realists or institutionalists, the constructivist school of thought argues that international politics are 'socially constructed'. That is, the basis of the structures of the international 'system' are not just the distribution of material resources but also include social interactions, and these shape the actors' identities and interests, not just their behaviour. For constructivists the structure not only includes the distribution of material capabilities but also social relationships. Alexander Wendt (1995: 71–3) argues that these social structures have three elements: shared knowledge, material resources and practice. Shared knowledge refers to the nature of the relationships between the actors in the system. The social patterns of enmity and amity are important here as competition will result when states are so distrustful of one another they make worst-case assumptions about each other. Cooperation, on the other hand, exists when amity exists between states such that there is a sufficient level of trust among the states that none will use force to resolve their disputes. The distribution of material resources is also important but this only becomes problematic when assessed in relation to the shared knowledge of states. Wendt gives the example of 500 British nuclear missiles being less threatening to the United States than five North Korean nuclear weapons. The amity between the United States and Britain makes it impossible to conceive of a situation where the British would ever consider using their weapons against the United States, while the enmity between the United States and North Korea make such an event, although unlikely, conceivable. Finally, constructivists argue that such a social structure exists not only because we think it exists but also because the policy makers believe it exists and, as such, act in accordance with that shared knowledge – thereby recreating the social structure through practice. Wendt (1995: 74) gives the example that 'the cold war was a structure of shared knowledge that governed great power relations for 40 years, but once they stopped acting on this basis, it was "over".'

New regionalism theory

In identifying the importance of the need to manage the social structures of the region, Bjorn Hettne (2000) argues that there is a need for a region to have its own identity: that is, an identity, however nascent, as an independent actor that is different or distinct from that of the constituent member states. He refers to this as a 'new regionalism' or 'regionness': that is, 'the degree to which a particular region in various respects constitutes a coherent unit' (Hettne, 2000: xviii). Hettne (1997: 97) argues that the difference between 'old' and 'new' forms of regional security analysis is that in the past '[t]he region was not an actor itself, only a "level" or "space" of action.' It is through the development of its regionness that a region moves from being a passive part of the structure to an actor in its own right (Hettne and Soderbaum, 1998: 8). The degree to which a particular region achieves this distinct identity differs from region to region but can demonstrate the degree to which the individual states have internalized the shared values and norms of the regional identity (Ayoob, 1999: 249).

Hettne (1997: 97) argues that there are five distinct degrees of regionness. The first or most basic level is the simple geographic unit of states that exist in a natural physical collection. These states have limited or no interconnection with each other, especially in regards to security collaboration. They exist in the international system of anarchy, and their security interactions are limited to crises or conflicts with their immediate neighbours. States in such a region can only rely on their own resources, or at the most, limited or temporary alliances in their approach to their own security. The 'self-help' nature of the regional interactions will limit any such alliances to those that are temporary in nature and involve a small number of states. Cooperation is dependent on the existence of an imminent threat, or the perception of such a threat, and will dissolve once the threat has passed.

The second level involves a more complex set of social interactions among the states in the region, through what Barry Buzan (1991b) describes as a security complex. Here all the regional states are interconnected and dependent on each other in regards to their own security. This does not mean that the security interactions between all the states in a region need to be direct, however, as states at opposite edges of the region are unlikely to have a great deal of contact with each other, but they may both be drawn into the same set of alliances and crises. Informal institutions or norms to help govern security relations across the region may also exist at this level. These may range from the informal alliances similar to those of the first level, to the development of other types of institutions or norms to govern state behaviour.

The third level is where any form of organized cooperation exists through the establishment of formal regional institutions such as a collective defence organization. Collective defence organizations or formal alliances are structures whereby regional actors seek to ally themselves with other like-minded states against a perceived common threat or enemy. Robert Osgood (1968: 17–31) defines an alliance as a formal agreement that commits states to combine their military forces against a certain state or group of states. Alliances usually also bind at least one of the participants to use force, or at the very least to consider using force in specifically defined circumstances. As alliances are primarily comprised of like-minded states, they form to meet an external threat or enemy and seldom contain any dispute settlement mechanisms for internal threats.

There can be a difference at this level between the 'formal' region (i.e. the institution) and the 'real' region. When they coincide, Hettne (1997: 97) argues, there is likely to be greater security but should the region be divided, as was common during the cold war, between two (or more) rival security institutions then regional security, if not stability, may be threatened. In the latter case, the approach of each sub-regional institution is likely to be one of collective defence where each alliance seeks to balance against the other. However, should the formal and real regions coincide then the region is more likely to adopt collective or cooperative security approaches.

Collective security differs from alliances in that in the former, members are not necessarily like-minded states but have agreed not to use force to resolve differences and to respond collectively to any violation of this rule. That is, unlike collective defence where the commitment is to act in defence against a known or perceived aggressor, in a collective security system the commitment is to respond to an unspecified aggressor in support of an unspecified victim.

Cooperative security differs from both collective defence and collective security in that it attempts to deepen understandings of the mutuality of security as well as to broaden the definition of security beyond the traditional military concerns to include environmental, economic and social concerns. Cooperative security adopts a gradual process that seeks to shape policy makers' attitudes to security and offer alternatives to the definition of security from the narrow military-only focus. It attempts to change the motives of state behaviour from competition with other states to cooperation with those states. What cooperative security really provides is a means to challenge long-held or emergent fears, to overcome the hesitancy that accompanies political risk-taking, to lower the walls which have been erected between societies, governments, and countries in the wake of colonial, pre-independence and cold war periods, and to transcend the barriers of sectarian and national interests (Dewitt, 1994: 8).

The fourth level of regionness exists when the relationships among the states have developed to such a degree that a civil society has been developed throughout the region. In this, the organizational framework of the regional institutions facilitates and promotes social communication and convergence of values throughout the states and people of the region. Here the region attains the status of a security community. A security community, as defined by Karl Deutsch (1957), exists when a shared sense of belonging to a community, or 'we-ness', is developed throughout the region. Through a security community, an expectation of only peaceful relations between states is developed. This does not imply that tensions and disputes cannot emerge within the region but that the disputants will seek only peaceful means to resolve these issues.

Hettne's fifth level of regionness occurs when a 'region-state' is developed. A region-state has its own distinct identity, capability and legitimacy. In addition to being a collection of states with common objectives, ideas and policies, there is a need for the region itself to have a decision-making structure independent of the member states for conflict-resolution for issues not only between the member states but also within them.

The new regionalism theory takes from constructivism and critical security studies the notion of social interaction as the main defining feature of a region. 'Regional identity' while a contested topic, plays a significant role in regards to the degree of regionalization that is developed. 'To a certain extent, all regions are "imagined", subjectively defined and cognitive constructions. To be successful, regionalization necessitates a certain degree of homogeneity of compatibility of culture, identity and fundamental values' (Hettne and Soderbaum, 1998: 13).

Critics of this approach such as Ndayi (2006) argue that the social constructivist aspect of the new regionalism theory confuses the structure with the process. The degree to which a region has established its 'regionness' is determined by the extent that the member states adopt the ideology of regionalism through regionalization. In this, 'people develop awareness of their interdependence because they are from the same geographic area. Because of the commonalities and developed shared interests, they establish amongst other factors, a sense of belonging together' (Ndayi, 2006: 123). It is important to note here that the degree of regionalism can *increase* or *decrease* in a particular region, and when it increases it leads to regionalization. This approach to regions, while acknowledging the necessity of geographic contiguity for a region, cautions that its importance should not be exaggerated and that regionalism can be applied to communities such as the Anglosphere.

Development of regional security

Regionalization has developed throughout the various regions of the world at radically different paces. Again, the process is not linear. In some regions it has decreased and in others it has increased. Europe and the Asia Pacific have both developed the highest degree of regionalization, but even these are well below Hettne's fifth level of a region state. Moreover, even in these two regions there is unevenness in regards to both the geographic scope of regionalization and the degree of integration that has occurred across different sectors. In these, and indeed globally, economic integration has been the most successful, with political will and security integration lagging behind.

European regionalization was built on the foundations of West European economic, political and security integration developed during the cold war through institutions such as NATO, the Council of Europe, the Organization for Security and Cooperation in Europe, and the European Union (EU) and their predecessors. Following the end of the cold war this success was extended to all of Europe, albeit slowly (see Snyder, 1996). Over time, the degree of regionness in Europe has deepened and extended beyond the initial West European states to include almost all of Europe, with the important exception of the Balkans. However, the Europeans remain stalled at Hettne's fourth level of regionness. The pace of regionalization in Europe has also been sporadic with debate emerging over the pace and scope of integration. While the Europeans have been relatively successful in the development of common market conditions throughout the EU members, they are reluctant to transfer too much political power to the regional level.

In regards to regional security, the Europeans have tended to rely on the US-led NATO for their security cooperation. Indeed, there exists a divide in Europe over the role of the United States in European security. While most support a continued US role as the principal state in NATO, some in Europe, led by the French, would prefer a European-only security and defence structure. The tensions between these competing visions for Europe are not new, and indeed were responsible for the demise of the European Defence Community in the 1950s. In 2003 these tensions re-emerged over the US-led war in Iraq. In this, a division within Europe emerged between what the then US Secretary of Defense Donald Rumsfeld (2003) famously described as 'old' and 'new' Europe. Old Europe comprised those states in Western Europe, especially France and Germany, who were opposed to the war and new Europe was mainly made up of Central and East European states that were more supportive of the US actions. While the dispute was formally over support for the US action in Iraq, it was much more a reflection on divisions between France and many of the Central and East European states over the direction of European regionalism. The French vision was for a more independent (of the United States) Europe, with regional security integration overseen by the EU. The Central and East Europeans were more opposed to this as they were concerned as to the level of control France sought to continue to exert over the EU.

As a result of these tensions, the Europeans have found it difficult to develop a common foreign and security policy or a European security and defence policy beyond agreements to adopt multilateral approaches and to develop military forces geared toward humanitarian, peacekeeping and peace-making tasks. These are referred to as the Petersberg Tasks after the hotel near Bonn, Germany, where the Council of the Western European Union met in 1992 and first articulated this goal (see Anderson and Seitz, 2006).

While the level of regional security institutionalization in Southeast Asia is not at the same level as in Europe, the region has been successful in developing its own sense of regionness. As in Europe, the basis of the contemporary Asia Pacific regional integration rests on the foundations of sub-regional regionalization developed during the cold war and extended region-wide following the end of the cold war. The Association of South-East Asian Nations (ASEAN), formed in 1967, has successfully developed the political and economic integration of the non-communist states of Southeast Asia. While ASEAN did not officially deal with security issues, the underlying emphasis of its security outlook was that regional stability was the responsibility of the indigenous states (Acharya, 1993; Snyder, 1996). The success of ASEAN was that it sought to promote the goal of 'regional reconciliation through a gradual process based on functional cooperation' (Zhang, 2005: 60).

Again like Europe, the ASEAN states also sought to extend the rules and norms of what came to be known as the 'ASEAN Way', first to all of Southeast Asia, but also to the wider Asia-Pacific Region. While some success has occurred, through the establishment of institutions such as the ASEAN Regional Forum, the Asia Pacific Economic Cooperation group, ASEAN plus Three and the East Asian Summit, some problems still exist. The Asian financial crisis of the late 1990s derailed, or at least delayed, progress in economic integration as well as putting pressure on the political institutions of regionalization that had been developed. Moreover, continuing tensions and mistrust in Northeast Asia prevent deeper region-wide integration (see Acharya, 2001; Severino, 2006).

Progress in regionalization in other regions is much more sporadic and is often focused around a specific sector, most often economic cooperation or free trade groupings. The largest of the free trade areas is the North American Free Trade Agreement (NAFTA), formed in 1994 between the United States, Canada and Mexico. While NAFTA has been successful in removing barriers to trade among the three states, no further regionalization has occurred in North America. Canada and the United States maintain close relations and cooperate over a number of continental defence and border security issues. They jointly operate the North American Aerospace Defense (NORAD) Command that provides surveillance and control over North American airspace (NORAD, 2007). In addition, following the 11 September 2001 attacks, Canada has sought to work closely with the United States to coordinate their border protection measures in order to maintain ease of access to the United States for Canadian goods and services (Canada, Department of Foreign Affairs and

International Trade, 2007). However, despite close ties and similar cultural backgrounds, Canada has been reluctant to participate in other US-led hemispheric regionalization activities. Canada only joined the Organization of American States (OAS) (founded in 1948) in 1990 as it considered the OAS simply a tool for US foreign policy in the hemisphere (Kilgour, 1999).

Despite these concerns, the OAS has facilitated some degree of regionness within the western hemisphere. The founding principles of the OAS are of collective defence and promoting the peace and prosperity of the region. In 1990 the OAS transformed this role to focus on cooperation in several broad areas: anti-terrorism, illegal drugs and other threats to public security; the promotion of democratic governance; and social and sustainable development (OAS, 2007).

In regions such as South Asia, Africa, Central Asia and the Western Pacific a degree of regionalization has also emerged. In each, a nascent regionness exists. Organizations such as the South Asian Association for Regional Cooperation (SAARC), the African Union (AU), the Shanghai Cooperation Organization (SCO), and the Pacific Islands Forum (PIF) have had some success in promoting regionness. Economic cooperation agreements have increased regionalization in South Asia, Central Asia and the Pacific. The AU and PIF have also had success in organizing peacekeeping operations in the Sudan (AU), Bougainville and the Solomon Islands (PIF). In addition, these regional organizations have been successful in promoting dialogue on issues of regional interest. Despite these successes, further regionalization is hampered by high degrees of mistrust and periodic tensions between many of the regional powers. In general, these regions have only been able to achieve Hettne's third level of regionalization.

Finally, in the Middle East regionness is the least developed. Despite several regional or sub-regional organizations, such as the Gulf Cooperation Council and the Arab League, very little integration has occurred among the states. The region has experienced a high degree of conflict sparked by ethnic and religious differences, interference by extra-regional powers, problems of undemocratic governance and the impact of globalization. It is these sources of conflict, not only in the Middle East, but also in other regions of the globe, that will be discussed in the final section of this chapter.

Regional security threats

The nature of the threats that are likely to be faced by regional security institutions can be grouped into four categories. Bjorne Hettne (1998: 54) identifies three main types of conflicts: traditional balance of power contests between great or regional powers, 'grass fire' conflicts which emerge from the more primitive security complexes, and intra-state conflicts. However, a fourth category needs to be added for those conflicts that, as discussed in Chapter 4, arise from transnational threats caused by such things as environmental degradation, resource scarcity etcetera. It should be noted that these categories are highly porous and a particular conflict or security threat may fit within more than one category.

In regards to the first two categories, many of these conflicts are sparked by local issues (territorial disputes; competition over scarce resources; access to major geophysical resources such as deep water or warm water ports; or political, religious or ethnic tensions) between neighbouring states. The causes of these conflicts are often multi-faceted and involve both 'trigger' events and longer-term underlying conditions. The 1990 Iraqi invasion of Kuwait is a particular case in point. The trigger event was accusations by Iraq of illegal Kuwaiti slant drilling within the Rumaila oilfield along the Iraq–Kuwait border. However, the longer-term cause of the conflict was the relative wealth of Kuwait as compared with Iraq in general, and a dispute over the level of debt that Iraq had accumulated with Kuwait during Iraq's 1980–8 war with Iran in particular. There was also the perception, in Iraq, that an independent Kuwait was an accident of history caused by British colonial administration. Added to this were the regional leadership goals of the Iraqi leader, Saddam Hussein, who felt that control of Kuwait would strengthen his claim to the role of leader of the Arab world.

The third category is arguably the most likely source of conflict to emerge in the early twenty-first century. These are conflicts that exist primarily within the territory of one state. However, they may also draw in other states or sub-national groups, or may involve an attempt to create a new political entity, either as a state in its own right or a semi-autonomous entity within the state. These low-intensity civil wars arise from ethno-nationalism or micro-regionalism (Hettne, 1998: 54–5). Joseph Nye (2005: 196–7, 248) argues that these types of conflict arise when the forces of globalization and modernization challenge societal identity.

As discussed in Chapter 3 ethno-nationalist conflicts arise from issues of societal security where sub-national groups raise claims for increased autonomy or even separation from the dominant ethnic majority within a multi-ethnic state. Ethno-national movements question the legitimacy of the established state structure. Such conflict usually involves violence and is a reactive phenomenon. Examples of this type of conflict are the wars over the break-up of Yugoslavia, where at one time or another Serbian, Croatian, Bosnian and Kosovar nationalist forces clashed. Likewise in Africa 'modern and premodern societal referents continue to exist simultaneously' (Sheehan, 2005: 97). In this case states have been created that contain many societal groups, such as clans or tribes, that have little in common with each other while at the same time having close cultural and language associations with others outside the formal state. Conflicts between the Hutu and Tutsi ethnic forces in Central Africa and between Muslim and Christian-backed nationalist forces in

East Africa are examples of where the tensions between the modern and premodern societal referents have led to violent conflict. Finally, in the Middle East ethnic and religious nationalist cleavages reinforce each other, leading to near-internecine warfare between Israel and its Arab neighbours (including the Palestinian Authority) and between the various ethnic and religious groups in the region. As in Africa, the societal boundaries in the Middle East do not coincide with the formal state boundaries. Arab nationalism as well as tribal loyalty competes with notions of state nationalism that also clashes with the religious divisions between the two main forms of Islam and with the minority religions that exist in the region as well as between Arabs and non-Arabs.

Unlike these ethno-nationalist conflicts, micro-regional conflicts are less likely to result in violence. Micro-regional conflicts exists where a high degree of regionalization exists in a smaller, economically dynamic subnational or transnational region that seeks to gain direct access to the larger economic system, bypassing the nation-state and the national capital. Multi-ethnic states, with little integration between their various parts, will also show a particular vulnerability to micro-regionalism. For example, the former state of Czechoslovakia broke up when the Czech and Slovak sections proved incapable of maintaining political harmony between them. Similarly, the disintegration of the Yugoslavian federation was caused by Croatia and Slovenia's push for independence in protest against Serbian attempts to equate its nationalist agenda with that of the Yugoslav state (Hettne, 1998: 54–5).

Like ethno-nationalism and micro-regionalism that involve crises of identity, another form of intra-state conflict exists in the disputes between and among the state and anti-state or anti-society groups. That is the organized violence of social deprivation, alienation and frustration. The types of groups covered by this concept include organized crime gangs but also right-wing extremists such as white supremacist groups. The importance of the regional dimension here lies in the need for supranational coordination of police activities against these forms of crime (Hettne, 1998: 55).

Mary Kaldor (1999) identifies this type of conflict as 'new wars'. These conflicts, she argues, blur the distinction between traditional understandings of interstate conflict, organized crime and 'large-scale violations of human rights'. Such conflicts tend to emerge within states where the governing authority begins to lose its monopoly in the use of legitimate organized violence. This loss of autonomy or sovereignty is usually challenged from above (through the growing constraints the international community puts on the exercise of state power) as well as below (that is, from organized criminal gangs or paramilitary forces). New wars are wars based on identity politics. They contrast to the 'old wars' which, while they could also be considered to be based on identity politics (that is, wars between nations or ideologies), are often based on notions of how society should be organized. New wars, in contrast, are the result of increased globalization. 'The new wave of identity politics is both local and global, national as well as transnational' (Kaldor, 1999: 7). It uses information revolution technology to speed political mobilization. New wars also differ in their mode of warfare. They tend to blend guerrilla and counter-insurgency strategies. Like guerrilla warfare, the new warfare seeks to win though political control of a population rather than by physically gaining territory through conventional battle. However, unlike guerrilla warfare, political control is not sought by winning the 'hearts and minds' of the population but rather, like counter-insurgency warfare, through destabilizing tactics designed to instil 'fear and hatred'. The objective is to control the population by removing the 'other', or those with a different identity, from the territory (Kaldor, 1999: 7–8).

The fourth category of regional conflict is that which emerges from non-traditional security issues. As discussed in Chapter 4, many threats to regional security also come from non-traditional or non-military issues such as conflicts over natural resources, access to economic resources or issues of migration, both legal and illegal. These threats are different from the traditional inter-state military threats or the intra-state threats identified above in that they do not readily lend themselves to military responses and the threats are transnational rather than state or intra-state based. While these issues may spark inter-state conflict, the source of the conflict is transnational; in many cases, conflict will not resolve the problem but may position one state in an advantageous position vis-à-vis the other. These conflicts also need international and regional attention as they are embedded in the history and socio-ethnic tensions of the region but are beyond the political capability of any one government to resolve. The tension in Southeast Asia over the multiple overlapping territorial claims to the Spratly Islands in the South China Sea is an example of this type of conflict (see Snyder, 1996–7, 1997). The Spratly Islands are resource rich (at least in fish if not oil and gas) and crises between the various claimant states (China, Vietnam, the Philippines, Malaysia, Brunei and Taiwan) arise from time to time as they attempt to exercise sovereignty in the area. For example, tensions can increase when the individual states improve the infrastructure on the islands, such as erecting lighthouses and building or upgrading military outposts on the various features in the chain, or when one state arrests fishing boats from one of the other claimants that are fishing in disputed waters. While embedded in traditional security issues of sovereignty and control of territory, the disputes over the Spratly Islands are exacerbated by non-traditional security issues; these include access to scarce resources such as the potential hydrocarbon bonanza that sits beneath the island group or to the rich fishing grounds that surround the islands. Other issues such as environmental pollution and control over strategic shipping lanes also influence state behaviour over the islands (see Snyder, 1996–7).

Energy security is also a potential source of regional conflict. For many in the Asia-Pacific, for example, access to energy resources is constructed not only in terms of traditional national security but also in terms of economic and political development. For many, reliance on foreign oil and gas supplies has had a major influence on their security policies. While at the present these states are seeking political and economic solutions to securing the supply of these resources, they have also sought to develop military capability as insurance should these efforts fail. Japan, for example, has focused on building a high-tech maritime self-defence force with the ability to operate out to 1000 nautical miles beyond Japanese territory, while at the same time it has engaged in a policy of assisting the Southeast Asian states to protect the shipping in the Straits of Malacca. China has adopted a similar dual strategy of diplomacy and cooperation with the Southeast Asian states while also increasing its air and maritime power projection capabilities, although there has been a specific decision not to build a force that can single-handedly secure its energy supply (see Tang, 2006: 31–3; Katsumata, 2006: 41–2).

Access to potable water is another potential source of conflict. Water has been a key security concern for the states in the Levant (Israel, Jordan, Syria and the Palestinian Authority) for at least several decades. J. A. Allan (2002: 16) argues that 'it was one of three issues on the table in the 1992–3 negotiations between Jordan and Israel, along with peace and territory/borders. It is one of five major unresolved and contentious issues in the relations of Israel and Palestine'. However, Helle Munk Ravnborg (2004: 5–15) argues that it is overly simplistic to link water scarcity to international conflict. Between 1948 and 1999, out of some 1288 water events, over two-thirds were cooperative in nature; only 28 per cent were conflictive and none of these involved formal conflicts between states. Rather, these were trans-boundary disputes between locals. It is likely that water-related violence is much more liable to be in the form of 'water riots', that is, social unrest within a state, than 'water wars' or conflicts across national boundaries.

Conclusion

As we have seen throughout both this chapter and the book as a whole, regional security is an issue that encompasses all aspects of security. At a very basic level, all conflicts are local and as such involve forces within the same region. As discussed in Chapter 10, even the so-called global war on terror stems from local conditions in the Middle East. That the terrorists have identified Western, and in particular US, support for what they see as morally and politically corrupt regimes has led them to the very Clausewitzian strategy of striking the most powerful member of an alliance.

Many contemporary security issues are not ones where it is possible for a single state or political actor to resolve the problem. Be they traditional issues of state-to-state conflicts, or global military issues such as nuclear war or non-traditional security threats, it is at the regional level that these issues can best be addressed. They are beyond the capabilities of individual states to manage and at the global level the issues are often marginalized or consumed within a wider political or security agenda. Rather, it is at the regional level that groupings of states can combine their efforts to deal with specific issues. By focusing on the specific regional aspect of a global problem, the regional powers are more likely to be able to identify the local influences on the issue and more effectively address both the regional and global aspects. However, it is important to note that regionalism is not a panacea for all the world's security problems, but can be one of many tools that policy makers can chose from when seeking to resolve these problems.

Further reading

Acharya, A. and Stubbs, R. (2006) 'Theorizing Southeast Asian Relations: An Introduction', *The Pacific Review*, 19: 125–34.

Beeson, M. (2005) 'Rethinking Regionalism: Europe and East Asia in Comparative Historical Perspective', *Journal of European Public Policy*, 12: 969–85.

Bennett, J.C. (2004) *The Anglosphere Challenge: Why the English-Speaking Nations will Lead the Way in the Twenty-first Century*, Lanham: Rowman and Littlefield.

Dewitt, D. (1994) 'Common, Comprehensive and Cooperative Security', *The Pacific Review*, 7: 1–15.

Hettne, B. (1997) 'Development, Security and World Order: A Regionalist Approach', *European Journal of Development Research*, 9: 83–106.

Hettne, B. (1998) 'Globalization, Regionalism and the Europeanization of Europe', *Politeia*, 17, 3: 44–59.

Hettne, B. (2000) 'The New Regionalism: A Prologue', in Hettne, B. (ed.), *The New Regionalism and the Future of Security and Development*, Vol. 4, London: Macmillan.

Hettne, B. and Soderbaum, F. (1998) 'The New Regionalism Approach', *Politeia*, 17, 3: 6–21.

Hettne, B. and Soderbaum, F. (2002) 'Theorising the Rise of Regionness', in Breslin, S., Hughes, C., Philips, N. and Rosamond, B. (eds), *New Regionalisms in the Global Political Economy: Theories and Cases*, London: Routledge.

Kaldor, M. (1999) *New and Old Wars: Organized Violence in a Global Era*, Cambridge: Polity.

Kriesberg, L. (1994) 'Regional Conflicts in the Post-Cold War Era: Causes, Dynamics, and Modes of Resolution', in Klare, M.T. and Thomas, D.C. (eds), *World Security: Challenges for a New Century*, New York: St Martin's.

Nye, J.S. Jr. (2005) *Understanding International Conflicts: An Introduction to Theory and History*, 5th edn, New York: Pearson Longman.

Sheehan, M. (2005) *International Security: An Analytical Survey*, Boulder: Lynne Rienner.

Snyder, C.A. (1996) 'Emerging Regional Security Cooperation in Europe and the Asia Pacific', *The Pacific Review*, 9: 553–76.

Bibliography

Acharya, A. (1993) *A New Regional Order in South-East Asia: ASEAN in the Post-Cold War Era*, Adelphi Paper 279, London: Brassey's for the International Institute for Strategic Studies.

Acharya, A. (2001) *Constructing a Security Community in Southeast Asia: ASEAN and the Problem of World Order*, London: Routledge.

Acharya, A. and Stubbs, R. (2006) 'Theorizing Southeast Asian Relations: An Introduction', *The Pacific Review*, 19: 125–34.

Adamson, F.B. (2005) 'Globalization, Transnational Political Mobilization and Networks of Violence', *Cambridge Review of International Affairs*, 18, 1: 31–49.

Aggestam, L. and Hyde-Price, A.G.V. (2000) *Security and Identity in Europe: Exploring the New Agenda*, New York: St Martin's.

Akan, M. (2003) 'Contextualizing Multiculturalism', *Studies in Comparative International Development*, 38: 57–75.

Alam, U.Z. (2002) 'Questioning the Water Wars Rationale: A Case Study of the Indus Waters Treaty', *Geographical Journal*, 168: 341–53.

Alkire, S. (2003) *A Conceptual Framework for Human Security*, CRISE Working Paper 2, Centre for Research on Inequality, Human Security and Ethnicity (CRISE), University of Oxford.

Allan, J.A. (2002) *Water Security in the Middle East: The Hydro-Politics of Global Solutions*, New York: Columbia International Affairs Online (CIAO), <www.ciaonet.org>. Accessed March 2007.

Allenby, B.R. (2000) 'Environmental Security: Concept and Implementation', *International Political Science Review*, 21: 5–21.

Allison, G. (1971) *The Essence of Decision: Explaining the Cuban Missile Crisis*, New York: Harper Collins.

Allison, G. (2004) *Nuclear Terrorism: The Ultimate Preventable Catastrophe*, New York: Henry Holt.

Allison, G. and Treverton, G.F. (eds) (1992) *Rethinking America's Security: Beyond Cold War to New World Order*, New York: W.W. Norton.

Anderson, G. (2007) 'US-Imposed Sanctions Against Russia are "Illegal", Says Ivanov', *Jane's Defence Weekly*, 44, 3: 21.

Anderson, S. and Seitz, T.R. (2006) 'European Security and Defense Policy Demystified', *Armed Forces & Society*, 33: 24–42.

Annan, K. (1999) 'Balance State Sovereignty with Individual Sovereignty!', speech before the U.N. General Assembly 20 September, from Toward Democratic World Federation website,
<www.dwfed.org/pp_annan_on_sov.html> Accessed 19 August 2007.

Aron, R. [1962] (1966) *Peace and War: A Theory of International Relations*, London: Weidenfeld and Nicholson.

Arquilla, J. and Ronfeldt, D. (1997) *In Athena's Camp*, Santa Monica: RAND Corporation.

Ashley, R. (1986) 'The Poverty of Neorealism', in Keohane, R.O. (ed.), *Neorealism and its Critics*, New York: Columbia University Press.

Aslan, R. (2006) *No God But God: The Origins, Evolution and Future of Islam*, 2nd edn, New York: Arrow.

Ayoob, M. (1999) 'From Regional System to Regional Society', *Australian Journal of International Affairs*, 53: 247–60.

Ayson, R. (2005) 'Regional Stability in the Asia-Pacific: Towards a Conceptual Understanding', *Asian Security*, 1: 190–213.

Bacevich, A. (2006) 'The Islamic Way of War', *American Conservative*, 11, <www.amconmag.com/2006/2006_09_11/cover.html>. Accessed January 2007.

Baer, G. (1994) *One Hundred Years of Sea Power: The US Navy, 1890–1990*, Stanford: Stanford University Press.

Baldwin, D.A. (1995) 'Security Studies and the End of the Cold War', *World Politics*, 48: 117–41.

Baldwin, D.A. (1997) 'The Concept of Security', *Review of International Studies*, 23, 1: 5–26.

Barber, B. (2003) *Jihad vs. McWorld: Terrorism's Challenge to Democracy*, new revised edn, London: Corgi Adult.

Bauman, Z. (2001) 'Wars in the Era of Globalization', *European Journal of Social Theory*, 4, 1: 11–28.

Beck, M. and Gahlaut, S. (2003) 'Creating a New Multilateral Export Control Regime', *Arms Control Today*, 33, 3: 12–18.

Beckett, I.F.W. (2001) *Modern Insurgencies and Counter-Insurgencies*, London: Routledge.

Beckett, I.F.W. (2005) *Insurgency in Iraq: An Historical Perspective*, Carlisle, Pa.: Strategic Studies Institute.

Beeson, M. (2005) 'Rethinking Regionalism: Europe and East Asia in Comparative Historical Perspective', *Journal of European Public Policy*, 12: 969–85.

Beier, J.M. (2005) *International Relations in Uncommon Places: Indigeneity, Cosmology, and the Limits of International Theory*, New York: Palgrave Macmillan.

Beier, J.M. (2006) 'Outsmarting Technologies: Rhetoric, Revolutions in Military Affairs, and the Social Depth of Warfare', *International Politics*, 43: 266–80.

Bell, C. (1971) *The Conventions of Crisis: A Study in Diplomatic Management*, Oxford: Oxford University Press.

Bellamy, A.J. and Williams, P.D. (2005) 'Who's Keeping the Peace? Regionalization and Contemporary Peace Operations', *International Security*, 29, 4: 157–195.

Benbow, T. (2004) *The Magic Bullet? Understanding the Revolution in Military Affairs*, London: Brassey's.

Bennett, J.C. (2004) *The Anglosphere Challenge: Why the English-Speaking Nations will Lead the Way in the Twenty-first Century*, Lanham: Rowman and Littlefield.

Bergen, P. (2002) *Holy War Inc: Inside The Secret World of Osama Bin Laden*, London: Pheonix.

Betts, R.K. (1982) *Surprise Attack: Lessons for Defense Planning*, Washington: Brookings Institution Press.

Betts, R.K. (1997) 'Should Strategic Studies Survive?' *World Politics*, 50: 7–33.

Bilgin, P. (2003) 'Individual and Societal Dimensions of Security', *International Studies Review*, 5: 203–22.

Bisley, N. (2006) 'Enhancing America's Alliances in a Changing Asia-Pacific', *Journal of East Asian Affairs*, 20: 47–73.

Bisley, N. (2007) *Rethinking Globalization,* Basingstoke: Macmillan.

Blair, T. (1999) 'Doctrine of the International Community', Speech to the Economic Club of Chicago, Chicago, Ill., 22 April, <www.pm.gov.uk/output/Page1297.asp>. Accessed 1 August 2006.

Blair, T. (2006) 'Foreword', *The Future of the United Kingdom's Nuclear Deterrent*, UK: Ministry of Defence, <www.mod.uk/NR/rdonlyres/AC00DD79–76D6–4FE3–91A1–6A56B03C092F /0/DefenceWhitePaper2006_Cm6994.pdf>. Accessed January 2007.

Blaufarb, D.S. (1977) *The Counterinsurgency Era: U.S. Doctrine and Performance – 1950 to the Present*, New York: Free Press.

Blinken, A.J. (2003–4) 'From Pre-empion to Engagement', *Survival*, 45, 4: 33–60.

Blix, H. (2005) *Disarming Iraq*, revised edn, London: Bloomsbury.

Bloom, M. (2005) *Dying to Kill: The Allure of Suicide Terrorism*, New York: Columbia University Press.

Böhning, W.R. (1972) *The Migration of Workers in the United Kingdom and the European Community,* London: Oxford University Press for the Institute of Race Relations.

Böhning, W.R. (1984) *Studies in International Labour Migration*, New York: St Martin's.

Boot, M. (2003) 'The New American Way of War', *Foreign Affairs*, 82: 41–59.

Boot, M. (2006) *War Made New: Technology, Warfare and the Course of History*, New York: Gotham.

Booth, K. (1991) 'Security and Emancipation', *Review of International Studies*, 17: 315–26.

Booth, K. (2005a) 'Beyond Critical Security Studies', in Booth, K. (ed.), *Critical Security Studies and World Politics,* Boulder: Lynne Rienner.

Booth, K. (ed.) (2005b) *Critical Security Studies and World Politics*, Boulder: Lynne Rienner.

Borjas, G.J. (1990) *Friends or Strangers: The Impact of Immigrants on the American Economy*, New York: Basic Books.

Bouchard, J.F. (1991) *Command in Crisis: Four Case Studies*, New York: Columbia University Press.

Boutin, J.D.K. (2004) *Technological Globalization and Regional Security in East Asia*, Working Paper No. 65, Singapore: Institute of Defence and Strategic Studies, Nanyang Technological University.

Bowen, W.Q. (2006) *Libya and Nuclear Proliferation: Stepping Back from the Brink*, Adelphi Paper No.380, London: International Institute for Strategic Studies.

Bracken, P. (2003) 'The Structure of the Second Nuclear Age', *Orbis,* 47: 399–413.

Breslin, S. and Higgott, R. (2000) 'Studying Regions: Learning from the Old, Constructing the New', *New Political Economy*, 5: 333–52.

Brodie, B. (ed.) (1946) *The Absolute Weapon: Atomic Power and World Order*, New York: Harcourt, Brace and Company.

Brooks, S. (1997) 'Dueling Realisms', *International Organization*, 51: 445–77.

Brooks, S.G. and Wohlforth, W.C. (2000–1) 'Power, Globalization, and the End of the Cold War: Reevaluating a Landmark Case for Ideas', *International Security*, 25, 3: 5–53.

Brown, C. (2004) 'Do Great Powers Have Great Responsibilities? Great Powers and Moral Agency', *Global Society*, 18: 5–19.

Brown, L. (1997) 'Redefining National Security', *Worldwatch Paper*, Washington: Worldwatch Institute.

Brown, M.E., Coté, O.R. Jr., Lynn-Jones, S.M. and Miller, S.E. (eds) (2004a) *New Global Dangers: Changing Dimensions of International Security*, Cambridge: MIT Press.

Brown, M.E., Coté, O.R. Jr., Lynn-Jones, S.M. and Miller, S.E. (eds) (2004b) *Offense, Defense, and War*, Cambridge: MIT Press.

Brown, M.E., Lynn-Jones, S.M. and Miller, S.E. (eds) (1996) *Debating the Democratic Peace*, Cambridge: MIT Press.

Bull, H. [1977] (1995) *The Anarchical Society: A Study of Order in World Politics*, 2nd edn, Basingstoke: Macmillan.

Bunker, R.J. (1998) *Five-Dimensional (Cyber) Warfighting: Can the Army after Next be Defeated through Complex Concepts and Technologies?* Carlisle Barracks: Strategic Studies Institute, US Army War College.

Burke, J. (2004) *Al-Qaeda: The True Story of Radical Islam*, London: I.B. Tauris.

Butfoy, A. (2002) 'Perpetuating US Nuclear First-Use Into The Indefinite Future: Reckless Inertia or Pillar of World Order?' *Contemporary Security Policy*, 23: 149–68.

Butler, J.P. (2004) *Precarious Life: The Power of Mourning and Violence*, London: Verso.

Butterfield, H. (1950) *History and Human Relations*, London: Collins.

Buzan, B. (1983) *People, States and Fear: The National Security Problem in International Relations*, New York: Wheatsheaf.

Buzan, B. (1987) *An Introduction to Strategic Studies: Military Technology and International Relations*, London: Macmillan.

Buzan, B. (1991a) 'New Patterns of Global Security in the Twenty-First Century', *International Affairs*, 67: 431–51.

Buzan, B. (1991b) *People, States and Fear: An Agenda for International Security Studies in the Post-Cold War Era*, 2nd edn, Boulder: Lynne Rienner.

Buzan, B., Kelstrup, M., Lemaitre, P. and Tromer, E. (1990) *The European Security Order Recast: Scenarios for the Post-Cold War Era*, London: Pinter.

Buzan, B., Wæver, O. and de Wilde, J. (1998) *Security: A New Framework for Analysis*, Boulder: Lynne Rienner.

Byman, D.L. (2005a) 'A Corrective Which Goes Too Far', *Terrorism and Political Violence*, 17: 511–16.

Byman, D.L. (2005b) *Deadly Connections: States That Sponsor Terrorism*, Cambridge: Cambridge University Press.

Cable, L.E. (1986) *Conflict of Myths: The Development of American Counterinsurgency Doctrine and the Vietnam War*, New York: New York University Press.

Callwell, C.E. (1897) *The Effect Of Maritime Command On Land Campaigns Since Waterloo*, Edinburgh: William Blackwood and Sons.

Callwell, C.E. (1905) *Military Operations and Maritime Preponderance*, Edinburgh: William Blackwood and Sons.

Campbell, D. (1998a) *National Deconstruction: Violence, Identity and Justice in Bosnia*, Minneapolis: University of Minnesota Press.

Campbell, D. (1998b) *Writing Security: United States Foreign Policy and the Politics of Identity*, revised edn, Minneapolis: University of Minnesota Press.

Canada, Department of Foreign Affairs and International Trade (DFAIT) (2007) 'Border Cooperation', <geo.international.gc.ca/can-am/main/border/default-en. asp>. Accessed March 2007.

Carr, E.H. (1942) *The Twenty Years' Crisis, 1919–1939: An Introduction to the Study of International Relations*, London: Macmillan.

Cashman, G. (2000) *What Causes War? An Introduction to Theories of International Conflict*, Lanham: Lexington Books.

Castex, R. (1994) *Strategic Theories*, Annapolis: Naval Institute Press.

Ceyhan, A. and Tsoukala, A. (2002) 'The Securitization of Migration in Western Societies: Ambivalent Discourses and Policies', *Alternatives: Global, Local, Political*, 27: 21–39.

Chan, S. (1997) 'In Search of Democratic Peace: Problems and Promise', *Mershon International Studies Review*, 41, supplement 1: 59–91.

Chaturvedi, S. (1998) 'Common Security? Geopolitics, Development, South Asia and the Indian Ocean', *Third World Quarterly*, 19: 701–24.

Chen, L.C. (2004) 'Health as a Human Security Priority for the 21st Century', paper presented to the Human Security Track III, Helsinki Process, 7 December, <www.helsinkiprocess.fi/netcomm/ImgLib/24/89/LCHelsinkiPaper12%5B1%5 D.6.04.pdf>. Accessed March 2007.

Chen, L.C. and Narasimhan, V. (2002) 'Health and Human Security: Pointing a Way Forward', paper presented to the Commission on Human Security, Stockholm, 9 June, <www.fas.harvard.edu/~acgei/Publications/Chen/ LCC_Health_and_HS_way_forward.pdf>. Accessed March 2007.

Chernavin, V. (1982) 'On Naval Theory', *Morskoi Sbornik* (Moscow), No. 1.

Chomsky, N. (2003) *Hegemony or Survival: America's Quest for Global Dominance*, London: Hamish Hamilton.

Christensen, T.J. (1997) 'Perceptions and Alliances in Europe, 1865–1940', *International Organization*, 51: 65–97.

Christensen, T.J. and Snyder, J. (1990) 'Chain Gangs and Passed Bucks: Predicting Alliance Patterns in Multipolarity', *International Organization*, 44: 137–68.

Cirincione, J. (2003) 'How Will the Iraq War Change Global Nonproliferation Strategies?' *Arms Control Today*, 33, 3: 3–6.

Clancy, T. and Seitz, R. (1991–2) 'Five Minutes Past Midnight: And Welcome to the Age of Proliferation', *The National Interest*, 26: 3–12.

Claude, I.L. (1962) *Power and International Relations*, New York: Random House.

Clausewitz, C. von [1832] (1949) *On War*, Graham, J.J. (trans.), London: Routledge and Kogan Paul.

Clausewitz, C. von [1832] (1982) *On War*, Rapoport, A. (ed.), London: Penguin.

Clausewitz, C. von [1832] (1993) *On War*, Howard, M. and Paret, P. (ed. and trans.), London: David Campbell.

Clausewitz, C. von [1832] (2002) *Vom Kriege*, München: Ullstein.

Coady, T. (2005) 'Intervention, Political Realism and the Ideal of Peace', in Coady, T. and O'Keefe, M. (eds), *Righteous Violence: The Ethics and Politics of Military Intervention*, Melbourne: Melbourne University Press.

Cohen, E.A. (1985) *Citizens and Soldiers: The Dilemmas of Military Service*, Ithaca: Cornell University Press.

Cohn, C. (1987) 'Sex and Death in the Rational World of Defense Intellectuals', *Signs: Journal of Women in Culture and Society*, 12: 687–718.

Coker, C. (2001) *Humane Warfare*, Boulder: Lynne Rienner.

Coker, C. (2002) *Waging War Without Warriors*, Boulder: Lynne Rienner.

Collins, R. (1978) 'Long-term Social Change and the Territorial Power of States', *Research in Social Movements, Conflicts and Change*, 1: 1–34.

Collins, R. (1986) *Weberian Sociological Theory*, Cambridge: Cambridge University Press.

Collins, R. and Waller, D. (1992) 'What Theories Predicted the State Breakdowns and Revolutions of the Soviet Bloc', *Research in Social Movements, Conflicts and Change*, 14: 31–47.

Commission on Human Security (2003) *Human Security Now: Protecting and Empowering People*, New York: Commission on Human Security.

Congressional Research Service (CRS) (2000) *Trafficking in Women and Children: The U.S. and International Response*, Washington: United States Congress.

Cooley, J.N. (2003) 'Integrated Nuclear Safeguards: Genesis and Evolution', in Findlay, T. (ed.), *Verification Yearbook 2003*, London: The Verification Research, Training and Information Centre.

Copeland, D.C. (2000a) 'The Constructivist Challenge to Structural Realism: A Review Essay', *International Security*, 25, 2: 187–212.

Copeland, D.C. (2000b) *The Origins of Major War*, Ithaca: Cornell University Press.

Corbett, J. [1911] (1988) *Some Principles of Maritime Strategy* with an introduction by Eric Grove, Annapolis: Naval Institute Press.

Corera, G. (2006) *Shopping for Bombs: Nuclear Proliferation, Global Insecurity, and the Rise and Fall of the A.Q. Khan Network*, Melbourne: Scribe.

Cornell, S.E. (2005) 'The Interaction of Narcotics and Conflict', *Journal of Peace Research,* 42: 751–60.

Cox, M. (2003) 'The Empire's Back in Town: Or America's Imperial Temptation – Again', *Millennium: Journal of International Studies*, 32: 1–27.

Cox, R.W. (1981) 'Social Forces, States and World Order', *Millennium: Journal of International Studies, 10*, 2: 126–55.

Cox, R.W. (1986) 'Social Forces, States and World Orders: Beyond International Relations Theories', in Keohane, R.O. (ed.), *Neorealism and its Critics*, New York: Columbia University Press.

Crenshaw, M. (1981) 'The Causes of Terrorism', *Comparative Politics,* 13, 4: 379–99.

Crenshaw, M. (2005) 'Political Explanations', in Neumann, P.R. (ed.), *Addressing the Causes of Terrorism: The Club de Madrid Series on Democracy and Terrorism, Volume 1*, Madrid: Club de Madrid.

Daalder, I.H. and Lindsay, J.M. (2003) *America Unbound: The Bush Revolution in Foreign Policy*, Washington: Brookings Institution Press.

Daams, C.A. (2003) *Criminal Asset Forfeiture: One of the Most Effective Weapons Against (Organized) Crime? A Comparative Analysis*, Nijmegen: Wolf.

Dalby, S. (1992) 'Security, Modernity, Ecology: The Dilemmas of Post-Cold War Security Discourse', *Alternatives*, 17: 95–134.

Dalby, S. (1996) 'Reading Rio, Writing the World: *The New York Times* and the "Earth Summit"', *Political Geography*, 15: 593–613.

Dalby, S. (1997) 'Contesting an Essential Concept: Reading the Dilemmas in Contemporary Security Discourse', in Krause, K. and Williams, M.C. (eds), *Critical Security Studies: Concepts and Cases,* Minneapolis: University of Minnesota Press.

Dalby, S. (2000) *Geopolitical Change and Contemporary Security Studies: Contextualizing the Human Security Agenda,* Working Paper No. 30, Vancouver: Institute of International Relations, The University of British Columbia.

Dalby, S. (2002) 'Environmental Change and Human Security', *ISUMA,* 3: 71–9.

Dalby, S. (2006) *Security and Environment Linkages Revisited*, Singapore: Institute for Defence and Strategic Studies, Nanyang Technological University.

De Ruyver, B. (2002) *Strategies of the EU and the US in Combating Transnational Organized Crime,* Antwerp: Maklu.

Der Derian, J. (1993) 'The Value of Security: Hobbes, Marx, Nietzsche, and Baudrillard', in Dillon, D.C.M. (ed.), *The Political Subject of Violence,* Manchester: Manchester University Press.

Der Derian, J. (2001) *Virtuous War: Mapping the Military-Industrial-Media-Entertainment Network*, Boulder: Westview.

Der Derian, J. and Shapiro, M. (eds) (1989) *International/Intertextual Relations,* Lexington: Lexington Books.

Desch, M.C. (1998) 'Culture Clash: Assessing the Importance of Ideas in Security Studies', *International Security*, 23, 1: 141–70.

Deudney, D. (2006) *Bounding Power: Republican Security Theory from the Polis to the Global Village,* Princeton: Princeton University Press.

Deutsch, K.W. (1957) *Political Community and the North Atlantic Area: International Organization in Light of Historical Experience*, Princeton: Princeton University Press.

Dewitt, D. (1994) 'Common, Comprehensive and Cooperative Security', *The Pacific Review*, 7: 1–15.

Dillon, M. (1996) *Politics of Security: Towards a Political Philosophy of Continental Thought,* London: Routledge.

Dobbins, J. (2004) *Testimony: Stabilization and Reconstruction Civilian Management Act of 2004*, testimony presented to the Senate Committee on Foreign Relations on 3 March 2004, CT–218, Santa Monica: RAND Corporation.

Doty, R.L. (1993) 'Foreign Policy as Social Construction: A Post-Positivist Analysis of U.S. Counterinsurgency Policy in the Philippines', *International Studies Quarterly*, 37: 297–320.

Douhet, G. (1983) *The Command of the Air*, Washington: Office of Air History.

Doyle, M.W. (1983) 'Kant, Liberal Legacies, and Foreign Affairs', *Philosophy and Public Affairs*, 12: 205–35 and 323–53.

Duffield, M.R. (2001) *Global Governance and the New Wars: The Merging of Development and Security*, London: Zed Books.

Elman, C. (1996a) 'Horses for Courses: Why *Not* Neorealist Theories of Foreign Policy?' *Security Studies*, 6: 7–53.

Elman, C. (1996b) 'Cause, Effect, and Consistency: A Response to Kenneth Waltz', *Security Studies*, 6: 58–61.

Elman, M.F. (1997) 'Introduction: The Need for a Qualitative Test of the Democratic Peace Theory', in Elman, M.F. (ed.), *Paths to Peace: Is Democracy the Answer?* Cambridge: MIT Press.

Elman, C. (2004) 'Extending Offensive Realism: The Louisiana Purchase and America's Rise to Regional Hegemony', *American Political Science Review*, 98: 563–76.

Enloe, C. (1989) *Bananas, Beaches and Bases: Making Feminist Sense of International Politics*, London: Pandora.

Erickson, S.A. (2001) 'Economic and Technological Trends Affecting Nuclear Nonproliferation', *The Nonproliferation Review*, 8, 2: 40–54.

Eriksson, J. (1999) 'Observers or Advocates? On the Political Role of Security Analysts', *Cooperation and Conflict*, 34: 311–30.

Faist, T. (2004) *The Migration–Security Nexus: International Migration and Security Before and After 9/11*, Malmö: Malmö University.

Ferguson, C. and Potter, W. (2004) *The Four Faces of Nuclear Terrorism*, Monterey: Center for Nonproliferation Studies, Monterey Institute of International Studies.

Fettweiss, C.J. (2006) 'A Revolution in International Relation Theory: Or, What if Mueller Is Right?' *International Studies Review*, 8: 677–97.

Fischer, M. (1992) 'Feudal Europe, 800–1300: Communal Discourse and Conflictual Practices', *International Organization*, 46: 427–66.

Fitzpatrick, M. (2006) 'Lessons Learned from Iran's Pursuit of Nuclear Weapons', *The Nonproliferation Review*, 13: 527–37.

Flank, S. (1993–4) 'Exploding the Black Box: The Historical Sociology of Nuclear Proliferation', *Security Studies*, 3: 259–94.

Foucault, M. (1972) *The Archaeology of Knowledge and the Discourse on Language*, Sheridan Smith, A.M. (trans.), New York: Pantheon.

Freedman, L. (1995) 'Great Powers, Vital Interests and Nuclear Weapons', *Survival*, 36, 4: 35–52.

Freedman, L. (1998) 'International Security: Changing Targets', *Foreign Policy*, 109: 48–63.

Frost, R. (2005) *Nuclear Terrorism After 9/11*, Adelphi Paper 378, London: Routledge for the Institute for International and Strategic Studies.

Fuller, J.F.C. (1925) *The Foundations of the Science of War*, London: Hutchinson.

Fuller, W.C. (1992) *Strategy and Power in Russia 1600–1914*, New York: Free Press.

Gaddis, J.L. (1992–3) 'International Relations Theory and the End of the Cold War', *International Security*, 17: 5–58.

Galeotti, M. (2002) *Russian and Post-Soviet Organized Crime*, Aldershot: Ashgate/Dartmouth.

Galeotti, M. (2006) 'Dealing with the Russian "Arsenal of Anarchy"', *Jane's Intelligence Review*, 18, 2: 48–9.

Galtung, J. (1969) 'Violence, Peace, and Peace Research', *Journal of Peace Research*, 6: 167–91.

Galula, D. (1966) *Counterinsurgency Warfare: Theory and Practice*, New York: Praeger.

Gansler, J. (2006) Interview with Jacques Gansler, Chairman, U.S. Defense Science Board Task Force, published in *Jane's Defence Weekly*, 43, 51: 34.

Garnett, J. (1987) 'Strategic Studies and its Assumptions', in Baylis, J., Booth, K., Garnett, J. and Williams, P., *Contemporary Strategy: Vol 1 Theories and Concepts*, London: Holmes and Meier.

Gause, F.G. (2005) 'Can Democracy Stop Terrorism?' *Foreign Affairs*, 84, 5: 62–76.

George, J. (1994) *Discourses of Global Politics: A Critical (Re)introduction to International Relations*, Boulder: Lynne Rienner.

Ghai, D. (1997) *Economic Globalization, Institutional Change and Human Security*, Geneva: United Nations Research Institute for Social Development.

Giap, V.N. (1962) *People's War: People's Army*, New York: Prager.

Giddens, A. (1985) *The Constitution of Society: Outline of the Theory of Structuration*, Los Angeles: University of California Press.

Gilbert, A. (1999) *Must Global Politics Constrain Democracy? Great-Power Realism, Democratic Peace and Democratic Internationalism*, Princeton: Princeton University Press.

Gilpin, R. (1981) *War and Change in World Politics*, Cambridge: Cambridge University Press.

Gilpin, R. (1986) 'The Richness of the Tradition of Political Realism', in Keohane, R.O. (ed.), *Neorealism and its Critics*, New York: Columbia University Press.

Gilpin, R. (1987) *The Political Economy of International Relations*, Princeton: Princeton University Press.

Gilpin, R. (1996) 'No One Loves a Political Realist', *Security Studies*, 5: 3–26.

Giordano, M., Giordano, M. and Wolf, A.T. (2002) 'The Geography of Water Conflict and Cooperation: Internal Pressures and International Manifestations', *Geographical Journal*, 168: 293–312.

Glaser, C.L. (1994–5) 'Realists as Optimists: Cooperation as Self-Help', *International Security*, 19, 3: 50–90.

Glaser, C.L. and Kaufmann, C. (1998) 'What is the Offense–Defense Balance and How Can we Measure it?' *International Security*, 22, 4: 44–82.

Gleick, P.H. (1990) 'Environment, Resources, and International Security and Politics', in Arnett, E. (ed.), *Science and International Security: Responding to a Changing World*, Washington: American Association for the Advancement of Science.

Gleick, P.H. (1993) 'Water and Conflict: Fresh Water Resources and International Security', *International Security*, 18, 1: 79–112.

GlobalSecurity.org (2002) *Nuclear Posture Review [Excerpts]*, <www.global security.org/wmd/library/policy/dod/npr.htm> Accessed January 2007.

Goertz, G. and Diehl, P.F. (1992) *Territorial Changes and International Conflict*, London: Routledge.

Goldstein, L.J., Hattendorf, J. and Zhukov, Y. (eds) (2005) 'The Cold War at Sea: An International Appraisal', *Journal of Strategic Studies*, 28: 151–439.

Gorshkov, S. (1979) *The Seapower of the State*, London: Pergamon.

Gray, C.H. (1997) *Postmodern War: The New Politics of Conflict*, New York: Guildford Press.

Gray, C.S. (2004) *The Sheriff: America's Defence of the New World Order*, Lexington: University Press of Kentucky.

Gray, C.S. (2005) *Strategic Surprise*, Carlisle: US Army War College.

Gray, C.S. (2006) 'Stability Operations in Strategic Perspective: A Skeptical View', *Parameters*, 36: 4–14.

Greenhill, K. (2007) 'Draining the Sea, or Feeding the Fire? Evaluating the Role of Population Relocation in Counter-insurgency Operations', Unpublished manuscript.

Grieco, J.M. (1990) *Cooperation Among Nations: Europe, America and Non-Tariff Barriers to Trade*, Ithaca: Cornell University Press.

Grieco, J.M. (1993) 'Anarchy and the Limits of Cooperation: A Realist Critique of the Newest Liberal Institutionalism', in Baldwin, D.A. (ed.), *Neorealism and Neoliberalism: The Contemporary Debate*, New York: Columbia University Press.

Gruber, L. (2000) *Ruling the World: Power Politics and the Rise of Supranational Institutions*, Princeton: Princeton University Press.

Guevara, C. [1961] (2003) *Guerrilla Warfare*, London: Souvenir.

Gunaratna, R. (2003) *Inside al-Qaeda: Global Network of Terror*, New York: Berkeley.

Gunaratna, R. (2004) 'The Post-Madrid Face of al-Qaeda', *The Washington Quarterly*, 27, 3: 91–100.

Haass, R.N. (1999) *Intervention: The Use of American Military Force in the Post-Cold War World*, Washington: Brookings Institution Press.

Hall, B.S. and Devries, K. (1990) 'Essay Review: The "Military Revolution" Revisited', *Technology and Culture*, 31, 3: 500–7.

Halperin, M.H. (1963) *Limited War in the Nuclear Age*, New York: John Wiley.

Halperin, M.H. (1972) *Contemporary Military Strategy*, London: Faber and Faber.

Handel, M.I. (1986) 'Clausewitz in the Age of Technology', in Handel, M.I. (ed.), 'Clausewitz and Modern Strategy', *Journal of Strategic Studies*, 9.

Handel, M.I. (2001) *Masters of War: Classical Military Thought*, London: Frank Cass.

Hanson, V.D. (1989) *The Western Way of War: Infantry Battle in Classical Greece*, Oxford: Oxford University Press.

Hardouin, P. and Weichhardt, R. (2006) 'Terrorist Fund Raising Through Criminal Activities', *Journal of Money Laundering Control*, 9: 303–8.

Hastedt, G. (2006) *American Foreign Policy: Past, Present, Future*, 6th edn, Upper Saddle River, N.J.: Pearson/Pentice Hall.

Hattendorf, J.B. (ed.) (1991) *The Influence of History on Mahan*, Newport: Naval War College Press.

Hawley, S. (2005) *The Imjin War: Japan's Sixteenth-Century Invasion of Korea and Attempt to Conquer China*, Berkeley: University of California Press, 2005.

Heisler, M.O. and Layton-Henry, Z. (1993) 'Migration and the Links between Social and Societal Security', in Wæver, O., Buzan, B., Kelstrup, M. and Lemaitre, P., *Identity, Migration and the New Security Agenda in Europe*, London: Pinter.

Hemenway, D., Shinado-Tagawa, T. and Miller, M. (2002) 'Firearm Availability and Female Homicide Victimization Rates in 25 High-Income Countries', *Journal of the American Medical Women's Association*, 57: 100–4.

Herz, J.H. (1962) *International Politics in the Atomic Age*, New York: Columbia University Press.

Hettne, B. (1997) 'Development, Security and World Order: A Regionalist Approach', *European Journal of Development Research*, 9: 83–106.

Hettne, B. (1998) 'Globalization, Regionalism and the Europeanization of Europe', *Politeia*, 17, 3: 44–59.

Hettne, B. (2000) 'The New Regionalism: A Prologue', in Hettne, B. (ed.), *The New Regionalism and the Future of Security and Development*, Vol. 4, London: Macmillan.

Hettne, B. and Soderbaum, F. (1998) 'The New Regionalism Approach', *Politeia*, 17, 3: 6–21.

Hettne, B. and Soderbaum, F. (2002) 'Theorising the Rise of Regionness', in Breslin, S., Hughes, C., Philips, N. and Rosamond, B. (eds), *New Regionalisms in the Global Political Economy: Theories and Cases*, London: Routledge.

Heuser, B. (2002) *Reading Clausewitz*, London: Pimlico.

Hibbs, M. (2006) 'The Unmaking of a Nuclear Smuggler', *Bulletin of the Atomic Scientists*, 62, 6: 35–41, 63.

Hobsbawm, E.J. (1975) *The Age of Capital, 1848–1875*, London: Weidenfeld and Nicolson.

Hobsbawm, E.J. (1995) *The Age of Extremes: The Short Twentieth Century 1914–1991*, London: Abacus.

Hoffman, B. (2004) 'The Changing Face of al-Qaeda and the Global War on Terrorism', *Studies in Conflict and Terrorism*, 27: 549–60.

Hoffman, B. (2006) *Inside Terrorism,* 2nd edn, New York: Columbia University Press.

Hoffman, B. and McCormick, G.H. (2004) 'Terrorism, Signalling and Suicide Attack', *Studies in Conflict and Terrorism,* 27: 243–81.

Hollis, M. and Smith, S. (1990) *Explaining and Understanding International Relations,* Oxford: Oxford University Press.

Holloway, S. (2000) 'U.S. Unilateralism at the UN: Why Great Powers Do Not Make Great Multilateralists', *Global Governance*, 6: 361–82.

Holsti, K. (1996) *The State, War and the State of War*, New York: Cambridge.

Homer-Dixon, T. (1991) 'On the Threshold: Environmental Changes as Causes of Acute Conflict', *International Security,* 16, 2: 76–116.

Homer-Dixon, T. (1994) 'Environmental Scarcities and Violent Conflict: Evidence from Cases', *International Security,* 19, 1: 5–40.

Homer-Dixon, T.F. and Levy, M.A. (1995–6) 'Correspondence: Environment and Security', *International Security*, 20: 189–98.

Honderich, T. (2002) *After the Terror*, Edinburgh: Edinburgh University Press.

Hopf, T. (1991) 'Polarity, the Offense–Defense Balance, and War', *American Political Science Review,* 85: 475–93.

Hopf, T. (1993) 'Correspondence: Getting the End of the Cold War Wrong', *International Security*, 18, 2: 202–10.

Horgan, J. (2005) *The Psychology of Terrorism,* London: Routledge.

Horgan, J. and Taylor, M. (2006) 'A Conceptual Framework for Addressing Psychological Problems in the Development of the Terrorist', *Terrorism and Political Violence*, 18: 585–601.

Howard, M. (2006–7) 'A Long War?' *Survival*, 48, 4: 7–14.

Hughes, D.M. (2000) 'The 'Natasha' Trade: The Transnational Shadow Market of Trafficking in Women', *Journal of International Affairs,* 53: 625–51.

Huth, P.K. (1996) *Standing Your Ground: Territorial Disputes and International Conflict,* Ann Arbor: University of Michigan Press.

Huysmans, J. (1995) 'Migrants as a Security Problem: Dangers of "Securitizing"

Societal Issues', in Miles, R. and Thänhardt, D. (eds), *Migration and European Integration: The Dynamics of Inclusion and Exclusion*, London: Pinter.

Huysmans, J. (1998) 'Security! What do you Mean? From Concept to Thick Signifier', *European Journal of International Relations*, 4: 226–55.

Ikenberry, G.J. (2002) 'America's Imperial Ambition', *Foreign Affairs*, 81, 5: 44–60.

India, Embassy of India to the United States (1999) *Draft Report of National Security Advisory Board on Indian Nuclear Doctrine*, <www.indianembassy. org/policy/CTBT/nuclear_doctrine_aug_17_1999.html>. Accessed January 2007.

India, Ministry of External Affairs (2003) 'The Cabinet Committee on Security Reviews Operationalization of India's Nuclear Doctrine', Press Release, 4 January, <meaindia.nic.in/pressrelease/2003/01/04pr01.htm>. Accessed January 2006.

International Commission on Intervention and State Sovereignty (ICISS) (2001) *The Responsibility to Protect: Report of the International Commission on Intervention and State Sovereignty*, Ottawa: International Development Research Centre.

Jackson, N.J. (2006) 'International Organizations, Security Dichotomics and the Trafficking of Persons and Narcotics in Post-Soviet Central Asia: A Critique of the Securitization Framework', *Security Dialogue*, 37: 299–317.

Jackson, T., Marsh, N., Owen, T. and Thurin, A. (2005) *Who Takes the Bullet? Understanding the Issues*, Oslo: Norwegian Church Aid.

Jenkins, B.M. (1974a) 'International Terrorism: A New Mode of Conflict', in Carlton, D. and Schaerf, C. (eds), *International Terrorism and World Security*, London: Croom Helm.

Jenkins, B.M. (1974b) 'Terrorism Works – Sometimes', The RAND Paper Series, P-5217, Santa Monica: RAND.

Jenkins, B.M. (1980) *The Study of Terrorism: Definitional Problems*, RAND Paper Series, P-6563, Santa Monica: RAND.

Jenkins, B.M. (1981) *The Psychological Implications of Media-Covered Terrorism*, The RAND Paper Series, P-6627, Santa Monica: RAND.

Jervis, R. (1976) *Perception and Misperception in International Politics*, Princeton: Princeton University Press.

Jervis, R. (1978) 'Cooperation Under the Security Dilemma', *World Politics*, 30: 167–214.

Jervis, R. (1988) 'War and Misperception', *Journal of Interdisciplinary History*, 18: 675–700.

Jervis, R. (1999) *System Effects: Complexity in Political and Social Life*, Princeton: Princeton University Press.

Johnson, T.P. (1991) 'Writing for *International Security*: A Contributors' Guide', *International Security*, 16: 171–80.

Johnston, A.I. (1995) 'Thinking About Strategic Culture', *International Security*, 19, 4: 32–64.

Johnston, C. (2004) *The Sorrows of Empire: Militarism, Secrecy and the End of the Republic*, New York: Holt.

Juergensmeyer, M. (2001) *Terror in the Mind of God: The Global Rise of Religious Violence*, Berkeley: University of California Press.

Kagan, F.W. (2006) *Finding the Target: The Transformation of American Military Policy*, New York: Encounter Books.

Kahn, H. (1961) *On Thermonuclear War*, Princeton: Princeton University Press.

Kahn, H. (1962) *Thinking about the Unthinkable*, New York: Avon Books.

Kahn, H. (1965) *On Escalation*, London: Pall Mall Press.

Kaldor, M. (1981) *Baroque Arsenal*, New York: Hill and Wang.

Kaldor, M. (1999) *New and Old Wars: Organized Violence in a Global Era*, Cambridge: Polity.

Kaldor, M. (2000) *Global Insecurity: Restructuring the Global Military Sector*, Vol. 3, London: Pinter.

Kaldor, M. (2001) *New and Old Wars: Organized Violence in a Global Era*, Cambridge: Polity.

Kaldor, M. (2003) *Global Civil Society: An Answer to War*, Cambridge: Polity.

Kalyvas, S. (2006) *The Logic of Violence in Civil Wars*, Cambridge: Cambridge University Press.

Kampani, G. (2002) 'Second Tier Proliferation: The Case of Pakistan and North Korea', *The Nonproliferation Review*, 9, 3: 107–16.

Kapstein, E.B. (1995) 'Is Realism Dead?' *International Organization*, 49: 751–74.

Katsumata, H. (2006) 'Japan', in Pardesi, M.S., Acharya, A., Somasundram, P., Chang, Y.H., Ruey, J.L.S., Katsumata, T.S.H. and Ivanov, V.I., *Energy and Security: The Geopolitics of Energy in the Asia-Pacific*, Singapore: Institute of Defence and Strategic Studies, Nanyang Technological University.

Katzenstein, P. (ed.) (1996) *The Culture of National Security: Norms and Identity in World Politics*, New York: Columbia University Press.

Katzenstein, P.J. (1997) 'Introduction: Asian Regionalism in Comparative Perspective', in Katzenstein, P.J. and Shiraishi, T. (eds), *Network Power: Japan and Asia*, Ithaca: Cornell University Press.

Katzenstein, P.J. (2000) 'Regionalism and Asia', *New Political Economy*, 5: 353–68.

Keegan, J. (1976) *The Face of Battle: A Study of Agincourt, Waterloo, and the Somme*, New York: Viking.

Keegan, J. (1999) *Daily Telegraph*, 6 June.

Kegley, C.W. Jr. (1993) 'The Neoidealist Moment in International Studies? Realist Myths and the New International Realities', *International Studies Quarterly*, 37: 131–46.

Kennan, G.F. (1954) *Realities of American Foreign Policy*, Princeton: Princeton University Press.

Kennedy, P. (1988) *The Rise and Fall of the Great Powers: Economic Change and Military Conflict From 1500 to 2000*, New York: Random House.

Kennedy, P. (2002) 'The Greatest Superpower', *New Perspectives Quarterly*, 19, 2: 2–18.

Keohane, R.O. (1984) *After Hegemony: Cooperation and Discord in the World Political Economy*, Princeton: Princeton University Press.

Keohane, R.O. (1986a) 'Realism, Neorealism and the Study of World Politics', in Keohane, R.O. (ed.), *Neorealism and its Critics*, New York: Columbia University Press.

Keohane, R.O. (1986b) 'Reciprocity in International Relations', *International Organization*, 40: 1–27.

Keohane, R.O. (1986c) 'Theory of World Politics: Structural Realism and Beyond', in Keohane, R.O. (ed.), *Neorealism and its Critics*, New York: Columbia University Press.

Keohane, R.O. and Martin, L.L. (1995) 'The Promise of Institutionalist Theory', *International Security*, 20: 39–51.

Keohane, R.O. and Nye, J.S. Jr. (1987) '*Power and Interdependence* Revisited', *International Organization*, 41: 725–53.

Keohane, R.O. and Nye, J.S. Jr. (1977) *Power and Interdependence: World Politics in Transition*, Boston: Little, Brown.

Kicinger, A. (2004) *International Migration as a Non-Traditional Security Threat and the EU Responses to this Phenomenon*, Warsaw: Central European Forum for Migration Research.

Kilcullen, D. (2005) 'Countering Global Insurgency', *Journal of Strategic Studies*, 28: 597–617.

Kilcullen, D. (2006–7) 'Counter-Insurgency Redux', *Survival*, 48, 4: 111–30.

Kilgour, D. (1999) 'Canada and the OAS: Engaging Our Neighbours', *One World*, 36. <www.david-kilgour.com/secstate/oas2.htm>. Accessed March 2007.

Kindleberger, C.P. (1973) *The World in Depression, 1929–1939*, Berkeley: University of California Press.

Kiras, J.D. (2007) 'Irregular Warfare: Terrorism and Insurgency', in Baylis, J., Wirtz, J., Grey, C.S. and Cohen, E. (eds), *Strategy in the Contemporary World*, 2nd edn, Oxford: Oxford University Press.

Kissinger, H.A. (1957) *A World Restored: Metternich, Castlereagh and the Problems of Peace* 1812–1822, Boston: Houghton Mifflin.

Kitson, F. (1960) *Gangs and Counter-Gangs*, London: Barrie and Rockliff.

Kitson, F. (1971) *Low Intensity Operations,* London: Faber and Faber.

Klein, B. (1990) 'How the West was Won: Representational Politics of NATO', *International Studies Quarterly*, 34: 311–25.

Klein, B. (1994) *Strategic Studies and World Order*, Cambridge: Cambridge University Press.

Kliot, N. (1994) *Water Resources and Conflict in the Middle East*, London: Routledge.

Knopf, J.W. (2006) 'Deterrence or Pre-empion?' *Current History*, 105: 395–9.

Knox, M. and Murray, W. (2001) *The Dynamics of Military Revolution, 1300–2050*, Cambridge: Cambridge University Press.

Kolodziej, E.A. (1993) 'Whither Security Studies After the Cold War?' in Bajpai, K.P. and Cohen, S.P. (eds), *South Asia After the Cold War: International Perspectives*, Boulder: Westview.

Koser, K. (2005) 'Irregular Migration, State Security and Human Security', a paper Prepared for the Policy Analysis and Research Programme of the Global Commission on International Migration, Geneva. <test.gcim.org/attachements/TP5.pdf>. Accessed March 2007.

Koser, K. (2006) 'Human Security and International Migration in Western Europe' (unpublished manuscript).

Krasner, S.D. (1976) 'State Power and the Structure of International Trade', *World Politics*, 28: 317–43.

Krasner, S.D. (1991) 'Global Communications and National Power: Life on the Pareto Frontier', *World Politics*, 43: 336–66.

Krause, K. (1998) 'Critical Theory and Security Studies: The Research Programme of 'Critical Security Studies', *Cooperation and Conflict,* 33: 298–333.

Krause, K. and Williams, M.C. (1996) 'Broadening the Agenda of Security Studies: Politics and Methods', *Mearshon International Studies Review*, 40: 229–54.

Krause, K. and Williams, M.C. (1997a) 'From Strategy to Security: The Foundations of Critical Security Studies', in Krause, K. and Williams, M.C. (eds), *Critical Security Studies: Concepts and Cases*, Minneapolis: University of Minnesota Press.

Krause, K. and Williams, M.C. (1997b) 'Preface: Toward Critical Security Studies', in Krause, K. and Williams, M.C. (eds), *Critical Security Studies: Concepts and Cases*, Minneapolis: University of Minnesota Press.

Krause, L. (1972) 'Private International Finance', in Keohane, R.O. and Nye, J.S. (eds), *Transnational Relations and World Politics*, Cambridge: Harvard University Press.

Kreisler, H. (2002) 'Through a Realist Lens: Conversation with John Mearsheimer, University of California at Berkeley, 8 April, <http://globetrotter.berkeley.edu/people2/Mearsheimer/
mearsheimer-con5.html>. Accessed January 2006.

Krepinevich, A.F. Jr. (1996) *The Conflict Environment of 2016: A Scenario-Based Approach*, Washington: Center for Strategic and Budgetary Assessments.

Kriesberg, L. (1994) 'Regional Conflicts in the Post-Cold War Era: Causes, Dynamics, and Modes of Resolution', in Klare, M.T. and Thomas, D.C. (eds), *World Security: Challenges for a New Century*, New York: St Martin's.

Kurth, J. (2005) 'Humanitarian Intervention after Iraq: Legal Ideals vs. Military Realities', *Orbis*, 50: 87–101.

Kydd, A. (1997) 'Why Security Seekers do not Fight One Another', *Security Studies*, 7: 114–54.

Labs, E.J. (1997) 'Beyond Victory: Offensive Realism and Why States Expand Their War Aims', *Security Studies*, 6: 1–49.

Laclau, E. (2005) 'On "Real" and "Absolute" Enemies', *CR: The New Centennial Review*, 5: 1–12.

Lambeth, B.S. (2005) *Air Power Against Terror: America's Conduct of Operation Enduring Freedom*, Santa Monica: RAND Corporation.

Laqueur, W. (1998) *Guerrilla Warfare: A Historical and Critical Study*, New Brunswick: Transaction.

Laqueur, W. (1999) *The New Terrorism: Fanaticism and the Arms of Mass Destruction,* Oxford: Oxford University Press.

Laqueur, W. (2003) *No End to War: Terrorism in the Twenty First Century*, New York: Continuum.

Latham, A. (2002) 'Warfare Transformed: A Braudelian Perspective on the Revolution in Military Affairs', *European Journal of International Relations, 8,* 1: 247–60.

Lavoy, P., Sagan, S. and Wirtz, J.J. (2000) *Planning the Unthinkable: How New Powers Will Use Nuclear, Biological, and Chemical Weapons*, Ithaca: Cornell University Press.

Layne, C. (1993) 'The Unipolar Illusion: Why New Great Powers Will Rise', *International Security*, 17, 4: 5–51.

Layne, C. (2006) 'The Unipolar Illusion Revisited: The Coming End of the United States' Unipolar Moment', *International Security*, 31, 2: 7–41.

Lebow, R.N. (1994) 'The Long Peace, the End of the Cold War, and the Failure of Realism', *International Organization*, 48: 249–77.

Lebow, R.N. and Risse-Kappen, T. (eds) (1995) *International Relations Theory and the End of the Cold War*, New York: Columbia University Press.

Lebow, R.N. and Stein, J.G. (1998) 'Nuclear Lessons of the Cold War', in Booth, K. (ed.), *Statecraft and Security: The Cold War and Beyond*, Cambridge: Cambridge University Press.

Lemaitre, P., Gerner, K. and Hansen, T. (1993) 'The Crisis of Societal Security in the Former Soviet Union', in Wæver, O., Buzan, B., Kelstrup, M. and Lemaitre, P., *Identity, Migration and the New Security Agenda in Europe*, London: Pinter.

Lemke, D. (2002) *Regions of War and Peace*, Cambridge: Cambridge University Press.

Levy, J.S. (1983a) 'Misperception and the Causes of War: Theoretical Linkages and Analytical Problems', *World Politics*, 36: 76–99.

Levy, J.S. (1983b) *War in the Modern Great Power System, 1495–1975*, Lexington: University Press of Kentucky.

Levy, J.S. (1987) 'Declining Power and the Preventive Motivation for War', *World Politics*, 40: 82–107.

Levy, J.S. (1989a) 'Domestic Politics and War', in Rotberg, R.I. and Rabb, T.K. (eds), *The Origin and Prevention of Major Wars*, Cambridge: Cambridge University Press.

Levy, J.S. (1989b) 'The Causes of War: A Review of Theories and Evidence', in Tetlock, P.E., Husbands, J.L., Jervis, R., Stern, P.C. and Tilly, C. (eds), *Behaviour, Society, and Nuclear War*, Vol. 1, New York: Oxford University Press.

Levy, M.A. (1995) 'Is the Environment a National Security Issue?' *International Security*, 20: 35–62.

Lewis, B. (2002) *What Went Wrong? The Clash Between Islam and Modernity in the Middle East*, New York: Harper Collins.

Liddell Hart, B.H. (1932) *The British Way in Warfare*, London: Faber and Faber.

Liddell Hart, B.H. (1967) *Strategy: The Indirect Approach*, London: Faber and Faber.

Lieber, K. and Press, D. (2006) 'The End of MAD? The Nuclear Dimension of US Primacy', *International Security*, 30, 4: 7–44.

Linklater, A. (1990) *Beyond Realism and Marxism: Critical Theory in International Relations*, London: Macmillan.

Lipschutz, R.D. (1995) *On Security*, New York: Columbia University Press.

Lipson, C. (2003) *Reliable Partners: How Democracies Have Made a Separate Peace*, Princeton: Princeton University Press.

Livezey, W.E. (1981) *Mahan on Sea Power*, Norman: University of Oklahoma Press.

Lomperis, T.J. (1996) *From People's War to People's Rule: Insurgency, Intervention, and the Lessons of Vietnam*, Chapel Hill: University of North Carolina Press.

Long, A. (2006) *On 'Other War': Lessons from Five Decades of RAND Counter-insurgency Research*, Santa Monica: RAND.

Lonsdale, D. (2004) *The Nature of War in the Information Age: Clausewitzian Future*, London: Routledge.

Luttwak, E.N. (1987) *Strategy: The Logic of War and Peace*, Cambridge: Belknap.

Luttwak, E.N. (1995) 'Toward Post-Heroic War', *Foreign Affairs*, 7, 3: 109–22.

Lynn-Jones, S.M. (1995) 'Offense–Defense Theory and its Critics', *Security Studies*, 4: 660–91.

Lynn-Jones, S.M. (1998) 'Realism and America's Rise: A Review Essay', *International Security*, 23, 2: 157–82.

Machiavelli, N. [1532] (1961) *The Prince*, London: Penguin.

Mack, A. (1975) 'Why Big Nations Lose Small Wars: The Politics of Aysmmetric Conflict', *World Politics*, 27: 175–200.

Mackenbach, J.P. (2005) *Health Inequalities: Europe in Profile*, an independent, expert report commissioned by, and published under the auspices of, the UK Presidency of the EU, <www.fco.gov.uk/Files/kfile/HI_EU_Profile,0.pdf>. Accessed March 2007.

Mahan, A.T. (1890) *The Influence of Sea Power upon History, 1660–1783*, London: Sampson, Low, Marston.

Mahan, A.T. (1911) *Naval Strategy: Compared and Contrasted with the Principles and Practice of Military Operations on Land*, Boston: Little, Brown.

Mann, M. (1988) *States, War and Capitalism*, New York: Blackwell.

Manwaring, M. (1995) 'Peru's Sendero Luminoso: The Shining Path Beckons', *Annals of the American Academy of Political and Social Science*, 541: 157–66.

Mao Tse-Tung [1961] (2000) *On Guerrilla Warfare*, Griffiths, S.B. (trans.), Urbana: University of Illinois Press.

Maoz, Z. (1997) 'The Controversy Over the Democratic Peace: Rearguard Action or Cracks in the Wall?' *International Security*, 22, 1: 162–98.

Marighella, C. (1968). 'Mini-Manual of the Urban Guerrilla'. In Moss, R. (ed.), *Urban Guerrilla Warfare*, Adelphi Paper No. 79, London, International Institute for Strategic Studies: 20–42.

McCauley, C. (2002) 'Psychological Issues in Understanding Terrorism and the Response to Terrorism', in Stout, C.E. (ed.), *The Psychology of Terrorism, Volume III: Theoretical Understandings and Perspectives*, Westport: Praeger.

McDonough, D. (2006) *Nuclear Superiority: The New Triad and the Evolution of Nuclear Strategy*, Adelphi Paper 383, London: Routledge for the Institute for International and Strategic Studies.

McInnes, C. (2002) *Spectator-Sport War*, Boulder: Lynne Rienner.

McLean, J. (1988) 'Marxism and International Relations: A Strange Case of Mutual Neglect', *Millennium*, 17: 295–319.

McSweeney, B. (1996) 'Identity and Security: Buzan and the Copenhagen School', *Review of International Studies*, 22: 81–93.

McSweeney, B. (1999) *Security, Identity and Interests: A Sociology of International Relations*, Cambridge: Cambridge University Press.

Mearsheimer, J.J. (1983) *Conventional Deterrence*, Ithaca: Cornell University Press.

Mearsheimer, J.J. (1990) 'Back to the Future: Instability in Europe after the Cold War', *International Security*, 15: 5–56.

Mearsheimer, J.J. (1994–5) 'The False Promise of International Institutions', *International Security*, 19, 3: 5–49.

Mearsheimer, J.J. (2001) *The Tragedy of Great Power Politics*, New York: W.W. Norton.

Mearsheimer, J.J. and Walt, S.M. (2002) *Can Saddam be Contained? History Says Yes*, Cambridge: Belfer Center for Science and International Affairs, Harvard University.

Meilinger, P.S. (ed.) (1997) *The Paths of Heaven: The Evolution of Airpower Theory*, Maxwell Air Force Base, Ala.: Air University Press.

Miller, B. (1995) *When Opponents Cooperate: Great Power Conflict and Collaboration in World Politics*, Ann Arbor: University of Michigan Press.

Milner, H. (1992) 'International Theories of Cooperation Among Allies: Strengths and Weaknesses', *World Politics*, 44: 466–96.

Moody, R.A. (1997) 'Armageddon for Hire', *Jane's International Defense Review*, 30, 2: 21–3.

Morgenthau, H.J. (1946) *Scientific Man versus Power Politics*, Chicago: University of Chicago Press.

Morgenthau, H.J. (1948) *Politics Among Nations: The Struggle for Power and Peace*, New York: Knopf.

Mozley, R.F. (1998) *The Politics and Technology of Nuclear Proliferation*, Seattle: University of Washington Press.

Mueller, J. (1989) *Retreat from Doomsday: The Obsolescence of Major War*, New York: Basic Books.

Mueller, J. (2005) 'Six Rather Unusual Propositions About Terrorism', *Terrorism and Political Violence*, 17: 487–505.

Münkler, H. (2002) *The New Wars*, London: Polity.

Mutimer, D. (2006) 'Critical Security Studies: A Schismatic History', in Collins, A. (ed.), *Contemporary Security Studies,* Oxford: Oxford University Press.

Nagl, J. (2005) *Learning to Eat Soup With a Knife: Counter-Insurgency Lessons from Malaya and Vietnam*, 2nd edn, Chicago: University of Chicago Press.

Naveh, S. (1997) *In Pursuit of Military Excellence: The Evolution of Operational Theory*, London: Frank Cass.

Ndayi, Z.V. (2006) '"Theorising the Rise of Regionness" by Bjorn Hettne and Fredrik Soderbaum', *Politikon*, 33: 113–24.

Neufeld, M. (1995) *The Restructuring of International Relations Theory*, Cambridge: Cambridge University Press.

Niebuhr, R. (1944) *The Children of Light and the Children of Darkness*, New York: Charles Scribner's Sons.

North American Aerospace Defense Command (NORAD) (2007) 'About Us: North American Aerospace Defense Command', NORAD Website, <www.norad.mil/about_us.htm>. Accessed March 2007.

Nye, J.S. (2002) *The Paradox of American Power: Why the World's Only Superpower Cannot Go it Alone*, Oxford: Oxford University Press.

Nye, J.S. Jr. (2005) *Understanding International Conflicts: An Introduction to Theory and History*, 5th edn, New York: Pearson Longman.

O'Hanlon, M. (1997) *Saving Lives with Force: Military Criteria for Humanitarian Intervention*, Washington: Brookings Institution Press.

O'Hanlon, M. (2000) *Technological Change and the Future of Warfare*, Washington: Brookings Institution Press.

Ohmae, K. (1990) *The Borderless World*, New York: Harper Business.

Organization of American States (OAS) 2007, 'OAS at a Glance', Organization of American States Website, <www.oas.org/key%5Fissues/eng/KeyIssue_Detail.asp?kis_sec=20>. Accessed March 2007.

Organski, A.F.K. (1968) *World Politics*, New York: Knopf.

Organski, A.F.K. and Kugler, J. (1980) *The War Ledger*, Chicago: University of Chicago Press.

Orme, J. (1997–8) 'The Utility of Force in a World of Scarcity', *International Security*, 22, 3: 138–67.

Osgood, R.E. (1957) *Limited War: The Challenge to American Strategy*, Chicago: University of Chicago Press.

Osgood, R.E. (1962) *NATO: The Entangling Alliance*, Chicago: Chicago University Press.

Osgood, R.E. (1968) *Alliances and American Foreign Policy*, Baltimore: Johns Hopkins Press.

Osgood, R.E. (1979) *Limited War Revisited*, Boulder: Westview.

Owen, J.M. IV. (1997) *Liberal Peace, Liberal War: American Politics and International Security*, Ithaca: Cornell University Press.

Palmer, M.A. (1988) *Origins of the Maritime Strategy: American Naval Strategy in the First Postwar Decade*, Washington: Naval Historical Center.

Pape, R.A. (2003) 'The Strategic Logic of Suicide Terrorism', *American Political Science Review*, 97: 343–61.

Pape, R.A. (2005a) *Dying to Win: The Strategic Logic of Suicide Terrorism*, New York: Random House.

Pape, R.A. (2005b) 'Soft Balancing Against the United States', *International Security*, 30, 1: 7–45.

Paul, T.V. (2005) 'Soft Balancing in the Age of US Primacy', *International Security*, 30, 1: 46–71.

Pike, D. (1966) *Viet Cong*, Cambridge: MIT Press.

Porter, P. (2007) 'Good Anthropology, Bad History: The Cultural Turn in Studying War', *Parameters*, 37, 2: 45–58.

Posen, B.R. (1984) *The Sources of Military Doctrine: France, Britain, and Germany Between the World Wars,* Ithaca: Cornell University Press.

Posen, B.R. (1993) 'The Security Dilemma and Ethnic Conflict', *Survival*, 35: 27–47.

Prins, G. (2002) *The Heart of War*, London: Routledge.

Quinlan, M. (2004) 'The British Experience', in Sokolski, H. (ed.), *Getting MAD: Nuclear Assured Destruction, its Origins and Practice*, Carlisle, Pa.: Strategic Studies Institute of the US Army War College, <www.strategicstudiesinstitute. army.mil/pubs/display.cfm?pubID=585>. Accessed January 2007.

Race, J. (1972) *War Comes to Long An: Revolutionary Conflict in a Vietnamese Province*, Berkley: University of California Press.

Rathbun, N.S. (2006) 'The Role of Legitimacy in Strengthening the Nuclear Nonproliferation Regime', *The Nonproliferation Review*, 13: 227–52.

Ravnborg, H.M. (2004) 'Introduction: From Water "Wars" to Water "Riots"?' in Boesen, J. and Ravnborg, H.M. (eds), *From Water 'Wars' to Water 'Riots'? – Lessons From Transboundary Water Management*, DIIS Working Papers, No. 6/2004, Copenhagen: Danish Institute of International Studies, <www.diis.dk>. Accessed March 2007.

Ray, J.L. (1995) *Democracy and International Conflict: An Evaluation of the Democratic Peace Proposition*, Columbia, S.C.: University of South Carolina Press.

Richardson, L. (2006) *What Terrorists Want: Understanding The Enemy, Containing the Threat*, New York: Random House.

Roberts, B. (1990) 'Human Rights and International Security', *Washington Quarterly*, 13: 65–75.

Roberts, M. (1956) *The Military Revolution, 1560–1660*, Belfast: Queen's University Press.

Robertson, G. (1999) *Crimes Against Humanity*, London: Penguin.

Roe, P. (2004) 'Securitization and Minority Rights: Conditions of Desecuritization', *Security Dialogue*, 35: 279–94.

Rogers, C.J. (2000) '"Military Revolutions" and "Revolutions in Military Affairs": A Historian's Perspective', in Gongora, T. and von Reikhoff, H. (eds), *Defence and Security at the Dawn of the Twenty-First Century: Toward a Revolution in Military Affairs*, Westport, Conn.: Greenwood Press: 21–36.

Rogers, M. (1992) 'Institute to Halt "Brain Drain"', *Jane's Defence Weekly*, 17, 12: 472.

Romm, Joseph J. (1993) *Defining National Security: The Nonmilitary Aspects*, Council on Foreign Relations Occasional Paper, New York: Council of Foreign Relations.

Rosato, S. (2003) 'The Flawed Logic of Democratic Peace Theory', *American Political Science Review*, 97: 585–602.

Rose, G. (1998) 'Neoclassical Realism and Theories of Foreign Policy', *World Politics*, 51: 144–72.

Rosecrance, R. and Stein, A.A. (eds) (1993) *The Domestic Bases of Grand Strategy*, Ithaca: Cornell University Press.

Rosen, S.P. (1991) *Winning the Next War: Innovation and the Modern Military*, Ithaca: Cornell University Press.

Rotberg, R.I. and Rabb, T.K. (eds) (1989) *The Origin and Prevention of Major Wars*, Cambridge: Cambridge University Press.

Rothschild, E. (1995) 'What is Security?' *Daedalus*, 124: 53–98.

Ruggie, J.G. (1986) 'Continuity and Transformation in the World Polity: Towards a Neorealist Synthesis', in Keohane, R.O. (ed.), *Neorealism and its Critics*, New York: Columbia University Press.

Rumsfeld, D.H. (2003) *Secretary Rumsfeld Briefs at the Foreign Press Center*, News Transcript, 22 January, Washington: US Department of Defense, <www.defenselink.mil/Transcripts/Transcript.aspx?TranscriptID=1330>. Accessed January 2007.

Russett, B. (1993) *Grasping the Democratic Peace: Principles for a Post-Cold War World*, Princeton: Princeton University Press.

Russett, B. and Oneal, J. (2001) *Triangulating Peace: Democracy, Interdependence, and International Organizations*, New York: Norton.

Sageman, M. (2004) *Understanding Terror Networks*, Philadelphia: University of Pennsylvania Press.

Sandell, R. (2006) *Pandemics: A Security Risk?* Madrid: Real Instituto Elcano.

Savranskaya, S. (2005) 'New Sources on the Role of Soviet Submarines in the Cuban Missile Crisis', *Journal of Strategic Studies*, 28: 233–59.

Schafer, D.M. (1988) 'The Unlearned Lessons of Counterinsurgency', *Political Science Quarterly*, 103: 57–81.

Scheuer, M. (2004) *Imperial Hubris: Why the West is Losing the War on Terror*, Dulles: Brassey's.

Schmid, A. (1988) *Political Terrorism*, 2nd edn, Amsterdam: North-Holland Publishing Company.

Schmid, A. (2004) 'Frameworks for Conceptualizing Terrorism', *Terrorism and Political Violence,* 16: 197–221.

Schmid, A. (2005) 'Terrorism as Psychological Warfare', *Democracy and Security,* 1: 137–46.

Schmitt, C. (2004) *The Theory of the Partisan: A Commentary/Remark on the Concept of the Political,* Goodson, A.C. (trans.), East Lansing: Michigan State University Press.

Scholte, J.A. (2000) *Globalization: A Critical Introduction,* New York: St Martin's.

Schweller, R.L. (1994) 'Bandwagoning for Profit: Bringing the Revisionist State Back In', *International Security,* 19: 72–107.

Schweller, R.L. (1996) 'Neorealism's Status-quo Bias: What Security Dilemma?' *Security Studies,* Vol. 5: 90–121.

Schweller, R.L. (2003) 'The Progressiveness of Neoclassical Realism', in Elman, C. and Elman, M.F. (eds), *Progress in International Relations: Appraising the Field,* Cambridge: MIT Press.

Schweller, R.L. (2004) 'Unanswered Threats: A Neoclassical Realist Theory of Underbalancing', *International Security,* 29: 159–201.

Selby, J. (2005) 'Oil and Water: The Contrasting Anatomies of Resource Conflicts', *Government and Opposition,* 40, 2: 200–24.

Severino, R.C. (2006) *Southeast Asia in Search of an ASEAN Community: Insights from the Former ASEAN Secretary-General,* Singapore: Institute of Southeast Asian Studies Publications.

Shafer, D.M. (1988) *Deadly Paradigms: The Failure of US Counterinsurgency Policy,* Princeton: Princeton University Press.

Shaw, M. (1991) *Post-Military Society,* Philadelphia: Temple University Press.

Shaw, M. (2000) *Theory of the Global State: Globality as Unfinished Revolution,* Cambridge: Cambridge University Press.

Shaw, M. (2005) *The New Western Way of War: Risk-Transfer War and its Crisis in Iraq,* Cambridge: Polity.

Sheehan, M. (2005) *International Security: An Analytical Survey,* Boulder: Lynne Rienner.

Simon, J.L. (1999) *The Economic Consequences of Immigration,* Ann Arbor: University of Michigan Press.

Simon, S. and Benjamin, D. (2005) *The Next Attack: The Globalization of Jihad,* London: Hodder and Stoughton.

Simpson, G. (2003) *Great Powers and Outlaw States: Unequal Sovereigns in the International Legal Order,* Cambridge: Cambridge University Press.

Sinha, U.K. (2005) 'Water Security: A Discursive Analysis', *Strategic Analysis,* 29: 317–31.

Smith, R. (2006) *The Utility of Force: The Art of War in the Modern World,* London: Penguin.

Smith, S. (2005) 'The Contested Concept of Security', in Booth, K. (ed.), *Critical Security Studies and World Politics,* Boulder: Lynne Rienner.

Snyder, C.A. (1996) 'Emerging Regional Security Cooperation in Europe and the Asia Pacific', *The Pacific Review,* 9: 553–76.

Snyder, C.A. (1996–7) 'The Implications of Hydrocarbon Development in the South China Sea', *International Journal,* 52: 142–58.

Snyder, C.A. (1997) 'Building Multilateral Security Cooperation in the South China Sea', *Asian Perspective,* 21: 5–36.

Snyder, G.H. (2002) 'Mearsheimer's World: Offensive Realism and the Struggle for Security', *International Security*, 27, 1: 149–73.

Snyder, J. (1977) *The Soviet Strategic Culture: Implications for Limited Nuclear Operations*, Santa Monica: RAND Corporation.

Snyder, J. (1991) *Myths of Empire: Domestic Politics and International Ambition*, Ithaca: Cornell University Press.

Snyder, J. (2000) *From Voting to Violence: Democratization and Nationalist Conflict*, New York: W.W. Norton.

Sondhaus, L. (2006) *Strategic Culture and Ways of War*, London: Routledge.

Sorensen, G. (1996) 'Individual Security and National Security: The State Remains the Principal Problem', *Security Dialogue*, 27: 371–86.

Sperandei, M (2006) 'Bridging Deterrence and Compellence: An Alternative Approach to the Study of Coercive Diplomacy', *International Studies Review*, 8, 253–80.

Sprout, H. and Sprout, M. (1965) *The Ecological Perspective on Human Affairs with Special Reference to International Politics*, Princeton: Princeton University Press.

Spykman, N.J. [1942] (1970) *America's Strategy in World Politics: The United States and the Balance of Power*, Hamden, Conn.: Archon Books.

Starr, B. (1993) 'Woolsey Tackles Proliferation as the Problem Gets Worse', *Jane's Defence Weekly*, 20, 20: 23.

Starr, Joyce R. (1991) 'Water Wars', *Foreign Policy*, 82: 17–36.

Steinbruner, J. (2003) 'Confusing Means and Ends: The Doctrine of Coercive Preemption', *Arms Control Today*, 33, 1: 3–5.

Stern, J. (1999) *The Ultimate Terrorists*, Cambridge: Harvard University Press.

Stix, G. (1995) 'Fighting Future Wars', *Scientific American*, 273, 6.

Stoessinger, J.G. (2005) *Why Nations Go to War*, 9th edn, Belmont: Wadsworth.

Suganami, H. (2002) 'Explaining War: Some Critical Observations', *International Relations*, 16: 207–26.

Suhrke, A. (1999) 'Human Security and the Interest of States', *Security Dialogue* 30: 265–76.

Sumida, J.T. (1997) *Inventing Grand Strategy and Teaching Command: The Classic Worlds of Alfred Thayer Mahan Reconsidered*, Baltimore: Johns Hopkins University Press.

Sun Tzu. (1971) *The Art of War* (trans. and intro. by Griffith, S.B.), Oxford: Oxford University Press.

Svechin, A.A. (1926) *Strategiia*, Moscow: Voenizdat.

Sylvester, C. (1994) *Feminist Theory and International Relations in a Postmodern Era*, Cambridge: Cambridge University Press.

Talentino, A. (2005) *Military Intervention after the Cold War: The Evolution of Theory and Practice*, Athens: Ohio University Press.

Taliaferro, J.W. (2000–1) 'Security Seeking Under Anarchy: Defensive Realism Revisited', *International Security*, 25, 3: 128–61.

'Taming Nuclear Tigers' (1991) *Jane's Defence Weekly*, 16, 23: 1106.

Tang Shiping (2006) 'China', in Pardesi, M.S., Acharya, A., Somasundram, P., Chang, Y.H., Ruey, J.L.S., Katsumata, T.S.H. and Ivanov, V.I. (eds), *Energy and Security: The Geopolitics of Energy in the Asia-Pacific*, Singapore: Institute of Defence and Strategic Studies, Nanyang Technological University.

Taureck, R. (2006) 'Securitization Theory and Securitization Studies', *Journal of International Relations and Development*, 9: 53–61.

Tellis, A.J. (2002) 'Toward a "Force in Being": The Logic, Structure, and Utility of India's Emerging Nuclear Posture', *Journal of Strategic Studies*, 25, 4: 61–108.

Thompson, R. (1972) *Defeating Communist Insurgency*, London: Chatto and Windus.

Thompson, W. (1988) *On Global War: Historical-Structural Approaches to World Politics*, Columbia: University of South Carolina Press.

Thucydides (1954) *History of the Peloponnesian War*, Warner, R. (trans.), Finley, M.I. (ed.), Harmondsworth: Penguin.

Tickner, J.A. (1992) *Gender in International Relations*, New York: Columbia University Press.

Tickner, J.A. (1995) 'Re-visioning Security', in Booth, K. and Smith, S. (eds), *International Relations Theory Today*, Oxford: Oxford University Press.

Till, G. (2004) *Seapower: A Guide for the 21st Century*, London: Frank Cass.

Till, G. (ed.) (2006) *The Development of British Naval Thinking*, London: Routledge.

Toffler, A. and Toffler, H. (1993) *War and Anti-War: Survival at the Dawn of the Twenty-First Century*, New York: Diane Publishing.

Toynbee, A.J. (1926) *The World After the Peace Conference*, Oxford: Oxford University Press.

Trager, R. and Zagorcheva, D.P. (2005–6) 'Deterring Terrorism: It Can Be Done', *International Security*, 30, 3: 87–103.

Tuchman, J. (1989) 'Redefining Security', *Foreign Affairs*, 68, 2: 162–77.

United Kingdom Ministry of Defence. (2004) *The Military Contribution to Peace Support Operations*, Joint Warfare Publication 3–50, UKMOD: Director General, Joint Doctrine and Concepts.

United Kingdom Ministry of Defence. (2006) *The Future of the United Kingdom's Nuclear Deterrent*, <www.mod.uk/NR/rdonlyres/AC00DD79-76D6-4FE3-91A1-6A56B03C092F/0/DefenceWhitePaper2006_Cm6994.pdf>. Accessed January 2007.

United Nations (1945) *Charter of the United Nations*, <www.un.org/aboutun/charter/index.html>. Accessed July 2006.

United Nations Development Programme (UNDP) (1994) *Human Development Report 1994*, Oxford: Oxford University Press for the UNDP.

United States Arms Control and Disarmament Agency (1995) *World Military Expenditures and Arms Transfers 1993–1994*, Washington.

United States, Department of Defense (2002) *News Briefing with Donald Rumsfeld*, 12 February, <www.defenselink.mil/transcripts/transcript.aspx?transcriptid=2636>. Accessed January 2007.

US Department of State (2002) *Patterns of Global Terrorism 2001*, Washington: Department of State.

US Department of the Army (2006) *Counterinsurgency*, FM-324, Washington: Headquarters, Department of the Army (US).

US White House (2002) *National Security Strategy of the United States of America 2002* <www.whitehouse.gov>. Accessed August 2006.

US White House (2005) 'Joint Statement Between President George W. Bush and Prime Minister Manmohan Singh', <www.whitehouse.gov>. Accessed January 2007.

Valencia, M.J. (2005) *The Proliferation Security Initiative: Making Waves in Asia*, Adelphi Paper No.376, London: International Institute for Strategic Studies.

van Crevald, M. (1977) *Supplying War: Logistics from Wallenstein to Patton*, Cambridge: Cambridge University Press.

van Crevald, M. (1985) *Command in War*, Cambridge: Harvard University Press.

van Creveld, M. (1986) 'The Eternal Clausewitz', in Handel, M.I. (ed.), 'Clausewitz and Modern Strategy', *Journal of Strategic Studies*, 9.

van Creveld, M. (1991a) 'The Clausewitzian Universe and the Law of War', *Journal of Contemporary History*, 26: 403–29.

van Creveld, M. (1991b) *The Transformation of War*, New York: Free Press.

Van Evera, S. (1984) 'The Cult of the Offensive and the Origins of the First World War', *International Security*, 9, 1: 58–107.

Van Evera, S. (1990–1) 'Primed for Peace: Europe after the Cold War', *International Security*, 15, 3: 33–40.

Van Evera, S. (1998) 'Offense, Defense, and the Causes of War', *International Security*, 22, 4: 5–43.

Van Evera, S. (1999) *Causes of War: Power and the Roots of Conflict*, Ithaca: Cornell University Press.

Van Ness, P. (2006) 'Bush's Search for Absolute Security and the Rise of China', in Beeson, M. (ed.), *Bush and Asia: America's Evolving Relations with East Asia*, London: Routledge.

Vasquez, J.A (1993) *The War Puzzle*, Cambridge: Cambridge University Press.

Vasquez, J.A. (1997) 'The Realist Paradigm and Degenerative Versus Progressive Research Programmes: An Appraisal of Neotraditional Research on Waltz's Balancing Proposition', *American Political Science Review*, 91: 899–912.

Von Laue, T.H. (1950) *Ranke: The Formative Years*, Princeton: Princeton University Press.

Wæver, O. (1993) 'Societal Security: The Concept', in Wæver, O., Buzan, B., Kelstrup, M. and Lemaitre, P., *Identity, Migration and the New Security Agenda in Europe*, London: Pinter.

Wæver, O. (1995) 'Securitization and Desecurization', in Lipschutz, R. (ed.), *On Security*, New York: Columbia University Press.

Wæver, O. (1997) *Concepts of Security*, Copenhagen: University of Copenhagen.

Wæver, O. (2000) 'What is Security? The Securityness of Security', in Hansen, B. (ed.), *European Security Identities – 2000*, Copenhagen: Copenhagen Political Studies Press.

Wæver, O., Buzan, B., Kelstrup, M. and Lemaitre, P. (1993) *Identity, Migration, and the New Security Agenda in Europe*, London: Pinter.

Walker, R.B.J. (1993) *Inside/Outside: International Relations as Political Theory*, Cambridge: Cambridge University Press.

Walker, R.B.J. (1997) 'The Subject of Security', in Krause, K. and Williams, M.C. (eds), *Critical Security Studies: Concepts and Cases*, Minneapolis: University of Minnesota Press.

Walker, W. (2004) *Weapons of Mass Destruction and International Order*, Adelphi Paper 370, London: Routledge for the Institute for International and Strategic Studies.

Walt, S.M. (1987) *The Origins of Alliances*, Ithaca: Cornell University Press.

Walt, S.M. (1989) 'The Case for Finite Containment: Analysing U.S. Grand Strategy', *International Security*, 14, 1: 5–49.

Walt, S.M. (1991) 'The Renaissance of Security Studies', *International Studies Quarterly*, 35: 211–39.

Walt, S.M. (2000–1) 'Beyond bin Laden: Reshaping US Foreign Policy', *International Security*, 26, 3: 56–78.

Walt, S.M. (2002) 'The Enduring Relevance of the Realist Tradition', in Katznelson, I. and Milner, H.V. (eds), *Political Science: The State of the Discipline*, New York: W.W. Norton.

Walt, S.M. (2005) *Taming American Power: The Global Response to US Primacy*, New York: W.W. Norton.

Waltz, K.N. (1959) *Man, the State, and War*, New York: Columbia University Press.

Waltz, K.N. (1979) *Theory of International Politics*, Reading: Addison-Wesley.

Waltz, K.N. (1986) 'Reflections on *Theory of International Politics*: A Response to My Critics', in Keohane, R.O. (ed.), *Neorealism and Its Critics*, New York: Columbia University Press.

Waltz, K.N. (1988) 'The Origins of War in Neorealist Theory', in Rotberg, R.I. and Rabb, T.K. (eds), *The Origin and Prevention of Major Wars*, Cambridge: Cambridge University Press.

Waltz, K.N. (1994) 'The Emerging Structure of International Politics', *International Security*, 18, 2: 44–79.

Waltz, K.N. (1996) 'International Politics is Not Foreign Policy', *Security Studies*, 6: 54–57.

Waltz, K.N. (2000) 'Structural Realism after the Cold War', *International Security*, 25, 1: 5–41.

Walzer, M. (1992) *Just and Unjust Wars: A Moral Argument with Historical Illustrations*, 2nd edn, New York: Basic Books.

Warden, J.A. III. (1988) *The Air Campaign: Planning for Combat*, Washington: Pergamon Brassey's.

Warden, J.A. III. (1995) 'The Enemy as a System', *Airpower Journal*, 9: 40–55.

Wardlaw, G. (1989) *Political Terrorism: Theory, Tactics, and Counter-Measures*, Cambridge: Cambridge University Press.

Weigley, R.F. (1973) *The American Way of War: A History of United States Military Strategy and Policy*, New York: Macmillan.

Weiner, M. (1992–3) 'Security, Stability and International Migration', *International Security*, 17: 91–126.

Weinstein, J. (2003) 'A New Threat of Terror in the Western Hemisphere', *SAIS Review*, 23, 1: 1–17.

Wendt, A. (1987) 'The Agent-Structure Problem in International Relations', *International Organization*, 41: 335–70.

Wendt, A. (1992) 'Anarchy is What States Make of It: The Social Construction of Power Politics', *International Organization*, 46: 391–425.

Wendt, A. (1995) 'Constructing International Politics', *International Security*, 20: 71–81.

Wendt, A. (1999) *Social Theory of International Politics*, Cambridge: Cambridge University Press.

Westing, A.H. (1986) *Global Resources and International Conflict*, Oxford: Oxford University Press.

Wight, M. [1946] (1978) *Power Politics*, Bull, H. and Holbraad, C. (eds), London: Leicester University Press and the Royal Institute of International Affairs.

Williams, P. (1994) 'Transnational Criminal Organizations and International Security', *Survival*, 36: 96–113.

Windsor, J.L. (2006) 'Promoting Democratization Can Combat Terrorism', *The Washington Quarterly*, 26, 3: 43–58.

Wirtz, J. and Larsen, J. (eds) (2005) *Nuclear Transformation: The New US Nuclear Doctrine*, New York: Palgrave Macmillan.

Wohlforth, W.C. (1994–5) 'Realism and the end of the Cold War', *International Security*, 19, 3: 91–129.

Wohlforth, W.C. (1999) 'The Stability of a Unipolar World', *International Security*, 24, 1: 5–41.

Wohlforth, W.C. and Brooks, S.G. (2002) 'American Primacy in Perspective', *Foreign Affairs*, 81, 4: 20–33.

Wolf, A.T. (1995) *Hydropolitics along the Jordan River: Scarce Water and its Impact on the Arab-Israeli Conflict*, Tokyo: United Nations University Press.

Wolf, A.T. (1999) 'Water and Human Security', *AVISO: An Information Bulletin on Global Environmental Change and Human Security*, Bulletin No. 3: 29–37.

Wolfers, A. (1962) *Discord and Collaboration: Essays on International Politics*, Baltimore: Johns Hopkins Press.

World Health Organization (2002) *Food and Health in Europe: A New Basis for Action, Summary*, Copenhagen: World Health Organization.

Wright, Q. [1942] (1964) *A Study of War*, Wright, L.L. (abridged version), Chicago: University of Chicago Press.

Wyn Jones, R. (1995) '"Message in a Bottle?" Theory and Praxis in Critical Security Studies', *Contemporary Security Policy*, 16: 299–319.

Wyn Jones, R. (1999) *Security Strategy and Critical Theory*, London, Lynne Rienner.

Yergin, D. (1991) *The Prize: The Epic Quest for Oil, Money and Power*, New York, Simon and Schuster.

Yergin, D. (2007) *The Fundamentals of Energy Security*, Washington: Committee on Foreign Affairs, US House of Representatives.

Yost, D. (2005) 'France's Evolving Nuclear Strategy', *Survival*, 47, 3: 117–46.

Zakaria, F. (1992) 'Realism and Domestic Politics: A Review Essay', *International Security*, 17, 1: 177–98.

Zakaria, F. (1992–3) 'Is Realism Finished?' *The National Interest*, 30: 21–32.

Zakaria, F. (1996) *From Wealth to Power: The Unusual Origins of America's World Role*, Princeton: Princeton University Press.

Zalewski, M. (1996) '"All These Theories Yet the Bodies Keep Piling Up": Theories, Theorists, Theorising', in Smith, S., Booth, K. and Zalewski, M. (eds), *International Theory: Positivism and Beyond*, Cambridge: Cambridge University Press.

Zhang, Y. (2005) 'Emerging New East Asian Regionalism', *Asia-Pacific Review*, 12: 55–63.

Index